Rediscovering Community

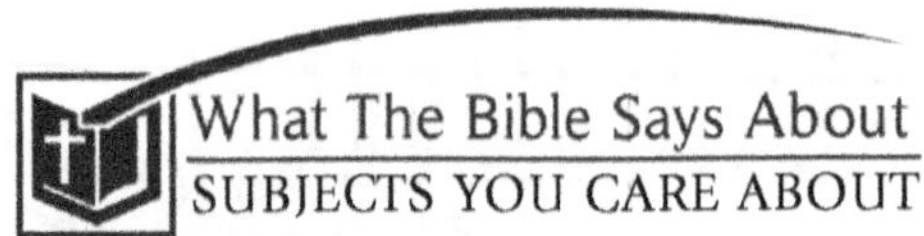

His Story — Our Response: What the Bible Says about Worship
Dinelle Frankland

The Life to Come: What the Bible Says about the Afterlife
Kenny Boles

Listening to His Heartbeat: What the Bible Says about the Heart of God
Harold Shank

Power from On High: What the Bible Says about the Holy Spirit
Jack Cottrell

Rediscovering Purposeful Community: What the Bible Says about the Church
Daniel Overdorf

Set Free: What the Bible Says about Grace
Jack Cottrell

Where Is God When We Suffer? What the Bible Says about Suffering
Lynn Gardner

Other Topics in the Planning:

The Doctrine of God, Prayer

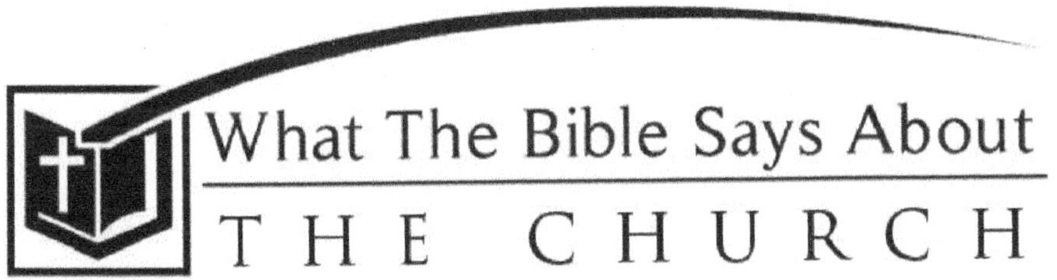

Daniel Overdorf

COLLEGE PRESS
Joplin, Missouri

College Press Publishing Co
Since 1959, publishers of resources for preachers, teachers, and Bible students
Order toll-free 800-289-3300
On the web at www.collegepress.com

International Standard Book Number: 978-0-89900-993-3

To

my mother,

Becky Overdorf,

in gratitude for thirty-seven years
of encouragement (and counting).

Abbreviations Used in this Book and Others in the Series

AD..................*Anno Domini*
ASV ....American Standard Version
BC..................Before Christ
KJV.................King James Version
LXX ....Septuagint (Greek Translation of OT)
MT ....Masoretic Text (Standard Hebrew OT)
NASB ....New American Standard Bible
NIV ....New International Version
NRSV ....New Revised Standard Version
NT..................New Testament
OT..................Old Testament
RSV ....Revised Standard Version

ABOUT THE SERIES

"What does the Bible say about that?" This is a question that should concern every Bible-believing Christian, whatever the particular subject being discussed. Granted, we know there are situations and activities that are not directly addressed by the Bible, because of changes in society, culture, and technology. However, if we truly believe that the Bible is to be our guide for living and especially for developing our relationship with God, then we need to look to it for information that will impact our everyday decisions. Even what may seem like abstract doctrinal matters will affect our religious practices, and if the Bible is indeterminate on a particular issue, then we need to know that too, so that we don't waste time on the kinds of controversies Paul warns about in 1 Timothy 1:4.

College Press Publishing Company is fully committed to equipping our customers as Bible students. In addition to commentary series and small study books on individual books of the Bible, this is not the first time we have done a series of books specifically dedicated to this question: "What DOES the Bible say?" Part of this stems from the background of CPPC as a publishing house of what has generally been known as the "Restoration Movement,"[1] a movement that gave rise to Churches of Christ and Christian Churches. The "restoration" of the movement's name refers to the desire to restore biblical teaching and emphases to our religious beliefs and activities.

[1] In order to be more specific and recognize that these churches are not necessarily unique in the plea to restore the church of the apostles, it is also known as the "Stone-Campbell Movement," after the names of some of the 19th-century leaders of the movement.

It is important to understand what this series can and cannot do. Every author in the series will be filtering the exact words of the biblical text through a filter of his or her own best understanding of the implications of those words. Nor will the Bible be the only source to be quoted. Various human authors will inevitably be referenced either in support of the conclusions reached or to contradict their teachings. Keeping this in mind, you should use them as tools to direct your own study of the Bible, and use the "Berean principle" of studying carefully every part of the Bible to see "whether these things [are] so" (Acts 17:11, ASV). We would not be true to our own purpose if we encouraged you to take any book that we publish as the "last word" on any subject. Our plea, our desire, is to make "every Christian a Bible Student."

A Word about Format

In order to emphasize the theme of "What the Bible Says," we have chosen to place Scripture quotations and Scripture references in distinct typestyles to make them stand out. Use of these typestyles within quotations of other works should not be taken as an indication that the original author similarly emphasized the highlighted text.

ACKNOWLEDGMENTS

My deepest appreciation to Dru Ashwell and the team at College Press for the opportunity to write about a topic for which I have great passion, to Drew Keane for extensive assistance in research and refining the manuscript (and to the Appalachian College Association for a grant that made Drew's research possible), to Ken Overdorf and Debbie Keller for proofreading each chapter, to Matt Zingraf for assistance with the bibliography and indexes, and to my colleagues at Johnson Bible College for lunchtime conversations and swapped emails that helped sharpen the ideas and biblical study represented in the book. I also want to thank my family—Carrie, Peyton, Tyler, and Claire—for their patience and encouragement.

IN THIS BOOK

Part 2 — The Church in the Gospels and Acts

6 Intimately Connected 141

Jesus taught and demonstrated that healthy relationships among believers require an intimacy far deeper than the superficial. The early church, in its better moments, provided illustrations of such intimacy.

7 Kingdom Advancing 167

Through a series of parables and other teachings, Jesus described God's reign—both its "already" and "not yet" aspects—as "the Kingdom"—a Kingdom in which the church plays a critical part.

8 Mission Focused 193

While New Testament believers developed intimate relationships with one another, they also displayed keen awareness of their mission to minister to others and to draw them into the fold.

9 Spirit Empowered 221

Jesus promised the indwelling of His Spirit to empower the church. Acts describes how the Spirit led the early church to purposeful, fruitful ministry.

10 Sacramentally Participating 241

God gave the church baptism as the means through which we, in faith, enter into a covenant with Christ. He gave the Lord's Supper as the means through which we find continual nourishment in our covenant relationship with Him.

Part 3 — The Church in the Epistles and Revelation

11 Purposefully Designed 269

As it began ministering, the early church organized itself to minister most effectively in its context, keeping Christ as the head of the body, and with all members of the body leading and/or ministering as they were gifted.

12 Graciously United 299

God designed and desires a unified church. Our selfishness, however, has often divided it. The restoration of unity will require a humble confluence of grace and truth, and a commitment to implement Jesus' command to "love one another."

13 Word Driven 325

God gave His Word to empower and equip the church for maturity and ministry. Biblical churches, therefore, seek, study, and submit to the authoritative Word of God, giving it priority in church life and worship.

14 Radically Perseverant 347

Jesus warned that His followers would face persecution. His prediction proved true, as the early church met opposition from unbelieving Jews and later from the Romans. Early believers remained extraordinarily undeterred, however, in their dedication to the cause of Christ, demonstrating for the contemporary church how to persevere.

Charts and Special Studies

INTRODUCTION

What life have you if you have not life together?
There is no life that is not in community,
And no community not lived in praise of God.
T.S. Eliot[1]

Researcher Jim Henderson hired a friend-of-a-friend, self-identified atheist Matt Casper, to join him in attending twelve churches around the United States. They visited some congregations that featured preachers whose names appear on best-seller lists; they visited other congregations that labor in obscurity. After a series of worship services that, from Casper's perspective, would pass only as mediocre facsimiles of community theater performances, smoke machines and background tracks fully functioning, the befuddled atheist turned to his Christian friend and asked, "Is this what Jesus asked you guys to do?" (**Henderson and Casper, 18**).

- I. An Uphill Battle
  - A. Criticisms of the Church
  - B. The Bride of Christ
- II. The Individualization of the Church
  - A. An Individualistic Society
  - B. A Distinction in Language
- III. The Biblical Concept of Community
  - A. Biblical Evidence of God's Desire for Community
  - B. Personal Reflection
  - C. Products of a Healthy Community
- IV. Defining "Church"
  - A. Linguistic Background
  - B. Biblical Teaching
  - C. A Definition of "Church"
- V. Getting the Most Out of This Book
  - A. Book Title
  - B. Outline and Study Aids

Granted, we cannot expect the unbaptized to fully comprehend the gravity and mystery of Christian worship. Casper's bafflement, however, did not stem from gravity or mystery, but from what he perceived as simplistic, self-absorbed superficiality: "I don't understand why they need

[1]T.S. Eliot, "Choruses from the 'The Rock,'" in *The Complete Poems and Plays, 1909–1950* (New York: Harcourt, Brace, 1952). In Hanson, 1.

to do the big show. Why don't they just help people and call it good? Why the fog machine, camera crane, multiple screens, PowerPoint, and the lights, lights, lights? . . . For one to have a connection with God seems so astounding in and of itself. Why give it such a formulaic treatment?" (**Ibid., 18, 20**).

Since reading of Henderson and Casper's experience, Casper's questions have haunted me. What did Jesus ask us to do? What does God intend for the church? Have we missed the mark? If so, how might we rediscover and reimplement His intentions?

What does God intend for the church?

My family and I enjoy our church. Each Sunday we leave refreshed and fulfilled; or, when needed, convicted and motivated. The community thrives throughout the week on service, encouragement, and prayer. Nevertheless, while sitting with my wife in "our" pew on Sunday mornings, I occasionally wonder what thoughts would pass through Jesus' mind if He sat next to us. "Jesus," I'd relish the opportunity to ask, "what do you intend for us?"

This book represents my imagined response. To be clear, the book's contents grow not from my fanciful imagination, but from my understanding of Jesus' intentions as the Bible reveals them. Though He never disclosed His intentions in a manner as systematic as this book does, our survey of both testaments of Scripture will reveal certain common threads concerning what God desires of His people, His community, His church.

AN UPHILL BATTLE

Criticisms of the Church

We should grant at the outset that, for some, the term "church" evokes negative images and emotions.

At an extreme, we hear comments such as those by former professional wrestler and Minnesota governor, Jesse Ventura, "Organized religion is a sham and a crutch for weak-minded people who need strength in numbers. It tells people to go out and stick their noses in other people's business" (**Associated Press, "Ventura"**). Or, from fiction writer Stephen King, "I'm not a vampire type, when somebody shows me the cross or something like that. But organized religion gives me the creeps" (**ABC News**).

> **To have Jesus without the church is an impossible venture.**

Less extreme but equally disheartening frustrations commonly float around local coffee shops and Little League parks, such as, "I want Jesus, but not the church;" or, "I'm a spiritual person, I'm just not into church." Though I feel sympathy toward this perspective, it breaks my heart. To have Jesus without the church is an impossible venture—by definition the church consists of all Jesus' followers. The prominence of this disillusioned perspective, however, magnifies the need for the church to authentically admit our mistakes, and to tenaciously pursue what Jesus truly intends of us.

Churches, church leaders, and church members have made numerous mistakes over the years. We have embarrassed ourselves, damaged our effectiveness, and worst of all we have disappointed God. When someone barks, "The church is full of hypocrites!" we must admit the comment has some validity. Churches include members who act hypocritically (often I'm one of them). When someone sneers, "Preachers are just money-hungry and sex-crazed!" my head drops and heart sinks, not only because of the sneer, but because the statement proves true in far too many cases; it has been documented and splashed across newspapers and newscasts worldwide. Churches have provided fodder sufficient for decades of criticism.

The Bride of Christ

Even so, I love the church. Really, I do. I do not write these words because I work at a Bible college. My salary does not depend on glowing descriptions of all that's ecclesiastical. Warts and all, I love the church.

The church at its worst is still the bride of Christ. He loves us—not just individually, but corporately. "The reason that we are committed to the church," writes John Stott, "is that God is so committed. True, we may be dissatisfied, even disillusioned, with some aspects of the institutional church. But still we are committed to Christ and his church" (**20**).

In exalting the church, we fight an uphill battle. But the battle needs to be fought.

THE INDIVIDUALIZATION OF THE CHURCH

AN INDIVIDUALISTIC SOCIETY

In addition to battling a contemporary disdain for the church, we also battle against the bias of an individualistic society that has for three hundred years dismissed the need for community. The eighteenth-century Enlightenment, which continues to significantly influence current thought and practice, emphasized the reason, intellect, and logic of the individual, delivering a destructive blow against the horizontal, relational foundations of the church. "The notion that participation in some form of communal way of life is necessary for right knowledge and action was no longer self-evident," wrote Nicholas Healy of the Enlightenment (**279**).

This individualization of society crept into the church. Much of modern preaching and teaching focuses on the private aspects of faith. We speak often of a personal relationship with God, and an individual walk with Christ. Such terminology would have sounded odd in the ears of first-century Christians, and appears nowhere in the Bible.[2] This misdirected focus continues unchecked until someone raises the jarring question, "Well, then, why do we need the church?"

A DISTINCTION IN LANGUAGE

The language barrier between English-speaking believers and the original biblical texts further contributes to this problem of individualization. While the original biblical languages distinguish between the singular "you" and the plural "you," the English language makes no such distinction. As a result, we often read "you" as singular—about me, for me, centered on me—when the Bible intends to make a statement about us, for us, centered on the community.

For example, consider Paul's encouragement to the Philippians, *"He who began a good work in you will carry it on to completion until the day of Jesus Christ"* (***Php 1:6***). Numerous sermons, lessons, and devotions have personalized the passage and led listeners to contem-

[2] Obviously faith includes personal elements, such as an individual's decisions and actions. Jesus Himself, for example, often prayed privately. In both the OT and the NT, however, followers of God understood these personal elements of faith not in isolation, but as they functioned in the larger context of community.

plate how God works in them individually. While God does mold individual lives, this particular passage depicts God's ministry to the life of the community—the "you" is plural. God began a work in the Philippian church, and He would continue that work. Our teaching from this passage should, therefore, lead listeners to contemplate not how God works in "me" but how God works in "us."

Or, consider Paul's reminder to the Corinthians, *"Don't you know that you yourselves are God's temple and that God's Spirit lives in you? If anyone destroys God's temple, God will destroy him; for God's temple is sacred, and you are that temple"* (***1Cor 3:16-17***). While a couple of chapters later Paul speaks of the individual believer's body as a temple (***1Cor 6:19***), in chapter three Paul wrote in the plural—you together, you corporately, you the community are the temple of God in which His Spirit dwells, and anyone who destroys this community will stand accountable before God. A reader who misses the plurality of Paul's teaching simply misses the teaching.

While we tend to emphasize the parts, the Bible emphasizes the whole, and the parts as they relate to the whole.

THE BIBLICAL CONCEPT OF COMMUNITY

Biblical Evidence of God's Desire for Community

God aches to redeem, nourish, and empower a people, a community. From His initial covenant with Abraham (*"I will make you into a great nation,"* ***Gen 12:2***) to the vision He gave John concerning Heaven (*"Now the dwelling of God is with men, and he will live with them. They will be his people, and God himself will be with them and be their God,"* ***Rev 21:3***), God's heart for His community casts a glow across the entire biblical narrative. The cross of Jesus, which stands central to the biblical narrative, serves not only *"to redeem us from all wickedness"* but also to *"purify for himself a people that are his very own"* (***Tts 2:14***).

Through Abraham God birthed His people. Through Moses God set apart His people. Through David God led His people. Through Nehemiah God restored His people. Through Jesus God redeems His people. Through

God's heart for His community casts a glow across the entire biblical narrative.

Paul God expanded His people. Through the church God nourishes His people.

One cannot read of Jesus' relationship with His disciples without recognizing the power of community. This ragamuffin twelve talked with Jesus during their long walks from village to village, asking questions and probing the wisdom of the great I AM. They sat at His feet around the evening campfires, drinking in story after story drawn from the annals of God's history. They stood beside Jesus, intrigued, while He taught the crowds. They watched while He stretched His hand to heal the leper, to comfort the grieving, and to brush back the wisp of hair from the eye of the curious child who sat on His knee. The disciples listened, learned, and observed in community with one another and with Jesus.

The disciples listened, learned, and observed in community with one another and with Jesus.

One cannot read of Paul's adventures in ***Acts***, or the conclusions of epistles such as ***2 Timothy*** and ***Romans***, without recognizing the power of community in his life and ministry. Yes, Paul served as the great pioneer missionary. But he did not serve alone. Silas, Timothy, Barnabas, Luke, Mark, Priscilla and Aquila, Titus, Gaius—the list could continue for pages. To Paul, however, these names represented far more than a list. Such saints battled arm-in-arm with the great missionary apostle, often with intense personal sacrifice, stretching the boundaries of the church until it penetrated the furthest reaches of the Mediterranean world. They united with Paul in a purpose far larger than themselves. As a community, they banded together and extended the gospel.

Personal Reflection

My own faith and ministry did not develop, nor does it continue, in isolation. When I reflect across the years, numerous names come to mind of those who influenced me. Diane, Roland, Dane, Leta, Doug, and Kim taught me. Burt, Rick, and Dave mentored me. Tommy, David, Wayne, Bob, and Haddon molded me. Jason, Greg, Drew, Danny, Kenna, Mike, Adam, Helen, Lamar, my own family. . . . I could continue listing names infinitely. Yet, these names are much more than a list. Each individual, every face and memory that rolls through my mind, comprise the community of saints who have loved and nurtured me, and who have given me the privilege of ministering alongside of them.

"Christian brotherhood," observed Dietrich Bonhoeffer, "is not an ideal which we must realize; it is rather a reality created by God in Christ in which we may participate" (***Life*, 30**). When we follow the biblical design, believers band together for growth, nourishment, and to further the purposes and love of the One who redeemed us. The resulting church reflects this description offered by N.T. Wright:

> Church is a place of welcome and laughter, of healing and hope, of friends and family and justice and new life. It's where the homeless drop in for a bowl of soup and the elderly stop by for a chat. It's where one group is working to help drug addicts and another is campaigning for global justice. It's where you'll find people learning to pray, coming to faith, struggling with temptation, finding new purpose, and getting in touch with a new power to carry that purpose out. It's where people bring their own small faith and discover, in getting together with others to worship the one true God, that the whole becomes greater than the sum of the its parts. No church is like this all the time. But a remarkable number of churches are partly like that for quite a lot of the time" (***Simply*, 123**).

Products of a Healthy Community

I recall teaching on more than one occasion that "healthy Christians produce a healthy church." A church that prays consists of individuals who pray, I would argue, and a church that evangelizes consists of individuals who evangelize. To grow toward community health, the thought continues, we should focus on the personal spiritual health of the individuals who make up the church.

Healthy churches produce healthy individuals.

This argument contains some truth, but it misses the critical contribution of community to individual health. In fact, we might more accurately phrase the argument in the opposite manner: healthy churches produce healthy individuals. A community saturated with prayer will produce individuals who pray. A community ingrained with a passion for evangelism will produce individuals who evangelize. Spiritually healthy churches produce spiritually healthy believers.

DEFINING "CHURCH"

Linguistic Background

As often proves true when attempting to define a word, defining "church" creates more confusion than one might initially expect. The English "church" derives from the Greek *kuriakon* ("belonging to the Lord," **BAGD, 458**), which appears only twice in the NT, and, in neither case, is translated "church." In both occurrences, *kuriakon* translates as the possessive "Lord's"—the Lord's supper (***1Cor 11:20***) and the Lord's Day (***Rev 1:10***). In later centuries, Greek Christians began using *kuriakon* to refer to their houses of worship—the Lord's house, and the believers who met there—the Lord's people. As its usage evolved, believers shortened these to simply "the Lord's" (*kuriakon*).

When we read "church" in our contemporary English Bibles, however, the term translates not from *kuriakon* but from *ekklesia* ("assembly, gathering, congregation," **BAGD, 240**). This term occurs well over one hundred times in the New Testament; scholars almost always render it "church." In the NT, *ekklesia* referred to a people, the assembly of God's followers, the community of those who belong to Him.[3]

Biblical Teaching

Beyond this linguistic background, the Bible offers an abundance of teaching concerning the origin, nature, and ministry of the church.

God called the people from among the nations to be His very own.

Far from a divine afterthought, or a midhistorical adjustment, God intended from the beginning to call out from the world a people who would glorify him. He hinted at this desire through His relationships with Adam and Noah, and initiated the process through His covenant with Abraham. Then, through the covenant God gave Moses, He called the people from among the nations to be His very own: *"I will take you as my own people, and I will be your God. . . . Out of all nations you will be my treasured possession. Although the whole earth is mine,*

[3]The NT uses *ekklesia* both to describe local communities of Christians (such as those in Antioch in ***Acts 11:26***, and in Ephesus in ***20:17***), and to describe Christians on the whole, regardless of location (***Acts 9:31, 20:28***). This implies that "each local group of Christians is not merely related to the total church but in fact is the total church in the place where it exists" (**Barrett, lxxxviii**).

you will be for me a kingdom of priests and a holy nation" (**Ex 6:7; 19:5-6**). The remainder of the OT traces the development of the Israelites into a people for whom Yahweh longed with the passion of an often-jilted but always faithful lover, and through whom He intended to glorify Himself among all nations.

During this era, God promised to send His people an anointed Messiah who would redeem them and transform the community into a divinely empowered, eternal Kingdom. When this redeemer, Jesus Christ—God incarnate—sacrificed Himself, He began mediation of a new covenant based on His blood that brought to fruition the community that began development under the former covenant. This new community finds grace in the once-and-for-all sacrifice of its Great High Priest, gains empowerment from the Holy Spirit, and extends the Kingdom to the ends of the earth in a manner that glorifies God.

A Definition of "Church"

Growing from this linguistic and biblical basis, for the purposes of this book we will define "church" as follows:

> The church is the community of God's people,
> rooted in His eternal plan,
> initiated in His covenant with Abraham,
> expressed through His covenant with Moses,
> brought to fruition through Christ's covenant of blood,
> empowered by the Holy Spirit to
> minister to one another and to
> extend the grace and truth of Christ to the world,
> glorifying God throughout all generations and into eternity.

As this book progresses, it will unpack the biblical teachings and concepts that lie behind each element of this definition.

GETTING THE MOST OUT OF THIS BOOK

Book Title

The topic of "What the Bible Says about the Church" proves far more expansive than what one volume could cover.[4] Every chapter, in

[4] I searched for the term "church" in book titles on Amazon.com—the search returned almost 900,000 results.

fact, could easily expand into an entire book. To narrow its focus, this book will attempt to survey biblical teaching concerning the development of community among God's people, in hopes of encouraging the contemporary church to return to this biblical ideal.

The phrase "purposeful community" from the book's title deliberately contains a double meaning. The book will argue that 1) God desires a church that purposefully cultivates community, and 2) He calls this church community to pursue a definite purpose.

Outline and Study Aids

Concerning the outline of the book, a brief glance at the table of contents reveals that the book surveys the Bible by section—the Old Testament, the Gospels and Acts, the Epistles and Revelation—seeking to discover recurring themes as they appear in each section. The discussions in each chapter will not, however, limit themselves only to passages in the defined section. For example, though the chapter about the church community being "Intimately Connected" appears in the section from the Gospels and Acts, the chapter will not limit itself only to passages from Matthew–Acts; it will also include appropriate passages from other sections of the Bible.

Each chapter will include sidebars that provide additional, related information, and discussion questions to spur both individual consideration and group discussion.

Ultimately, I pray that by the end of the book we will have fallen in love with Christ's bride all over again.

Part 1

The Old Testament Covenant Community

CHAPTER ONE
COVENANT GRACED

My wife and I recently refinanced our house. We sat with a representative of our mortgage company in front of a sixty-seven page contract, initialed and signed everywhere the mortgage broker pointed, and tried to at least skim each page as he rambled through a series of explanations in a manner reminiscent of an old country auctioneer. After we signed the final page, we shook our hands to relieve the writer's cramp and shook our heads to relieve our headaches. The broker offered to let me keep the pen. "Thanks," I said, after having signed my life away, "this fifteen cent pen will make it all better."

Sixty-seven pages, tens of thousands of dollars, and thirty years of impending payments—the thought still slows my blood flow. I wonder why they will not just take my word for it?

On the way home, we stopped to fill our car with gasoline. As I removed the nozzle from the gas pump, my eyes rested on a banner hanging above me: "So good, they've guaranteed it in writing. Amoco Fuels."

"Why do they think this banner will make me feel better about their gasoline?" I wondered. "Why do I care if they put it in writing?"

A few days later I visited a friend in the hospital. He had neared the end of an extended battle with cancer. The medication had taken his hair and most of his

"How do I know He'll keep His word?" "He guaranteed it with a cross and a covenant."

clear thoughts. I read some Scripture passages to him about God's promises, unsure if he even heard me, then I prayed. As I turned to leave the room, he mumbled, "How do I know He'll keep His word?" At such questions the theories of classroom debate and the clichés of the church sanctuary pass by the wayside.

"He guaranteed it," I responded after gathering my thoughts, "with a cross and a covenant."

Our filing cabinets brim with contracts, from mortgages to agreements with exterminators and warranties on MP3 players. But a contract with God? An agreement with the Almighty? The biblical term is "covenant," but the idea compares.

A discussion of the church community begins with a recognition of the covenant in which we participate. At the most basic level, a covenant is "an agreement between two people or two groups that involves promises on the part of each to the other" (**Lockyer, 259**). As this chapter continues, however, it will reveal that God's covenant with His people holds far greater significance than a contract we share with an exterminator.

A COVENANT ESTABLISHED

The OT Roots of the NT Church

In a book subtitled *What the Bible Says about the Church,* the reader might wonder why the first chapter begins in the OT. Is not the church a NT institution?

The "church" does, indeed, find its definition in the death and resurrection of Jesus Christ, which occurred during the NT era. Prior to the crucifixion, Jesus proclaimed, *"I will build my church"* (***Mt 16:18,*** note the future tense). Later, the NT describes the church as *"the body of Christ"* (***1Cor 12:27***), pictures the church as the bride of Christ (***Eph 5:31-33***), and depicts the church as a building constructed with Christ as its cornerstone (***Eph 2:20-21***).

We cannot understand the NT church in its full glory, majesty, and gravity, however, without exploring its OT roots. "The New Testament doctrine of the church, like most New Testament doctrines, is built on Old Testament doctrine," explained Charles Briggs. "Those who attempt to understand New Testament doctrine by itself alone may be compared to those who look at a beautiful castle whose foundations, supporting hillsides, and adjoining valleys are all shrouded in mist and cloud" (2).

We cannot understand the NT church in its full glory, majesty, and gravity without exploring its OT roots.

Furthermore, while the church proper is a NT entity, the community of God's people (the focal point of this book), stretches far further back into history. In fact, God recognizes man's need for community as early as Eden: *"It is not good for the man to be alone"* (***Gen 2:18***).[1] God saved not only Noah in the ark, but also Noah's family; and after God released them from the ark He set the rainbow in the sky as *"my covenant with you and with all your descendants after you"* (***Gen 9:9***).

From the beginning, God desired a people—not just persons—who would follow Him.

God's Covenant with Abraham

God set the wheels in motion for the formation of this community with the covenant He offered Abraham, in which God promised the patriarch, *"I will make you into a great nation"* (***Gen 12:2***). Through Abraham and his descendants God would develop a community through whom *"all peoples on earth will be blessed"* (***Gen 12:3***). God further defined this covenant in ***Genesis 15 and 17***.

In ***Genesis 15***, God defined His side of the covenant: He would show faithfulness to Abraham. Specifically, God would bless Abraham with a son, through whom Abraham would have innumerable descendants. God took Abraham outside and said, *"Look up at the heavens and count the stars—if indeed you can count them. . . . So shall your offspring be"* (***Gen 15:5***). Additionally, God would express His faithfulness to Abraham by giving him and his descendants the land on which Abraham stood (***Gen 15:7***), which stretched *"from the river of Egypt to the great river, the Euphrates"* (***Gen 15:18***).

[1] With poetic repetition, ***Genesis 1*** describes God looking upon His creation at various phases of development and repeating, *"It is good."* This refrain changes in ***Genesis 2:18***, when God looks upon Adam's loneliness and says for the first time, *"It is not good."*

God sealed the covenant through a ceremony in which Abraham cut a heifer, a goat, and a ram in half, and arranged the pieces opposite one another. Later, *"When the sun had set and darkness had fallen, a smoking firepot with a blazing torch appeared and passed between the pieces"* (***Gen 15:17***). Though the ceremony strikes the modern reader as odd and grotesque, Abraham knew the significance of God's gesture. God used a ceremony typical in the ancient world to give Abraham tangible assurance of His promise. "If I break this promise," God indicated to Abraham via the ceremony, "may I meet the same fate as these animals."[2]

In ***Genesis 17***, God defined Abraham's side of the covenant—as God would show faithfulness to Abraham, Abraham would, in turn, show faithfulness to God. While the seed of Abraham's faithfulness occurred in ***Genesis 15*** (*"Abram believed the LORD, and he credited it to him as righteousness,"* ***Gen 15:6***), his belief found further definition in ***Genesis 17***: *"When Abram was ninety-nine years old, the LORD appeared to him and said, 'I am God Almighty; walk before me and be blameless'"* (***Gen 17:1***). Abraham, you believe; now, live out that belief.

Just as God provided a tangible expression of His commitment with a ceremony, He instructed Abraham to provide an expression of his commitment: *"You are to undergo circumcision,"* God commanded, *"and it will be the sign of the covenant between me and you"* (***Gen 17:11***).

Word Study
Berith (Covenant)[3]

The noun form of *berith* refers to a legally binding agreement between two people or parties—a covenant. The verb form (which never appears in the OT) carries the image of cutting. Thus, the idiom "to cut a covenant" developed to describe a ceremony in which a covenant is established through animal sacrifice (***Gen 15:9-21***).

[2] ***Jeremiah 34:18-20*** describes and provides further details concerning this type of ceremony, *"[18]The men who have violated my covenant and have not fulfilled the terms of the covenant they made before me, I will treat like the calf they cut in two and then walked between its pieces. [19]The leaders of Judah and Jerusalem, the court officials, the priests and all the people of the land who walked between the pieces of the calf, [20]I will hand over to their enemies who seek their lives. Their dead bodies will become food for the birds of the air and the beasts of the earth."*

[3] Sources consulted: "Berit Obligation," by E.W. Kutch; "Covenant," by Lawrence Richards; "Berit," by Elmer B. Smick; and "Covenant" by Scot McKnight.

In the Ancient Near East, some covenants represented agreements between two equal parties, such as Abraham's covenant with the Amorites (***Gen 14:3***). Other covenants, however, represented agreements between a greater party and a lesser party, such as Abraham's covenant with God (***Genesis 12, 15, 17***). Ancient Near East covenants often contained five parts, listed below. Many scholars believe that the covenants described in the OT follow this pattern, such as those found in ***Joshua 24*** and in the 10 Commandments. The entire book of ***Deuteronomy***, in fact, appears to follow this basic pattern.

1. A preamble identifying the parties involved (***Deu 1:1-5***).
2. A historical prologue describing the prior relationship between the parties (***Deu 1:6–4:43***).
3. Stipulations and demands (***Deu 4:44–26:19***)
4. Swearing of allegiance, including blessings and curses for obedience or disobedience (***Deuteronomy 27–28***).
5. Witnesses and directions for implementation of the covenant (***Deuteronomy 29–34***).

God chose a concept familiar to His people—the Ancient Near East covenant—to promise His faithfulness and to call for their faithfulness.

Observations

A few observations deserve mentioning before we continue.

First, both sides of the covenant involve faithfulness—God's faithfulness to Abraham and his descendants, and Abraham's and his descendants' faithfulness to God. This fact will remain true throughout the remainder of the Bible and throughout the covenant's various modifications and additions, such as the expansions of the covenant through Moses and David. Even in the new covenant through Christ, which fulfills the old covenant originally offered to Abraham,[4] the heart of the covenant remains unchanged: God offers faithfulness to His people, and demands faithfulness from His people.

Second, God initiated the covenant as an act of grace. Though man shares a covenant with God, this does not imply that man shares

[4] The covenant through Christ "fulfills" the former covenant (***Mt 5:17***), as opposed to expanding or modifying it, as happened through Moses and David.

God initiated the covenant as an act of grace.

equal status with God. God, as the superior participant in the covenant, approached Abraham, the inferior participant, as an expression of love and compassion—as an expression of grace.[5]

When David praised God for the covenant, his use of parallelism demonstrated that the covenant finds its origin in God:

> [15]*He remembers his covenant forever,*
> *the word he commanded, for a thousand generations,*
> [16]*the covenant he made with Abraham,*
> *the oath he swore to Isaac.*
> [17]*He confirmed it to Jacob as a decree,*
> *to Israel as an everlasting covenant.* (**1Chr 16:15-17**)

David parallels *"his covenant"* with *"the word he commanded," "the oath he swore,"* and the *"decree"* that *"he confirmed."* This demonstrates that "the emphasis is on God's initiative—his promise, his decrees, his ordinances" (**Ferguson, 3-4**).

Why would God offer such a covenant? Moses explained,

> [7]*The LORD did not set his affection on you and choose you because you were more numerous than other peoples, for you were the fewest of all peoples.* [8]*But it was because the LORD loved you and kept the oath he swore to your forefathers that he brought you out with a mighty hand and redeemed you from the land of slavery, from the power of Pharaoh king of Egypt.* [9]*Know therefore that the LORD your God is God; he is the faithful God, keeping his covenant of love to a thousand generations of those who love him and keep his commands.* (**Deu 7:7-9**)

God's offer of the covenant "is not grounded in anything other than God's own resolve to be in the relationship" (**Brueggemann, *Reverberations*, 37**).

Third, recognizing that the superior God initiated the covenant with inferior man, mankind's obedience to the covenant grows from our gratitude for the grace God extended. Believers express gratitude for grace by honoring the stipulations set forth in the covenant. "God acts first and calls people to respond," explains C.J.H. Wright. "This

[5]While some biblical covenants consisted of a mutual agreement between equal parties, such as the covenant between David and Jonathan (***1 Samuel 18, 23***), the covenant between God and His people better reflects ancient Near East covenants offered by those of socially greater positions, such as kings, with those of socially lesser positions, such as the king's constituents.

is the starting point for the moral teaching of the Old Testament. God takes the initiative in grace and redeeming action and then makes his ethical demand in light of it. Ethics then becomes a matter of response and gratitude within a personal relationship, not of blind obedience to rules or adherence to timeless principles" (25).

Teachers and preachers sometimes proclaim that the OT involved only law, while the NT involves only grace. Such a statement oversimplifies and thus naively misses the relationship between law and grace. God's extension of the law to man, couched in the covenant, was itself an act of grace. Law and grace interrelate. In both testaments, in fact, and in all expressions of God's covenant with man, the grace of God precedes and provides the foundation for man's obedience.

In the 1950s, OT scholar Berend Gemser observed, and others have since concurred, that unlike other law codes in the Ancient Near East, within the OT laws rest "motive clauses"—reasons, based on God's character, that should motivate His followers to obedience (52). God desired His people's obedience to sprout from the fertile soil of His goodness.[6] A few examples, all taken from *Deuteronomy*, demonstrate Gemser's thesis (the motive clauses are bolded):

God desired His people's obedience to sprout from the fertile soil of His goodness.

> *Deut 10:17-22:* ***"For the LORD your God is God of gods and Lord of lords, the great God, mighty and awesome, who shows no partiality and accepts no bribes. He defends the cause of the fatherless and the widow, and loves the alien, giving him food and clothing.*** *And you are to love those who are aliens,* ***for you yourselves were aliens in Egypt.*** *Fear the LORD your God and serve him. Hold fast to him and take your oaths in his name.* ***He is your praise; he is your God, who performed for you those great and awesome wonders you saw with your own eyes. Your forefathers who went down into Egypt were seventy in all, and now the LORD your God has made you as numerous as the stars in the sky."***

[6] This discussion admittedly simplifies Gemser's observations. Some motive clauses center, for example, on obedience in light of God's justice (*Ex 20:4-5*) or character (*Lev 26:1-2*). The inclusion of motive clauses of any kind, however, makes the OT law unique when compared to other Ancient Near East law codes and demonstrates God's concern not only for obedience, but for the motivation behind the obedience.

📖 ***Deuteronomy 14:1-2***: *"**You are the children of the Lord your God.** Do not cut yourselves or shave the front of your heads for the dead, **for you are a people holy to the Lord your God. Out of all the peoples on the face of the earth, the Lord has chosen you to be his treasured possession.**"*

📖 ***Deuteronomy 24:21-22***: *"When you harvest the grapes in your vineyard, do not go over the vines again. Leave what remains for the alien, the fatherless and the widow. **Remember that you were slaves in Egypt. That is why I command you to do this.**"*

While man should obey God simply in recognition of His position, and while God could demand obedience simply because He is God, God desires a deeper motivation for man's obedience—a desire deeper than compelled obligation. He desires obedience that grows from gratitude.

In grace He offers us a covenant; in gratitude we obey its stipulations.

A COMMUNITY EMERGING

My wife and I recently read *Sacred Marriage* by Gary Thomas.[7] Despite its title, the book does not focus primarily on marriage, but on the spiritual maturity that Thomas believes God uses marriage to develop. Marriage, he asserts, provides a magnifying glass that displays where we need to grow spiritually, and a laboratory in which this growth can take place. An intimate relationship with another human being will display, for example, how patient we really are. And that relationship will provide an atmosphere in which patience can be developed. The relationship provides a laboratory for spiritual growth.

As our OT survey transitions from Abraham to Moses, a similar dynamic appears. In Moses' day, circumstances forced God's people to live in close community, an atmosphere through which God attempted to lead them into significant growth as His covenant people.

Community in the Mosaic Covenant

A few hundred years after God established a covenant with Abraham and his descendants, one of those descendants—Moses—

[7] Grand Rapids: Zondervan, 2000.

served as God's mouthpiece for an expansion of the covenant. In a sense, the Mosaic covenant brought a new agreement between God and man, but not in a manner that left the former covenant obsolete. Moses, in fact, tied the new version of the covenant directly to what God *"swore to your fathers, Abraham, Isaac, and Jacob"* (**Deu 29:13**). This "new" covenant reaffirmed, revalidated, and expanded the original promises and stipulations.

Of particular relevance to this book, the Mosaic covenant offered the first concrete expression of God's call for His followers to live, worship, and relate to one another as a distinct community. God instructed the people through Moses, *"If you obey me fully and keep my covenant, then out of all nations you will be my treasured possession. Although the whole earth is mine, you will be for me a kingdom of priests and a holy nation"* (***Ex 19:5-6***). Later Moses reminded the people that God offered the covenant *"to confirm you this day as his people"* (**Deu 29:13**).

Prior to the Exodus, Scripture focused on individuals such as Abraham, Isaac, Jacob, Joseph, and their immediate families. After the slavery of Joseph's descendants in Egypt, however, during which time the number of people multiplied exponentially, God told Moses, *"I have seen the misery of **my people** in Egypt"* (***Ex 3:7***, bolding mine—this is the first time in Scripture God used the phrase *"my people"*). God promised the Israelites, *"I will take you as my own people, and I will be your God"* (***Ex 6:7***).[8] Throughout the plagues in Egypt, God echoed through Moses the constant refrain to Pharaoh, *"Let my people go"* (***Ex 5:1; 7:16; 8:1,20; 9:1,13; 10:3***).

Immediately following the Exodus, during which the Israelites witnessed God's power through the plagues and the dividing of the Red Sea, Moses and the people sang of their newfound position as God's precious community:

> [13]*In your unfailing love you will lead*
> *the people you have redeemed.*
> *In your strength you will guide them*
> *to your holy dwelling.*

[8] Immediately after this promise to make the people into His community, God said, *"I will bring you to the land I swore with uplifted hand to give to Abraham, to Isaac and to Jacob. I will give it to you as a possession. I am the LORD"* (***Ex 6:8***). Recall that part of God's original covenant with Abraham included the land; this promise would find its fulfillment when the Israelites settled in the Promised Land.

[14]The nations will hear and tremble;
anguish will grip the people of Philistia.
[15]The chiefs of Edom will be terrified,
the leaders of Moab will be seized with trembling,
the people of Canaan will melt away;
[16]terror and dread will fall upon them.
By the power of your arm
they will be as still as a stone—
until your people pass by, O Lord,
until the people you bought pass by.
[17]You will bring them in and plant them
on the mountain of your inheritance—
the place, O Lord, you made for your dwelling,
the sanctuary, O Lord, your hands established.
[18]The Lord will reign
for ever and ever. (***Ex 15:13-18***)

The redeemed slaves found hope, security, and promise in their position as God's people.

Community Stipulations That Reflect God's Character

After they left Egypt, and as they wandered in the wilderness, the Israelites found difficulty in living out the implications of community. God's covenant with Abraham had remained relatively broad in terms of its stipulations; this newly formed community needed additional guidance. The Mosaic covenant, therefore, contained numerous specific instructions to teach the people how they, as God's community, should live.

The particular stipulations of the Mosaic covenant grow from God's imperative, *"Be holy because I, the Lord your God, am holy"* (***Lev 19:2***). God called His people to reflect His character in their own lives, including how they functioned with one another in community. "The entire history of the biblical notion of community," explains Paul Hanson, "points to the same transcendent referent—the God who creates out of nothing, delivers the enslaved, defends the vulnerable, nurtures the weak, and enlists in a

The Mosaic covenant contained numerous specific instructions to teach the people how they, as God's people, should live.

universal purpose of *salom* all those responsive to the divine call" (5). God calls us to relate to those around us in a manner that mirrors how He has related to mankind from the beginning.

The Ten Commandments—the heart of the law God delivered through Moses—exemplify this principle. Before launching into the "Thou shalt not's," God prefaced the commandments with a statement of His identity and redemptive nature: *"I am the LORD your God, who brought you out of Egypt, out of the land of slavery"* (**Ex 20:2**). The first four commandments, then, grow from this preface by establishing man's response to God directly: worship no other god (commandments one and two), honor His name (commandment three), and respect Him by recognizing the Sabbath (commandment four). The remaining six commandments call mankind to live out the nature and compassion of God through their relationships with one another: honor the covenant relationship of family, recognize the sanctity of human life, and maintain purity in word and heart (commandments five through ten)—all relational gestures through which believers mimic God's character.

A second example appears through an examination of the law's instructions concerning the Israelites' responsibility to the poor, displaced, and oppressed. The following series of commands from ***Exodus 22:21-27*** demonstrate God's call for the Israelites to reflect His heart in their treatment of others:

> *[21]Do not mistreat an alien or oppress him, for you were aliens in Egypt.*
>
> *[22]Do not take advantage of a widow or an orphan. [23]If you do and they cry out to me, I will certainly hear their cry. [24]My anger will be aroused, and I will kill you with the sword; your wives will become widows and your children fatherless.*
>
> *[25]If you lend money to one of my people among you who is needy, do not be like a moneylender; charge him no interest. [26]If you take your neighbor's cloak as a pledge, return it to him by sunset, [27]because his cloak is the only covering he has for his body. What else will he sleep in? When he cries out to me, I will hear, for I am compassionate.*

God instructed the Israelites to treat the alien as He treated them when they were aliens in Egypt, to care for the widow and orphan recognizing God's concern for them, and to express generosity to one another using the compassion that God Himself displays. God's character provides the basis for His covenant community.

I recently spoke for a church in southern Illinois, just across the Indiana state line. The church reserved a room for me in New Harmony, Indiana. I toured New Harmony on foot, and learned of its interesting history. Robert Owen, an atheist who believed man could achieve a perfect society apart from God, bought the town in 1825 and invited others to join him in a utopian experiment. Residents covenanted with one another to exist in a communal way, with no money or property ownership. The experiment failed within three years, however, because of constant quarreling and, ironically, *dis*harmony.[9]

A covenant that exists only between people, with no thought of God, will fail. If contemporary believers consider only the horizontal aspects of their relationships (regardless of their level of commitment to these relationships), they face certain disharmony. Instead, enduring communities—enduring churches—share a commitment to God, and reflect the very character of God in their relationships with one another.

A covenant that exists only between people, with no thought of God, will fail.

Prophetic Reminders

Later in the OT era, when the prophets confronted Israel's moral decline, the prophets constantly pointed the community back to the covenant. If the Israelite community failed to repent, the severe consequences of such failure loomed over them. The prophets, therefore, in an effort to reform the Israelites' behavior, reminded them of God's faithfulness to them through the covenant, and God's character reflected in the covenant. Ezekiel, for example, included the phrase *"and you shall know that I am the Lord"* eighty-six times amid his calls for repentance (**Hanson, 217**).

Jeremiah 11:1-5 provides another example. In these verses, God called the people to reform their behavior so that it realigned with covenant stipulations. Woven throughout this call to reform, God offered continual reminders of His character and faithfulness (note these reminders in bold).

> *[1]This is the word that came to Jeremiah from the Lord: [2]"Listen to the terms of this covenant and tell them to the people of Judah*

[9] Stone-Campbell Restoration Movement scholars will recall that Alexander Campbell debated Robert Owen in 1829, soon after the failure of the New Harmony utopian experiment.

and to those who live in Jerusalem. [3]Tell them that this is what ***the LORD, the God of Israel,*** *says: 'Cursed is the man who does not obey the terms of this covenant—[4]the terms I commanded your forefathers when* ***I brought them out of Egypt, out of the iron-smelting furnace.*** *' I said, 'Obey me and do everything I command you, and* ***you will be my people, and I will be your God. [5]Then I will fulfill the oath I swore to your forefathers, to give them a land flowing with milk and honey'—the land you possess today.*** *"*

If covenant obedience grows from man's gratitude for God's faithfulness, and reflects God's character, then moral failure indicates that man has forgotten God. Wise preachers and teachers, like the prophets, recognize this principle and call their listeners to reform based not only on guilt and fear of punishment (though these may play a part), but more so based on God's character and faithfulness. "Remember who He is; and remember what He has done," the teacher might exhort her listeners. "These memories leave us desiring to please Him, to honor Him, and to live in a manner that reflects Him." Such teaching may leave contemporary listeners responding like Jeremiah's listeners responded:

[20]O LORD, we acknowledge our wickedness
and the guilt of our fathers;
we have indeed sinned against you.
[21]For the sake of your name do not despise us;
do not dishonor your glorious throne.
Remember your covenant with us
and do not break it.
[22]Do any of the worthless idols of the nations bring rain?
Do the skies themselves send down showers?
No, it is you, O LORD our God.
Therefore our hope is in you,
for you are the one who does all this. (***Jer 14:20-22***)

The Israelites repented in acknowledgement of God's character (*"for the sake of your name . . . your glorious throne . . . LORD our God"*) and faithfulness (*"remember your covenant with us . . . our hope is in you, for you are the one who"* brings rain and sends showers).[10]

[10] The validity of the Israelites' repentance is certainly questionable (God questioned it in ***Jeremiah 15***). Even so, the process exemplifies the manner through which the prophets attempted to lead the people toward genuine repentance.

In the midst of such calls to repentance, God sought to remind His people of His passion for them—the covenant meant far more to the Lord than a legal agreement. The covenant represented love, not just legalities. To illustrate this, the prophets (and God through the prophets) often used the analogy of marriage. *"For your Maker is your husband,"* penned Isaiah, *"the LORD Almighty is his name"* (**Isa 54:5**). When Israel rejected Him in favor of other gods, God's heart throbbed with the angst of a husband whose wife committed adultery: *"You adulterous wife!"* God bellowed to Israel. *"You prefer strangers to your own husband!"* (**Eze 16:32**). If the Israelites would repent, the Lord promised that He would accept them back and restore the relationship:

> 14*Therefore I am now going to allure her;*
> *I will lead her into the desert*
> *and speak tenderly to her.*
> 15*There I will give her back her vineyards,*
> *and will make the Valley of Achor a door of hope.*
> *There she will sing as in the days of her youth,*
> *as in the day she came up out of Egypt.*
> 16*"In that day," declares the LORD,*
> *"you will call me 'my husband';*
> *you will no longer call me 'my master.'"* . . .
> 19*I will betroth you to me forever;*
> *I will betroth you in righteousness and justice,*
> *in love and compassion.* . . .
> 23*I will plant her for myself in the land;*
> *I will show my love to the one I called "Not my loved one."*
> *I will say to those called "Not my people," "You are my people;"*
> *and they will say, "You are my God."* (**Hos 2:14-23**)

God aches for His community with the passion of a smitten lover. Thus He offers and enters into a covenant with His bride that requires, of both, everything—utterly, entirely, wholly everything. God offers His complete faithfulness and demands ours.

A CROSS ERECTED

A NEW COVENANT PROMISED

The old covenant required faithfulness from both parties—God and His people. Only the Lord kept His side of the agreement. He knew from the beginning, of course, the inadequacy of the covenant offered through Abraham and further defined through Moses—an

Major Biblical Covenants

Representative Person	Text	Description
Noah	Genesis 9:8-17	God committed that He would never again destroy the earth with a flood. He signified this covenant with the rainbow.
Abraham	Genesis 12:1-3; 15:1-21; 17:1-16	God promised Abraham land, descendants, and to bless all nations through him; Abraham promised faithfulness to God and signified the promise through circumcision
Moses	Exodus 19–24	God pledged His protection and blessing on Israel as their God; Israel pledged its holiness through obedience to God's commands.
David	2 Samuel 7:4-17	God committed to keep a descendant of David on the throne of Israel forever.
Jesus	Jeremiah 31:31-34; Luke 22:20	Through the cross, Christ mediated a new covenant through which God grants grace and eternal life to all who respond to Christ in faith. This covenant fulfills all the promises made in the previous covenants.

inadequacy found not in the covenant itself, but in man's inability to keep it. As the OT narrates the attempts of God's people to keep the covenant, it reveals a seemingly never-ending cycle of faithfulness, complacency, rebellion, then repentance. Time and again the OT community demonstrated what Paul would later write, *"In my inner being I delight in God's law; but I see another law at work in the members of my body, waging war against the law of my mind and making me a prisoner of the law of sin at work within my members"* (***Rom 7:22-23***).

A hotel in Galveston, Texas, that overlooks the Gulf of Mexico, faced a unique problem. The edge of the hotel hangs over the water. Before the hotel opened, someone thought, "What if someone decides to fish out of the windows?" This person then erected signs throughout the structure that read, "No fishing out of the hotel windows." As a result, when the hotel opened, its guests tossed their fishing lines out the hotel windows—something they would never have thought to do had they not read the signs. Lines became snared with one another. People in the hotel restaurant saw fish slapping against the picture windows. Rather than preventing a problem, the signs had the opposite effect and simply exposed humankind's rebellious nature (**H. Robinson, 100**). *"Through the law,"* Paul says similarly, *"we become conscious of sin"* (***Rom 3:20***).

This consciousness of sin, and the old covenant that brought it, stood as a necessary step in the process through which God would eventually fulfill His promise to Abraham that *"all nations on earth will be blessed through you"* (***Gen 12:3***). Before arriving at the new covenant, mankind needed the old covenant to learn of God's holiness, their sinfulness, and their need for a savior (***Rom 3:20-21***). God never intended this first step to conclude the journey. All along, God intended the old covenant to pave the way for a new one. The Lord revealed through Jeremiah, among others, that He would unveil this new covenant for His people:

All along, God intended the old covenant to pave the way for a new one.

[31]"The time is coming," declares the LORD,
"when I will make a new covenant
with the house of Israel
and with the house of Judah.
[32]It will not be like the covenant
I made with their forefathers

when I took them by the hand
to lead them out of Egypt,
because they broke my covenant,
though I was a husband to them,"
declares the LORD.
33 *"This is the covenant I will make with the house of Israel*
after that time," declares the LORD.
"I will put my law in their minds
and write it on their hearts.
I will be their God,
and they will be my people.
34 *No longer will a man teach his neighbor,*
or a man his brother, saying, 'Know the LORD,*'*
because they will all know me,
from the least of them to the greatest,"
declares the LORD.
"For I will forgive their wickedness
and will remember their sins no more." (***Jer 31:31-34***)

These verses indicate that, while the new covenant would result in the same relationship God desired all along (*"I will be their God, and they will be my people"*), the covenant itself would involve considerable differences from the old (*"it will not be like the covenant I made with their forefathers"*).

Most significantly, God would write the new covenant *"in their minds"* and *"on their hearts."* Instead of a law delivered externally on tablets of stone, God would deliver the new covenant to the hearts and minds of His people. While the Lord never desired only external obedience (***Isa 1:10-20***), the nature of the old covenant, with its numerous ceremonies and rituals, more easily lent itself to superficial, outward-only, compliance. In contrast, the new covenant would begin with matters of the heart, allowing these matters to naturally lead into outward obedience (***Mt 5:20-48***).

Furthermore, God would base the new covenant on forgiveness. The Hebrews writer explained the inadequacy of the old covenant,

> *It can never, by the same sacrifices repeated endlessly year after year, make perfect those who draw near to worship. If it could, would they not have stopped being offered? For the worshipers would have been cleansed once for all, and would no longer have felt guilty for their sins. But those sacrifices are an annual reminder of sins, because it is impossible for the blood of bulls and goats to take away sins.* (***Heb 10:1-4***)

In contrast, through the new covenant, *"We have been made holy through the sacrifice of the body of Jesus Christ once for all"* (**Heb 10:10**).

The differences between the old and new covenants

> are not in what God requires, but in the internalizing of his law and in the means of forgiveness for violation. The consequence of everyone knowing the Lord indicates that, instead of coming into a covenant relationship by natural birth, one would enter the new covenant by a conscious choice based on personal knowledge of the Lord. (**Ferguson, 6-7**)

The Former Covenant Fulfilled

The first words of the NT demonstrate that Jesus fulfilled the various evolutions of the old covenant: *"A record of the genealogy of Jesus Christ the son of David, the son of Abraham"* (**Mt 1:1**). Jesus bears the title "Christ," which indicates that Jesus was the "anointed one," the Messiah, whom the law and prophets taught would redeem God's people (***Isa 49:7***). Jesus entered the world as the descendant of Abraham through whom *"all peoples on earth will be blessed"* (**Gen 12:3**), and the descendant of David who would reign forever (**2Sa 7:13**).

"The law was put in charge to lead us to Christ," explained Paul to the Galatians, *"that we might be justified by faith. Now that faith has come, we are no longer under the supervision of the law"* (**Gal 3:24-25**). When the law, this supervisor, passed the baton to Christ, the transition made many of the specific stipulations of the old covenant and the manner in which mankind expressed its faith to God "obsolete" (**Heb 8:13**). Lest we underestimate the significance of the law to the new covenant, however, Jesus specified, *"Do not think that I have come to abolish the Law or the Prophets; I have not come to abolish them but to fulfill them"* (**Mt 5:17**). The law's lessons and longings provide the foundation on which Jesus built the new covenant. At the interchange of the old covenant to the new, the old did not pass away, instead it found new depth, expression, and fullness in Christ Jesus.

The law's lessons and longings provide the foundation on which Jesus built the new covenant.

Specifically, the grace provided through the blood of Christ, through which He established the new covenant, leads mankind to a deeper commitment to God's law than the old covenant required. Jesus provided examples of this truth in His Sermon on the Mount. While the old covenant required believers to refrain from such sins as murder, adultery, and divorce, Christ calls His followers to deeper commitment—genuine community, pure thoughts, and marital commitment (***Mt 5:21-32***). Certainly, God wished for the deeper commitment all along. While the OT law served well to identify sin, however, it proved inadequate to produce righteousness (***Gal 3:19-22***). The grace of the cross succeeds where the law failed—leading mankind to a righteousness deeper than what a law could specify.

Erwin McManus writes of a conversation he shared with a gentleman who had visited the church were McManus preaches. "Are you a law or a grace church?" the visitor asked.

Aware that the question presented a trap, McManus replied, "Well, of course we're a grace church."

"I thought so," the man replied. "I was concerned that you were one of those law churches that told people they had to tithe."

"Oh, no," McManus answered. "We're a grace church. The law says, 'Do not murder.' Grace says you don't even have to have hatred in your heart; you can love your enemy. The law says, 'Do not commit adultery,' but grace says you don't even have to have lust in your heart for another woman. The law says, 'Give ten percent,' but grace always takes us beyond the law. You can give 20, 30, or 40 percent. We would never stop you from living by grace."

"Oh," came the man's profound response (**McManus, 204-205**).

Christ fulfills the law by providing the grace that produces in mankind the genuine righteousness toward which the law pointed.

The Covenant Community Continued

One key element of the old covenant that continues through the new covenant involves God's desire for community. God established the old covenant with a people—Abraham's descendants. He established the new covenant with the church, which consists of Abraham's *spiritual* descendants—all who have followed his pattern of belief by

God established the old covenant with a people, the new covenant with the church.

placing their faith in Jesus Christ (***Gal 3:7***). *"If you belong to Christ,"* explained Paul, *"then you are Abraham's seed, and heirs according to the promise"* (***Gal 3:29***). God's promises to Abraham find their ultimate fulfillment in the church, the community of God's people by means of the new covenant.

As Israel enjoyed her standing as God's covenant people in the OT, the church enjoys the same standing in the NT and beyond. The concept of a covenant people far from dissipated at the onset of the new covenant. Instead, the concept of the covenant stands critical to an accurate theology of the church. Stanley Grenz explained, "Fundamentally, the church of Jesus Christ is neither a building nor an organization. Rather, it is a people, a special people, a people who see themselves as standing in relationship to the God who saves them and to each other as those who share in this salvation. . . . Stated theologically, the church is a people in covenant" (**605**).

What God initiated through Abraham, He fulfills through Christ and His church. The church, Abraham's spiritual descendants, serves as God's people fulfilling His purposes on His planet. As the Lord's community, we extend the blessings of His grace to all nations.

What Do You Say?

1. What would be missing from our understanding of the church if we neglected to read the OT?
2. How does knowing that God offered us a covenant influence our perspective of Him?
3. How do the concepts of law and grace relate to one another?
4. When God called the recently released Hebrew slaves "my people," how might this designation have affected the Hebrews' thoughts, feelings, perspectives, and behaviors? How might thinking of ourselves as "God's people" affect us today?
5. What needs to change in today's church so that our horizontal relationships with each other better reflect our vertical relationship with God?
6. Why do you think God often uses the image of a marriage to describe His relationship with His people?
7. What are the similarities and differences between the old covenant and the new covenant through Christ?

CHAPTER TWO
CULTURALLY DISTINCT

God calls His people to remain distinct from our culture. Churches who seek distinctiveness, however, often do so in ways that damage, rather than further, God's purposes. One "church" has appeared in newspapers numerous times over recent years because of their hateful picketing of military funerals. "These deaths represent God's punishment on our nation for our acceptance of immorality," they sneer as they thrust signs into the air that read "God hates fags!" and "You're going to Hell!" The same group recently touted their message by picketing the funeral of four teenagers who died in a car accident near where I live in Tennessee. While the group certainly sets itself apart from the culture, their rhetoric seems grossly inconsistent with Paul's exhortation, *"Be wise in the way you act toward outsiders. . . . Let your conversation be always full of grace, seasoned with salt"* (***Col 4:5-6***).

- I. The Call to Distinctiveness
  - A. A Community Set Apart
  - B. A Distinctiveness Based on Allegiance to God
- II. The Implications of the Call to Distinctiveness
  - A. Distinctiveness in the OT Law
  - B. Distinctiveness Tangibly Expressed
- III. When God's People Blend In
  - A. The Failure to Remain Distinct
  - B. The Consequences of Blending In
- IV. Distinctiveness as It Relates to Evangelism
  - A. Israel as a Blessing to the Nations
  - B. Distinction in Morality
  - C. Distinction Furthering Evangelism
- V. A Case Study: Daniel
  - A. Pearls against Black Velvet
  - B. A Resolve Not to Defile
  - C. Wisdom in Action

Other efforts toward distinctiveness may not appear as blatantly antagonistic, but they present dilemmas for believers who seek to emulate Jesus' example of balancing grace and truth. I recall a particular Tuesday morning when I served as the minister of a church. A local Christian businessman called my office and asked that I make a petition available for our church on the following Sunday morning and that I encourage our members to sign it. The restaurant Hooters planned to open an establishment a mile from our church building, complete with their trademark attractive waitresses in skimpy outfits. Several local churches and Christians sought to stop it. The businessman asked if I would lead our church to "take a moral stand against this atrocity," that we might "keep such decadence out of our neighborhood."

I sympathize with such requests. As Dietrich Bonhoeffer said, "There are things for which an uncompromising stand is worthwhile" (***Testament***, **322**). The manner in which we take that stand, however, and our choices concerning which issues to stand for or against, require great wisdom.

Perhaps our distinctiveness should find definition in more than just those matters we passionately *oppose*.

God calls us to remain distinct from our culture. I fear, however, that when we seek distinctiveness, we often do so with a sneer that repels the very people God called us to reach. Perhaps our distinctiveness should find definition in more than just those matters we passionately oppose.

THE CALL TO DISTINCTIVENESS

A Community Set Apart

The roots of God's call for His people's distinctiveness stretch back into the OT. As chapter one observed, the idea of community appears in the Garden of Eden. The concept develops further through God's promises to Abraham, and emerges more concretely through Moses and the Israelites after they leave Egypt. One particular aspect of God's concept of community involved the distinctiveness of His people from their surrounding culture. *"If you obey me fully and keep my covenant,"* the Lord instructed the Israelites through Moses, *"then out of all nations you will be my treasured possession. Although the whole earth is mine, you will be for me a kingdom of priests and a holy nation"* (***Ex 19:5-6***). Out of all the nations God would set apart His people as a holy community.

Its covenant with God required Israel to break significantly from the normal social, cultural, and ethical patterns of its day. God sought to establish "an alternative community with an alternative memory and an alternative social perception rooted in a peculiar text, identified by a peculiar genealogy, signed by peculiar sacraments, peculiar people not excessively beholden to the empire, and not lusting after domestication into the empire" (**Brueggemann, "Rethinking," 137**).

A Distinctiveness Based on Allegiance to God

Rather than an identity based on worldly matters, Yahweh's community would find their identity exclusively in their standing as His people. Walter Brueggemann explains, "The theological self-understanding of Israel permitted a new people that had no other identity—linguistic, racial, ethnic, or territorial—except exclusive allegiance to its God" (***Social*, 18**). The Israelite community's exclusive allegiance to God would result in distinctiveness from the surrounding nations. Distinctiveness, in and of itself, was not the goal. God sought believers devoted solely to Him. This devotion, then, would set the Israelite community apart.

God desires the church of all ages to stand out from its culture. When Paul wrote to the Ephesians, he addressed the letter to *"the saints [holy ones] in Ephesus, the faithful in Christ Jesus"* (***Eph 1:1***). Paul explained that Christ loved the church *"to make her holy"* (***Eph 5:26***). Believers live in a distinct manner because, in Christ, we have *"put on the new self, created to be like God in true righteousness and holiness"* (***Eph 4:24***).

Similar to God's call to the Israelites, His call for the distinctiveness of the church grows from our identity in Christ. Distinctiveness is not the ultimate goal; rather it results from an exclusive allegiance to Jesus. Because we serve God and Him only, we stand out from the culture. We do not stand out simply for the sake of standing out.

Distinctiveness is not the ultimate goal but results from an exclusive allegiance to Jesus.

Like the Pharisees Jesus confronted, who sought distinctiveness by setting numerous, particular boundaries that set them apart from the culture, churches today often seek to stand out by keeping superficial rules that draw external lines between them and society. Churches define themselves by how they dress, what style of music they listen to, or what petitions they sign. "Who are we?" they imply, "We are the church who boycotted such-

and-such." Instead, our distinction should come, not as an end in itself, but as a by-product of living and functioning as a Christ-like, holy community. Our identity hinges on our standing in Christ. "Who are we?" this would imply, "We are the church who seeks to reflect Christ in all we say and do."[1]

THE IMPLICATIONS OF THE CALL TO DISTINCTIVENESS

The truth outlined in the previous section—the church's distinctiveness should grow from an identity in Christ, not from external rules—does not abrogate the external implications of an identity in Christ. While the church's distinctiveness grows from an allegiance to God, rather than from superficial outward expressions, the church's allegiance to God certainly holds great implications for external behavior.

Distinctiveness in the OT Law

God's call for the OT Israelites' holiness required them to guard themselves from the pagan behaviors common to their surrounding culture. Numerous OT laws grow from this basis. For example, in ***Leviticus 20*** God outlined several prohibitions concerning sexual behavior. A man would face punishment who:

- ✗ commits adultery with another man's wife (***Lev 20:10***).
- ✗ sleeps with his father's wife (***Lev 20:11***).
- ✗ sleeps with his daughter-in-law (***Lev 20:12***).
- ✗ lies with a man as one lies with a woman (***Lev 20:13***).
- ✗ marries both a woman and her mother (***Lev 20:14***).
- ✗ has sexual relations with an animal (***Lev 20:15***).
- ✗ marries his sister (***Lev 20:17***).
- ✗ lies with a woman during her monthly period (***Lev 20:18***).
- ✗ [has] sexual relations with the sister of either your mother or father (***Lev 20:19***).
- ✗ sleeps with his aunt (***Lev 20:20***).
- ✗ marries his brother's wife (***Lev 20:21***).

[1] Our identity in Christ will certainly lead to some external distinctions, just as held true for the Israelites, and as we will discuss below. My argument here deals more with the cause of the distinctions—are we simply trying to be different, or are we seeking to reflect Christ? Furthermore, we should consider that if we sought to reflect Christ, our distinctions would appear at least as much in what we do (such as ministering to the needy or displaying integrity in business) as in what we do not do.

Why would God outline such specific prohibitions? Would not a command to remain faithful to marriage suffice? Immediately following the list, the Lord explained why He outlined these specifics:

> [22]*Keep all my decrees and laws and follow them, so that the land where I am bringing you to live may not vomit you out.* [23]*You must not live according to the customs of the nations I am going to drive out before you. Because they did all these things, I abhorred them.* [24]*But I said to you, "You will possess their land; I will give it to you as an inheritance, a land flowing with milk and honey." I am the* Lord *your God, who has set you apart from the nations. . . .* [26]*You are to be holy to me because I, the* Lord*, am holy, and I have set you apart from the nations to be my own.* (**Lev 20:22-24,26**)

God specified these particular sins because the pagan nations *"did all these things."* To maintain their purity, the Israelites must set themselves apart from these pagan elements of the surrounding nations. God called His community *"to be holy."* As Everett Ferguson points out, "'Holy' means 'separated,' 'set apart,' or 'consecrated.' Holiness has to do with setting boundaries and making distinctions: some things are acceptable to God, some things are not. When these boundaries are defined by God's standards of purity and sanctification, the holiness is neither impractical 'otherworldliness' nor legalistic self-righteousness" (**Ferguson, 363**). Holiness, which grows from allegiance to God, necessarily includes purity in external behavior.

Holiness has to do with setting boundaries and making distinctions.

Another particular issue that receives much emphasis in the OT relates to the intermarriage of the Israelites with those of surrounding pagan nations. If the Israelite families grew intermeshed with the pagans, the relationships would inevitably dilute the holiness and distinctiveness of God's people. Therefore, before the people entered the Promised Land, Moses instructed them,

> [1]*When the* Lord *your God brings you into the land you are entering to possess and drives out before you many nations—the Hittites, Girgashites, Amorites, Canaanites, Perizzites, Hivites and Jebusites, seven nations larger and stronger than you—*[2]*and when the* Lord *your God has delivered them over to you and you have defeated them, then you must destroy them totally. Make no treaty with them, and show them no mercy.* [3]*Do not intermarry with them. Do not give your daughters to their sons or take their*

daughters for your sons, [4]for they will turn your sons away from following me to serve other gods, and the LORD's anger will burn against you and will quickly destroy you. (**Deu 7:1-4**)

Centuries later, when Nehemiah and Ezra helped the nation rebuild after the Babylonian exile, the two leaders showed particular concern for this issue of intermarriage. Ezra, in fact, devoted the final two chapters of his book to this specific issue (even listing the names of those who had fallen guilty to this sin!). Ezra described his response to the news of the Israelites' guilt of intermarriage with the pagans, *"When I heard this, I tore my tunic and cloak, pulled hair from my head and beard and sat down appalled. Then everyone who trembled at the words of the God of Israel gathered around me because of this unfaithfulness of the exiles. And I sat there appalled until the evening sacrifice"* (**Ezra 9:3-4**). Ezra then led the people through a ceremony of repentance, and exhorted them, *"Do not give your daughters in marriage to their sons or take their daughters for your sons. Do not seek a treaty of friendship with them at any time, that you may be strong and eat the good things of the land and leave it to your children as an everlasting inheritance"* (**Ezra 9:12**).

Regaining purity in the Israelites' relationships stood critical to regaining their purity as God's people. "To a community battered by internal strife and beleaguered by foreign adversaries, self-preservation seemed to necessitate both the stringent ordering of the structures regulating the internal life of the people and a strict separation from non-Jews," explains Paul Hanson. "Nehemiah introduced an era whose energies were dedicated to establishing a community intent on defining its identity as opposed to 'all those of foreign descent' (**Neh. 13:3**)" (294-295).

DISTINCTIVENESS TANGIBLY EXPRESSED

The NT continues the OT emphasis on the holiness of God's community. *"Just as he who called you is holy,"* Peter wrote, *"so be holy in all you do; for it is written: 'Be holy, because I am holy'"* (**1Pet 1:15-16**). Peter extends the thought in the next chapter, *"You are a chosen people, a royal priesthood, a holy nation, a people belonging to God, that you may declare the praises of him who called you out of darkness into his wonderful light"* (**1Pet 2:9**). Paul often referred to believers as *hagios* (**Rom 1:7; 2Cor 1:1; Eph. 1:1**; et al.), a term usually translated "saints" or "holy" that

Word Study
Qodesh[2]

Qodesh refers to that which is distinct, holy, and sacred. The term appears frequently in Jewish and other Ancient Near East dialects and texts, almost always in a religious manner (around 400 times in the OT). It refers not simply to something different, but to something sacred and holy. ***Numbers 16:38***, for example, gives instructions about certain censers: *"Hammer the censers into sheets to overlay the altar, for they were presented before the LORD and have become holy."* The censers had become "holy" (a form of *qodesh*) because they *"were presented before the LORD."* They held special significance because they had been dedicated to God. The OT often uses the term in a manner similar to this occurrence in ***Numbers 16***, speaking of articles dedicated to God that thus entered the realm of the holy (e.g., ***Ex 29:37; 30:29; Lev 6:18***). Such articles merited careful, special treatment. OT Israelites maintained a clear distinction between the holy and the common—refusing to treat what is holy in a casual manner, but instead treating it with fear and a sense of awe (***Num 18:32***).

God serves as the ultimate example of *qodesh*—what is holy, sacred, and entirely pure. The OT sometimes refers to God as *"the Holy One of Israel"* (e.g., ***2Kgs 19:22; Ps 89:18; Isa 5:19***); Isaiah shows particular affinity for this title, as 25 of the title's 31 occurrences appear in ***Isaiah***. The OT also uses *qodesh* to refer to the "Holy Spirit" (***Ps 51:11; Isa 63:10-11***). God's holiness provides the basis for faithfulness to His promises (***Ps 105:42***) and His ability to deliver His people (***Ex 15:11***).

God calls His followers to reflect this divine, perfect holiness in their own lives (***Lev 19:2***). In response to His holiness (note *"Be holy* ***because*** *I am holy"* in ***Lev 19:2***, bold added) we strive for moral purity and sacred distinction in ourselves.

implies "separation, consecration, devotion to the service of Deity, sharing in God's purity and abstaining from earth's defilement" (**Zodhiates, 70**). Paul implied in his terminology that the communities of believers receiving his letters must maintain a holy distinction from

[2] Sources Consulted: "Qodesh," by Thomas E. McComiskey; "Holiness, Holy," by Stephen Renn ; "Qds," by Jackie A. Naude.

worldly surroundings. Churches who find an authentic identity in Christ exhibit tangible distinctions from their surrounding culture.

I recall standing in the parking lot outside of a church building where I used to minister, talking with a fellow we hired to complete some minor repairs on our facility. He did not attend our church, but told me of his involvement with another congregation. He taught Sunday School, served on the leadership team, and sang in the choir. During our conversation, his cell phone buzzed. He politely excused himself from our conversation and answered the call. The person on the other end of the call, his coworker, delivered frustrating news about another job. I watched and listened as this Sunday School teacher turned red in the face, then unleashed a fuming tirade, laced with profanity and threats.

Churches who find an authentic identity in Christ exhibit tangible distinctions from their surrounding culture.

As the phone call ended, I thought, "I hope, in the very least, he is as embarrassed as I am right now."

He was not embarrassed. Instead, he dropped the phone back into its holster on his belt and chuckled, "That's business. Now, where were we . . ."

If we—the church, Christians—act no differently than the world acts, how can we claim an identity in Christ? If we conform our actions to the cultural norm, rather than to God's holiness, we lose the very distinction to which God called us.

In contrast to that conversation in the church parking lot, I recall another conversation in the same church's gymnasium. A lady I had not met previously stopped by to see our new gym floor—she worked as a custodian for another church who had a similar floor, and she wanted to see how we cleaned ours. After we chatted for a while she said, "Fayetteville Christian Church . . . I think my son's baseball coach goes here—Lamar Knight?"

"Yes," I responded, "He's one of our faithfuls."

"My son just loves him. There's just something different about Coach Knight. Do you know he prays with the kids before every practice and game? He constantly encourages them; he cares about them. He's teaching those boys a lot more than just baseball."

On another occasion I chatted with a gentlemen who stood behind me in line at the local coffee shop. "Fayetteville Christian Church?" he asked when I mentioned where I worked. "Larry Coleman goes to church out there, doesn't he? I buy building materials from Larry. He's always so helpful, and honest—not like most people I have to deal with."

Honesty, integrity, purity, authentic love—such virtues have fallen into short supply in our culture. Such virtues, however, gush like Niagara Falls from communities of believers who find their identity in Christ Jesus. These communities, therefore, are distinct.

WHEN GOD'S PEOPLE BLEND IN

THE FAILURE TO REMAIN DISTINCT

Though God, through the law, attempted to keep His people distinct from the surrounding pagan nations, the community failed often and miserably. Describing the Israelites just a couple of generations after they settled in the Promised Land, ***Judges*** strikes a sour note:

> [11]*Then the Israelites did evil in the eyes of the LORD and served the Baals.* [12]*They forsook the LORD, the God of their fathers, who had brought them out of Egypt. They followed and worshiped various gods of the peoples around them. They provoked the LORD to anger* [13]*because they forsook him and served Baal and the Ashtoreths.* [14]*In his anger against Israel the LORD handed them over to raiders who plundered them. He sold them to their enemies all around, whom they were no longer able to resist.* [15]*Whenever Israel went out to fight, the hand of the LORD was against them to defeat them, just as he had sworn to them. They were in great distress.* (***Jdg 2:11-15***)

Even in the midst of their disobedience, however, God did not forget His people. He raised up leaders for them—judges—who led them to repentance, restored peace, and reestablished their military protection. Notice, however, as the Judges narrative continues, the despairing cycle of Israel's disobedience, and the consequences this behavior earned them:

> [16]*Then the Lord raised up judges, who saved them out of the hands of these raiders.* [17]*Yet they would not listen to their judges but prostituted themselves to other gods and worshiped them. Unlike their fathers, they quickly turned from the way in which their fathers had walked, the way of obedience to the LORD's com-*

mands. 18Whenever the LORD raised up a judge for them, he was with the judge and saved them out of the hands of their enemies as long as the judge lived; for the LORD had compassion on them as they groaned under those who oppressed and afflicted them. 19But when the judge died, the people returned to ways even more corrupt than those of their fathers, following other gods and serving and worshiping them. They refused to give up their evil practices and stubborn ways.

> *20Therefore the LORD was very angry with Israel and said, "Because this nation has violated the covenant that I laid down for their forefathers and has not listened to me, 21I will no longer drive out before them any of the nations Joshua left when he died."* (***Jdg 2:16-21***)

By blending in with their pagan neighbors, the Israelites shattered numerous elements of their covenant with God, including idol worship and the flagrant sexual immorality that often accompanied it. And, though God had warned them of the dangers of intermarriage, *"The Israelites lived among the Canaanites, Hittites, Perizzites, Hivites and Jebusites. They took their daughters in marriage and gave their own daughters to their sons, and served their gods"* (***Jdg 3:5-6***). The very behaviors from which God had attempted to protect the Israelites through the laws reappear frequently in the Israelite narrative. God's call for distinctiveness faded into the miry fog of compromise.

God's call for distinctiveness faded into the miry fog of compromise.

By some counts, sadly, the same could be said of the contemporary American church. In *unChristian*, David Kinnaman, president of The Barna Group, discussed some disheartening research concerning the failure of contemporary Christians to remain distinct:

> In virtually every study we conduct, representing thousands of interviews every year, born-again Christians fail to display much attitudinal or behavior evidence of transformed lives.[3]

[3] Kinnaman clarifies that the group labeled "born-again Christians" does not simply refer to the broad group of people who identify themselves as Christians (around four out of every five Americans). Instead, "born-again Christians" is a more narrowly defined group (about two out of every five Americans). To be classified as born-again Christians, people must affirm that they have made personal commitments to Jesus that are still important and that they believe they will go to heaven at death because they have confessed their sin and accepted Christ as Savior (**Kinnaman, 46**).

For instance, based on a study released in 2007, we found that most of the lifestyle activities of born-again Christians were statistically equivalent to those of non-born-agains. When asked to identify their activities over the last thirty days, born-again believers were just as likely to bet or gamble, to visit a pornographic website, to take something that did not belong to them, to consult a medium or psychic, to physically fight or abuse someone, to have consumed enough alcohol to be considered legally drunk, to have used an illegal, nonprescription drug, to have said something to someone that was not true, to have gotten back at someone for something he or she did, and to have said mean things behind another person's back. (**47**)

Today's church, like OT Israel, too often fails to exhibit the moral distinction God demands.

As the period of the Judges ended, Israel asked for a king. *"We want a king over us,"* the people begged, ***"then we will be like all the other nations"*** (***1Sa 8:19-20***, bold added). Despite Samuel's warnings, the people persisted. God explained to the heartbroken Samuel, *"It is not you they have rejected, but they have rejected me as their king"* (***1Sa 8:7***). The community's rebellion against God's kingship and their insistence on blending in with the pagans sent them down a path that led, by the end of Solomon's reign (their third king), to a state of disarray and upheaval.

Solomon himself chronically ignored God's laws concerning intermarriage:

> *King Solomon, however, loved many foreign women besides Pharaoh's daughter—Moabites, Ammonites, Edomites, Sidonians, and Hittites. They were from nations about which the LORD had told the Israelites, "You must not intermarry with them, because they will surely turn your hearts after their gods." Nevertheless, Solomon held fast to them in love. He had seven hundred wives of royal birth and three hundred concubines, and his wives led him astray.* (***1Kgs 11:1-3***)

Similarly, "Solomon entered into military and economic treaties, symbolized cultically by the introduction of shrines to the gods of those nations into his acropolis. This of course constituted a frontal attack on the cher-

Like OT Israel, we too often fail to exhibit the moral distinction God demands.

ished belief of early Yahwism that Yahweh was the sole guarantor of the people's security" (**Hanson, 106**).

Though the narrative offers occasional bright spots—God continued to work and make His glory known through many of David's exploits, for example—the overall momentum of God's community pushed them continually further from the covenant with which Yahweh blessed them, and the cultural distinctiveness Yahweh demanded of them.

The Consequences of Blending In

Later, prophets attempted to lead the nation back to its roots of holiness, but to no avail. As the unrepentant people continued neglecting their covenant with God, God promised His wrath would pour on them in the form of enemy armies. Through Jeremiah, for example, the Lord remembered fondly *"the devotion of your youth, how as a bride you loved me and followed me through the desert, through a land now sown. Israel was holy to the Lord, the firstfruits of his harvest"* (***Jer 2:2-3***). *"But,"* Yahweh continued, *"my people have exchanged their Glory for worthless idols. Be appalled at this, O heavens, and shudder with great horror. . . . My people have committed two sins: They have forsaken me, the spring of living water, and have dug their own cisterns, broken cisterns that cannot hold water"* (***Jer 2:11-13***). Therefore, God bid Jeremiah,

> *"Announce in Judah and proclaim in Jerusalem and say: 'Sound the trumpet throughout the land!' Cry aloud and say: 'Gather together! Let us flee to the fortified cities!' Raise the signal and go to Zion! Flee for safety without delay! For I am bringing disaster from the north, even terrible destruction."* (***Jer 4:5-6***)

God takes His call to holiness seriously, and He expects us to take that call just as seriously.

I recently heard of a church who established as its mission statement, "Our mission is to blur the lines between church and community" (**M. Scott, "Love"**). I assume the church's leaders established this mission statement with noble intentions. Churches need to don the hats of missionaries and speak relevantly and authentically to our communities. We must cease to hide behind stained glass windows, insulating ourselves from those whom God has called us to reach. I assume this church sees service to its community as a core value. I would encourage such a church, however, to show greater care with its terminology. When God's people have "blurred the lines" between themselves and their culture, such a blurring has not pleased the Almighty.

DISTINCTIVENESS AS IT RELATES TO EVANGELISM

Israel as a Blessing to the Nations

When God called OT Israel to holiness, this call did not diminish His desire to bless all nations; in fact, the call to distinctiveness served as a critical part of God's missional plan. Moses explained to the Israelites that when God's people live according to God's standards,

> *this will show your wisdom and understanding to the nations, who will hear about all these decrees and say, "Surely this great nation is a wise and understanding people." What other nation is so great as to have their gods near them the way the* Lord *our God is near us whenever we pray to him? And what other nation is so great as to have such righteous decrees and laws as this body of laws I am setting before you today?* (**Deu 4:6-8**)

Furthermore, when God commanded His community to serve as *"a kingdom of priests and a holy nation"* (**Ex 19:6**), this implied "a pastoral and missionary function on the part of Israel, witnessing on God's behalf to the other nations and mediating on their behalf before the Lord. They would become co-laborers with Him in effecting the world's redemption" (**D. Smith, 210**). C.J.H. Wright explains concerning OT Israel's distinctiveness,

> The purpose of Israel's existence was to be a vehicle both for God's revelation and for the blessing of humanity. They were not only the bearers of redemption, but were to be a model of what a redeemed community should be like, living in obedience to God's will. Their social structure, aspirations, principles and policies, so organically related to their covenantal faith in the Lord, were also part of the content of that revelation, part of the pattern of redemption. God's message of redemption through Israel was not just verbal; it was visible and tangible. They, the medium, were themselves part of the message. Simply by existing and being obedient to the covenant law of the Lord, they would raise questions among the nations about the nature of their God and the social justice of their community. (**62**)

Distinction in Morality

Though at first glance the concepts appear antithetical, God's people most effectively influence the nations when they remain distinct from the nations. This holds true when one understands "distinction" in terms of ethics and morality. As Jesus Himself exemplified, the Lord's mission requires the Lord's people to relate in an authentic, compassionate manner with people of the world. *"It is not the healthy who need a doctor, but the sick,"* Jesus explained to those suspicious of His relationships with *"tax collectors and 'sinners'"* (***Mt 9:11-12***). Jesus remained sinless, but deliberately related with sinful people. Our distinction, then, if we follow His example, lies in the realm of morality rather than locality.

Our distinction lies in the realm of morality rather than locality.

Consider, to extend this discussion further, the issue of intermarriage discussed previously in this chapter. God strictly prohibited His community from intermarrying with men and women of the surrounding pagan nations. God knew that such intimate interaction would allow immorality and idol worship to seep into His community. Israel ignored this command and brought disastrous consequences onto themselves. As before, however, God's desire had to do with morality—in this case more so than ethnicity. Consider Ruth and Rahab, two ladies of foreign descent whom God welcomed into the community. Both ladies married into the Israelite community and are counted among the ancestors of David and Jesus. Ruth has long been exalted as an example of faithful love. Rahab's name appears in the faith hall of fame (***Heb 11:31***). God always held compassion for people outside of Israel;[4] He simply did not want His community infected with the pagan, immoral, idolatrous aspects of their neighboring nations.

Distinction Furthering Evangelism

God calls His community to be *"the salt of the earth"* (***Mt 5:13a***), which requires deliberate interaction with the world. In the midst of this interaction, however, we keep in mind that *"if the salt loses its saltiness . . . it is no longer good for anything"* (***Mt 5:13b***). Evangelism

[4]Another example lies in God sending Jonah to Nineveh.

requires us to relate with people of the world; holiness requires our moral distinction from the same people. Rather than the two matters opposing one another—evangelism and distinction—one (distinction) actually furthers the other (evangelism). Salt impacts the world not despite its saltiness, but because of its saltiness.

Salt impacts the world not *despite,* but *because* of its saltiness.

In contrast to the church's mission statement mentioned in the previous section ("Our mission is to blur the lines between church and community"), consider the comment of J.K. Jones, a professor of Lincoln Christian University, "We are best for our communities when we are most unlike our communities" (**M. Scott, "Love"**). Ironically, our very distinctiveness enables us to minister most effectively to our culture—a world adrift in relativism seeks an anchor of truth; a culture of superficiality seeks substance; a society of aimlessness seeks purpose; a community burdened by relational manipulation seeks relational authenticity. God's church offers what the godless world seeks. If we lose our distinctiveness, therefore, we lose our ability to evangelize. If we offer the world only those things the world already has on its own, such as flashy programs, entertainment, or even opportunities to serve, we lose our reason for being. To effectively reach our world, we must hold to and never diminish the covenant-based, truth-honoring, Christ-exalting holiness which sets us apart.

A CASE STUDY: DANIEL

Pearls against Black Velvet

The first chapter of Daniel provides a picture of the distinctiveness God requires of His community, putting flesh on God's call to holiness. The first two verses of Daniel set the scene:

> *In the third year of the reign of Jehoiakim king of Judah, Nebuchadnezzar king of Babylon came to Jerusalem and besieged it. And the Lord delivered Jehoiakim king of Judah into his hand, along with some of the articles from the temple of God. These he carried off to the temple of his god in Babylonia and put in the treasure house of his god.* (**Dan 1:1-2**)

Though the reader may feel tempted to skim these verses, they provide the backdrop necessary to understand the remainder of the narrative.

In about 600 BC God directed the pagan king of Babylon to conquer His children living in Judah, and to deport many of them back to Babylon. The pagan king of Babylon, Nebuchadnezzar, did not know God directed him, but He did. God's hand manipulated the entire event because Judah had fallen into deep wells of sinful indulgence, and they wallowed around in it. Through prophet after prophet, for decade upon decade, God warned His children that if they did not repent He would send a band of pagans to conquer them. Time and again the people thumbed their noses at God: *"They mocked God's messengers, despised his words and scoffed at his prophets until the wrath of the Lord was aroused against his people and there was no remedy"* (***2Chr 36:16***). At one point God sent a warning directly to Jehoiakim, the king of Judah. Jehoiakim responded by shredding the scroll with a knife and throwing it into the fire. He did the same thing three times (***Jeremiah 36***).

Idol worship, illicit sex, mockery of all that is good and right and pure—the people of Judah covered all the sinfully indulgent bases.

Against this backdrop of a faithless nation, the book of ***Daniel*** highlights the faithfulness of a godly few. When a jeweler wants to display a string of pearls, the jeweler sets the pearls against black velvet. The dark backdrop provides a contrast that causes the pearls to gleam. The book of ***Daniel*** takes a similar approach. The first two verses describe God's punishment inflicted on His unfaithful people. The remainder of the book describes how God honored a faithful few. Daniel is one of a few Bible heroes who, as far as we know, had no major flaw on his résumé. Noah had his drunkenness, Abraham his lies, Jacob his scheming, David his Bathsheba, and Peter his denials. But Daniel, despite the impure culture in which he lived, stayed pure. He managed to help a few of his friends stay pure, also.

When I grew up in West Virginia, I had a friend named J.W. who devoted his life to Christ, and whose life reflected holiness. In comparison, I tried too often to live in both worlds. I played on the basketball team, which in my home town put me in the realm of the elite. I enjoyed sitting with the popular crowd at lunch, flirting with the cheerleaders, and swaggering through the hallways with the other athletes.

I was never a bad kid; for the most part, I did not do the things I was not supposed to do. But instead of a pearl set against black velvet, on too many occasions I tried to blend into the velvet as much as I could without actually getting it on me. I recall specific instances when someone mentioned Christianity, or asked if I went to church—blood rushed to my face and I tried to answer as quietly as I could. I did not lie, but I hoped to stay incognito in my faith.

One particular semester, some youth ministers from area churches started a chapter of Fellowship of Christian Athletes at our high school. My youth minister guilted me into attending the first meeting. I found excuses to bow out of the rest. J.W. served as the president of the Fellowship of Christian Athletes. The last I heard, J.W. served as a youth minister with a church in Kentucky. I imagine he does a good job teaching his students about Daniel, because J.W. lived the distinct life that the book teaches.

A Resolve Not to Defile

After Daniel, who was probably around fifteen years old at the time, and the other captives arrived in Babylon, King Nebuchadnezzar instructed his officials to choose the cream-of-the-crop Jewish boys—those who were handsome, intelligent, and had royal blood in their veins—to enter training for service in the King's administration. Probably, Nebuchadnezzar would use them to manage the affairs concerning the captive Jews. Nebuchadnezzar changed the boys' names to reflect a submission to Babylonian gods. He immersed them in a study of Babylonian language and literature—literature heavily steeped in pagan worship and mythology. Finally, he sat the boys at his own banquet table that they might enjoy a steady diet of royal proportions. The banquet table presented a dilemma for Daniel. Imagine the scene. . . .[5]

Daniel twirls his fork like a baton. Then he uses it to shuffle his prime rib from one side of the plate to the other. He pretends to sip the wine that was placed in front of him, however his lips remain closed so that no wine actually enters his mouth. He salts the prime rib again, and pours on another dollop of steak sauce. Daniel picks up the steak knife and cuts the meat, then puts the knife back down. He pretends to take another sip of wine, then adds a little more salt, and another dollop of steak sauce. He picks up the knife again, cuts a little more.

[5] I will take literary license in imagining Daniel's story. I trust the reader will humor me.

Daniel fidgets, but doesn't eat or drink. Everybody around him does, and they seem to enjoy the feast. The steak, the wine—they do look awfully tasty. And the aroma—Daniel's mouth begins watering.

The guys sitting around Daniel notice that he isn't eating. They nudge him and whisper, "Come on, Daniel. Don't make an issue out of this. There's no need to cause any ripples. We're prisoners here, we don't want trouble. Just blend in. It's not that big of a deal. God will understand. Just eat." But to Daniel it was a big deal. Though complying would please everyone around him, Daniel knew it would not please God.

As a faithful Jew, Daniel lived under certain dietary restrictions. The law prohibited particular foods, and allowable foods must be prepared in a specific manner—all the fat had to be cut off before cooking it, for example, and all the blood drained out. God made such commands for health reasons, and to ensure that His children didn't blend in with the pagan cultures around them. God set His people apart as a holy nation—even their diet reflected this distinctiveness.

Most certainly, the food sitting before Daniel had not been prepared in the proper Jewish manner. And, perhaps more noteworthy, Daniel knows the meat came from animals that had been sacrificed to pagan gods. The first portion of the wine had been poured out on pagan altars. By partaking of such food and wine, Babylonians expressed their appreciation for and sought the blessings of their gods. If he partook alongside them, Daniel would, in a sense, participate in pagan worship. All in all, Daniel knows that eating and drinking would displease God. He faces a complicated, momentous issue.

Thus, he cuts the meat into ever small pieces, and sprinkles on a little more salt.

The issues we face may not seem so large; that is, until we face them. Coworkers at the office need everyone to skew the numbers on their expense reports, or no one can. At school, the cheat sheet circles around the classroom. At home, the computer connects easily to the internet which connects quickly to lust-inducing images and chat rooms. The pagan culture lures like a seductress.

The pagan culture lures like a seductress.

After fidgeting with his food, Daniel returns the fork to the table. He sets his jaw, straightens his back, and lifts his chin. *"Daniel resolved not to defile himself with the royal food and wine"* (***Dan 1:8***). Daniel knew his options and weighed the consequences. He understood that if he defied Nebuchadnezzar's order, the king might have Daniel's head on a platter. But Daniel resolved not to defile himself.

Every December 31 numerous people sit down with pen and paper and list aspirations for the coming year: "This year I'll lose weight (and I mean it this time!). I'll exercise more. I'll read three chapters of the Bible every day. I'll buy my wife flowers and take my kids fishing at least once a month." Wouldn't Daniel's resolution provide a great addition to the list? Maybe it should *be* the list: "This year I resolve not to defile myself. Come what may, I will stay pure. Go ahead, Satan, throw 'em at me—lust, greed, pride, gossip—I refuse to submit to your devious enticements."

Then, when temptations arrive, the decision for purity has already been made. We will not have to re-decide with every temptation. Nate Saint, a missionary who along with Jim Elliot died as a martyr in South America, once noted in his journal, "Obedience is not a momentary option . . . it is a die-cast decision made beforehand" (**Hitt, 232**).

Wisdom in Action

Resolve by itself, however, will not keep us pure. In addition to his resolve, Daniel developed and executed a wise plan.

We left Daniel fidgeting at the king's banquet table. He resolved not to defile himself with the royal food and wine. Immediately his mind began formulating a plan. He rose from the table and strode toward the man in charge. Daniel explained his plan to the official. Rather than eating from the royal cupboard, Daniel suggested that he and a few of his friends eat only vegetables and drink only water for ten days. After ten days the official could judge whether this diet made the boys more or less healthy.

When asked to do something that would compromise his integrity, Daniel spewed no hate or vengeance. He wrote no angry emails. He did not storm out of the banquet room and march with a picket sign around the palace. Instead, Daniel used tact, showed respect for his superiors, and displayed careful judgment and wisdom. Daniel kindly offered an alternative—a way to both respect the authorities over him, and keep a pure conscience.

We can do the same. Christians, I fear, have too often damaged our ultimate mission with our hatefulness. Scathing letters, angry voicemails, and wagging fingers win few people to Christ.

After some hesitation, the official agreed to Daniel's plan. The result? *"At the end of the ten days they looked healthier and better nourished than any of the young men who ate the royal food"* (**Dan 1:15**). Daniel wisely developed, tactfully presented, and diligently executed a plan for holiness. As a result, God blessed his efforts.

In one of his books, Bob Russell tells of the time when the Southeast Christian Church established the third of their four Crisis Pregnancy Centers in Louisville, Kentucky. The lady who directs these centers felt convicted to start a center as near as possible to an abortion clinic. She prayed about her conviction, then drove into Louisville and turned onto the street that held the second largest abortion clinic in Kentucky.

When she turned her car down that street, her heartbeat quickened as she discovered a house for sale immediately next door to an abortion clinic. The house not only sat next to the clinic, but the walls of the two buildings butted up against one another. Within months, the church purchased and renovated the house, and opened a Crisis Pregnancy Center.

The ministry made a quick and astounding impact. Women would turn onto the street, and, sometimes even by accident, enter the Crisis Pregnancy Center instead of the abortion clinic. When a young woman realized her mistake, the receptionist would graciously say, "The abortion clinic is next door . . . but while you're here would you like to see a free ultrasound of your baby?" Almost every woman who viewed the ultrasound and heard her baby's beating heart decided to keep her baby.

The staff of the clinic did not change mothers' minds by picketing, yelling insults, or writing angry letters to the newspaper. They changed mothers' minds by wisely and kindly showing them another option.

The Crisis Pregnancy Center staffers treated the clinic workers next door with kindness, and prayed for them. And, the staffers placed their hands on the adjoining wall and prayed that God would stop the abortions in the neighboring building. Just a few months later the abortion clinic closed its doors (**Russell, 127-128**).

God calls His church to remain distinct from our culture. Sadly, many churches who seek distinctiveness do so in a manner that hinders, rather than helps, our mission to the world. When churches follow Christ's own example of grace and truth, of purity demonstrated alongside of love, the world takes notice, and our distinctiveness itself becomes one of the most effective tools God uses to accomplish His mission.

> **Many churches seek distinctiveness in a way that hinders, rather than helps, our mission.**

What Do You Say?

1. How might a church's efforts toward distinction hinder its ability to accomplish God's mission?
2. What criteria might Christians use in deciding when, and concerning what issues, to take a public stand?
3. In what specific ways should today's church stand out from our culture?
4. What consequences did the Israelites face when they blended in with their pagan surroundings? What consequences might today's church face if we blend in to our culture?
5. What did J.K. Jones mean when he said, "We are best for our communities when we are most unlike our communities"?
6. How did Daniel remain distinct from the pagan culture in which he lived?
7. What might we learn from Daniel's example?

CHAPTER THREE

COMMUNALLY RESPONSIBLE

Older baseball fans remember when Jackie Robinson, the first African American to play Major League baseball, joined the Brooklyn Dodgers. Wherever the Dodgers traveled, opposing players and fans spewed hateful words and racial slurs at Robinson. Pitchers threw fastballs at his head. Opposing base runners attempted to gouge him with the spikes on their shoes as they slid into second base, where Robinson played. Fans threw trash and spat upon him as he returned to the dugout between innings.

During a particular game in Boston, the jeers escalated. As fans screamed their venomous prejudice, one of Robinson's teammates, a white southerner named Pee Wee Reese, called time out. Reese walked from his position at shortstop and stood next to Robinson. Reese put his arm around Robinson's shoulder and simply stood there with him, accepting the jeers alongside his friend. Jackie Robinson later commented that the gesture saved his career; he learned from such friendships that "a life is not important except in the impact it has on other lives" (**www.baseball-almanac.com**).

COMMUNAL RESPONSIBILITY

Reese's gesture and Robinson's wisdom stand in contrast to Cain. Among the first few chapters of the Bible, Cain scoffed before God, *"Am I my brother's keeper?"* (**Gen 4:9**). While God did not respond directly to Cain, the remainder of the OT answers in the affirmative, defining God's desire that the Hebrew people share responsibility for one another's physical and spiritual condition.

The modern Western world, however, too often neglects or ignores such communal ties. N.T. Wright observes,

> Anyone growing up in an average African town has dozens of friends up and down the street; indeed, many children live within what to the Western eyes would look like a massive and confusing extended family, with virtually every adult within walking distance being treated as an honorary aunt or uncle in a way that is unimaginable in the modern West. In such a community, there exist multiple networks of support, encouragement, rebuke, and warning, a corporate repository of folk wisdom (or, as it might be, folk folly) which keeps everyone together and gives people a shared sense of direction or at least, when things are bad, a shared sense of misfortune. Those who live in today's Western world mostly don't even realize what they're missing. In fact, they might be alarmed at the thought of all that togetherness. In such a community, everyone is in it together, for good or ill. (***Simply*, 31**)

When someone enters the realm of God's family, he or she enters a community in which individuals hold responsibility for one another, where "everyone is in it together, for good or ill" (**ibid.**). "Biblically oriented community," explains Paul Hanson, "offers as its sign-up bonus a promissory note signifying that the adherent need no longer live for self, but henceforth can be free to live for God and neighbor" (**xviii**).

One who enters God's family enters a community where individuals are responsible for one another.

When an individual belongs to a community, that individual's actions—either positive or negative—impact everyone. An old Jewish parable describes a group of men sailing on a ship. One of the men began boring a hole beneath his seat. When the others saw, they objected to him, "What are you doing?"

"What concern is it of yours? Am I not just drilling under my own seat?"

"But the water will come up and flood the ship for all of us," they replied (**Kaminsky, 1**).

In contrast to "current ethical thinking that seems to treat society as nothing more than a collection of unrelated individuals who happen to live together" (**ibid., 188**), God calls individuals to recognize their responsibility for the community; conversely, He calls the community to recognize its responsibility for the individual.

PROVIDING CARE WITHIN THE COMMUNITY

God calls His people to care for one another both physically and spiritually.

Physical Care

God's people hold responsibility for the physical care of the individuals among them. Numerous biblical laws and commands spell out specific aspects of this responsibility. The examples below offer a small sampling from the OT:

- *[7]If there is a poor man among your brothers in any of the towns of the land that the LORD your God is giving you, do not be hard-hearted or tightfisted toward your poor brother. [8]Rather be open-handed and freely lend him whatever he needs* (**Deu 15:7-8**).
- *Do not charge your brother interest, whether on money or food or anything else that may earn interest* (**Deu 23:19**).
- *[14]Do not take advantage of a hired man who is poor and needy, whether he is a brother Israelite or an alien living in one of your towns. [15]Pay him his wages each day before sunset, because he is poor and is counting on it. Otherwise he may cry to the LORD against you, and you will be guilty of sin* (**Deu 24:14-15**).
- *[17]Do not deprive the alien or the fatherless of justice, or take the cloak of the widow as a pledge. [18]Remember that you were slaves in Egypt and the LORD your God redeemed you from there. That is why I command you to do this* (**Deu 24:17-18**).
- *[19]When you are harvesting in your field and you overlook a sheaf, do not go back to get it. Leave it for the alien, the fatherless and the widow, so that the LORD your God may bless you in all the work of your hands. [20]When you beat the olives from your trees, do not go over the branches a second time. Leave what remains for the alien, the fatherless and the widow. [21]When you harvest the grapes in your vineyard, do not go over the vines again. Leave what remains for the alien, the fatherless and the*

widow. [22]Remember that you were slaves in Egypt. That is why I command you to do this (***Deu 24:19-22***).

[13]Do not have two differing weights in your bag—one heavy, one light. [14]Do not have two differing measures in your house—one large, one small. [15]You must have accurate and honest weights and measures, so that you may live long in the land the LORD *your God is giving you. [16]For the* LORD *your God detests anyone who does these things, anyone who deals dishonestly* (***Deu 25:13-16***).

"The sum of them," explains Walter Brueggemann about such laws, "is a vision of a radically alternative society in which neighborly commitments supersede all the requirements of commodity and production and consumption" (***Mandate*, 167**). God's followers care more about one another than they care about profit or the accumulation of wealth.

As they administered physical care to one another, the Lord called His people to recognize that "every individual was equally precious to God, regardless of social standing, and thus to be protected from exploitation and oppression by the structures intrinsic to the covenant between God and people" (**Hanson, 23**). Several laws specified that the Israelites must give particular attention to groups commonly marginalized in society—aliens, orphans, and widows. Aliens often lived as homeless nomads, working as cheap laborers and facing exploitation because they lacked family protection or inheritance. Because husbands/fathers provided a family's income, security, and protection, orphans and widows faced particular vulnerability. For these reasons God frequently reminded His people to remember *"the aliens, the fatherless and the widows"* (this phrase appears eleven times in ***Deuteronomy*** alone). God held such compassion for these marginalized of society that He warned the Israelites,

> *Do not mistreat an alien or oppress him, for you were aliens in Egypt. Do not take advantage of a widow or an orphan. If you do and they cry out to me, I will certainly hear their cry. My anger will be aroused, and I will kill you with the sword; your wives will become widows and your children fatherless.* (***Ex 22:21-22***)

God cares for those—such as the alien, orphan, and widow—whose circumstances make life difficult; and He calls His followers to pay particular attention to such people. Members of the LifeBridge Christian Church in Longmont, Colorado, developed a heart for the "orphans" of their community—foster children who have no place to go. Their county, like most, had far more foster children waiting for families than they had families willing to house the children. They developed a program labeled "Change Who Waits," which established the goal of recruiting so many families willing to provide foster care that the county had more homes than foster children. As a result, families would be waiting for children, rather than children waiting for families. By December of 2008, for the first time in three decades, and thanks in large part to LifeBridge Christian Church, Boulder County had enough homes to house all of their foster children (**Mavis, 10-12**).

God calls His followers to pay particular attention to people with greater needs.

The alien, orphan, and widow—and similar counterparts today—need the attention of God's people.

Lest we confine these principles to the pages of OT Israelite history, the NT repeats the emphasis to provide physical care for those among us who face need. *"Suppose a brother or sister is without clothes and daily food,"* writes James. *"If one of you says to him, 'Go, I wish you well; keep warm and well fed,' but does nothing about his physical needs, what good is it?"* (***Jas 2:15-16***). John explained to his readers that Jesus provides the ultimate example of brotherly love:

> [16]*This is how we know what love is: Jesus Christ laid down his life for us. And we ought to lay down our lives for our brothers.* [17]*If anyone has material possessions and sees his brother in need but has no pity on him, how can the love of God be in him?* [18]*Dear children, let us not love with words or tongue but with actions and in truth.* (***1Jn 3:16-18***)

One of my older sisters and her husband served for twelve years as missionaries in Haiti. Among various other ministries, such as church plants, a school, and feeding programs, they discipled a few young men who today lead various churches and ministries. One participant in this discipleship group, a shy young man named Miltador, showed a heart to obey even the most radical aspects of the gospel.

Like most Haitians, Miltador lived in poverty. He did have one possession, however, that gave him unusual opportunity. Miltador owned a cow—a feat that may not sound all that impressive to American ears, but one that would give Miltador's family an opportunity for ongoing nourishment from the cow's milk and ongoing income by breeding the cow and selling its calves.

Miltador came into possession of the cow after several years of work. A local farmer hired Miltador, then just a boy, to take care of a calf. Each morning and evening Miltador retrieved the calf from the neighboring farm, found a place for it to graze (not an easy task in Haiti), then returned it to its home. Miltador cared for the calf, with no pay, until it had grown and could be bred. When the farmer finally bred the cow, the farmer gave Miltador a calf—his only payment for years of work.

As the discipleship group, including Miltador, studied through the NT, they came upon ***1 John 3:16-18*** (quoted above), which teaches believers to use their material possessions to help their brothers in need. Paul, my brother-in-law who led the study, struggled with whether or not to teach the passage. American Christians need this message; we typically think of Haitians, however, as the ones who need help. Because the passage is in the Bible, however, and because even the poor need to recognize the need to help others, he taught the text.

The next week, when Miltador arrived at discipleship group meeting, Paul casually asked about his cow—had it stayed healthy? Miltador hung his head. "I don't have the cow anymore," he confessed.

"What?" Paul responded, his voice implying the obvious, "Are you crazy? Did you not realize what this cow would mean for your family?"

"My brother has been sick, and needed to see a doctor," explained Miltador in quiet, broken English. "He had no money to pay a doctor. Last week you told us that if we have material possessions, and see our brother in need, but don't help—how could the love of God be in us? So I sold the cow and gave the money to my brother so he could see the doctor."

Such sacrifice occurs in biblical community. Such sacrifice occurs too infrequently, however, in the American church that often misses the depth of community to which God has called us.

God's call for His people to care for one another's physical needs reflects His own character. God reached out to the Israelites in their poverty, oppression, and destitution. Then, He called them to reach out in the same way to the poor, oppressed, and destitute among them—to grant the needy the same grace they had received: *"He defends the cause of the fatherless and the widow, and loves the alien, giving him food and clothing. And you are to love those who are aliens, for you yourselves were aliens in Egypt"* (**Deu 10:18-19**).

Scholars sometimes use the terms *imitatio dei,* a Latin phrase that roughly translates "imitating God," to describe the virtue of reflecting the character and holiness of God. The concept finds its roots in God's seminal ethical instruction, *"Be holy because I, the LORD your God, am holy"* (***Lev 19:2***). C.J.H. Wright points out concerning this passage,

> We are inclined to think of "holiness" as a matter of personal piety or, in the Old Testament terms, of ritual cleanliness, proper sacrifices, clean and unclean food, and the like. Certainly, the rest of ***Leviticus 19*** includes some of these dimensions of Israel's religious life. But the bulk of the chapter shows us that the kind of holiness that reflects God's own holiness is thoroughly practical. It includes generosity to the poor at harvest time, justice for workers, integrity in judicial processes, considerate behaviour to other people (especially the disabled), equality before the law for immigrants, honest trading and other very "earthy" social matters. And all through the chapters runs the refrain "I am the LORD," as if to say, "*Your* quality of life must reflect the very heart of *my* character. This is what I require of *you* because this is what reflects *me*. This is what I myself would do." (39)

The Lord, who has great concern for the physical needs of individuals, requires that His community reflect the same concern.

The Lord requires that His community reflect the same concern as He has.

SPIRITUAL CARE

In addition to physical care, God's community holds responsibility for the spiritual care of the individuals among them. While this responsibility includes behavioral accountability—a matter we will discuss below—it also includes mutual encouragement to persevere and to grow in faith.

The friendship shared by David and Jonathan provides an example of such spiritual care. David, already anointed as the next king, and Jonathan, the eldest son of the existing king, culturally speaking should have battled one another for the throne. Instead of battling, however, the two men cultivated a significant friendship through which they encouraged one another's faith. The narratives that describe their relationship, such as those found in ***1 Samuel 18:1-4, 19:1-7, and 20:1-42,*** continually emphasize the godly basis of David and Jonathan's friendship. In fact, these narratives—at first glance about the two men—mention the Lord seventeen times. Thirteen of these seventeen occurrences include God as a part of an oath or covenant. For example, on one occasion, *"Jonathan said to David, 'Go in peace, for we have sworn friendship with each other in the name of the LORD, saying 'The LORD is witness between you and me, and between your descendants and my descendants forever'"* (**1Sa 20:42**).

One particular incident gives insight into the spiritual care that nourished David and Jonathan's friendship:

> *While David was at Horesh in the Desert of Ziph, he learned that Saul had come out to take his life. And Saul's son Jonathan went to David at Horesh and helped him find strength in God. "Don't be afraid," he said. "My father Saul will not lay a hand on you. You will be king over Israel, and I will be second to you. Even my father Saul knows this." The two of them made a covenant before the LORD.* (**1Sa 23:15-18**)

When faced with exhaustion, confusion, and frightening circumstances, David needed a friend who would come alongside him and help him *"find strength in God."* Jonathan provided the spiritual care David needed.

Mindy Caliguire refers to such relationships as "soul friendships."

> Soul friends do a very unique thing: They help you find strength in God. They do not try to fix you. They do not try to convince you everything is okay. They do not try to be God for you. They are not even concerned primarily with helping you get happy again. They want to help reconnect you with God, which is what you most need in that moment. (**90**)

In his book *Stories for the Journey*, William White tells of a European seminary professor and his wife, named Hans and Enid. During World War II they escaped to America, where Hans began teaching in a seminary. Students loved this warm, gentle Bible teacher; and, they enjoyed observing the tender love that Hans and Enid displayed as the couple often walked hand in hand around campus.

Enid's unexpected death sent Hans into a pit of sorrow. The seminary president and three other friends began visiting Hans, but he remained lonely and depressed. "I am no longer able to pray to God," Hans confided in the men. "In fact, I am not certain I believe in God any more."

After an awkward moment of silence, the seminary president responded, "Then we will believe for you. We will make your confession for you. We will pray for you." In the following weeks the four men met daily to pray with Hans, asking God to help Hans experience God's presence and healing.

Biblical communities help one another find strength in God.

Months later, as the four men gathered once again in Hans's living room, Hans greeted them with a smile. "It is no longer necessary for you to pray for me," he said. "Instead, I would like you to pray with me" (**White, 48-49**).

Biblical communities provide this kind of spiritual care to the individuals among them who need encouragement. They help one another find strength in God.

Word Study
Qahal[1]

Qahal refers to any kind of assembly, gathering, or congregation. Depending on its context, the word may portray a generic, nontheological assembly, or it may carry theological implications.

The OT uses the term in reference to those gathered for evil purposes (***Gen 49:6***), for war (***Num 22:4***), an assembly of "holy ones" in heaven (***Ps 89:5***), and to describe God's people on earth (***Ezra 10:12***). When God repeated to Jacob the covenant He had made with Abraham, including the promise of numerous descendants, God used *qahal* to describe the resulting covenant community (***Gen 28:3***). Jacob repeated the same promise to Joseph, again using *qahal* to describe the community (***Gen 48:4***). Generations later, when God promised Jeremiah that He would bring His people back from exile, He promised the return of *"a great throng"* ("throng" translated from *qahal*, ***Jer 31:8***)—a promise fulfilled seventy years later.

The OT sometimes pairs *qahal* with other terms that specifically designate the assembly as the people of God, such as *qehal YHWH* (*"the LORD's assembly,"* ***Num 16:3***), and *qehal elohim* (*"the assembly of God,"* ***Neh 13:1***).

The most occurrences of *qahal* in the OT, however, reference the assembling of God's people for ritual ceremony—such as sacrifices (***Lev 4:13-14; Num 15:15***), festivals (***Ex 12:6; 2Chr 20:5***), worship (***Deu 23:1-3; 1Kgs 8:14***), and to renew their covenant with God (***2Chr***

[1] Sources consulted: "Qahal," by Jack P. Lewis; "Qhl," by Eugene Carpenter; "Assemble/Assembly," by Stephen Renn.

23:3). In some cases, a person deemed unclean may not enter the *qahal* (*Deu 23:1-8*).

In sum when used in a religious context, *qahal* refers to the assembly of God's covenant community.

Interestingly, the Septuagint (the "LXX," the Greek translation of the Hebrew OT used widely during the NT era) usually translates the Hebrew *qahal* as the Greek *ekklesia*—a Greek term used throughout the NT, most often translated "church." Though this linguistic fact does not sufficiently warrant referring to an "Old Testament church," it does demonstrate that NT writers believed the NT covenant community—the church (*ekklesia*)—has foundations in the OT covenant community (*qahal*).

THE COMMUNITY ACCOUNTABLE TO GOD

SHARING THE GUILT OF THE INDIVIDUAL

In addition to spiritual and physical care, OT teaching concerning communal responsibility extends to another, less comforting concept: God's people stand accountable for any sin that infects the community. The community bears the guilt of each individual. "The covenant was deemed to have been entered into both with each individual Israelite and with Israel as a people," explains Anthony Phillips. "Thus on its breach, both individual and communal liability arose, a man being liable not only for his own acts, but also, by reason of his membership in the covenant community, for the acts of others" (**Kaminsky, 93**).

God's people stand accountable for any sin that infects the community.

In light of this, as ***Deuteronomy*** proceeds through various laws, on ten occasions Moses repeats this same refrain to the Israelites: *"You must purge the evil from among you"* (***Deu 13:5; 17:7,12; 19:13,19; 21:9,21; 22:21,22,24***). Those who had infected the community with sin could no longer remain a part of the community; in fact, they faced the punishment of death—usually a stoning at the hands of the community (notably not at the hands of a single executioner). This communal execution of justice demonstrated corporate responsibility for sin, and corporate desire for purity.

Achan's Folly

A clear example of communal accountability lies in the story of Achan, recorded in ***Joshua 7***. Immediately after God empowered the Israelites to defeat Jericho (***Joshua 6***), Joshua states that *"the Israelites acted unfaithfully in regard to devoted things"* (***Josh 7:1***). Had the people taken a majority vote to act unfaithfully? Did each Israelite cast his or her ballot in support of sin? Had the leaders convened a public forum in which everyone had a voice, at the end of which the entire community reached a consensus to rebel against God? No—though the opening phrase speaks of the Israelites as a whole, ***Joshua 7:1*** continues by describing how one individual had been unfaithful *"in regard to devoted things"*: *"Achan son of Carmi, the son of Zimri, the son of Zerah, of the tribe of Judah, took some of them. So the LORD's anger burned against Israel."*

When the Israelites destroyed Jericho, God commanded them to keep away from Jericho's valuable plunder. Instead, as a gesture of devotion to God, they must destroy everything except for the precious metals, which they were to add to the Lord's treasury (***Josh 6:18-19***). Achan, however, greedily took some of this plunder for himself and hid it in the ground inside his tent (***Josh 7:20-21***). His disobedience brought guilt to the entire community. In fact, though the one man sinned, note the repetition of the plural pronoun "they" in God's accusation: *"Israel has sinned; they have violated my covenant, which I commanded them to keep. They have taken some of the devoted things; they have stolen, they have lied, they have put them with their own possessions"* (***Josh 7:11***).

One man sinned, unbeknown to everyone else; yet God's anger burned against the whole community. The community bore the guilt of the individual. As a result, when Israel waged war against Ai—a small band of people who should have easily folded beneath the strength of the more numerous Israelites—the soldiers of Ai defeated Israel, killing *"about thirty-six of them"* (***Josh 7:4***). When they attacked Jericho, the Lord was present among His people. When they attacked Ai, however, God explained that the community had *"been made liable to destruction"* (***Josh 7:12***) because God no longer dwelt among them. Achan's sin resulted in God's absence from the community. *"I will not be with you anymore,"* the Lord explained, *"unless you destroy whatever among you is devoted to destruction"* (***Josh 7:12***).

To regain God's presence among them, therefore, *"Joshua, together with all Israel, took Achan son of Zerah, the silver, the robe, the gold wedge, his sons and daughters, his cattle, donkeys and sheep, his tent and all that he had, to the Valley of Achor. . . . Then all Israel stoned him, and after they had stoned the rest, they burned them."* As a result, *"Then the LORD turned from his fierce anger"* (***Josh 7:24-26***).

The Hebrew text contains a play on the term *cherem* throughout ***Joshua 6 and 7***. The term means "devoted to ban, dedicated to destruction" (**Holladay, 117**); and furthermore implies "the exclusion of an object from the use or abuse of man and its irrevocable surrender to God . . . a ban for utter destruction, the compulsory dedication of something which impedes or resists God's work, which is considered to be accursed before God" (**Archer, Harris, and Waltke, 324-325**).

In ***Joshua 6***, God warned the Israelites concerning the destruction of Jericho, *"Keep away from the devoted things [**cherem**], so that you will not bring about your own destruction [**cherem**] by taking any of them. Otherwise you will make the camp of Israel liable to destruction [**cherem**] and bring trouble on it"* (***6:18***). God set aside the physical wealth of Jericho to be destroyed for His glory. If the people did not keep this command, God would set apart the Israelites themselves for destruction.

Chapter seven reveals that, through Achan, what God warned came to pass:

> *[11]"Israel has sinned; they have violated my covenant, which I commanded them to keep. They have taken some of the devoted things [**cherem**]. . . . [12]That is why the Israelites cannot stand against their enemies; they turn their backs and run because they have been made liable to destruction [**cherem**]. I will not be with you anymore unless you destroy whatever among you is devoted to destruction [**cherem**]."* (***Josh 7:11-12***)

Because they stole those things God had set apart for destruction, the Israelite community was set apart for destruction, until they destroyed the one (Achan) among them who had brought this evil into the camp.

Standing or Falling Together

God held the entire community responsible to maintain purity. God's presence, in fact, required this purity. For Israel to enjoy His blessing, including military victory, they must create and maintain a holy environment in which God would dwell. Any sin present among God's people threatens the purity of the community and, therefore, places that community in an impure state in which God will not dwell and will not bless. Any sin within the community places the entire community beneath a blanket of guilt.

> **Any sin present among God's people threatens the purity of the community.**

Modern readers may balk at the corporate punishment God inflicted on the Israelites because of Achan's sin. Such punishment seems unfair; should not God treat every individual as autonomous? "One wonders," speculates Joel Kaminsky concerning this perspective, "whether this narrative might not offer an implicit critique of the modern predisposition to view individuals as autonomous entities who only relate to their society when they freely choose to do so" (95). God tied His people together with a web of relationship that remains for better or worse. We succeed together. We fail together. We face consequences together. We repent together.

A healthy church, then—a church who seeks God's presence and blessing—cares deeply for the spiritual condition of every member. A healthy church recognizes the absurd impossibility of the statement, "I'm hurting no one but myself," or the incongruity of the phrase "victimless sin" (one can imagine similar thoughts seeping through Achan's mind). Any sin within a church threatens the entire church's standing before God, and blessing from God, who wishes to dwell among His holy people.

INDIVIDUALS ACCOUNTABLE TO ONE ANOTHER

When believers recognize that God's presence and blessing requires the holiness of the community, they intentionally seek to facilitate holiness in one another through sharpening, confession, and reproof.

Sharpening

"As iron sharpens iron," **Proverbs** explains, *"so one man sharpens another"* (***Prov 27:17***). Believers dedicated to communal holiness sharpen one another's faith, *"until we all reach unity in the faith and in the knowledge of the Son of God and become mature, attaining to the whole measure of the fullness of Christ"* (***Eph 4:13***).

One of my early experiences in vocational ministry involved a men's discipleship group dedicated to sharpening one another. Five of us established a covenant to meet weekly for study, prayer, and accountability. We read books related to biblical manhood that consistently challenged our faith and our roles as men, husbands, and church members. Every week, each participant set one or two goals that grew from what we had read. "This week I will pray with my wife three times," someone might say, or, "This week I will memorize four Scriptures that will help me control my anger." When we met the following week, each participant had to look the others in the eye and explain how well he met (or didn't meet) his goals. The group continued—with a few members coming and going—for three years, until I relocated to another ministry.

I recently visited the church and had time to reconnect with some of the men from this discipleship group that ended ten years ago. We had a cookout at one of their homes. That evening, two thoughts struck me. First, our conversations quickly reverted to the depth we shared ten years before. Genuine, godly relationships have a timeless quality that does not exist in superficial relationships. Second, as I looked around the room at these gentlemen, I thought about how much each of us has grown since we first began meeting. When we began, most of the group were new or nominal Christians. Now, the living room in which we chatted included an elder, a worship leader, a ministry team leader, a small group teacher, and a Bible College professor. I recognize that our growth did not extend exclusively from the discipleship group; however, I believe the time we spent intentionally sharpening one another played a definite, significant part in the process.

Some friendships spur us into a more passionate pursuit of God.

Some friendships spur us into a more passionate pursuit of God. My old friends had this very effect on me. They challenged me, encouraged me, loved me, and helped me grow in righteousness.

The right relationships leave us more holy, not less. The right relationships sharpen us.

Confession

Sharpening will often include confession of sin.

Some occasions call for corporate confession of sin by the community. For example, as God reiterated the stipulations of the law in ***Leviticus 26***, He reminded His people of the consequences of disobedience—terror, defeat at the hands of their enemies, and various other afflictions (***26:14-39***). *"But if they will confess their sins and the sins of their fathers—their treachery against me and their hostility toward me,"* God continued, *"then when their uncircumcised hearts are humbled and they pay for their sin, I will remember my covenant with Jacob and my covenant with Isaac and my covenant with Abraham, and I will remember the land"* (***26:40-42***).[2] The confession of His people served as the catalyst for God to restore them. Modern examples of corporate confession include the Roman Catholic Church's formal acknowledgement in 1998 that they remained silent during the Holocaust; or the public confession of many predominantly white churches for a history of hate and racial prejudice. Many congregations, as a part of their weekly liturgy, include a prayer of confession offered corporately by the community. For example, a local church recently included the prayer below in their Sunday bulletin—a confession made by the community during worship:

> Most merciful Father, we confess before you our sinfulness: we hunger and thirst for that which satisfies our own selfish desires, rather than for a righteousness that goes beyond ourselves; we love mercy for us, but are reluctant to give it, or even desire it, for others, especially if they have wronged us; we honor only those who are in power or who have wealth, rather than all who are on our path; and we act out of pride and arrogance to seek our own advancement rather than in humility and meekness to serve others. Lord, forgive our many sins. Bring us low, so that we can receive the riches of your mercy. Satisfy us with your steadfast love. In Jesus' name we pray. Amen.[3]

[2] ***Nehemiah 9*** contains an extended example of a corporate confession of sin offered by the Israelites.

[3] This prayer was taken from the September 28, 2008, Sunday bulletin of the Redeemer Church of Knoxville, Tennessee.

Through such corporate expression of sin, a community of believers stands together exposed before the holy God, reminding one another with joint voices of their human frailty, need for God's grace, and need to help one another remain on paths of righteousness.

While some occasions call for corporate confession by the community, other occasions call for individual confession within the community. The same book of ***Leviticus*** that teaches corporate confession also teaches personal confession. For example, after listing various sins one might commit, the text instructs,

> *When anyone is guilty in any of these ways, he must confess in what way he has sinned and, as a penalty for the sin he has committed, he must bring to the LORD a female lamb or goat from the flock as a sin offering; and the priest shall make atonement for him for his sin.* (**Lev 5:5-6**)

The same book that teaches corporate confession also teaches personal confession.

The confession, we should note, did not occur simply between the individual and God—the individual had to bring the matter before the priest. Because sin impacts the community, confession takes place within community. In the NT, James instructed his readers, *"Confess your sins to each other and pray for each other so that you may be healed"* (***5:16***). Spiritual, emotional, and communal healing requires confession.

In her insightful and helpful book, *Spiritual Friendship*, Mindy Caliguire offers practical advice both to the person making a confession, and to the person hearing the confession. To the person making a confession, she writes,

> A helpful way for me to think about confession has been to recognize that it consists of three parts: (1) an acknowledgment of the wrong that was done, (2) a "confession" that I was the one who did it and (3) a willingness to go public with this fact. We say, in effect, "Here's the line. Here's where I crossed it. I need to be known in this." . . . The phrase "I need to be known in this" is a powerful one. If you're like me, this is not exactly what you'd call a "felt need." Nothing in me wants to be known where and when I have failed. Instead, I want to hide. But at a deeper level, I know this: if I want to grow, if I want to heal, if I want to be free, then "I need to be known in this." (**64-65**)

Regarding receiving the confession of a friend, Caliguire reflects,

> I want to be present with them in a way that receives their confession as a fellow struggler—which I very much am—who deeply respects their choice to bring their darkness into the light. I've learned . . . to always thank them for sharing . . . for being willing to entrust to us this essential ingredient in their own development. (**67**)

Furthermore, she advises,

> While we don't want to recoil in horror at the [confession], the other extreme to avoid is this: do not minimize. Don't pretend it's not there. When someone risks their "image" to expose an area of struggle or sin, many nice and well-meaning folks respond by minimizing their venture into confession. We might say, "Anyone would struggle with that; it's no big deal; don't worry about it." Even if it seems quite small to you, it is a big deal to the person and to God, and we should respect it as such. (**69-70**)

I recall one Sunday morning when, immediately after the morning worship service, a burly road construction worker in his fifties approached me after the service. Hank had attended our church for several months. He and I had never shared more than superficial conversation; however, on this morning tears streamed from his eyes as he said, "We need to talk." We retreated to my office, where he promptly blurted, "I need to make a confession." My mind raced. Perhaps he had committed adultery, or abused his kids. Maybe the downturned economy sent him looking for less than legal ways to balance his budget.

Amid these thoughts I did my best to keep a pastoral demeanor. "I'm glad you felt you could come talk to me. What's on your heart?"

Between sobs, he responded, "I haven't been getting along with my boss at work. And, my mind keeps filling with ugly, vengeful thoughts about him. I know these thoughts are wrong."

I almost blurted, "Is that all?! You've come to me weeping because you thought mean things about your boss?" Thankfully, though, I held my tongue.

"The Bible teaches that if we confess our sins to one another," he continued, "we will be healed. So, I'm confessing this to you and I'd like you to pray with me for God's forgiveness."

We prayed; then he left. I felt the size of an ant. Hank looked to me as a spiritual leader, yet I am unsure if I have ever felt so convicted of sin. Later, as I reflected on the encounter, I sensed that the brief conversation provided a significant jolt to both his and my spiritual lives, and a significant jolt to the community to which we belonged—a step of growth we would not have experienced had he not willingly confessed his sin.

Reproof

God holds believers responsible to keep themselves from sin, and to intentionally keep one another pure. When a believer falls into sin but refuses to repent and confess, fellow believers must confront that person. "Reproof is unavoidable," wrote Dietrich Bonhoeffer. "God's Word demands it when a brother falls into open sin. . . . Nothing can be more compassionate than the severe rebuke that calls a brother back from the path of sin. It is a ministry of mercy, an ultimate offer of genuine fellowship" (***Life*, 107**).

When a believer refuses to repent and confess, fellow believers must confront.

When David committed adultery with Bathsheba, and subsequently murdered her husband Uriah, the sage and prophet Nathan knew the sin could not remain unchallenged. With great tact and compassion, Nathan used a story to confront David with the heinousness of his actions (though David did not immediately connect himself with the story). When David expressed outrage over the story, Nathan could hold back no longer, *"You are the man!"* (***2Sa 12:7***). The next words from David's mouth were a confession, *"I have sinned against the Lord"* (***2Sa 12:13***)—a confession that may never have surfaced without Nathan's reproof.

Loving believers care enough to confront sin; and, in wisdom they recognize that sin cannot remain unchecked in healthy communities.

In such love and wisdom, Paul offered a stiff reproof to the community of believers in Corinth for refusing to confront a particular situation that had arisen among them: *"It is actually reported that there is sexual immorality among you, and of a kind that does not occur even among pagans: A man has his father's wife. And you are proud!"* (***1Cor 5:1-2***). Paul instructed the community to take the action they should have already taken—to expel the man from the community. Paul, in fact, quotes the refrain repeated throughout ***Deuteronomy***, *"Expel the wicked man from among you"* (***1Cor 5:13***).

The text outlines the general principle communities should apply to such situations: *"You must not associate with anyone who calls himself a brother but is sexually immoral or greedy, an idolater or a slanderer, a drunkard or a swindler. With such a man do not even eat"* (**1Cor 5:11**). When a person claims a faith in Christ and membership in the community, but refuses to repent of sin, the community must expel the person.[4] Why would God require such drastic action? Note the purpose clause in Paul's instructions, *"Hand this man over to Satan, so that the sinful nature may be destroyed and his spirit saved on the day of the Lord"* (**1Cor 5:5**). We offer reproof because we love and because we hope the reproof itself, by God's grace, will spur repentance.

> **We offer reproof because we love and because we hope the reproof itself will spur repentance.**

Apparently the church in Corinth followed Paul's instructions; and, apparently the unrepentant man repented when he endured church discipline. In ***2 Corinthians***, just a few months later, Paul instructed the church (presumably about the same situation), *"The punishment inflicted on him by the majority is sufficient for him. Now instead, you ought to forgive and comfort him, so that he will not be overwhelmed by excessive sorrow. I urge you, therefore, to reaffirm your love for him"* (**2Cor 2:5-8**). The church confronted the sin and thus saved the soul of the sinner.

I once met with the leaders of a church who struggled with these passages from the Corinthian letters. A married man in the congregation had been accused of extending unwanted advances toward other women. The church leaders investigated the situation and concluded, based on the testimony of several witnesses, that the accusations were true. The heartbroken leaders hurt for the offended women, and for the man tangled in sin. They wept and they prayed. They asked me to walk with them through the Corinthian letters and other relevant Scriptures to discern how to best handle the situation.

Following biblical teaching, two elders met with the man and confronted him with the accusations and the evidence, and asked him to repent. He refused to admit any wrongdoing. Next, they asked him to attend a meeting with the whole eldership. At this meeting, they again

[4] Obviously, in the preferable scenario the person in sin repents when confronted, thus saving himself from expulsion from the community.

gently confronted him with the accusations and the evidence, and with a Christ-like combination of directness and grace they tried to lead him to face up to his sin, repent, and receive the grace of God. Again, he refused. Left with no other option, the leaders said, "You are no longer welcome here until you face up to this sin."

The man burst out in anger, made threats of legal action, then stormed out of the room. After he left, the room fell silent, and remained silent for a couple minutes. Every man in the room had to brush tears from their eyes.

Six months later the same man sat in the same room with the same elders—except, the "same man" had changed. "I've confessed to God and to my wife, asked forgiveness of the women I hurt, and I have been in counseling," he explained to the elders. "I want to ask your forgiveness, also. And, I want to thank you. Thank you for loving me enough to confront my sin. Thank you for caring enough to do what must have been incredibly difficult to do." Every leader in the room—eyes filled, once again, with tears—smiled as wide as the ocean, hugged their now repentant brother, and welcomed him back home.

The Conversation of Confrontation

Any believer who has confronted a brother or sister in sin can attest to the heart-wrenching apprehension involved in such a conversation. We do not want to appear (or to be) judgmental or self-righteous, but to demonstrate our love through our words and demeanor.

How can we make certain that we confront the person with the proper motives and heart? If you imagine the conversation, do you imagine:

- ***Furrowed brow or teary eyes?*** Are you approaching your brother or sister with anger and condemnation, or with empathy? Do you see yourself as judge and jury, or as a fellow struggler?
- ***Crossed arms or an open embrace?*** Are you shutting your friend out, having built a wall between you, tossing angry grenades over the wall? Or have you put your arm on their shoulder, eager to give them a comforting hug?
- ***Wagging finger or wringing hands?*** A wagging finger indicates a hypocritical, judgmental spirit. Wringing hands indicate nervousness. You should be a little nervous! If you're

looking forward to confrontation, if you're eager to raise the issue of a friend's sin, this indicates your heart is not yet in the right condition.

- ***Storm away or stay and pray?*** Does the conversation end in anger or humility? Do you see yourself firing off words of judgment then storming out? Or do you see yourself as a sinner, going to God with a fellow sinner, asking for help on the journey?

A LESSON ON COMMUNITY

Cain's question has echoed across the ages, *"Am I my brother's keeper?"* (**Gen 4:9**). Both the OT and NT answer with a resounding "Yes." The community of God's people holds responsibility for the physical and spiritual needs of the individuals within the community.

> **The church is responsible for the physical and spiritual needs of the individuals within it.**

As I contemplate the communal responsibility of God's people, I recall an old friend named Bob Smith. When I began ministering with a church in Georgia, Bob, a retired man who served as a deacon, became one of my golfing buddies. One afternoon while we golfed, Bob shared his life story. Bob battled alcoholism for much of his life. He described how his addiction cost him jobs and relationships. He did not care for his children like he should have, he confessed, and through his life and behavior he scoffed at God for decades. "But," Bob continued with a twinkle in his eye, and motioning with the putter in his hand, "God never let go of me. I can look back on all my mistakes and failures, and through all of it I can see the hand of God protecting me and trying to get me back on the straight and narrow. Throughout all of my life God has been this golden thread holding it all together. Even when I was at the lowest of lows, God never forgot about me."

After we teed off on the next hole, Bob told me that his Alcoholics Anonymous group had planned a celebration to mark his twenty-fifth year of sobriety. He asked if I would attend with him.

The next week I walked with Bob and his wife down a set of stairs into the musty basement of an old church building. The diversity of the participants amazed me. The room held rich and poor, politicians and the unemployed; black, white, Latino, and Asian. Some wore expensive suits, others wore T-shirts that revealed needle scars on their arms. Introductions took place just as I had seen on television: "Hi, I'm John, and I'm an alcoholic." Everyone responded, "Hi, John!"

Different people stood to report on their progress and their battles with alcohol and drug addiction. The room was thick with compassion and warmth, laughter and tears. Everyone enjoyed spending this hour each week with others who could see into their souls. There was no reason to wear masks and no room for superficiality.

Alcoholics Anonymous originated when Bill Wilson, who had been sober for six months, found himself out of town on a business trip. The deal fell through, leaving Bill depressed and wandering through the hotel lobby. He felt drawn toward the bar, thinking, "I need a drink." Before reaching the bar, though, a new thought stopped him midstride. "I don't need another drink—I need another alcoholic!" Instead of the hotel bar, he headed toward the telephone, where a sequence of calls put him in touch with a fellow alcoholic. The two men later founded Alcoholics Anonymous.

The original intent of Bill Wilson manifests itself in the meeting I attended with my friend. Someone had brought a cake for Bob. Everyone patted him on the back and congratulated him for twenty-five years of refusing the bottle. Someone called out, "Speech! Speech!" My friend stood and choked through a testimony similar to what he shared with me on the golf course. "God has been a golden thread throughout my life," he repeated.

A few days later I encouraged Bob to share his testimony at our church. "Others need to hear your story," I said. He hesitated. Only a handful of people in the congregation knew of his past struggles. And, Bob did not want to embarrass his wife. They talked through it, however, and spent a few days praying about the possibility. He called me on the phone and said, "I'll do it."

The following Sunday—the Sunday before Thanksgiving—Bob told of his thankfulness for "the golden thread" that held his life together.

Church is the last place most people would feel comfortable standing and declaring, "Hi, I'm John, and I'm an alcoholic." Or, "I struggle with pornography." Or even, "Our marriage is on the rocks and we need your prayers." This should trouble us. God designed the church as a community in which Christians *"carry each others' burdens"* (***Gal 6:2***). The Bible admonishes believers, *"Confess your sins to each other and pray for each other so that you may be healed"* (***Jas 5:16***). And, *"If one part suffers, every part suffers with it; if one part is honored, every part rejoices with it"* (***1Cor 12:26***). Reclaiming God's design for the church community begins when each of us says, unashamedly, "I don't need to sin. I need another sinner. I need you to keep me accountable. I need you to help me stay on the path of Christian growth."

> **Church is the last place most people would feel comfortable publicly admitting their faults.**

Philip Yancey interviewed a young alcoholic who had formerly been an active church member, but had allowed Alcoholics Anonymous to take the place of church. When questioned why, the young man responded, "Mainly I'm trying to survive, and AA helps me in that struggle far better than any local church."

Yancey explored further, "Name one quality missing in the local church that AA somehow provides."

The young alcoholic stared at his coffee, watching it go cold. Finally he looked up and whispered one word: dependency. He explained, "Most church people give off a self-satisfied air of piety or superiority. I don't sense them consciously leaning on God or on each other. . . . Maybe God is calling us alcoholics to teach the saints what it means to be dependent on Him and on His community on earth" (***Church*, 51**).

Maybe He is.

Bob Smith passed away in the summer of 2000. I'll never see a gold-colored thread without thinking of my friend, and of what he taught me about community.

What Do You Say?

1. In what ways might an individual's actions positively or negatively impact the community?
2. Aliens, orphans, and widows were the most marginalized groups in the culture in which the Israelites lived, therefore God called His people to give them special care. To what people might God want us to offer special care today?
3. Can you give an example from your own life of a friend who helped you *"find strength in God"* (from David and Jonathan narrative, ***1Sa 23:16***)? How, specifically, did this person help you find strength in Him?
4. What should the contemporary church learn from the story of Achan? How does his story compare to that of Ananias and Sapphira in ***Acts 5:1-11***?
5. How might the contemporary church create an environment where believers more readily confess their sins to one another?
6. Why do we typically shy away from confronting our brothers or sisters who are in sin? Why should we confront them? How might we go about confronting them in a Christ-like manner?
7. What might the church learn from Alcoholics Anonymous?

CHAPTER FOUR

STORY ORIENTED

This chapter makes its initial appearance on my computer screen during the Christmas season. A few days ago I celebrated the holiday with my family: twenty of us crammed into my parents' three-bedroom house in Beckley, West Virginia. When our family gathers, the room fills with chocolate, giggles, and stories—often the same stories retold year after year. "Remember the Christmas when we hiked across the Patton's farm in the snow looking for the perfect Christmas tree to cut? When we got it home, it barely fit into the house! Or the first Christmas after Rachel and Paul got married, and Rachel got up at 3:00 a.m. ready to open presents? 'Rachel, you get back in here!' Paul's frustrated voice echoed through the house." Every time I get a glass of milk someone reminds me of the Christmas evening I spilled eight ounces onto my sister Debbie's new Monopoly game. This story often leads to the time I stepped on and broke my brother's new electric race track (apparently I caused a lot of damage in those days!). A family expresses its heritage through its stories—told and retold, remembered and relished.

If someone asked me to explain God, conversely, I would respond with bullet points. God is creator. God is just. God is full of grace. If pressed, I could list twenty such attributes of God, and provide a handful of Scripture references to support each attribute. "Look at this list;" I'd say, "these bullet points explain who God is."

If you had asked an OT Israelite to explain God, he would have responded with a story. "Ah, Elohim. Our Lord and God," the old Jewish man might begin while stoking the embers of the evening campfire. "We were slaves of Pharaoh in Egypt, but the LORD brought us out of Egypt with a mighty hand. Before our eyes the LORD sent miraculous signs and wonders—great and terrible—upon Egypt and Pharaoh and his whole household. But he brought us out from there to bring us in and give us the land that he promised on oath to our forefathers" (***Deu 6:21-23***). The story of God's relationship with the descendants of Abraham—not just the bare facts, but the story—framed the identity of God's OT people. The Israelites "were communities bound by a common commitment to a central story" (**Brueggemann, "Rethinking," 132**). The Creator, the God of Abraham, Isaac, and Jacob, loved and redeemed them. This narrative of God served as their "metanarrative," the overall, grand story that gave life a sense of connectedness, purpose, and hope.

This story, therefore, and all of its accompanying stories, passed as treasures from generation to generation. The OT believers "learned and handed on that accumulated store of revelation and experience, of tradition and challenge, of glowing examples and spectacular failures, that make up the ethical tapestry of the Old Testament. Israel was a community of memory and hope. It was in the remembering and retelling of their past, and in the hope that this generated for the future, that Israel most learned the shape of its own identity and mission and the ethical quality of life appropriate to both. Israel's community was shaped by Israel's story" (**C.J.H. Wright, 26**).

GROUNDED IN GOD'S STORY

EARLY CHRISTIANS' CONNECTION WITH GOD'S METANARRATIVE

The early believers, as described in ***Acts***, grounded their message and hope in God's story. The sermons of Peter, Stephen, and Paul—recorded in such texts as ***Acts 2:14-36; 3:12-26; 7:2-53; and 13:16-41***—

portray Jesus as the continuation of God's story. *"The God of Abraham, Isaac, and Jacob, the God of your fathers, has glorified his servant Jesus,"* preached Peter.

> *"Indeed, all the prophets from Samuel on, as many as have spoken, have foretold these days. And you are heirs of the prophets and of the covenant God made with your fathers. He said to Abraham, 'Through your offspring all peoples on earth will be blessed.'"* (**Acts 3:13,24-25**)

Stephen's message in ***Acts 7*** provides a detailed narrative of the eras of Abraham, Isaac, Jacob, Joseph, and Moses, demonstrating the historical propensity of the Israelites to reject God's redemption. Then, based on their collective story, Stephen issued the challenge that led to his stoning:

> *"You stiff-necked people, with uncircumcised hearts and ears! You are just like your fathers: You always resist the Holy Spirit! Was there ever a prophet your fathers did not persecute? They even killed those who predicted the coming of the Righteous One. And now you have betrayed and murdered him—you who have received the law that was put into effect through angels but have not obeyed it."* (**Acts 7:51-53**)

In Pisidian Antioch, Paul traced God's story from the Exodus through David through the birth of Christ. He continued, *"Brothers, children of Abraham, and you God-fearing Gentiles, it is to us that this message of salvation has been sent. . . . We tell you the good news: What God promised our fathers he has fulfilled for us, their children, by raising up Jesus"* (**Acts 13:26,32**).

God's metanarrative drove the first-century church. The Christian faith blossomed through story.

Acts, itself offered in narrative form, comes to a conspicuously abrupt ending in ***chapter 28***. The book of ***Acts*** offers no conclusion, as if to bid the reader to continue the story. What God began in ancient days and continued through the NT church, He hopes to continue through all generations. God's story continues unfolding.

The Christian faith blossomed through story.

Modern Believers' Connection with God's Metanarrative

A church disengaged from God's story floats about like a helium balloon that escapes a child's grasp on a windy afternoon, blown this way and that by whims, fads, and personalities.

A church with a sense of story, however, who recognizes its place in God's metanarrative and who constantly retells the stories of how God's faithfulness manifests itself in the community, offers people the opportunity to connect with something bigger than life's day-to-day chaos. "Human beings fundamentally require framing narratives," explain Emily Griesinger and Mark Eaton, "if for no other reason than because we need answers to fundamental questions: Who am I? Why am I here? Given life's difficulties—evil, suffering, death—how shall I respond, act, live?" (**x**). Furthermore, metanarratives "ground human experience in some larger framework, some idea or purpose that makes sense of our lives. Without metanarratives or grand stories, we lose hope for understanding the past, making sense of the present, and imagining and working towards a better future" (**ibid.**). A church grounded in its story offers stability, clarity, and hope.

Modern believers can find great comfort by recalling and retelling God's story as it appears through the centuries. We can sit in the back pew of the Congregational Church in Enfield, Connecticut, grasping the pews in horror alongside of other listeners as Jonathan Edwards describes the fate of "sinners in the hands of an angry God." We can peer around the corner as Martin Luther nails ninety-five theses to the door of the church in Wittenberg, peek over John Wycliffe's shoulder as he pens the final brushstrokes on his English translation of the Bible, listen from the next room as Thomas Aquinas explains to his appalled family why he must shun the lifestyle of nobility to enter a monastery, kneel beside Francis of Assisi as he dresses the oozing sores of a leper, and stand beside the road and weep for John Chrysostom as soldiers march the weary saint to his death. When we further turn back through the pages of God's story, we shield our eyes from the glory John experiences while caught up in a vision on the island of Patmos, run beside Peter from the empty tomb, stand intrigued beside a soldier at the foot of the cross, high-five the shepherds beside the manger of the Christ-child, cheer as Nehemiah places the final stone in the rebuilt Jerusalem wall, duck as David slings a stone toward Goliath, coo when Abraham pulls back the blanket to reveal the face of his promised newborn son, gawk at the enormity of Noah's ark, and drop our eyes to the floor of the garden when Eve picks the fruit from the tree.

Today's church steps into the stream of God's story that has flowed for millennia, and will flow for eternity. We do not exist in a historical vacuum; rather we stand on the shoulders and stories of our brothers and sisters from years gone by. "The church is called to find its identity and mission," explains Richard Hays, "within this epic story stretching from Adam to Abraham to Moses to Isaiah to Christ to the saints" (147).

We stand on the shoulders and stories of others from years gone by.

Stories within the Story

In addition to our connection with God's metanarrative, believers today can also find hope and comfort in the stories of God's work and faithfulness in their own churches. Believers of past generations built the communities that nourish us. Wise preachers, teachers, and church leaders constantly remind church members of those who saved, sacrificed, and served in years gone by.

The church in which I was raised, the Oak Grove Christian Church in Beckley, West Virginia, enjoys its stories. Well over one hundred years old, the community boasts a rich history of faithfulness and sacrifice. In the 1930s, during the Great Depression, the church almost closed its doors. Attendance dwindled to around ten people. They could not afford a preacher. The ten remained faithful, however, and continued meeting each Sunday to share in the Lord's Supper. Some say the Lord's Supper kept them together, and kept the congregation from dying.

Old-timers smile as they tell of a concrete, outdoor baptistery that sat beside their old church building. The congregation felt strongly concerning the importance of immersing new believers, so they built the baptistery in the churchyard in the 1940s. They sealed the baptistery with an iron cover that took four men to remove. They also kept a lead pipe handy to break the ice for winter baptisms—subfreezing temperatures might leave a layer of ice atop the water, but it would not deter the church nor new believers from obeying Christ's Great Commission.

Later, in the 1950s, the church leaders felt a full-time minister would help the congregation grow and minister more effectively. They lacked funds to support such a step, but they hired a preacher anyway, and rented a house for him. God provided and they never missed a payment on the house or a paycheck for their preacher.

Such stories become a part of a community's ethos; they shape our identity and motivate us toward faithfulness in the future. Aware of this dynamic, the Hebrews writer offered his readers numerous examples of faith, such as Abraham, Noah, Moses, and Rahab. On the heels of these examples, the writer bid his readers, *"Therefore, since we are surrounded by such a great cloud of witnesses, let us throw off everything that hinders and the sin that so easily entangles, and let us run with perseverance the race marked out for us"* (***Heb 12:1***). We stand in the tradition of believers who have, for centuries, persevered. Their examples encourage us. When faith seems too difficult, temptation intolerable, life unlivable, struggles unbearable, and hope unattainable, when the race feels all uphill, let us listen to the voices of the past. Let us hear their stories. Let us hear God's story. Let us, then, proceed in assurance.

We stand in the tradition of believers who have, for centuries, persevered.

RELIVING THE STORY THROUGH FESTIVALS

Dramatizing God's Story

Recognizing the value of His people remembering His story, God instructed the Israelites to celebrate a series of festivals through which they remembered key elements of God's history. "The Hebrew word translated 'feasts' means *appointed times,*" explain Kevin Howard and Marvin Rosenthal. "The idea is that the sequence and timing of each of these feasts have been carefully orchestrated by God himself. Each is part of a comprehensive whole. Collectively, they tell a story" (13). As the Israelites progressed through the specified series of festivals each year, they reminded themselves, reviewed, and even relived God's story—the story from which their communal identity grew.

Leviticus 23 outlines the series of festivals. In the opening words of the chapter, God instructed Moses, *"Speak to the Israelites and say to them: 'These are my appointed feasts, the appointed feasts of the* Lord*,* *which you are to proclaim as sacred assemblies.'"* The chapter then describes seven feasts: Sabbath; Passover; Firstfruits; Feast of Weeks; Feast of Trumpets, Day of Atonement, and Feast of Tabernacles.[1]

Sabbath
Leviticus 23:3

Of the appointed festivals, only Sabbath holds a place in the Ten Commandments. Its origin, though, stretches back further than Sinai—it stretches to Eden: *"And God blessed the seventh day and made it holy, because on it he rested from all the work of creating that he had done"* (***Gen 2:3***). On the Sabbath, God commanded His people to rest from labor (***Ex 20:10***) and remember Him (***Deu 5:15***) as a sign of the covenant they shared (***Ex 31:16***). A refusal to honor the Sabbath brought severe consequences: *"Anyone who desecrates it must be put to death; whoever does any work on that day must be cut off from his people"* (***Ex 31:14***).

Through the Sabbath God called His people to reflect His pattern of creation: work, then rest for renewal. For the Jewish people, Sabbath celebration involves a period of worship, feasting, and rest, that stretches from sunset Friday until sunset Saturday. "The Jew is to embrace the Sabbath with his soul, celebrating it in joy, peace of mind, through meditation and festive meals," explains Jewish scholar Leo Trepp. "Throughout our history, even the poorest Jew saw in the Sabbath a beacon lighting up and transforming the degradation of the week. When it arrived, he was able to shake off his worries and sorrows. Even the mourner laid aside his grief. The Jew experienced a 'foretaste of the world to come,' as the Sabbath cast out all earthly concerns" (**68**).

[1] The Israelites also celebrated new moons (***Num 10:10***), and in later centuries added Purim to commemorate God's deliverance of His people through Esther around 460 BC, and Hanukkah to celebrate the cleansing of the Temple after it was desecrated during the Greco-Syrian oppression in 165 BC.

Enjoying the Sabbath, BC

Tahan and Tirzah lived in a small Jewish village east of the Mediterranean, several years before Jesus arrived in Bethlehem. From Sunday through Friday, they worked diligently. Tahan and Tirzah rose with the sun, and by the sweat of their brows fashioned a meager existence common for their day. Tahan labored in the fields, working the soil. Tirzah held down the home front, caring for family and home.

At the appearance of the first star on Friday evening, however, for a short while life took on a different flavor. A man specially designated climbed to the highest point of the village, atop the synagogue, and sounded three sharp blasts from his ram's horn trumpet. The sound signified the beginning of Sabbath.

By this time Tirzah and the other ladies had already cooked three meals, one for Friday evening and two for Saturday. They have checked all the lamps for oil, refilling any that ran low. The ladies made certain all the water jugs brimmed with cool, freshly drawn water. The ladies made these preparation to ensure that no work would need to be performed for the next twenty-four hours.

Tahan and the other men of the village assured that they and their families had bathed and cleansed their bodies. Tahan perfumed his body with special oils saved only for these occasions. Everyone donned their brightest, cleanest tunics.

The Friday evening meal brought much laughter and joy. Tirzah and the ladies had prepared special treats to honor this day, which honored the Lord. Tahan bounced his children on his knee, and told them stories of God's care for His people. The children never tired of hearing of Abraham, Isaac, and Jacob; of Joseph and Moses; and of the great King David.

The Sabbath brought extended hours for rest, renewal, and relationship.

This mood of quiet joy and thanksgiving continued through the next day, Saturday, until sunset, when the trumpeter would again climb atop the synagogue and sound the ram's horn, signifying the end of the Sabbath.

Passover/Unleavened Bread
Leviticus 23:5-8

The Passover feast celebrates God's saving the Israelite slaves during the tenth plague He inflicted on Egypt. The plague brought death to all the firstborn in Egypt—a final climactic attempt to convince Pharaoh to release the slaves. God instructed His children who lived in Egypt to smear the blood of a lamb on their doorposts. When God saw the blood on a doorframe, He would "pass over" that house, and inflict no harm on the family inside (*Ex 12:12-13*). The Israelites first celebrated the Passover feast in the Sinai desert, one year after the exodus from Egypt (*Num 9:1-5*). Since that time, aside from periods during which the people had rebelled against God and did not honor His feasts, the Jewish people have celebrated the Passover for well over three thousand years.

The Jewish people have celebrated the Passover for well over three thousand years.

The Passover feast centered on three symbolic foods—lamb, matzah, and bitter herbs. The lamb signified the lamb that provided the blood for the doorposts in Egypt—the perfect, pure blood sacrifice that saved them. Matzah (unleavened bread) signified the hasty manner in which the slaves left Egypt: they had no time to include leaven in the bread. Bitter herbs represented the suffering they faced as slaves.[2]

In comparison to the other appointed festivals, "There is a sense in which, as a key to Jewish identity, Passover outweighs all the others," notes Chaim Raphael. "The deliverance from slavery in Egypt that is celebrated at Passover has always been more than an important moment in history; it is the fulcrum around which the Jewish people has always identified its independence and pride" (**67**). Raphael further explains that during a ceremony on Passover eve, Jews recite these words: "In every generation every Jew must feel as if he himself came out of Egypt" (**ibid.**). God gave the Passover to enable

[2] In later years additional elements were added: Cups of wine filled four times to correspond with four aspects of God's work; a cup for Elijah signifying hope of his return to announce the Messiah; parsley representing the hyssop used to spread lamb's blood across the doorframes; salt water representing the tears of the Israelite slaves; and a mixture of apples, nuts, cinnamon, and wine signifying the bricks and mortar the slaves used in Egypt (**B. Scott, *Feasts*, 44-45**).

the Israelites to relive the story—God's story of deliverance. The annual commemoration "served to incorporate new generations into the identity of Israel that emerged from that memory" (**Brueggemann, *Reverberations*, 84**).

After the Passover festival—strictly speaking, a single-day feast—for the next seven days the Israelites celebrated the Feast of the Unleavened Bread. *"On the first day"* of the feast, God instructed, *"remove the yeast from your houses"* (***Ex 12:15***). Then, *"For seven days no yeast is to be found in your houses. And whoever eats anything with yeast in it must be cut off from the community of Israel"* (***Ex 12:19***). Furthermore, God instructed them not to work, and to begin and end the feast with sacred assemblies (***Ex 12:16***). Often the entire eight-day experience, including the Passover feast and the Feast of the Unleavened Bread, bears the label "Passover."

Firstfruits
Leviticus 23:10-14

Following the winter months, when the first spring harvest of grain arrived, God instructed the Israelites to honor Him with an offering of the first sheaf of grain harvested. They could not, in fact, eat any of the new grain nor use it to make bread until they had offered the firstfruits to God (***Lev 23:14***). The gesture "symbolized the dedication of the whole year's crop" (**Harris, 624**), and celebrated God's past provision for His people. As they brought the firstfruit offering, God instructed His children to recite the story of His provision throughout Jacob's wandering, the period of slavery in Egypt, then their redemption from Egypt (***Deu 26:5-8***). God instructed them to continue by bowing and placing the basket of firstfruits before the Lord, saying, *"He brought us to this place and gave us this land, a land flowing with milk and honey; and now I bring the firstfruits of the soil that you, O Lord, have given me"* (***Deu 26:9-10***).

The gesture celebrated God's past provision for His people.

Though Scripture remains vague concerning the timing of the Firstfruits festival, other than its occurrence *"on the day after the Sabbath"* (***Lev 23:11***), the celebration apparently occurred near—perhaps even during—the Feast of the Unleavened Bread (**Howard and**

Rosenthal, 76). The Mishnah describes Israelite farmers harvesting their firstfruits, then carrying them in baskets, with great celebration, on the pilgrimage to Jerusalem for the Passover and Feast of Unleavened Bread (***Bikkurim*, 3:1–3:12**).

The principle of offering God the firstfruits holds true throughout the OT, not only concerning grain, but also including other crops such as grapes and figs, and firstborn animals. Even firstborn males of the Israelites themselves were dedicated to the Lord (***Ex 22:29; 23:19***).

Feast of Weeks
Leviticus 23:15-21

Seven weeks after the Firstfruit festival, in which the Israelites offered the firstfruits of the spring harvest, they celebrated the Feast of Weeks. The Feast of Weeks lasted only a single day, and it marked the conclusion of the spring harvest and the beginning of the summer harvest. At the Feast of Weeks, the Israelites offered to God the firstfruits of the summer harvest. The celebration is also called the Feast of the Harvest; and, in the NT, Pentecost (which means "fiftieth" in Greek—it occurred on the fiftieth day after the Firstfruits festival). God instructed the participants to give their offerings and to

> *rejoice before the LORD your God at the place he will choose as a dwelling for his Name—you, your sons and daughters, your menservants and maidservants, the Levites in your towns, and the aliens, the fatherless and the widows living among you. Remember that you were slaves in Egypt, and follow carefully these decrees.* (***Deu 16:11-12***)

This festival "became in time the festival at which the enjoyment of all kinds of summer foods gave intense delight, with a highly decorative background of plants and flowers at home, in the synagogue and in the country generally" (**Raphael, 73**).

The Feast of Weeks (Pentecost) holds a significant place in the history of the NT church. During the Pentecost celebration, a little over seven weeks after Jesus' crucifixion, the Spirit came upon the disciples, and Peter preached to the large crowd of Jews who had gathered for the feast. In response, three thousand were baptized, and the snowball of the

During the festival to celebrate the firstfruits of the summer harvest, God harvested the firstfruits of the gospel.

conversions and ministry of the Acts church gathered great momentum (**Acts 2**). During this festival which celebrated the firstfruits of the summer harvest, God harvested the firstfruits of the gospel.

Feast of Trumpets
Leviticus 23:24-25

Also called *Rosh Hashanah,* the Feast of Trumpets celebrated the Jewish New Year, and began a ten-day observance that culminated with the Day of Atonement. This ten-day experience differed from the other festivals in that it bid worshipers into a more solemn mood of reflection, repentance, and recommitment. Believers sometimes referred to the ten day period as "The Days of Awe," or "Ten Days of Penitence" (**B. Scott, *Feasts*, 76**).

The Feast of Trumpets, which stood at the beginning of these ten days, included burnt offerings of a bull, a ram, and seven male lambs; grain offerings; and a goat sacrificed as a sin offering (***Num 29:2-5***). Together, these sacrifices created *"an aroma pleasing to the LORD"* (***Num 29:2***).

Additional traditions developed among the Jewish people that correlate with the passing of one year and the entrance of the next. Many Jews, still today, toss bread crumbs into water—perhaps a stream or a lake—to signify casting away their sins from the previous year. Also, they eat bread and apples dipped in honey to reflect the sweetness they hope the new year will bring (**Trepp, 104, 108**).

Day of Atonement
Leviticus 23:27-32

Ten days after the Feast of the Trumpets, at the climax of the ten days of reflection, repentance, and recommitment, the high priest led the Israelites through the Day of Atonement, a solemn day of extensive rituals through which Israel sought atonement for its sins. After ceremonially bathing himself, the high priest donned the sacred linen undergarments and tunic. He then sacrificed a bull to atone for his and his family's sins. Next, he entered the Most Holy Place of the Tabernacle with fragrant incense, and sprinkled some of the bull's blood before the Lord. The high priest then slaughtered a goat and sprinkled the goat's blood around the Most Holy Place and on the altar to atone for the sins of the whole community. Next, he laid his hands on the head of a live goat, symbolically transferring the sins of the Israelites to the animal, then sent the "scapegoat" into the desert. The high priest then removed the sacred garments, bathed again, put on his regular garments, and sacrificed burnt offerings for himself and the people (***Lev 16:3-25***).

The Day of Atonement (i.e., *Yom Kippur*) led

> people to put themselves in proper perspective, recognize their absolute spiritual bankruptcy, and acknowledge their total dependence on Almighty God. Thus, the Jewish people were expected to approach Yom Kippur, the day on which their sins were covered for another year by the awesome and exalted God of the universe, with humility of mind and soul. (**B. Scott, *Feasts*, 89-90**)

In light of this atmosphere, God commanded the Israelites to fast on the Day of Atonement—the only mandated annual fast of the OT (***Lev 23:27,32***).

The writer of **Hebrews** calls upon images of the Day of Atonement to exalt Christ, and His covenant of blood, as superior to the old covenant. Christ

> [12]*did not enter by means of the blood of goats and calves; but he entered the Most Holy Place once for all by his own blood, having obtained eternal redemption.* [13]*The blood of goats and bulls and the ashes of a heifer sprinkled on those who are ceremonially unclean sanctify them so that they are outwardly clean.* [14]*How much more, then, will the blood of Christ, who through the eternal Spirit offered himself unblemished to God, cleanse our consciences from acts that lead to death, so that we may serve the living God!* (**Heb 9:12-14**)

Furthermore, the sacrifices made year after year on the Day of Atonement were *"an annual reminder of sins, because it is impossible for the blood of bulls and goats to take away sins"* (**Heb 10:4**). On the other hand, *"We have been made holy through the sacrifice of the body of Jesus Christ once for all"* (**Heb 10:10**).

Feast of Tabernacles
Leviticus 23:34-36, 39-43

The final of the seven feasts listed in ***Leviticus 23***, the Feast of the Tabernacles, "is the most joyful and festive of all Israel's feasts. It is also the most prominent feast, mentioned more often in Scripture

The feast celebrated both God's past provision and present provision with the harvest.

than any other feast" (**Howard and Rosenthal, 135**). To remind His people of the forty years He cared for them in the desert, God instructed them to live for seven days in tent-like booths. The feast occurred after the final agricultural harvest of the year; therefore, it simultaneously celebrated God's past provision in the wilderness and God's present provision with the harvest.

This festival began on a Sabbath and concluded the following Sabbath. Each of the eight days included extensive animal sacrifices. On each of the first seven days they sacrificed two rams, fourteen lambs, and a goat. Additionally, they sacrificed a number of bulls that decreased each day—thirteen on the first day, decreasing by one per day until they sacrificed seven on the seventh day. On the eighth and final day (the second Sabbath), they sacrificed one bull, one ram, seven lambs, and one goat (***Num 29:12-39***). The extensive sacrifices emphasized both the importance and the celebratory nature of the feast.

Additional Observances

In addition to the seven festivals outlined in ***Leviticus 23***, God instructed His people to honor a Sabbatical Year and a Year of Jubilee.

The Sabbatical Year required Israelites to leave land fallow every seventh year:

> *For six years you are to sow your fields and harvest the crops, but during the seventh year let the land lie unplowed and unused. Then the poor among your people may get food from it, and the wild animals may eat what they leave. Do the same with your vineyard and your olive grove.* (***Ex 23:10-11***)

Furthermore, God commanded the Israelites to cancel any debts owed them by a fellow Israelite, and to release any Israelite slaves (***Deu 15:1-18***). Such gestures, as with other festivals, helped God's people to remember and relive God's story: *"Remember that you were slaves in Egypt and the Lord your God redeemed you. That is why I give you this command today"* (***Deu 15:15***).

The Year of Jubilee occurred every fifty years, after seven cycles of Sabbatical years. During this year, like the Sabbath Year, land remained fallow and Israelite slaves gained release. Furthermore, during the Year of Jubilee, all lands returned to their original owners (**Lev 25:10,13**). This practice preserved the identity of each family (an identity that depended heavily on the land it owned). In essence, to use modern terms, an Israelite could lease a parcel of land from a fellow Israelite for a time no longer than the number of years that remained until the next Year of Jubilee. If the next Jubilee would arrive in thirteen years, for example, one could "lease" land from a fellow Israelite for thirteen years or less. The Year of Jubilee, like the Sabbath Year, served to remind the Israelites of God's story. Couched amid the specific stipulations for the Year of Jubilee, God reminded His people, *"I am the LORD your God, who brought you out of Egypt to give you the land of Canaan and to be your God"* (**Lev 25:38**).

The appointed festivals led the Israelites to remember and relive the work and ministry God had performed for them and among them. They led God's people to relive God's story.

Jewish Festivals

Name	Description	Aspect of God's Story Relived
Sabbath	Rest on seventh day of week	Rest on seventh day of creation
Passover/ Unleavened Bread	Eat lamb, bitter herbs, unleavened bread	The Passover and exodus from Egypt
Firstfruits	Offer God first sheaf of spring grain harvested	God's provision through Jacob's wandering, the Exodus, and the Promised Land
Feast of Weeks	Offer God firstfruits of summer harvest	God's provision through the release from slavery in Egypt
Feast of Trumpets	Begin 10-day celebration of new year with sacrifices	The blessings of the previous year

Name	Description	Aspect of God's Story Relived
Day of Atonement	End 10-day celebration of new year with extensive ceremony and sacrifice for the atonement of sins	God's atonement for His people
Feast of Tabernacles	Live for 7 days in booths, numerous sacrifices each day	God's provision during the 40 years in the wilderness
Sabbath Year	Every seventh year, land lay fallow, Hebrew debts canceled, slaves freed	Redemption from slavery in Egypt
Year of Jubilee	Similar to Sabbath year, also land returned to original owners	God giving the Promised Land to His people

Pilgrimages to Jerusalem

Of the seven feasts outlined in ***Leviticus 23***, three held greater prominence in the Jewish life and calendar because they required pilgrimages to Jerusalem: *"Three times a year all your men must appear before the LORD your God at the place he will choose: at the Feast of Unleavened Bread [Passover], the Feast of Weeks [Pentecost] and the Feast of Tabernacles"* (***Deu 16:16***).

Large numbers of Jewish people journeyed to Jerusalem for these three feasts. Though many scholars warn that estimates of two or three million might represent hopeful exaggerations, in the latter parts of the OT era "the numbers were undoubtedly very great, with pilgrims coming not only from all parts of Palestine, but also from the Jewish Diaspora, which was now already very widespread and totaled a vast population" (**Raphael, 21**). *Acts 2* lists pilgrims who had journeyed to Jerusalem for Pentecost from Africa, Asia Minor, and the Middle East: *"Parthians, Medes and Elamites; residents of Mesopotamia, Judea and Cappadocia, Pontus and Asia, Phrygia and Pamphylia, Egypt* *and the parts of Libya near Cyrene; visitors from Rome (both Jews and converts to Judaism); Cretans and Arabs"* (***Acts 2:9-11***).

Not every individual Jew traveled to Jerusalem for all three feasts every year; instead, probably, individuals took turns in a system that sent representatives to each feast from each district. These pilgrims met in designated towns to caravan together (**Raphael, 22**). The Mishnah, a collection of oral laws and traditions that rabbis collected and recorded from around 200 BC until around 150 AD, contains a passage that describes the pilgrims gathering and traveling:

> [The male inhabitants of] all the towns in the priestly course gather in the [main] town of the priestly course [M. Ta. 4:2], and they sleep [outside] in the open area of the town, and they would not enter the houses [in the town, for fear of contracting corpse uncleanness].
>
> And at dawn, the officer would say, "Arise, and let us go up to Zion, to [the house of] the Lord our God (***Jer. 31:6***). Those [who come] from nearby bring figs and grapes, but those [who come] from afar bring dried figs and raisins. And an ox walks before them, its horns overlaid with gold, and a wreath of olive [leaves] on its head.
>
> A flutist plays before them until they arrive near Jerusalem. [Once] they arrive near Jerusalem, they sent [a messenger] ahead of them [to announce their arrival], and they decorated their firstfruits. The high officers, chiefs, and treasurer [of the Temple] come out to meet them. According to the rank of the entrants, they would [determine which of these officials would] go out. And all the craftsmen of Jerusalem stand before them and greet them [saying], "Brothers, men of such and such a place, you have come in peace."
>
> A flutist plays before them, until they reach the Temple mount. [Once] they reach the Temple mount, even Agrippa the King puts the basket [of firstfruits] on his shoulder, and enters, [and goes forth] until he reaches the Temple court. [Once] he reaches the Temple court, the Levites sang the song, "I will extol thee, O Lord, for thou has drawn me up, and hast not let my foes rejoice over me." (***Ps. 30:1***) (***Bikkurim*, 3:2b–3:4**)[3]

The pilgrims joyfully worshiped and sang as they traveled. Many scholars speculate that the travelers based much of this worship on

[3] The terms in brackets were added by the translator to provide clarity and explanation. Taken from *The Mishnah: A New Translation*, trans. by Jacob Neusner (New Haven, CT: Yale University Press, 1988).

Psalms 120–134. Each of these Psalms bear the label, "A Song of Ascents" (Hebrew *ma'aloth*, meaning "ascent, path of ascent, way up, steep path [**Holladay, 207**]) indicating, perhaps, their use as the pilgrims ascended to Jerusalem. The Mishnah connects the fifteen Psalms to the fifteen steps of the Temple where the Levites sang them (*Middoth* 2.5). "It is more likely," however, writes Willem Van Gemeren, "that the songs were sung in the three annual festival processions, as the pilgrims 'ascended' (*'-l-h*) to Jerusalem (cf. ***Exod 23:14-17; Deut 16:16***), hence the designation 'songs of ascents'" (***Psalms*, 769**).

Psalm 122 provides a good example. Imagine the pilgrims as they approached Jerusalem—the sparkle in their eyes, the spring in their steps, the warmth in their hearts—as they joined their voices to sing:

1I rejoiced with those who said to me,
"Let us go to the house of the LORD."
2Our feet are standing
in your gates, O Jerusalem.
3Jerusalem is built like a city
that is closely compacted together.
4That is where the tribes go up,
the tribes of the LORD,
to praise the name of the LORD
according to the statute given to Israel.
5There the thrones for judgment stand,
the thrones of the house of David.
6Pray for the peace of Jerusalem:
"May those who love you be secure.
7May there be peace within your walls
and security within your citadels."
8For the sake of my brothers and friends,
I will say, "Peace be within you."
9For the sake of the house of the LORD our God,
I will seek your prosperity.

Enjoying the Sabbath, AD

Jim and Jane both have good jobs and enjoy the pleasures these provide. They have two children who participate in various sports and activities.

Like many other families, Jim and Jane work hard and keep busy, but they have learned to balance work with rest, and with relating to God and other people. Their children participate in *some* activities, but not in *every* available activity. Jim and Jane work diligently and have progressed in their careers, but they seldom work overtime or bring work home with them.

Every Sunday Jim and Jane pack up the kids and worship together at their church. They love their Bible Fellowship Class. Every week they discuss different truths from God's Word, at the same time developing healthy Christian friendships with others in the class. Recently, when Jane had minor surgery and spent a couple of nights in the hospital, their friends from the Bible Fellowship Class brought meals and babysat the kids. One Saturday some class members helped Jane catch up on the laundry and housecleaning.

As much as they enjoy the time with their Christian friends, however, the most refreshing and encouraging part of the day comes when the family worships together. While Jim and Jane dedicate every day and every aspect of their lives to God, they take this special time every Sunday to focus exclusively on worshiping God. They join voices with other believers in songs of worship and in prayer. They open their Bibles together to learn from God's Word. During these times the Spirit of God pours over them a sense of peace—it envelops them like a refreshing waterfall. Life sometimes gets busy, confusing, frustrating, and painful, but this time of relating with God and God's people leaves Jim and Jane refocused, energized, encouraged.

After church on most Sundays, Jim and Jane keep certain family traditions with their kids. They prepare lunch together—sometimes the children's help proves adventuresome, but the laughs always outnumber the messes. After a leisurely dinner, everyone pitches in to clean the kitchen and the dishes. Then the family spends the remainder of the day enjoying one another—perhaps a game of touch football, riding bikes, or going for a swim at the pond. Occasionally they gather with the neighbors for a barbecue. Frequently the day includes naps.

Jim and Jane know that a mountain of work screams for their attention, but they also know that work will still be on their desks on Monday morning. Today, other matters hold greater importance.

IMPLICATIONS FOR THE CONTEMPORARY CHURCH

The various festivals described in this chapter stood central to the lives of God's OT covenant community. What significance do they hold for the contemporary church?

We Should Recognize Jesus as the Culmination of God's Story

While the OT feasts celebrated aspects of God's story that had taken place during the OT era, they also foreshadowed the coming Messiah. Festival sacrifices foreshadowed Jesus' sacrifice; the perfect lamb of the Passover foreshadowed the perfect Lamb of God; and God's provision and atonement during the OT foreshadowed the full provision and atonement Jesus provided on the cross. God's story leads to Christ. We cannot preach Christ in His fullness, therefore, without recognizing His supreme role in God's grand story.

We Should Use Terms Such as "Independent" and "Autonomous" Carefully

The church movement to which I belong, the Stone-Campbell Restoration Movement, seeks to follow the example of the NT church by remaining free of denominational structure and division. Each congregation functions independently and autonomously. A danger of such an approach, however, lies in taking the ideas of independence and autonomy to such an extreme that we disconnect ourselves from the history of the church, and disconnect ourselves from the contemporary church at large. We risk disregarding our place in God's grand story and inviting Him only into our smaller stories. While God's story certainly manifests itself in the smaller stories of each congregation, these are but pieces of something much more grand. In our stance of independence, we risk losing sight of this grandeur.

We Should Not Dismiss the Liturgical Calendar Too Quickly

Churches of a more liturgical nature recognize an annual calendar of observances, often called the Christian year. Those of us with a less liturgical heritage, though we generally celebrate Christmas and Easter, have shied from other aspects of the Christian year, fearing it restricts us with bindings not dictated by the Bible. Before completely dismissing the idea, however, we should consider the benefits of annual cycles of remembrance and celebration. As God directed OT believers to relive His story through annual festivals, elements of the Christian year can lead believers to relive the gospel story. While I do not advocate such remembrances as a matter of obligation, as the NT does not require them, I do encourage congregations to consider the potential benefits of living out the story of Christ in our annual worship and planning, connecting us in a tangible manner with the gospel story.

The Christian Year[4]

Day/Season	Date	Aspect of Jesus' Story Relived
Advent	Four Sundays before Christmas through December 24	Anticipation of Jesus' coming
Christmas	December 25–January 5	The birth of Jesus
Epiphany	January 6	The visit of the Magi
Ash Wednesday	The Wednesday seven weeks before Easter	Man's sinfulness and need for a Savior
Lent	Ash Wednesday through the Saturday before Easter (40 days)	Jesus' forty-day fast in the desert
HOLY WEEK:	Sunday through Saturday before Easter	The week of the crucifixion
• Palm Sunday	Sunday before Easter	Jesus' triumphal entry into Jerusalem
• Maundy Thursday	Thursday before Easter	The Last Supper
• Good Friday	Friday before Easter	Jesus' crucifixion

[4]This chart represents the most prominent and widely celebrated aspects of the liturgical year; some churches honor additional celebrations such as Trinity Sunday, Christ the King Sunday, All Saints Day, et al.

Day/Season	Date	Aspect of Jesus' Story Relived
EASTER SEASON:	Easter Sunday through seven weeks after Easter	Jesus' resurrection and post-resurrection ministry
• Easter	Easter Sunday	Jesus' resurrection
• Ascension Sunday	Sunday following the fortieth day after Easter	Jesus' ascension
Pentecost	The seventh Sunday after Easter	The birth of the church
Ordinary Time	Pentecost through Advent (and other times not designated)	The day-to-day life and ministry of Jesus and the church

WE SHOULD CELEBRATE MORE

No observant scholar could accuse the people of God in the OT, at least during their periods of faithfulness to God, of a lack of celebration. Their designated festivals assured a continual lifestyle in which God's people celebrated God's story. Such an accusation, however, could legitimately be levied against many contemporary churches. Whether through celebrations connected with the liturgical year, homecomings, anniversaries, appreciation dinners, or old-fashioned potluck dinners, believers need opportunities to gather with other believers to retell old stories, fellowship, and celebrate God's story. Christian Schwarz, who led research into thousands of healthy and unhealthy churches worldwide, noted a strong correlation between a church's health and the amount of laughter that occurs within the community (36-37). Church leaders need to create opportunities for people to laugh together.

Church leaders need to create opportunities for people to laugh together.

CONCLUSION

I mentioned above that I wrote this chapter during the Christmas season. A few days before Christmas, my two sons participated in a musical with the other children of our church. As happens every year,

I dreaded the hassle of driving them back and forth to rehearsals (we live forty minutes from our church), finding costumes, learning lines, and practicing songs. I made my annual speech to my wife, "This just isn't worth it. Next year let's bow out of the play—our boys won't mind."

Then, as happens every year, on the night of the play I wept as I watched my boys quote Scripture into a microphone—slowly and clearly just like we practiced at home—and sing of Bethlehem and Mary and baby Jesus. I remembered Christmas plays of past years, and reflected on how they have grown. I recalled when they were babies and played the role of Jesus in the manger. I reminisced of Christmas plays in which I participated when I was a little boy.

Our celebrations offer annual reminders, annual means of participating in the story of God. They help us recall what God has done in the past, which, in turn, aids us in moving into the future with confidence in His faithfulness.

What Do You Say?

1. What would change in our churches and our individual lives if we viewed God, not only in terms of His attributes, but also in terms of His story?
2. What is a metanarrative? Why do people need them?
3. What stories from the history of our congregation need to be continually retold? What benefit can congregations find in retelling such stories?
4. Why did God command the Israelites to progress through a series of festivals every year?
5. Recognizing that everyone's life circumstances differ, what would need to change in your own life for you to enjoy a weekly Sabbath like Jim and Jane from the sidebar "Enjoying the Sabbath, AD?"
6. Imagine yourself in the shoes of an Israelite making a pilgrimage to Jerusalem for one of the festivals. What emotions do you experience as you near the city?
7. What should the contemporary church learn from the OT feasts?

CHAPTER FIVE

SOVEREIGNLY PROTECTED

A few weeks ago a friend with whom I work and attend church poked his head into my office. Bypassing any greeting or small talk, he jumped immediately to theology: "What do we believe about God's sovereignty?"

I took a sip of my morning coffee—unsure if enough caffeine had yet entered my system to tackle such a question—then delayed answering by inquiring, "Why do you ask?"

- I. Job
  - A. The Issue of Suffering
  - B. God Answers
  - C. Job's Response
- II. Joseph
  - A. The Joseph Narrative
  - B. God's Unseen Hand
  - C. The Furtherance of God's Story
- III. Ezekiel
  - A. Historical Background
  - B. Ezekiel's Message
  - C. God's Purpose
- IV. Esther
  - A. The Story
  - B. God "Behind the Scenes"
- V. Implications for Today's Church
  - A. Trust
  - B. Submission
  - C. Praise
  - D. Loyalty
- VI. The Church in China
  - A. The Last Sixty Years
  - B. Current Status
  - C. One Man's Story

"I'm teaching about Esther in Sunday School this week," he explained, "and the commentaries I read keep talking about God's sovereignty. I don't know what to think about it. I think I'm supposed to believe God is sovereign, but these writers keep making it sound like God just controlled Esther and King Xerxes and those other people like puppets on a string. That's not how it works, is it?"

Resisting the temptation to send him to the office next door, to the professor who teaches Systematic Theology, I instead attempted to confirm his fears, and explained that "we" (meaning, "we in Christian Churches and Churches of Christ") typically struggle with this particular doctrine. "I don't believe we're just puppets on a string," I assured him, "but God does hold ultimate authority over everything. In His infinite wisdom, God allows, beneath the blanket of His sovereignty, humans to make choices and to face the consequences of those choices. Regardless of what we choose, however, He continues furthering His world and His people toward His purposes."

This principle emerges when one traces the history of God's people throughout the OT. Though the Israelites often frustrated the Lord with their moral and religious compromise, and though they often faced difficult consequences as a result of their decisions, God kept guiding, leading, and protecting them as He worked out His purpose among them—the blessing of all the earth through the descendants of Abraham (***Gen 12:3***).

Though numerous examples appear in the pages of the OT, four will prove most helpful for this particular discussion—God's sovereign guidance as seen in the stories of Job, Joseph, Ezekiel, and Esther.

JOB

The Issue of Suffering

Job's story of suffering has echoed through the ages. The narrative begins in the first couple of chapters with an odd exchange between God and Satan, during which Satan asserted that Job had remained faithful only because God protected and blessed him. After this accusation, God allowed Satan to pour unimaginable suffering into Job's life. Job lost his riches, herds, servants, health, and family. Throughout the ordeal, Job remained faithful (***Job 1–2***).

After these events recorded in ***Job 1–2***, the next thirty-five chapters relate conversations Job shared with four of his friends. In their dialogue, they attempted to make sense of the suffering Job faced. His friends believed that suffering came as a result of sin. Job, therefore, in light of the extensive suffering he faced, must have sinned grossly. If Job would simply confess this sin, the logic continued, God would restore blessing to Job. Job's friend Bildad said,

3 Does God pervert justice?
Does the Almighty pervert what is right?
4 When your children sinned against him,
he gave them over to the penalty of their sin.
5 But if you will look to God
and plead with the Almighty,

[6]*if you are pure and upright,*
even now he will rouse himself on your behalf
and restore you to your rightful place. (**Job 8:3-6**)

Job understood the logic, but it did not correlate with his experience. Job knew he had remained faithful to God—his integrity remained in check—yet he suffered. Job reflected,

[10]*But he knows the way that I take;*
when he has tested me, I will come forth as gold.
[11]*My feet have closely followed his steps;*
I have kept to his way without turning aside.
[12]*I have not departed from the commands of his lips;*
I have treasured the words of his mouth more than my daily bread.
[13]*But he stands alone, and who can oppose him?*
He does whatever he pleases.
[14]*He carries out his decree against me,*
and many such plans he still has in store.
[15]*That is why I am terrified before him;*
when I think of all this, I fear him. (**Job 23:10-15**)

Finally, in desperation, Job exclaimed, *"I cry out to you, O God, but you do not answer; I stand up, but you merely look at me. You turn on me ruthlessly; with the might of your hand you attack me"* (**Job 30:20-21**).

God Answers

Though Job's suffering, at first reading, stands central to the story, the book provides no definitive answer to the theological issue of suffering. "In the end," writes David Clines, "readers cannot discover from the book any one clear view about what the reason for their own particular suffering may be, nor any statement about the reason for human suffering in general; for the book is entirely about the suffering of one particular and unique individual" (**xxxviii**). Job suffered, and he swapped theories with his friends about its theological implications, but when God finally spoke up at the end of the book, He provided no answers. In fact, God asked more questions.

After the narrative of ***chapters 1–2***, and the dialogue between Job and his friends in ***chapters 3–37***, *"The LORD answered Job out of the storm"* (**Job 38:1**). *"Where were you,"* God asked, *"when I laid the earth's foundation? Tell me, if you understand. Who marked off its dimensions? Surely you know! Who stretched a measuring line across it?"* (**38:4-**

5). God continued immersing Job in a downpour of questions for the next four chapters. The questions forced Job to reconsider the mystery and complexity of creation; and, by implication, the mystery, complexity, and power of the Creator. "The only conclusion [Job] can come to," explains John Hartly, "is that Yahweh is the supreme Lord of the universe" (**534**).

The book of Job raises questions regarding suffering. It provides an answer, however, that deals with suffering only by implication. The book offers the assurance that God holds ultimate control over all that exists. "First and foremost," writes Stephen Hooks, "the God of Job is sovereign. He rules over the world he has made, and before him everyone and everything bows" (**36**).

The book of Job offers the assurance that God holds ultimate control over all that exists.

Job's Response

Job responded to God's questions in the only appropriate manner: *"Surely I spoke of things I did not understand, things too wonderful for me to know"* (***Job 42:3***). Rather than repeating his demand for God to respond to the issue of suffering, Job acknowledged his limited knowledge in light of God's sovereignty—his finiteness compared to God's infinite wisdom and power. Job continued, *"Therefore I despise myself and repent in dust and ashes"* (***42:6***).[1] Job expressed humility and turned away ("repented") from his attempts to understand God's ways.

In the end, Job "is finally reconciled to his Maker by acknowledging God's sovereignty and bowing before him in humble submission" (**Hooks, 37**).

[1] In the original Hebrew text, ***42:6*** does not contain an object for the verb "despise." The NIV inserts the term "myself." Francis Anderson asserts that Job, more likely than despising himself, despised the words he had spoken. He writes concerning this and the term "repent": "If we connect it with ***verse 3***, Job could be expressing regret at his foolish words, uttered hastily and in ignorance (this is how TEV takes it)—a fault deserving correction, but not a wickedness deserving punishment. . . . It is equally important not to misunderstand the word *repent* by reading into it too many conventional connotations of penitence for sins which weigh on the conscience. The whole story would collapse if this is the outcome. Job would have capitulated at last to the friends' insistent demand that he confess his sins. Job confesses no sins here" (**292**).

God operates in a manner beyond our ability to understand. Though our bookshelves sag under the weight of numerous books that attempt to explain Him and His ways, ultimately our only appropriate response is to join Job in bowing before His majestic sovereignty.

JOSEPH

The Joseph Narrative

Joseph's story brings the book of ***Genesis*** to a theologically meaningful conclusion, providing a significant example and additional insight concerning God's sovereign guidance of His community. Though space does not permit a detailed account, a basic overview of the Joseph narrative, recorded in ***Genesis 37–50***, will provide a basis for a few observations concerning God's sovereignty.

Joseph could wear the label "Valedictorian of the School of Hard Knocks." His jealous brothers beat him, threw him in a pit, then sold him as a slave to some passing travelers (***Genesis 37***). The travelers took Joseph to Egypt, where he gained a position of some prominence administering the household of an Egyptian official named Potiphar. When Potiphar's wife wrongfully accused Joseph of attempted rape, Joseph found himself imprisoned (***Genesis 39***). Despite these setbacks, through his God-given gift of dream interpretation, Joseph gained Pharaoh's respect and accepted an important government position (***Genesis 40–41***). When famine struck, Joseph administered Egypt's grain supply. His brothers—the same brothers who sold him into slavery—came to Egypt seeking food. The brothers did not immediately recognize Joseph. When Joseph revealed his identity, he comforted his brothers and assured them that God had been working through all of the circumstances. The brothers returned and gathered the rest of the family, including their father Jacob, and returned to Egypt, where they settled (***Genesis 42–50***).

God's Unseen Hand

Unlike God's more direct interaction with earlier patriarchs, Scripture records no words of God spoken to Joseph. God's only recorded verbal conversation with a person in ***Genesis 37–50***, the portion of the book that focuses on Joseph, appears at ***46:2-4***, where He assures Jacob that He will go with Jacob to Egypt when the family settles there.

Rather than overt, verbal guidance from God, the Joseph narrative includes numerous allusions to God through the words of human characters and through commentary provided by the biblical author, who attribute the working out of life's circumstances to the Lord's sovereign hand.

In **Genesis 39**, for example, the biblical author bookends the story of Joseph's encounter with Potiphar's wife with the repeated assurance, *"The LORD was with Joseph and he prospered"* (**Gen 39:2**); and *"The LORD was with Joseph and gave him success in whatever he did"* (**Gen 39:23**). Toward the end of the same narrative, the author reports that the LORD showed Joseph *hesed* (**39:21**)—loyal loving-kindness. Though the false accusation and imprisonment Joseph faced might cause the reader to question such statements, the author apparently intends to pull the reader away from the smaller picture and to view even Joseph's difficult days through broader lenses, this bigger picture demonstrating that God loyally and lovingly continued to keep His covenant and work out His purposes.

God loyally and lovingly continued to keep His covenant and work out His purposes.

A second example occurs in **Genesis 45**, as Joseph comforts his brothers in Egypt:

> *4Then Joseph said to his brothers, "Come close to me." When they had done so, he said, "I am your brother Joseph, the one you sold into Egypt! 5And now, do not be distressed and do not be angry with yourselves for selling me here, because it was to save lives that God sent me ahead of you. 6For two years now there has been famine in the land, and for the next five years there will not be plowing and reaping. 7But God sent me ahead of you to preserve for you a remnant on earth and to save your lives by a great deliverance. 8So then, it was not you who sent me here, but God."* (**Gen 45:4-8**)

Joseph believed, and explained to his brothers, that God sovereignly worked through his life circumstances, including the brothers' misdeed. A few chapters later, Joseph offered his brothers a similar reminder, *"You intended to harm me, but God intended it for good to accomplish what is now being done, the saving of many lives"* (**Gen 50:20**).

The Joseph narrative demonstrates a mysterious theological tension—an apparent incongruity—that often befuddles and divides scholars. On one hand, humans exercise free will in the ability to make choices, and they face the consequences or reap the rewards of these choices. On the other hand, God's unseen sovereign hand unmistakenly guides people, problems, and circumstances to achieve His purposes. C.J.H. Wright comments concerning this paradox,

> While holding firmly to this conviction, that the LORD was in overall control of events, these Israelite historians managed to avoid two extremes. On the one hand, they did not work with a mechanistic view of God's sovereignty, which would have eliminated human ethical freedom and responsibility. The best illustration of this is provided by the cycle of Joseph stories. Indeed, it is probably part of the narrator's purpose to exploit this very enigma of divine sovereignty and human moral decisions. From a human point of view, the whole story is one of free choices, some evil, some good; at no point does anyone act other than as a free agent according to his own choice. That applies to all the characters—Jacob, Joseph and his brothers, Potiphar and his wife, Pharaoh, Joseph's fellow prisoners, Jacob. Yet at the end of it all, Joseph acknowledges the sovereign control of God, whose redemptive purposes governed the whole story: 'You [his brothers] intended to harm me, but God intended it for good to accomplish what is now getting done, the saving of many lives' (***Gen. 50:20***). This is a wonderful statement of the paradox of divine sovereignty and human freedom. (**34-35**)

"In this extended story humans clearly bear responsibility for their deeds, as they reap what they sow," adds Lee Humphreys. "But more than they sow is reaped by God. Through the designs of a God who seeks good and the preservation of life, many people—Egypt, those others who come there for relief—and not just this family, are sustained alive. Joseph offers an expansive picture of God's activity as the story draws to its conclusion" (**229**).

Some use the image of a passenger airplane to illustrate the paradox of God's sovereignty over His community and the free will of individuals within the community. Imagine a jumbo jet, filled with passengers, flying from New York to Los Angeles. Passengers willingly choose to board the plane, and they can willingly choose to debark at any time. While on the flight, they can freely make numerous decisions. They can walk about the cabin or stay seated, they can talk or sleep, they can read or watch a movie. Regardless of what each individual chooses, however, the plane and its passengers will arrive in Los Angeles as scheduled.

God gives people freedom to make choices. Regardless of what we choose, though, He will direct the community of His people toward the accomplishment of His purposes.

The Furtherance of God's Story

Taken on its own, the Joseph narrative provides substantial teaching concerning God's sovereignty. Set within the larger framework of God's metanarrative, however, the teaching grows even more significant.

When readers stand in the Joseph narrative and look back in time, they discover echoes of God's covenant with Abraham (see chart below). While God's promises to Abraham did not come to full fruition through the Joseph narrative, God sovereignly and significantly advanced toward the fulfillment of these promises through Joseph and his family.

Abraham's Covenant and Joseph

Covenant with Abraham and Descendants	Corresponding Elements of Joseph Narrative
"I will make you into a great nation" (**Gen 12:2**).	*"Do not be afraid to go to Egypt, for I will make you into a great nation there"* (**Gen 46:3**).
"All peoples on earth will be blessed through you" (**Gen 12:3**).	*"God intended it for good to accomplish what is now being done, the saving of many lives"* (**Gen 50:20**).
"To your offspring I will give this land" (**Gen 12:7**).	*"God will surely . . . take you up out of this land to the land he promised"* (**Gen 50:24**).
"I . . . will greatly increase your numbers" (**Gen 17:2**).	*"Now the Israelites . . . were fruitful and greatly increased in number"* (**Gen 47:27**).
"Kings will come from you" (**Gen 17:6**).	*"So Pharaoh said to Joseph, 'I hereby put you in charge of the whole land of Egypt'"* (**Gen 41:41**).

When readers stand in the Joseph narrative and look forward in time, they discover that the events surrounding Joseph's life advance God's story toward significant elements that arise in later centuries. When Joseph's jealous brothers sold him into slavery, God's story shifted to Egypt. In Egypt, the number of God's people multiplied exponentially, enabling them to later conquer the Promised Land. During the last of the ten plagues in Egypt, God passed over the Israelites' homes that were marked with the blood of the lamb, an event which, as we discussed in chapter four, provided the basis for future annual Israelite celebrations and foreshadowed the blood of the Lamb (Jesus Christ) through whom God ultimately redeemed His people. After their release from Egypt, the Israelites spent forty years in the wilderness, during which God delivered the Law and gave them a forty-year tutorial on living in community before they entered the Promised Land.

These later developments hinge on a seemingly random happenstance—Joseph's brothers, after they had thrown their young brother into a pit, *"looked up and saw a caravan of Ishmaelites coming from Gilead. Their camels were loaded with spices, balm and myrrh, and they were on their way to take them down to Egypt"* (**Gen 37:25**). The brothers *just happened to* beat their brother that particular day and at that particular place. They *just happened to* look up and see the traveling caravan. The caravan *just happened to* need an additional slave and *just happened to* be traveling to Egypt. In Egypt Joseph *just happened to* be sold into Potiphar's household. In prison Joseph *just happened to* interpret the dream of one who would later *just happen to* remember Joseph and share this information with Pharaoh, who *just happened to* have dreams that needed to be interpreted.

The "just happen to's" continue infinitely. God unfolds His story through apparently random events by which He guides His people toward the accomplishment of His purposes. Who knows how God may use current circumstances, activities, or conversations to further what He intends to accomplish in the future? God uses today's apparently random events to achieve tomorrow's purposes.

God unfolds His story through apparently random events which lead to accomplishing His purposes.

EZEKIEL

The term "sovereign" appears 276 times in the NIV translation of the OT. Of these 276, 211 occur in Ezekiel. The term translates from the Hebrew *adonay*, which means "lord, master" (**Holladay, 4**). In every one of the term's 211 occurrences in Ezekiel, the prophet pairs *adonay* with *YHWH*, which the NIV translates as "Sovereign LORD." This significant linguistic clue points our study of God's sovereignty toward Ezekiel.

HISTORICAL BACKGROUND

When Solomon died in 930 BC, he left a kingdom in turmoil that soon split in two—Israel to the north, Judah to the south. By 605 BC, Babylon controlled most of the region, including the northern kingdom, Israel. Judah remained partially independent, but weak, and increasingly threatened by Babylon. Babylon took groups of captives from Judah in 605 BC (including Daniel) and 598 BC (including Ezekiel). In 588 BC, Zedekiah, the puppet king of Judah whom Babylon had placed on the throne, foolishly rebelled against Babylonian authority. This infuriated the king of Babylon, who then laid siege on Jerusalem. After a two-year siege, in July of 586 BC the Babylonians breached the walls of Jerusalem, essentially destroyed the city, and took a final group of captives back to Babylon. Judah never again existed as an independent, self-governing nation.

Ezekiel hailed from a privileged, priestly family in Judah (***Eze 1:1-3***), and began prophesying in 593 BC, five years after the Babylonians took him captive. He continued prophesying from Babylon until 571 BC. Outside of these bare facts, we know little concerning Ezekiel's personal history. "What God wanted us to have from this book was His divine message," conjectures Douglas Stuart, "not a portrait of the messenger" (**18**).

EZEKIEL'S MESSAGE

From 593–587 BC, Ezekiel warned Judah of impending doom (***Eze 1-24***). While a secular observer would note the political mistakes that led to Judah's fall, Ezekiel pointed to the spiritual undercurrents and to God's sovereignty that stands behind any political movement. From Ezekiel's perspective, Judah's fall to Babylon stemmed directly from their rebellion against God:

> [1]The word of the LORD came to me: [2]"Son of man, this is what the Sovereign LORD says to the land of Israel: The end! The end has come upon the four corners of the land. [3]The end is now upon you and I will unleash my anger against you. I will judge you according to your conduct and repay you for all your detestable practices. [4]I will not look on you with pity or spare you; I will surely repay you for your conduct and the detestable practices among you. Then you will know that I am the LORD. (**Eze 7:1-4**)

Judah's fall to Babylon stemmed directly from their rebellion against God.

After six years of hearing Ezekiel's pronouncements of doom, the captives in Babylon learned in 587 BC that Babylonian forces had broken through Jerusalem's walls, and that their beloved city—the physical and spiritual home for which their hearts yearned—would crumble. For the next sixteen years, then, from 587–571 BC, Ezekiel offered the captives hopeful glimpses of their future restoration (***Ezekiel 33–48***). He traveled about "proclaiming Yahweh's gracious intention of bringing back His dispersed people and of renewing them in heart and spirit, lifting the spirits of the captives with messages of hope" (**Brownlee, xxxv**). For example:

> [11]For this is what the Sovereign LORD says: "I myself will search for my sheep and look after them. [12]As a shepherd looks after his scattered flock when he is with them, so will I look after my sheep. I will rescue them from all the places where they were scattered on a day of clouds and darkness. [13]I will bring them out from the nations and gather them from the countries, and I will bring them into their own land. I will pasture them on the mountains of Israel, in the ravines and in all the settlements in the land. [14]I will tend them in a good pasture, and the mountain heights of Israel will be their grazing land. There they will lie down in good grazing land, and there they will feed in a rich pasture on the mountains of Israel. [15]I myself will tend my sheep and have them lie down, declares the Sovereign LORD. (**Eze 34:11-15**)

Ezekiel's

> work became increasingly one of bringing hope to a despairing people and of preparing his fellow exiles to see themselves as fulfilling a central place in this hope. They would one day return to the homeland and rebuild the temple. They would establish a new people of Israel, purged of the follies and sins of the past. They would be responsible for bringing to fruition

all the frustrated hopes and expectations that had been Israel's since its earliest beginnings with the great ancestral figures of Moses and David! (**Clements, 2**)

God's Purpose

God ultimately intended, both through Judah's fall and their restoration, to bring glory to Himself. Ezekiel's prophecies included the phrase *"And you shall know that I am the LORD"* eighty-six times—the prophet continually pointed his listeners to God's sovereignty (**Hanson, 217**). God sovereignly works through people, circumstances, and even nations to exalt His name: *"It is not for your sake, O house of Israel,"* the LORD explained, *"that I am going to do these things, but for the sake of my holy name, which you have profaned among the nations where you have gone. I will show the holiness of my great name, which has been profaned among the nations, the name you have profaned among them. Then the nations will know that I am the LORD . . . when I show myself holy through you before their eyes"* (***Eze 36:22-23***).

God restores broken people for His glory. Regardless of His community's wavering faith, God remains steadily faithful. He directs circumstances—indeed, He directs history—toward the day when *"at the name of Jesus every knee should bow, in heaven and on earth and under the earth, and every tongue confess that Jesus Christ is Lord, to the glory of God the Father"* (***Php 2:10-11***).

Regardless of His community's wavering faith, God remains steadily faithful.

ESTHER

The Story

A few decades after Ezekiel's ministry, while some of the Israelites remained captive in Babylon, neighboring Persia conquered Babylon. The Esther narrative occurred in the context of this Persian rule. The story begins when King Xerxes dismissed his queen, Vashti, for refusing to stand before the people and nobles. The king then invited the most beautiful women from across the land to vie for the queenship through what compares with a contemporary beauty pageant. Esther, whose Jewish ethnicity remained a secret, won the king's heart (***Esther 1–2***).

Soon thereafter, Xerxes' second-in-command, Haman, grew enraged when Mordecai, Esther's uncle, refused to bow to him. In his anger, Haman convinced King Xerxes, who remained unaware that his queen Esther was a Jew, to pass an edict calling for the extermination of all Jews who remained the land (**Esther 3**). When Mordecai learned of the edict, he convinced Esther to risk death by approaching King Xerxes to appeal for the Jews (**Esther 4**). *"Who knows,"* Mordecai famously said to Esther, *"but that you have come to royal position for such a time as this?"* (**Est 4:14**).

Meanwhile, during a bout with insomnia, the king ordered a servant to read to him from the records of his reign. The records included the story of Mordecai foiling a plot to assassinate the king—an act of bravery for which Mordecai never received honor. The king then ordered Haman to honor Mordecai in a parade of praise, which caused Haman to seethe all the more (**Esther 6**).

Finally, during a banquet, Esther revealed her Jewish identity to King Xerxes, and asked the king to extend a reprieve to her people. The king, enraged by Haman's craftiness, stormed out of the room. He soon returned to find Haman falling on the couch where Esther reclined, begging for mercy. The king assumed Haman was making sexual advances toward Esther, and ordered him hanged (ironically on the very gallows Haman had built for Mordecai). The king ordered Mordecai's exaltation to royal status, and granted the Jews permission to protect themselves (**Esther 7–8**).

God "Behind the Scenes"

During the exile—while they lived under the thumb of a pagan, foreign empire—the Jewish community worried about its position as God's people. Is God still with us? Are we still His people? Will He protect us? Does our covenant still stand? Do we have any hope of restoration? The Esther narrative answers all of these questions in the affirmative.

God placed Esther and Mordecai into positions from which they could act courageously to preserve the people. These human characters stood responsible to make critical decisions. Esther herself, for example,

God placed Esther and Mordecai into positions from which they could act courageously to preserve the people.

summoned great courage and risked her life by making a request of the king. Numerous "coincidences" in the story, however, point the reader to God's unseen hand of providence guiding the circumstances.

Similar to the Joseph narrative, the Esther narrative brims with "just happened to's." Queen Vashti *just happened to* refuse the king's command to stand before the people and nobles. Esther, among all the women of the kingdom, *just happened to* catch the eye of the king's servants, then the king himself. Mordecai *just happened to* overhear a plot to assassinate the king. Xerxes *just happened to* have difficulty sleeping. Xerxes' servant *just happened to* read the portion of the king's annals that recounted Mordecai's bravery in foiling the assassination plot. Haman *just happened to* throw himself before the couch on which Esther rested at the moment Xerxes returned to the room. "The story of Esther illustrates that human action is essential to divine providence," explains Karen Jobes, "yet God's triumph in history ultimately does not depend on what we do, but on what he does" (**48**).

Interestingly, though the narrative displays God's sovereignty, God's name never appears in Esther. This omission may represent a deliberate attempt by the author to teach something significant about God's providence: His work does not always appear obvious to the naked eye. God can accomplish His purposes with or without visible miracles. God did not act or speak overtly in Esther, but He guided and protected His people with an omnipotent hand. For this reason, the book has brought great encouragement to Jewish people over the centuries, particularly during their dark periods when God seemed absent.

God worked through Esther and Mordecai to preserve His people through which He would bring a Messiah to bless all nations. Despite appearances, despite circumstances, despite the efforts of any human or spiritual opponent, God will continue to unfold His story to accomplish His purposes. *"For the LORD Almighty has purposed, and who can thwart him? His hand is stretched out, and who can turn it back?"* (***Isa 14:27***).

IMPLICATIONS FOR TODAY'S CHURCH

Collectively, the stories of Job, Joseph, Ezekiel, and Esther point the Bible student toward this conclusion: God sovereignly protects and guides His people toward His purpose, which is His glory. This truth holds four implications for today's church—God's sovereignty elicits our trust, submission, praise, and loyalty.

Trust

God's sovereignty elicits our trust. We will not always understand His higher ways (***Isa 55:9***), but we must trust that, regardless what we see and experience in life, He remains on His throne (***Ps 11:4***).

Concerning the church specifically, we can trust that God's plans for the church will come to fruition. His church will endure. Those who predict the demise of the church have grossly underestimated God. *"I will build my church,"* Jesus promised, *"and the gates of Hades will not overcome it"* (***Mt 16:18***). Since its inception, the church has faced physical, intellectual, and cultural attack. Yet, it endures. And it will endure.

We can trust that God's plans for the church will come to fruition. His church will endure.

The church stands not on our shoulders, abilities, or creativity—in which case it would certainly spiral into nonexistence—rather it is *"built on the foundation of the apostles and prophets, with Christ Jesus himself as the chief cornerstone"* (***Eph 2:20***). We can trust that the church's future remains certain in the hands of our sovereign God.

Submission

God's sovereignty elicits our submission. Though our human nature may call for answers to all our questions and resolutions to all theological and philosophical dilemmas, and though we may wish to see and hear God acting and speaking overtly, "God must be allowed to know what he is doing, and lies under no obligation to give any account of himself" (**Clines, xlvi**). Stephen Hooks agrees, "As maker of heaven and earth and Lord of his creation he is not answerable to humans, obligated to explain his behavior to any mortal, or required to behave in accordance with anyone's systematic theology or self-righteous expectations" (**36-37**).

Our responsibility, then, lies not in complete understanding, but in obedience beyond understanding—submitting to His guidance and following His direction. Trusting Him with the results, we simply obey.

Praise

God's sovereignty elicits our praise—always. God stands above all. He does not change. He will work out His ultimate purpose.

I recall driving down the highway one afternoon while listening to a sermon by Jack Hayford, founding Pastor of The Church on the Way in Van Nuys, California. "Pastor Jack," as many affectionately call him, spoke in this message about the believer's response to adversity. When suffering strikes, he said, we should respond immediately by falling to our knees in worship, praising God specifically for His attributes. "Worship?" I thought. "That doesn't make sense." He continued by explaining that such worship will remind us of who He is—our all-powerful, all-knowing, sovereign God. The suffering we face does not change God's identity, nor does it change the surety of His promises and purposes, Hayford explained.

As Paul bid the Corinthians, therefore, *"We fix our eyes not on what is seen, but on what is unseen. For what is seen is temporary, but what is unseen is eternal"* (***2Cor 4:18***). A focus on our unseen, sovereign God elicits praise.

Loyalty

Trust, submission, and praise naturally lead us to a dogged loyalty to our sovereign God. When we trust His sovereignty, we gain the courage to put ourselves at His disposal, and obey regardless of the cost.

In his novel *The Source,* James Michener described a period in Jewish history around 170 BC when the Jews in Palestine faced severe persecution. Greek officials came to Jerusalem and read an edict that forbade any Jew from worshiping Yahweh, and ordered them to lay their hands on an unclean pig that the soldiers had scoffingly placed on the altar in the Temple. Any Jew who ignored this edict faced a scourging unto death. Michener described one old man who refused to lay his hands on the pig:

> They stripped the old man till he stood naked; they then tied him to a pillar, where ten swift blows of the lash tore at him terribly. The speeding lead tips caught at his face and ripped out one of his eyes. They tore away a corner of his mouth and laid bare the muscles of his neck. "Will you now acknowledge the pig?" asked the captain, and when the old man refused,

> the man with the lash directed his blows lower on the body, where the lead tips tore away at the old man. . . . At the fortieth blow the humane intention of the captain became apparent: he hoped that the scourging alone would kill the old man that he might be spared the agony of being flayed, but the old Jew had within him some profound source of resistance and he survived the hailstorm of pellets, so that he was finally thrown to the ground, where he lay quivering as men with sharp knives came to cut away the mutilated skin. And when it seemed that he must surely be dead, he raised his head and called the permanent prayer of all Jews: "Hear, O Israel, the Lord our God, the Lord is one." And on the long, wailing pronunciation of the last word he died. (**372**)

When God's people recognize God's sovereignty, they rise to an otherwise impossible level of devotion.

THE CHURCH IN CHINA

THE LAST SIXTY YEARS

God's sovereign guidance and protection of His people has evidenced itself in the Chinese church, particularly over the last sixty years. Around 1950, the Chinese Communist government began an intense expulsion of western missionaries and persecution of Chinese Christians. The wave of persecution swelled in 1966 when Chairman Mao instigated the Cultural Revolution (1966–1976), during which he "expelled the last of the old Western missionaries and ruthlessly persecuted what remained of their dwindling flock, which numbered less than half a million" (**Aitken, 44**). One western missionary, forced to leave in 1950, reported, "We felt so sorry for the church we left behind. They had no one to teach them, no printing presses, no seminaries, no one to run their clinics and orphanages. No resources, really, except the Holy Spirit" (**Yancey, "Discreet," 72**). The Holy Spirit, though—the Spirit of the sovereign God—managed to protect and grow the Chinese Christian community far more extensively than any missionary could have.

During the Cultural Revolution, the government's persecution sent Christians underground. They met in coal mines, sneaked into mountain caves, and huddled behind closed shutters in apartment buildings. In secret, they prayed, worshiped, shared in the Lord's Supper, and recited memorized Scriptures (or, on occasion, read from scraps or copies of Scriptures they managed to hide). The experience shaped Chinese Christians into a spiritual force that no government—despite its best efforts—could contain. "Through many decades of perseverance and suffering the Chinese church emerged through the suffering of the cross to the place of resurrection power," explains Paul Hattaway. "Broken and humble vessels have seen God move mightily in recent decades, and tens of millions of hungry people have repented and come into the kingdom of God" (**24**).

Current Status

At the onset of the Cultural Revolution, some observers predicted the end of the church in China. Instead, the community of half a million believers blossomed amid persecution, such that today in China

> there are at least 30 million regular churchgoers in the country (the official government estimate); probably over 50 million (the consensus figure among statisticians at Western embassies); and quite possibly around 100 million (the number proclaimed by underground church pastors, who say they are recruiting at the rate of 20,000 converts a day). (**Aitken, 44**)

Though persecution has lessened over the last three decades, the Chinese government still officially views any Christian who does not register with the government as a fugitive. In 2003, the China Soul Foundation, led by Yuan Zhiming, released the groundbreaking video *The Cross: Jesus in China,* documenting the enormous growth of the Chinese Christian community.[2] Soon thereafter, China's Public Security Bureau "launched a new crackdown on unregistered church leaders, arresting 50 or more people following the release" of the video (**Morgan, www.christianitytoday.com**). Prior to the 2008 Summer Olympics, held in Beijing, arrests of Chinese Christian leaders intensified. Just a few months before the Olympics, authorities raided a house church, arrested 249 Christians, then jailed the 21 most prominent leaders (**Aikman, 40**).

Even when His church faces such battles, God continues to protect, guide, and empower it. No government, no philosophy, and no measure of persecution will stop God's community. The Chinese

[2] *The Cross: Jesus in China,* DVD, directed by Yuan Zhiming (Petaluma, CA: China Soul for Christ Foundation, 2003). I watched this video with my eight-year-old son. That night he prayed, "Help me to feel that way about you. Help me to be a better Christian."

church brings to mind the words written of the Isrealites of old, *"The more they were oppressed, the more they multiplied and spread"* (*Ex 1:12*).

Even when His church faces such battles, God continues to protect, guide, and empower it.

One Man's Story

As held true for God's community of past generations, Chinese believers' faith in God's sovereignty has enabled them to remain extraordinarily loyal. Carl Lawrence and David Wang describe one such man, a doctor, who refused to say, "Chairman Mao is greater than Christ." The Red guard beat the doctor and left him to die on a hospital floor, covered by a blanket. A few days later they returned to find him still alive. His faith remained unchanged:

> "My Christ is the Lord of Lords and the King of Kings. He has been given a name above all names in heaven, on earth, and under the earth."
>
> More beatings followed, but the response remained the same: "Christ is the greatest." After several days, they decided to end this heresy once and for all. They stripped him naked and made him stand up on a narrow bench, barely six inches wide. "Now," they shouted, "if your Christ is bigger than Chairman Mao, let him save you! Our Chairman Mao can save you; just admit it."
>
> Quietly and barely audible, he repeated the story of the men in the fiery furnace. He raised his voice as he looked at his persecutors and told them, "They were not burned because the Lord stood with them, and He is with me now."
>
> The hours passed; not a muscle in his body moved. Five hours . . . ten hours—people began to take notice. "Where does this old man get his strength?" they asked. His very presence was becoming not only a witness to Christ, but also a source of conviction and embarrassment to the others that saw him standing, naked, on the bench.
>
> Finally, the cadre leader could stand it no longer. Naked and without a whimper, the man who believed that "Christ is greater than Chairman Mao" had stood, balancing himself on a narrow bench, from seven in the evening until ten the next morning—fifteen hours of what he called "peace and fellowship." The Red Guards promised him that there would be another day. It came a week later. After dragging him away from his patients, they hanged him.
>
> The Red Guards argued among themselves. They were

> frightened. Some wanted to cut him down before he died. After a scuffle, one cut the rope. As he fell to the floor, he preached his last message: "As I was hanging there, my heart was melting for you" (**17-18**).

God sovereignly protects and leads His church. When we recognize His sovereignty, we find the strength to remain faithful.

What Do You Say?

1. Why does the concept of God's sovereignty make many Christians uneasy?
2. If you had been in Job's shoes, how would you have felt when, instead of resolving the issue of Job's suffering, God responded by simply reminding Job of His sovereignty?
3. How do the biblical stories included in this chapter, particularly those of Joseph and Esther, shed light on the tension between God's sovereignty and man's ability to make choices?
4. Biblical narratives include many "just happen to" moments—instances when God accomplishes His purposes without visible miracles. Can you point to any "just happen to's" from your own life and experience?
5. How does our understanding of God's sovereignty elicit trust? Submission? Praise? Loyalty?
6. What lessons might the American church learn from the Chinese church?
7. How might persecution actually *benefit* the church?

Part 2

The Church in the Gospels and Acts

CHAPTER SIX

INTIMATELY CONNECTED

Legendary preacher Fred Craddock describes the annual tradition of a church in Rockwood, Tennessee, where he served as a young preacher. At sunset each Easter Sunday, the congregation held a baptismal service at nearby Watts Bar Lake. After everyone gathered, Craddock, as had preachers before him, walked onto a sandbar in the water. New believers followed him. Then he baptized them into Christ.

The new believers changed clothes in little booths on the shore that had been assembled using wires and blankets, then they gathered with the rest of the church around a fire. They cooked supper, told stories, sang, and laughed together. In the midst of the fellowship, Glen Hickey—always Glen, Craddock reports, in keeping with their annual custom—stood, raised his voice above the laughter, and invited the newly baptized to stand in the middle of the cluster of people. Glen then introduced the new believers one by one. He gave their names, told where they lived, and where they worked. After Glen's introductions, the other church members, standing in a circle around the new believers, introduced themselves: "My name is . . . , and if you ever need somebody to do washing and ironing. . . ." "My name is . . . , and if you ever need anybody to chop wood. . . ." "My name is . . . , and if you ever need anybody to babysit. . . ." "My name is . . . , and if you ever need a car to go to town. . . ." Such introductions and offers continued all around the circle. Then everyone ate together and enjoyed a square dance.

As the evening wound down, Percy Miller—always Percy, in keeping with annual custom—with thumbs in his bibbed overalls, stood up and said, "Time to go." The crowd dissolved, but Percy lingered behind, and with his big boot kicked sand over the smoldering fire. The first time Craddock experienced this annual tradition, he reports, Percy Miller "saw me standing there still, and he looked at me and said, 'Craddock, folks don't ever get any closer than this.'"

"In that little community," Craddock reports, "they have a name for that. I've heard it in other communities too. In that community, their name for that is 'church.' They call that 'church'" (151-152).

God designed His children to live in relationship with one another. And, He designed the context in which these relationships blossom and thrive—the church. The church provides an immediate family for all who confess faith in Christ—not a perfect family, by any means, but a family nonetheless. The Bible knows nothing of an orphaned Christian; rather, it describes believers as *"fellow citizens with God's people and members of God's household"* (***Eph 2:19***). Tied together by our common faith, we grow together as we grow toward Christ.

The Bible knows nothing of an orphaned Christian.

Some of the greatest joys of the Christian life grow from intimate relationships with other believers. When the church functions as God designed, it provides support, encouragement, challenge, and the vitality of belonging to something larger and more significant than ourselves. Healthy, biblical relationships provide extensive joy.

Unhealthy, unbiblical relationships, on the other hand, produce the opposite. As anyone invested significantly in the church could testify, some of the greatest heartaches of the Christian life grow from the same relationships that should bring joy. Life's deepest wounds often come at the hands of those we love, people in whom we have invested ourselves. Great investment requires great risk: the more of ourselves we invest in relationships, the more we risk heartache, disappointment, and betrayal.

Much stands at stake. The potential value of healthy, biblical relationships among God's people, coupled with the potential danger of unhealthy relationships, catapults our study toward the development of the former.

At this point we transition our study from God's community as taught in the OT to the church as taught in the NT. We can make this conversion with relative ease. As chapter one discussed, the OT and NT center on different covenants—one built on the mutual promises between God and Abraham (**Genesis 12, 17**), the other built on the blood of Jesus Christ (**Heb 12:24**). The new covenant did not replace the old so much as it fulfilled it (**Mt 5:17**). The essential elements of the old covenant—God's promise of faithfulness and His demand for our faithfulness—remain intact. Additionally, just as in the old covenant, in the new covenant God desires for His followers to live in community, reflecting His love and character in the ways we relate with one another and with the surrounding world.

JESUS' TEACHING ABOUT THE CHURCH COMMUNITY

JESUS' USE OF "CHURCH"

The Gospels record Jesus using the term "church" (translated from *ekklesia*) on only two occasions during His earthly ministry. Because the church finds its foundation in the death and resurrection of Jesus Christ (**Acts 20:28b**), unsurprisingly, usage of the term begins snowballing in **Acts**—which picks up the Gospel narrative just after the resurrection—and finds its most frequent usage in Paul's epistles.

The first occurrence of *ekklesia* in the Gospels appears just after Peter confessed that Jesus is *"the Christ, the Son of the living God"* (**Mt 16:16**). Jesus responded, *"I tell you that you are Peter, and on this rock I will build my church, and the gates of Hades will not overcome it"* (**Mt 16:18**). Scholars differ concerning the precise intention of Jesus' play on words with "Peter" (*Petros*, a masculine noun referring to a rock) and "rock" (*petra*, a feminine noun, also referring to a rock). Some believe the wordplay refers to the foundational role Peter would play at Pentecost and in the early church. Others—perhaps fearful of a Roman Catholic use of this text to support a papacy stemming from Peter—believe the feminine noun *petra* refers to Peter's prior confession of faith rather than to Peter himself.

An accurate interpretation includes elements of both possibilities. Peter indeed served in a key role in the early days of the church. In fact, in the following verse Jesus said to Peter, *"I will give you the keys to the kingdom of heaven"* (***Mt 16:19***). Other NT passages picture early leaders as foundations of the church. Paul, for example, wrote of *"God's household, built on the foundation of the apostles and prophets"* (***Eph 2:19-20***). On the other hand, the truth of Jesus' identity, which Peter revealed in ***Matthew 16:16***, serves as a necessary foundation of the church. Paul referred to his teaching about Christ as the foundation he laid (***Rom 15:20; 1Cor 3:11***). Either way, Christ Himself—whether as taught through Peter or through anyone else—is *"the chief cornerstone"* (***Eph 2:20***).[1] For this reason, *"the gates of Hades will not overcome it"* (***Mt 16:18***). In sum, both Peter and the truth Peter proclaimed served as foundational to the beginning of the church.

The second occurrence of *ekklesia* in the Gospels appears just two chapters later in ***Matthew***, where Jesus instructed His followers to confront those who sin against them. If such a person does not repent after a personal confrontation, nor after a confrontation including one or two others, *"tell it to the church; and if he refuses to listen even to the church, treat him as you would a pagan or a tax collector"* (***Mt 18:17***).[2] This second occasion of "church" in the Gospels places the term in a more intimate context. The church—the assembly, the community, those called in Christ to distinction from and for the world—must take seriously the holiness of its members. Jesus' followers hold responsibility, He taught, to keep one another from sin and to make every possible effort to lead those in sin to repentance and restoration.

The church must take seriously the holiness of its members.

Jesus followed this instruction with the assurance that *"whatever you bind on earth will be bound in heaven, and whatever you loose on earth will be loosed in heaven"* (***Mt 18:18***). This phrase, which implies the granting of authority, occurs only twice in the NT—both times from the lips of Jesus. Interestingly, the other occurrence of the phrase appears in

[1] Chapter 11 will offer more discussion of Jesus' primacy in the church.

[2] Jesus used *ekklesia* twice in ***Matthew 18:17***. So, in total, He used the term three times—once in ***Matthew 16:18***, and twice in ***Matthew 18:17***. To save confusion, I will refer to ***Matthew 18:17*** as the second *occasion* on which Jesus used the term (understanding that He used it two times on this second occasion).

Matthew 16, which we discussed above, just after Jesus promised Peter *"the keys to the kingdom of heaven"* (***Mt 16:19***). Jesus pairs the only two occasions of *ekklesia* in the Gospels with the only two occurrences of the phrase, *"Whatever you bind . . ."* in the NT (***Matthew 16 and 18***). When the church operates in accordance with Jesus' teaching and on His behalf, these passages indicate, it operates with His authority.

After this second occurrence of the phrase *"whatever you bind . . . ,"* following the second occasion of *ekklesia*, Jesus furthered the principle by adding, *"Again, I tell you that if two of you on earth agree about anything you ask for, it will be done for you by my Father in heaven. For where two or three come together in my name, there am I with them"* (***Mt 18:19-20***). While we often use ***verse 20*** to bolster our congregants' spirits when attendance dwindles—"Well, the Bible says 'wherever two or three are gathered . . .'"—Jesus first spoke these words in the context of a church confronting a sin in its midst. Again, if the community handles the situation *"in my name"* (i.e., in accordance with His will), Jesus explained, it functions with His authority.

With His death and resurrection still in the future, Jesus used *ekklesia* in the Gospels on only two occasions. His use of the term, however, offers critical teaching about the foundation of the church—the truth of His identity spoken through Peter and others—and the authority of the church to minister on His behalf.

Community Teachings in the Sermon on the Mount

Though in the Gospels Jesus used the term "church" on only two occasions, He taught much about the nature of the relationships He expects to develop among those who follow Him.

For example, immediately after telling His followers in the Sermon on the Mount, *"Unless your righteousness surpasses that of the Pharisees and the teachers of the law, you will certainly not enter the kingdom of heaven"* (***Mt 5:20***), Jesus discussed some of the communal implications of such righteousness:

> [21]*You have heard that it was said to the people long ago, "Do not murder, and anyone who murders will be subject to judgment."* [22]*But I tell you that anyone who is angry with his brother will be subject to judgment. Again, anyone who says to his brother, "Raca," is answerable to the Sanhedrin. But anyone who says, "You fool!" will be in danger of the fire of hell.*

> [23]*Therefore, if you are offering your gift at the altar and there remember that your brother has something against you,* [24]*leave your gift there in front of the altar. First go and be reconciled to your brother; then come and offer your gift.*
>
> [25]*Settle matters quickly with your adversary who is taking you to court. Do it while you are still with him on the way, or he may hand you over to the judge, and the judge may hand you over to the officer, and you may be thrown into prison.* [26]*I tell you the truth, you will not get out until you have paid the last penny.* (***Mt 5:21-26***)

Though some may stop short of murder and believe they have lived righteously, Jesus confronted the progression that leads to such dire outcomes. Anger leads to words of contempt ("Raca"), which leads to words of hate ("You fool!"). Left to follow their natural courses, strained relationships escalate in anger and lead to painful outcomes. Jesus' followers, however, must resist these natural tendencies and instead check the problems before they escalate. Before worshiping, Jesus' followers reconcile hurting relationships; believers cannot expect healthy vertical relationships with God when their horizontal relationships with other believers remain unhealthy.[3] Before disagreements reach legal action, Jesus' followers *"settle matters quickly."*

Jesus' followers reconcile hurting relationships.

Later in the Sermon on the Mount, Jesus extended his relational teaching to include one's enemies:

> [38]*You have heard that it was said, "Eye for eye, and tooth for tooth."* [39]*But I tell you, Do not resist an evil person. If someone strikes you on the right cheek, turn to him the other also.* [40]*And if someone wants to sue you and take your tunic, let him have your cloak as well.* [41]*If someone forces you to go one mile, go with him two miles.* [42]*Give to the one who asks you, and do not turn away from the one who wants to borrow from you.*
>
> [43]*You have heard that it was said, "Love your neighbor and hate your enemy."* [44]*But I tell you: Love your enemies and pray for those*

[3] ***Matthew 18***, discussed previously in this chapter, addresses those situations where *"your brother sins against you"* (***Mt 18:15***). This instruction in ***Mt 5:23*** speaks of instances where you *"remember that your brother has something against you."* Paired together, the passages make Jesus' intent obvious: if a problem exists between two of his followers, regardless of which follower caused the wrong, both hold responsibility to seek reconciliation. Any believer who senses a problem exists with another believer should take assertive action to address the difficulty.

who persecute you, [45]that you may be sons of your Father in heaven. He causes his sun to rise on the evil and the good, and sends rain on the righteous and the unrighteous. [46]If you love those who love you, what reward will you get? Are not even the tax collectors doing that? [47]And if you greet only your brothers, what are you doing more than others? Do not even pagans do that? [48]Be perfect, therefore, as your heavenly Father is perfect. (***Mt 5:38-48***)

The OT law of equal retribution (*"Eye for eye, and tooth for tooth"*) sought not to encourage revenge, but to limit punishment. The OT law allowed punishment to a level that corresponded with the wrong committed. Jesus called His followers to a love that surpasses what the law allowed.

Several years ago Tom Dace served as an active member of the South Side Christian Church in Springfield, Illinois. One morning after enjoying a prayer breakfast with some other men from the church, Tom went to continue his remodeling work on an apartment. When he started his circular saw, the noise awoke an upstairs neighbor, Frank Sherry. Frank, who had been sleeping off a hangover, stumbled down the stairs in a drunken stupor. He picked up a claw hammer and beat Tom Dace to his death.

A few days later, Tom's wife, Florence, visited the county jail that held Frank Sherry, her husband's killer. She asked to see Frank. She held a Bible in her hands as she looked into his cell. "You have done a terrible thing," she began. "You have taken away my husband, my livelihood, and my Christian partner. I am not here to condemn you, but to love you." She handed Frank the Bible. "You owe it to me to read this book. On the inside cover Tom wrote what one must do to become a Christian. I want you to read that." Frank accepted the Bible; Florence left.

Months later, Florence visited Frank at a maximum security prison, and there learned that Frank had accepted Christ. He asked God, and asked Florence, for forgiveness. She threw her arms around Frank Sherry, "God forgives you and so do I."

Years later, when Frank came up for parole, Florence wrote a letter to the parole board explaining that Frank no longer posed a danger to society. In fact, she argued, he now held great potential to improve society. Her letter helped convince the board to grant Frank parole.

Upon his release from prison, Frank Sherry established a prison ministry based in Arkansas that spread to other prisons across the southern United States. Frank passed from this life in 2004, leaving a legacy—not just a legacy of his own, but also that of Florence Dace—a legacy of the love of Christ expressed through Christians.[4]

Loving One Another

John 13 records Jesus' most concise summary of the love He expects among His followers: *"A new command I give you: Love one another. As I have loved you, so you must love one another. By this all men will know that you are my disciples, if you love one another"* (***Jn 13:34-35***).

The OT had previously commanded love (***Lev 19:18***), but Jesus gave the command new depth through His exhortation to love *"as I have loved you."* The love we express to others should mirror the love we receive from Him. The compassion, grace, and even the call to holiness we receive through the love of Christ, we, in turn, grant to others. He loves sacrificially, humbly, and unconditionally. He calls us to love in the same manner. When discerning how to relate with others, perhaps how to respond to a difficult relational situation or what words to speak, the faithful believer will first ask, "How would Jesus respond? What would He say? If He stood in my shoes, facing the circumstances I face, how would He express love?"

Furthermore, Jesus' command brings new motivation for love. "The new thing appears to be the mutual affection that Christians have for one another *on account of Christ's great love for them,*" writes Leon Morris. "A community has been created on the basis of Jesus' work for us, and there is a new relationship within that community" (**562**, emphasis added). In his first epistle, John elaborates on the same principle: *"We love because he first loved us. If anyone says, 'I love God,' yet hates his brother, he is a liar. For anyone who does not love his brother, whom he has seen, cannot love God, whom he has not seen. And he has given us this command: Whoever loves God must also love his brother"* (***1Jn 4:19-21***). Believers respond most naturally and gratefully to the love of Christ when they allow that love to flow through them to other people.

[4] I first read this story in *The Preacher's Teacher*, ed. Danny Clymer (Webb City, MO: Covenant Publishing, 2003) 85. Frank Sherry recounted further details of his life story in *The Lord Looseth the Prisoner* (Kearney, NE: Morris Publishing, 2000).

Jesus' new command also offers a significant outcome of the love shared among believers: *"By this all men will know that you are my disciples, if you love one another"* (**Jn 13:35**). The world will know we follow Jesus by the way we love each other—not by our impressive audio/visual effects, our Easter musicals, or our impressive church buildings, but by our love. A healthy community dynamic among God's people provides one of the most effective tools to proclaim the love of Christ to the world. The opposite also holds true: few things repulse unbelievers like the bickering of Christians. To the same degree that love shared between believers attracts outsiders, hatefulness between believers repels them.

Few things repulse unbelievers like the bickering of Christians.

A FAMILIAL INTIMACY

Jesus and the Family Image

In the midst of one of Scripture's more intriguing passages, Jesus attached His teaching about relationships to a helpful, familiar image.

As Jesus' ministry expanded, His mother and brothers grew uneasy concerning His mental state. *"They went to take charge of him, for they said, 'He is out of his mind'"* (**Mk 3:21**). They stood outside of a house in which Jesus taught, and sent a message in to Him.

> *They told him, "Your mother and brothers are outside looking for you." "Who are my mother and my brothers?" he asked. Then he looked at those seated in a circle around him and said, "Here are my mother and my brothers! Whoever does God's will is my brother and sister and mother."* (**Mk 3:32-35**)

Though the nature of His relationship with His mother and brothers at this point in time remains a question mark—Scripture makes clear they did, later, believe in Him—Jesus' provided significant teaching on this occasion concerning the relationships of His followers. In Christ, and with Christ, we are family. "It is in the Spirit of Christ, then," comments Robert Banks concerning the application of this passage, "that the early Christian communities sought to become communities of love, to become familial and familiar settings in which the art of love could be learned, to become places where the love that bound together Son and Father could be a visible, corporate reality in the lives of those who had committed themselves to the Gospel" (56).

As family, we share relationships with the same Father (***Gal 4:4-7***). We stand as heirs of the same glory (***Rom 8:17***). We serve as brothers and sisters (***Rom 12:10***). The usage of such familial terms in the NT "is an all impressive testimony to the prevalent sense of closeness and unity in the early church" (**Ferguson, 120**).

While many contemporary people—believers and unbelievers—hunger for such closeness, we often miss the opportunities that stand immediately before us. Tammy Harris of Roanoke, Virginia, began searching for her biological mother when she turned twenty-one. A year of searching proved fruitless. Tammy did not realize, however, that her mother, Joyce Schultz, had been searching for her for twenty years—the same Joyce Shultz who worked alongside her at the same convenience store. When Joyce overheard Tammy speaking with another coworker about her search for her biological mother, Joyce's ears perked. The two compared stories and birth certificates. When the coworkers realized they were, indeed, mother and daughter, "We held on for the longest time," Tammy said. "It was the best day of my life" (**Associated Press, "Friend"**).

Believers often sit side by side in the church pew, week after week, and fail to realize the depth of relationship they share in Jesus Christ.

Paul and the Family Image

The Apostle Paul showed great affinity for the family image. His use of the term "family" (*oikeioi*) "must be regarded as the most significant metaphorical usage of all. . . . More than any of the other images utilized by Paul, it reveals the essence of his thinking about community" (**Banks, 49**). Paul frequently referred to fellow Christians as brothers, such as Tychichus, Sosthenes, Apollos, Quartus, Philemon, and Epaphroditus. He called Apphia and Phoebe sisters. He viewed Timothy and Onesimus as children in the faith. Paul instructed Timothy concerning his relationships with others in the church, *"Do not rebuke an older man harshly, but exhort him as if he were your father. Treat younger men as brothers, older women as mothers, and younger women as sisters, with absolute purity"* (***1Tim 5:1-2***).

The fact that believers met in homes adds further depth to the family metaphor. Sharing meals, worship, and relationships in homes fostered more intimate connections than usually occurred in the more formal settings of the Temple and synagogues (see sidebar written by Gregory Linton for further discussion of the house church).

Philip Yancey offers additional insight and convicting application concerning the familial relationships in the church that will serve well to conclude this section:

> In an institution, status derives from performance. The business world has learned that human beings respond well to rewards of status; they can be powerful motivators. In families, however, status works differently. How does one earn status in a family? A child "earns" the family's rights solely by virtue of birth. An underachieving child is not kicked out of the family. Indeed, a sickly child, who "produces" very little, may actually receive more attention than her siblings. As novelist John Updike once wrote, "Families teach us how love exists in a realm beyond liking or disliking, coexisting with indifference, rivalry, and even antipathy."
>
> Similarly, in God's family, we are plainly told, "There is neither Jew nor Greek, male nor female, slave nor free." All such artificial distinctions have melted under the sun of God's grace. As God's adopted children we gain the same rights, clearly undeserved, as those enjoyed by the firstborn, Jesus Christ himself—a book like Ephesians underscores that astonishing truth again and again.
>
> For this reason, it grieves me to see local churches that run more like a business institution than a family (***Church*, 62-63**).

House Churches in New Testament Times

Gregory Linton[5]

For the first several centuries of Christianity, Christians gathered together primarily in domestic residences called house churches. Three times the book of ***Acts*** refers to Jesus' disciples gathering *"in a room upstairs"* (***1:13,15; 2:1***). Many houses in Palestine had rooms on the upper floors accessible by an exterior stairway. After Pentecost, believers met in large groups in the temple and then gathered in smaller groups in homes (***Acts 2:46; 5:42***). Very quickly, the church

[5] This information is condensed from Gregory Linton, "House Church Meetings in the New Testament Era," *Stone-Campbell Journal* 8 (Fall 2005) 229-244. Used by permission of the author.

grew to 8,000 disciples, who would have needed more than one hundred houses in which to hold their meetings (***Acts 2:41; 4:4***).

The churches that Paul planted around the Aegean Sea met in the homes of individuals who served as hosts and patrons (***1 Cor 16:19; Col 4:15; Phlm 2; Rom 16:5***). Occasionally they may have met together in the larger home of Gaius (***Rom 16:23***).

Christians most likely convened in the dining room of a house. During the course of the *"love-feasts"* (***Jude 12***), they would observe the Lord's Supper. After the meal, they gathered in an atrium for worship, prayer, and teaching.

Houses provided effective meeting places for Christians. Because they had few windows open to the outside, they offered inconspicuous meeting places for the persecuted Christians. Also, such houses had facilities for preparing, serving, and eating the Lord's Supper and fellowship meal. Most of these houses also contained baths and basins where Christians could baptize converts. House church meetings promoted closer interpersonal relationships because of the intimate family atmosphere.

As Christian groups grew larger, they sometimes converted houses into larger meeting spaces. Beginning around AD 250, some built large rectangular halls. When Constantine converted in AD 313, he constructed monumental church buildings called *basilica*. The public buildings increased the visibility of Christianity and enabled a greater variety of activities and ministries. However, they also deprived churches of the benefits of smaller meetings in homes—opportunities for participation, community, intimacy, and accountability that the larger buildings did not provide. Christians no longer gathered together to share love-feasts. Worship became more formal and less participatory because the seating was oriented toward the front. Distinctions between clergy and laity increased, and interpersonal interaction decreased.

The lessons of history reveal the need for larger meetings that are more public and less personal combined with smaller meetings that promote close relationships and personal discipleship. This balanced approach to ministry will allow churches to benefit from the strengths of both large and small gatherings.

AN INTIMACY DEEPER THAN FELLOWSHIP

Contemporary Use of "Fellowship"

The early church used a term to describe the intimate relationships that naturally develop among followers of Christ—*koinonia.* Contemporary scholars usually translate the term as "fellowship."

Unfortunately, the idea of fellowship in contemporary vernacular fails to capture the depth of *koinonia.* "There is a constant tendency for the meaning of words to be distorted, and for their currency to be devalued, so that words which once throbbed with life are now dead or dying," writes John Stott. "This is the case with the word 'fellowship.' It is an overworked and undervalued term. In common usage it means little more than a genial friendliness, a superficial gregariousness, what Australian Methodists call PSA (Pleasant Sunday Afternoon) or a good gossipy get-together over a nice cup of tea" (**86**).

Two men chitchat in the church hallway between Sunday School and worship, sipping coffee from styrofoam cups. In ninety seconds they rehash last night's ballgame, commiserate over the lack of rain, and solve the country's political woes. "Hey, nice fellowshipping with you," one says to the other as they grin, shake hands, and part ways.

Contrast this fellowship with a scene from the local funeral home. An older gentleman in our church passed away, and the widow asked that I perform the funeral. The evening before the service found several church members huddled around the new widow offering comfort. I joined the fray. I attempted to speak words of comfort, but they fell like pebbles to the carpet. I squeezed her shoulder, but struggled to look her in the eye. After I passed through the line, I remained in the room, milling around and speaking to other church members. I glanced back in time to see another woman arrive in front of the casket—a friend of the new widow who had lost her husband just a year before. The two widows embraced. The friend breathed a prayer into the ear of the new widow. They wept. They shared burdens. They fellowshipped.

The Intimacy of Koinonia

"It is time to reload this powerful word with its biblical content" (**M. Jones, 131**). *Koinonia* grows from the same root as *koine,* which means "common."[6] Speakers of the first century used cognates of the term to refer to various activities—legal, social, and religious—in which participants shared in something beyond themselves. In the NT, *koinonia* usually conveys the picture of community created when believers share a relationship in Christ, and together seek the purposes of His Kingdom (**Ferguson, 355; Moule, 352**). The NT use of *koinonia*, then, indicates that believers do not just share friendship with one another; rather, they partner with one another in Christ and for Christ. "In particular," writes John Stott, "*koinonia* bears witness to three things we hold in common. First, it expresses what we *share in* together (our common inheritance); second, what we *share out* together (our common service); and third, what we *share with* each other (our mutual responsibility)" (**90**).

With this understanding of the terms, rather than equating *koinonia* with fellowship, we will more accurately view fellowship as a by-product of *koinonia*. Believers partner in Christ (*koinonia*); this partnership results in gracious horizontal relationships (fellowship). Paul demonstrates this progression in his letter to the ***Philippians***. Paul explained that he prayed for them *"with great joy because of your partnership [koinonia] in the gospel"* (***Php 1:4-5***). His joy grew from their *koinonia*. In the next paragraph, Paul used the same progression, explaining, *"It is right for me to feel this way about you, since I have you in my heart. . . . I long for all of you with the affection of Christ Jesus"* (***1:7-8***). Paul explains the source of these feelings of affection, *". . . for, whether I am in chains or defending and confirming the gospel, all of you share [sunkoinonous][7] in God's grace with me"* (***1:7***). Their mutual sharing in God's grace—their partnership in His grace—resulted in feelings of affection.

In sum, Paul's joy (***1:4***) and affection (***1:7,8***) stemmed from *koinonia* (***1:5,7***). The gracious horizontal relationship (fellowship) grew from their partnership in Christ (*koinonia*).

This principle holds great implication for churches who seek to build a stronger sense of community among their members. Too often, we focus only on our horizontal relationships, believing this effort will result in biblical community. "We simply need to like each

[6] Scholars often refer to the marketplace language of first-century Palestine, for one example of the term's usage, as *koine* Greek.

[7] Paul here adds the prefix *sun* to *koinonia*. *Sun* implies "with," giving even greater emphasis to the partnernship depicted with *koinonia*.

other more, and build stronger friendships between us," we seem to believe. This approach fails because a primary focus on human relationships simply does not produce biblical community.[8] Instead, biblical community grows from our partnership in a shared purpose. When we partner in Christ and for Christ, community comes as a result.

This understanding holds consistent with what I heard an old country preacher say, "When I sense my people are beginning to bicker with one another, I preach on the Great Commission. Nothing creates unity like realizing that you're a part of a purpose bigger than yourselves."

Nothing creates unity like realizing that you're a part of a purpose bigger than yourselves."

Koinonia in Acts

Koinonia makes its first NT appearance in ***Acts 2:42***. After Jesus' ascension, the disciples obeyed His prior instruction to wait in Jerusalem for the gift of the Holy Spirit. The Spirit came on them early in ***Acts 2***, then Peter preached to the crowds who had gathered in Jerusalem for Pentecost. Following his sermon, three thousand people responded and were baptized.

What next? How will this new band of believers function? How will they relate to one another? How will they live out their new faith? How will they continue seeking Kingdom expansion? Luke, perhaps imagining our questions, responded by offering a snapshot of the church functioning in those earliest of days:

> *42They devoted themselves to the apostles' teaching and to the fellowship [**koinonia**], to the breaking of bread and to prayer. 43Everyone was filled with awe, and many wonders and miraculous signs were done by the apostles. 44All the believers were together and had everything in common [**koina**]. 45Selling their possessions and goods, they gave to anyone as he had need.*

[8] In fact, a primary focus on human relationships actually, inadvertently, hinders the development of community. When we focus primarily on relationships, we tend to place unrealistic expectations on them, setting up an ideal of community in our minds that no human relationship could ever live up to. We expect human relationships to provide fulfillment, peace, and joy—things that, in reality, only God can provide. A primary focus on human relationships, therefore, instead of producing biblical community, produces frustration and disillusionment.

[46]Every day they continued to meet together in the temple courts. They broke bread in their homes and ate together with glad and sincere hearts, [47]praising God and enjoying the favor of all the people. And the Lord added to their number daily those who were being saved. (**Acts 2:42-47**)

Luke offers another snapshot a couple of chapters later:

*[32]All the believers were one in heart and mind. No one claimed that any of his possessions was his own, but they shared [**koina**] everything they had. [33]With great power the apostles continued to testify to the resurrection of the Lord Jesus, and much grace was upon them all. [34]There were no needy persons among them. For from time to time those who owned lands or houses sold them, brought the money from the sales [35]and put it at the apostles' feet, and it was distributed to anyone as he had need.* (**Acts 4:32-35**)

Luke's description of the *koinonia* of the early church reflects the ideal of true friendship held among Greeks. Phrases such as "friends have everything in common," "one soul," and "nothing one's own" were commonly found in Greek literature to describe friendship. For example, in his work *Critias,* Plato pictured the early days of Athens as a time when "none of its members possessed any private property, but they regarded all they had as the common property of all" (**Johnson, *Acts,* 62**). Through his use of similar language, Luke sought to convince his readers that "the grace of God brought about a quality of life amongst the first Christians which answered even to the ideals of their own world" (**Seccombe, 52**). The church at its best, Luke taught in **Acts**, offers life at its best.

The wise scholar will recognize that the ideals portrayed in summary statements such as ***Acts 2:42-47*** and ***4:32-35*** are, in fact, ideals. Lest we exalt the early church to a level of perfection beyond human possibility, we must look beyond Luke's brief summary statements and also consider the larger, narrative portions of **Acts**, which display both joyous successes and dismal missteps of the first generation of Christians. Luke's inclusion of the good and the bad bids the modern reader to love and remain committed to the church despite its failure to always achieve the highest ideals. "Every human wish dream that is injected into the Christian community is a hindrance to genuine community and must be banished if genuine community is to survive," explained Dietrich Bonhoeffer. "He who loves his dream of a community more than the Christian community itself becomes a destroyer of the latter, even though his personal intentions may be ever so honest and earnest and sacrificial" (***Life***, **27**).

KOINONIA TODAY

What does *koinonia*—this partnership in Christ and for Christ—look like today? Several images come to mind:

- In a Sunday School class, someone stood and explained that another class member, who happened to be absent that day, faced serious financial difficulties. Someone else suggested, "How about the next time we get together, we bring our checkbooks and take up a collection?" The class patriarch responded, "We don't have a choice—this is who we are. This is what we do. Christians help each other."
- After our daughter Claire was born, friends from our church and from the Bible College where I teach brought us meals for twenty-four straight days.
- In a home Bible study a young couple spoke up and said, "We've got an announcement to make. We have a baby on the way! We wanted to tell you all first."
- In a men's accountability group, one group member confided, "Guys, I've been looking at things on the internet that I shouldn't be looking at. It's killing my marriage; I find it impossible to pray. You've got to help me stop." The others gathered in a circle around him and prayed for him. In coming weeks, every time they met, they asked him about his computer usage: "Have you kept pure this week?"
- I made a hospital visit to one of our church members. When I arrived, others from the church had already filled the room almost wall-to-wall.
- Each fall, the church my family attends conducts The Prom of the Stars, a formal dinner and dance for mentally and physically disabled adults. Last fall 100 volunteers from the church participated, hosting over 1,000 guests and their caretakers. In a letter to the church, one woman wrote, "I went to the Prom of the Stars with my Downs Syndrome sister. I have never in my 55 years seen happier people. I saw genuine love and caring generosity like I'd never seen before."

Just as Luke provided in ***Acts***, the contemporary church provides snapshots of *koinonia* in action. No church operates like this all the time, but most churches do at least some of the time—enough to give a glimpse, a glimmer of the glory of Christ's followers partnering together to accomplish Christ's purposes.

Pattern and Principle

When studying the NT, particularly *Acts* and the epistles, to learn what God desires of the church, wise interpreters guard against a hermeneutical pitfall often labeled "patternism." Elsewhere, I have described patternism as follows:

> Patternism turns biblical descriptions of people or events into universally normative prescriptions for behavior. Patternism turns descriptions into prescriptions, examples into mandates, and pictures into blueprints.
>
> Preachers with a strong legitimate desire to see the contemporary church reflect the ideals of the New Testament church (and I include myself in that category) face particular temptation to patternize. Scripture does, indeed, offer principles concerning the believer's life, service, and ministry. Some Scriptures, however, simply narrate the stories of believers attempting to live out these principles. Or, as in the case of the epistles, some texts discuss how these principles apply to particular circumstances in particular cultures and time periods. Simply because a biblical narrative or epistle mentions something that happened, or something that should happen in a particular circumstance, does not necessarily imply that God intends the church of all times to emulate that practice (**D. Overdorf, 80**).

For example, when the apostles cast lots to choose a new leader (*Acts 1:26*), this example does not prescribe a universal mandate to choose church leaders by casting lots. Instead, the example grows from an underlying principle—the principle, arguably, of seeking God's guidance when choosing church leaders. The pattern (casting lots) does not bind us, the underlying principle (seeking God's guidance) does.

While most readers, I imagine, will nod their heads when reading the previous paragraph—few churches (none that I know of) cast lots to choose leaders—we must recognize that the temptation to patternize creeps into our interpretations concerning more difficult issues such as church organization or the manner in which we partake of the Lord's Supper. Medford Jones, a Stone-Campbell Restoration Movement scholar of a generation ago, explained, "It is . . . disastrous to assume God blue printed the exact nature of every adaptation the churches would make in reaching people in different climates, cultures, and times. . . . We have done poorly in this and have at times superimposed our prejudices upon churches" (**Jones, 18**).

This hermeneutical approach does not render the patterns unimportant, but stresses their importance as they relate to larger principles. The wise reader seeks, therefore, to discern what principles lie behind biblical patterns, the "norms, Apostolic precedents and the spirit of the New Testament that must be understood and heeded" (**ibid.**).

A CASE STUDY OF CONTRAST

After his second summary statement in Acts (***4:32-35***, quoted above), Luke describes an individual who lived up to the ideals pictured in the summary, then a couple who failed to do so.

Barnabas's Sharing His Possessions

In ***Acts 4:32-35***, Luke pictures the believers as *"one in heart and mind,"* sharing *"everything they had."* More specifically, *"from time to time those who owned houses or lands sold them"* and gave the money to distribute to the needy.

Following this summary statement, Luke offers a particular example of one who showed such benevolent compassion: *"Joseph, a Levite from Cyprus, whom the apostles called Barnabas (which means Son of Encouragement), sold a field he owned and brought the money and put it at the apostles' feet"* (***Acts 4:36-37***).

Though the prior summary statement spoke of everyone sharing their possessions, this brief note about Barnabas makes clear that the early church did not require everyone to yield all their possessions to a communal purse (as though the summary statement

The early church did not require everyone to yield all their possessions to a communal purse.

supported Communism or Socialism). Barnabas had personal property—he owned a field—and willingly sold it. Early believers voluntarily sold their own properties and donated money to help those in need.[9]

When Christians, such as Barnabas, submitted to the Lordship of Christ, this submission included their complete selves, with nothing—including their possessions—held back. For this reason, explained F.F. Bruce, "Members regarded their private estates as being at the community's disposal; those who owned houses or lands sold these in order that they might be more conveniently available to the community in the form of money" (**101**). Believers placed their private possessions at the disposal of the community.

A single mother in a church I attended a few years ago struggled to make ends meet. With three small children and two jobs, the frazzled young lady could never seem to catch up. Her situation worsened when she learned that her car engine needed repairs that would cost more than the car's value, and far more than she could pay. While she sat weepy eyed in her living room on a Saturday afternoon, a friend from the church pulled into her driveway and gave her the keys to a slightly used, reliable car.

"How could you give away a *car*?" someone asked the friend a few days later.

"It's not my car," she responded, "it's God's. And if someone else in God's family needs it more than I need it, then I want her to have it."

Ananias and Sapphira's Hypocrisy

Apparently, Ananias and Sapphira watched as Barnabas gave the money from his property. The couple probably saw the respect generous believers such as Barnabas garnered from the rest of the community, and heard the glowing comments people made about Barnabas. People even gave him a nickname, "Son of Encouragement."

[9] Anthony Robinson and Robert Wall comment on the potential political implications of ***Acts 4:32-35***, "Make no mistake, this portrait of the Acts community *is* a challenge to an ownership society, to the way that most of us in twenty-first-century North American not only participate in a capitalist economy but have even internalized capitalism in our hearts and souls. But having said that, we must acknowledge that ***Acts*** is not offering a proposal for political policy but a picture of a community and a congregation's life together" (**83**).

Before Sunday School class, the men gathered around the coffee pot, trying to sneak donuts without their wives seeing them, and they said, "Did you hear what Barnabas did?"[10]

"Oh, yeah, he had that tract of land south of town. He sold it and brought every penny to the board meeting on Thursday. Told 'em to give the money to whoever needed it. That's Barnabas for you—he's the real deal."

Ananias stirred cream into his coffee, and thought, *I wish people would talk like that about me.*

That afternoon, over lunch at the Jerusalem lunch buffet, Ananias picked at his food. "Sapphira," he began, "I've been thinking." She had been thinking, as well. And the two hatched a plan. They would sell a couple of acres that they didn't need, pocket some of the money, and bring the rest to church. However—and here lies the genius of the plan—they would pretend they were giving the entire amount. Then, the next Sunday the men around the coffee pot would say, "Did you hear what Ananias and Sapphira did?"

The plan seemed foolproof. Of course, fool's plans usually do (at least to the fool). If only Ananias and Sapphira had access to Galatians, *"Do not be deceived: God cannot be mocked. A man reaps what he sows"* (**Gal 6:7**).

Ananias and Sapphira could have given part of the money and received commendation. No biblical or apostolic command required the giving of one hundred percent of the sale price of land. Yet, this couple apparently sought acclaim more than they sought to please God or to serve the community. They wanted the praise without the sacrifice. So, they gave part, told Peter they gave the full amount, and suffered the consequence of death (**Acts 5:1-11**). Their deaths stemmed not from the amount of the gift, but, as Peter explained, *"Satan has so filled your heart that you have lied to the Holy Spirit"* (**Acts 5:3**).

Barnabas personified *koinonia* by entering an intimate partnership with other believers—a partnership in Christ and for Christ. Ananias and Sapphira personified the opposite, showing more concern for personal acclaim than for other believers or for Christ Himself.

[10] As in a previous chapter, I will take literary liberties with the biblical story, attempting to imagine how it may have occurred in a contemporary church. I trust the reader will humor me.

IMPLICATIONS FOR TODAY

Though numerous implications grow from the principles presented in this chapter, three hold most relevance to our discussion in this book.

Conversion and Community

First, conversion propels believers into a new relationship not only with God, but also with God's people. **Acts 2** pictures the massive baptism of three thousand people on the Day of Pentecost. On the heels of this conversion, Luke describes the communal connotations of a new life in Christ. **Acts** weaves conversion and community together.

The church of today must recapture this emphasis. We too often teach new believers about their individual relationships with Christ, but fail to teach them about the community in which they now participate. Joseph Hellerman writes of "an American Christian paradigm that understands salvation to have everything to do with how the individual relates to God and nothing to do with how we relate to one another. . . . To become a Christian is to enter into a relationship with a new Father, with little or no emphasis on our relationship with a new set of brothers and sisters. In our typical gospel presentations, we introduce God's family only as a sort of utilitarian afterthought—church is there to help us grow in our newfound faith in Christ" (**122**). In contrast, "Church was unquestionably no afterthought for the early Christians" (**Ibid.**).

We often teach new believers about individual relationships with Christ, but fail to teach them about community.

Likewise, for biblical churches today, church is no afterthought. Conversion relates not only to individual salvation, but also to community incorporation.

"Our" Resources

Second, the intimate connection expressed in *koinonia* goes beyond just concept and philosophy to sacrificial expressions that will require putting "our" resources at Christ's disposal for use in His community. Those things that I consider "mine"—my car, house, time, checkbook, lawnmower, energy, clothes, books, boat, bicycle, and countless other things—I must hold with an open hand. For example, it may cause inconvenience (I hesitate to call this "hardship") to loan our family's second car to a missionary on furlough, helping him visit churches to raise support needed to continue his ministry. Such a gift should come as naturally to me, however, and with as minimal hesitation, as giving my son a quarter to play the video game at Pizza Hut. The car is not mine, it is Christ's. And if someone else in His community needs it, if I have internalized the concept of *koinonia*, I toss him the keys and consider myself his partner in ministry.

From Gratitude to Generosity

Third, the intimacy of *koinonia* grows from the gratitude of individuals who appreciate the work of Christ in their lives. Anthony Robinson and Robert Wall explain,

> Practically speaking, this suggests to us that significant giving and sharing, the practice of generosity, has its roots in transformative worship, bold witness, rich sacrament, and a vital life together. This generosity and sharing of goods is not born of imperatives such as "you should be generous," or "you should care for those in need," so much as it flows from the indicative of what God has done and is doing. To put it negatively, if there is no spirit of generosity alive in our congregations, it may be time to look at what is going on—or not going on—in worship and in our life together as a community. When people's deep hungers are being met, then generosity overflows naturally—or at least responsively. **(82)**

Much hinges on the intimate connection of Christians, including our individual ability to survive spiritually and physically, and the impact our churches will make on our surrounding communities. Churches in which individuals partner in Christ and for Christ offer great joy, and significant impact.

CONCLUSION

Bill Hybels wrote that after he preached one weekend, a young married couple approached him. The wife held a baby in her arms, wrapped in a blanket. The couple asked Bill to pray for their baby.

"Sure," he responded. The mother laid the baby in his arms, then pulled back the blanket to reveal the baby's face. Hybels said that at the sight of the baby's face, his knees buckled. In his arms he held the most horribly deformed baby he'd ever seen. The center of her tiny face had caved in. He could say nothing more than, "Oh my . . . oh my."

The mother explained, "Her name is Emily. We've been told she has about six weeks to live. We would like you to pray that before she dies she will know and feel our love."

Hybels prayed for the baby and the couple. As he handed Emily back to her mother, he said, "Is there anything we can do for you, any way that we as a church can serve you during this time?"

The father responded, "Bill, we're okay. Really we are. We've been in a loving small group in the church for years. Our group members knew that this pregnancy had complications. They were at our house the night we learned the news, and they were at the hospital when Emily was delivered. They helped us absorb the reality of the whole thing. They even cleaned our house and fixed our meals when we brought her home. They pray for us constantly and call us several times every day. They are even helping us plan Emily's funeral."

Three other couples then stepped forward and surrounded Emily and her parents. "We always attend church together as a group," they said.

Hybels wrote, "It was a picture I will carry to my grave, a tight-knit huddle of loving brothers and sisters doing their best to soften one of the cruelest blows life can throw. After a group prayer, they all walked up the side aisle toward the lobby.

"*Where,* I wondered as they left, *would that family be, where would they go, how would they handle this heartbreak, without the church?*

"There is nothing like the local church when it's working right. Its beauty is indescribable. Its power is breathtaking. Its potential is unlimited." **(22-23)**

What Do You Say?

1. This chapter provided several stories that pictured how community might look in a healthy church. Can you provide a similar story from your own experience?
2. Though He used the term on only two occasions in the Gospels, what insights should we draw from Jesus' use of the term *ekklesia*?
3. Jesus offered a "new" command: *"As I have loved you, so you must love one another"* (***Jn 13:34***). How does loving *as He loved us* add new depth to this command?
4. The NT often pictures the church as a family. What particular aspect of this analogy do you find most meaningful?
5. Compare and contrast our contemporary understanding of "fellowship" with the biblical term *koinonia*.
6. Why do you think God administered such severe punishment (death) on Ananias and Sapphira?
7. What would need to change in your church so that it better cared for people like Emily's parents, described by Bill Hybels at the end of this chapter?

CHAPTER SEVEN

KINGDOM ADVANCING

Not long ago, a friend emailed me an article penned by church historian Leroy Garrett. Garrett wrote the column on the day that would have marked Dietrich Bonhoeffer's one-hundredth birthday. "If Protestants made 'saints,'" wrote Garrett, "Dietrich Bonhoeffer would be a 'saint'" (**"Bonhoeffer at 100"**).

- I. Fulfilled Longings for the Kingdom
  - A. OT Longings
  - B. "The Kingdom Is Near"
- II. The Kingdom and the Church
  - A. Defining the Kingdom
  - B. The Relationship between the Church and the Kingdom
- III. The Kingdom Already
  - A. A Balanced Perspective
  - B. Jesus and the "Already" Kingdom
  - C. Today's Church and the "Already" Kingdom
- IV. The Kingdom Not Yet
  - A. "Eternal Life" in John
  - B. Understanding the "Not Yet" Factor
  - C. The Kingdom Eternal
  - D. The Hope of What's to Come
- V. The Kingdom Parables
  - A. The Sower and the Soils
  - B. The Wheat and the Weeds
  - C. The Mustard Seed and the Yeast
  - D. The Hidden Treasure and the Pearl of Great Value
  - E. The Net
- VI. Conclusion

When Bonhoeffer decided to enter the ministry, his family objected, saying he would waste his life on an inane and ineffective church. He responded, "If the church is feeble, I shall reform it." At age twenty-three, he completed his doctoral dissertation, which Karl Barth described as "a theological miracle." The dissertation, titled "The Communion of the Saints," displayed his passion that the church concretely and tangibly influence society. He described the church as "Christ existing as community."

He taught in Germany, ministered in Spain, then studied in New York. His friends encouraged Bonhoeffer to stay in America to avoid the rising Nazi threat in Germany. He felt morally obliged, however, to return home and to minister to the German church, even if it cost his life. In Germany he returned to teaching and writing, and continued to call the church to renewal and radical commitment. Such discipleship would prove costly, he taught, but the grace we receive demands nothing less.

Though they faced oppression by Hitler's earthly kingdom, Bonhoeffer reminded his flock that they belonged to Christ's kingdom, which "does not appear as one, visible, powerful empire, nor yet as the 'new' kingdom of the world; on the contrary, it manifests itself as the kingdom of the other world that has entered completely into the discord and contradiction of this world" (***Testament*, 97**). As the kingdom manifests itself in this world, it "assumes form in the church insofar as the church bears witness to the miracle of God. The function of the church is to witness to the resurrection of Christ from the dead, to the end of the law of death of this world that stands under the curse, and to the power of God in the new creation" (**ibid., 96**). Bonhoeffer spurned the thought that the kingdom exists only in the spiritual realm, waiting as a reward for Christians who manage to survive, even unnoticed, in this world. Instead, Bonhoeffer stressed that the kingdom infiltrates this world and miraculously changes it on behalf of Christ.

In 1943, Nazi soldiers arrested Bonhoeffer. Two years later, just one month prior to Hitler's suicide and the fall of the Nazis, a guard awoke Bonhoeffer at 5:00 AM, "Prisoner Bonhoeffer, get ready to come with us." He passed a note to a fellow prisoner that said, "This is the end; but for me it is the beginning."

A German camp doctor who witnessed Bonhoeffer's execution later recalled,

> Through the half open door in one room of the huts I saw Pastor Bonhoeffer before taking off his prison garb, kneeling on the floor praying fervently to his God. I was deeply moved by the way of this lovable man, so devout and so certain that God would hear his prayer. At the place of execution he again said a short prayer and then climbed the steps to the gallows, brave and composed. His death ensued after a few seconds. . . .
>
> In the almost fifty years that I worked as a doctor, I have hardly seen a man so entirely submissive to the will of God. **(Garrett, "Bonhoeffer at 100")**

Hitler's kingdom ended in a bunker with a self-inflicted pistol shot to the head and a cyanide capsule. Bonhoeffer's kingdom—more specifically, Christ's kingdom to which Bonhoeffer belonged and of which he tirelessly testified—continues, and will continue without end.

What had Bonhoeffer discovered about the kingdom that enabled his radical devotion?

FULFILLED LONGINGS FOR THE KINGDOM

OT Longings

When Jesus announced the coming of the kingdom, His listeners had some familiarity with the concept. "Old Testament passages . . . as well as writings from the apocrypha, the pseudepigrapha, and Qumran make evident that the concept of God's kingdom was prominent and quite intelligible among Jesus' Jewish hearers," explains Everett Ferguson (22).[1]

Old Testament writers viewed the kingdom as a past, present, and future reality, associating it with God's everlasting power and dominion:

- *"Yours, O Lord, is the greatness and power and the glory and the majesty and the splendor, for everything in heaven and earth is yours. Yours, O Lord, is the kingdom; you are exalted as head over all"* (**1Chr 29:11**).
- *"The Lord has established his throne in heaven, and his kingdom rules over all"* (**Ps 103:19**).
- *"How great are his signs, how mighty his wonders! His kingdom is an everlasting kingdom, and his sovereignty is from generation to generation"* (**Dan 4:3**).

God's kingdom manifested itself on earth through Israel, with Israel's kings serving as God's representatives:

- *"'Now if you obey me fully and keep my covenant, then out of all nations you will be my treasured possession. Although the whole earth is mine, you will be for me a kingdom of priests and a holy nation.' These are the words you are to speak to the Israelites"* (**Ex 19:5-6**).
- *"Of all my sons—and the Lord has given me many—he has chosen my son Solomon to sit on the throne of the kingdom of the Lord over Israel"* (**1Chr 28:5**).

[1]The next three paragraphs rely heavily on **Ferguson, 21-22**.

Because Israel repeatedly fell short of God's perfect reign, the prophets looked forward to a time when God would establish His kingdom on earth in a fuller, more pervasive way, through His anointed Savior (note the future tense in these passages):

- *"The LORD Almighty will reign on Mount Zion and in Jerusalem, and before its elders, gloriously"* (**Isa 24:23**)
- *"The LORD will be king over the whole earth. On that day there will be one LORD, and his name the only name"* (**Zec 14:9**).
- *"The LORD has made proclamation to the ends of the earth: 'Say to the Daughter of Zion, 'See, your Savior comes! See, his reward is with him, and his recompense accompanies him." They will be called the Holy People, the Redeemed of the LORD; and you will be called Sought After, the City No Longer Deserted"* (**Isa 62:11-12**).

The OT Jewish people pinned their hopes on God's anointed one, the Messiah, to bring God's kingdom in its fullness. Believers today share a similar hope. In *Jesus and the Kingdom of God,* G.R. Beasley-Murray offers application of this hope to people of all ages,

> Here is an expectation of the future firmly rooted in the Old Testament revelation and in Israel's history and experience of God, which corresponds to the hope of God's people in all ages; the prospect of "seeing God" and dwelling in his presence has always been viewed by his people as the ultimate blessing of the final order of existence. We should take care not to overlook one characteristic element in this expectation in particular, however: when Yahweh comes to bring his kingdom, it is to this world that he comes and in this world that he establishes his reign. The hope of Israel is not for a home in heaven but for the revelation of the glory of God in this world, when "the earth shall be full of the knowledge of the glory of the Lord as the waters fill the sea" (***Hab. 2:14***). As God's claim on man encompasses the totality of his life, so God's salvation for man encompasses the totality of human existence, including our historical existence. The claim and the promise alike find their fulfillment in the Messiah. In him man has his sufficient representative before God, and in him God's presence is signified and the rule of the world is actualized. In the person of the Messiah God's purpose in history finds its embodiment. (***Kingdom*, 25**)

Israel expected God to send an earthly king to establish a reign on earth. In Jesus, their hopes found fulfillment—not precisely as they expected, but in a manner that surpassed their (and our) expectations both for this world and beyond.

"The Kingdom is Near"

Jesus' first recorded words in the Gospel of Mark held great significance for those who longed for the fullness of God's reign: *"The kingdom of God is near. Repent and believe the good news!"* (***Mk 1:15***).[2] For centuries, even millennia, believers had ached for God to set right what had gone wrong. They sought the fulfillment of all God's promises, rescue from pagan oppression, judgment of evil, peace, and administration of justice. For Jesus to announce that the kingdom was near "was to summon up that entire narrative, and to declare that it was reaching its climax. God's future was breaking in to the present. Heaven was arriving on earth" (**N.T. Wright, *Simply*, 100**).

Unfortunately, many Jewish people of the day misunderstood significant elements of God's promised King and kingdom. In Jesus, God's kingdom would come to the earth; however, it had nothing to do with ousting the Romans from Palestine, as they anticipated. Even as late as ***Acts 1:6***, after Jesus' disciples heard Him teach about the kingdom for three years, and following His death and resurrection, *"They asked him, 'Lord, are you at this time going to restore the kingdom to Israel?'"*

While many of His followers anticipated an earthly kingdom of politics and military might, Jesus explained, *"My kingdom is not of this world. . . . My kingdom is from another place"* (***Jn 18:36***). It is not of this world—Jesus did not seek to establish an earthly kingdom with walls, armies, and political rule, but to establish a spiritual reign that would topple forces far more wicked than any Roman Caesar.

Jesus did not seek to establish an earthly kingdom with walls, armies, and political rule.

Though His kingdom *"is not of this world,"* this truth does not imply that Jesus' kingdom has no contact with or relevance in this world. The end of ***John 18:36*** indicates that the kingdom has indeed *come* to this world *"from another place."* Instead of a military uprising—which would prove petty in comparison—Jesus unleashed upon the world a dramatic spiritual uprising, one where people go the second mile, turn the other cheek, love their enemies, and pray for those who persecute them (***Mt 5:39-***

[2] Jesus used "The Kingdom of God" (primarily in Mark and Luke) and "The Kingdom of Heaven" (in Matthew) interchangeably.

44). Rather than blessing the ambitious, prideful, egocentric, and ruthless domination of earthly kingdoms, in Jesus' kingdom,

> [3]*Blessed are the poor in spirit,*
> *for theirs is the kingdom of heaven.*
> [4]*Blessed are those who mourn,*
> *for they will be comforted.*
> [5]*Blessed are the meek,*
> *for they will inherit the earth.*
> [6]*Blessed are those who hunger and thirst for righteousness,*
> *for they will be filled.*
> [7]*Blessed are the merciful,*
> *for they will be shown mercy.*
> [8]*Blessed are the pure in heart,*
> *for they will see God.*
> [9]*Blessed are the peacemakers,*
> *for they will be called sons of God.*
> [10]*Blessed are those who are persecuted because of righteousness,*
> *for theirs is the kingdom of heaven.* (***Mt 5:3-10***)

The first and last of these Beatitudes, bookending Jesus' summation of discipleship, make clear where such values appear—in the kingdom of heaven, which through Jesus has come to the earth.

THE KINGDOM AND THE CHURCH

DEFINING THE "KINGDOM"

Our discussion to this point leads to a definition of the phrase "kingdom of God." The English term "kingdom" generally refers to the realm over which a king rules. The Greek term used in the NT, however, refers primarily to the reign of a king, and secondarily to a physical realm. The term more often depicts the ruler's kingship than the territory he controls (see sidebar, "Word Study on *Basileia*").

In short, then, in the NT "the kingdom of God" refers to God's reign, sovereignty, and exercised power. To enter God's kingdom, one does not drive to a physical address—the corner of Fifth and Main, for example—nor does one cross a national border that appears in an atlas. Rather, one enters the kingdom by submitting to the rule of God. The NT offers several examples of such submission:

- having righteousness that surpasses the Pharisees (***Mt 5:20***);
- doing the will of the Father (***Mt 7:21***);

- becoming like little children (***Mt 18:3***);
- repenting and believing like the tax collectors and prostitutes (***Mt 21:31-32***);
- ministering to "the least of these" (***Mt 25:34-40***);
- refusing the trappings of wealth (***Mk 10:23***);
- being born of water and Spirit (***Jn 3:5***);
- avoiding wickedness (***1Cor 6:9***);
- accepting Christ's rescue from the dominion of darkness (***Col 1:13***); and
- being rich in faith (***Jas 2:5***).

The kingdom exudes God's character and pours His grace, compassion, and holiness into a world wracked by sin and its consequences—a world longing (albeit an often blind longing) for restoration. When people enter the kingdom, they join the restoration process, both in themselves and in the surrounding world.

Word Study on Basileia[3]

Everett Ferguson explains, "In Hebrew, Aramaic, and Greek, the primary meaning of 'kingdom' is 'kingship,' that is, royal power and kingly rule. The words more often refer to the 'reign' than to the 'realm' in which the rule is exercised, to the dominion rather than the domain" (19). Ferguson's evaluation stands consistent with *A Greek-English Lexicon of the New Testament and Other Early Christian Literature* by Bauer, Arndt, and Gingrich—a standard Greek lexicon used by many Greek scholars—which offers this primary definition of *basileia*: "kingship, royal power, royal rule, kingdom."

Basileia relates to *basileus* ("ruler"), and it originally described the position, power, or office of a king. Secondarily, it also grew to refer to the geographical realm over which a king rules. Primarily, though, it pointed to the power more so than to the locality.

The OT equivalent of *basileia, malak* (and its cognates, *melukah, malcuth,* and *mamlakah*), pictured the rule of dominion of a king: *"Yours, O LORD, is the greatness and the power and the glory and the majesty and the splendor, for everything in heaven and earth is*

[3] Sources consulted: Grenz, 616; Ferguson, 19; Ladd, *Theology*, 60-61; *"Basileia,"* in BAGD; *"Basileia,"* by Karl L. Schmidt; and *"Basileus,"* by Verlyn Verbrugge.

yours. Yours, O LORD, is the kingdom [**melukah**]; you are exalted as head over all" (***1Chr 29:11***); and *"For dominion [**melukah**] belongs to the LORD, and he rules over the nations"* (***Ps 22:28***). New Testament writers chose a Greek term that carries similar connotations. When Jesus proclaimed the *"The kingdom [**basileia**] of God is near"* (***Mk 1:15***), He drew upon the imagery of God's dominion and rule offered through the OT. And Jesus equated the "kingdom" with matters such as God's power over Satan and demons (***Mt 12:28-29***) and sickness (***Lk 10:9***).

Jesus and the NT writers also, in many texts, used the term more generically. For example, Jesus said of the poor in spirit and the persecuted, *"theirs is the kingdom of heaven"* (***Mt 5:3,10***). He also spoke of those who will or will not *"enter the kingdom"* (such as the wealthy in ***Mk 10:23-25***). Even in such cases, however, what one does or does not enter relates more with the reign and dominion of God than a particular locality or realm.

THE RELATIONSHIP BETWEEN THE CHURCH AND THE KINGDOM

The church and the kingdom relate, but they do not equate. Recall that the kingdom refers to the reign of God, more so than to the realm over which God reigns. The church (the people of God) rises out of the kingdom (the reign of God), testifies to it, and ministers to extend it, but the church is not itself the kingdom. Craig Blomberg explains, "The kingdom . . . is always bigger than the church, but it includes true Christians as its subjects. God's vision of building his church is always but one part of the much larger cosmic task of advancing his kingdom—his righteous reign in the entire universe" (125).

Much of what we have learned about the kingdom also holds true for the church. The church does not reside at a physical address, for example (members of the church often meet at particular physical addresses, obviously, but the church is more than a meeting or a building), and one enters the church through submission to Christ. The reign of God, however—His kingdom—extends beyond the church. God reigns over the cosmos (***Ps 50:1-6; 103:19-22***), for instance, and over governments (***Rom 13:1***). God's reign (His kingdom) includes each of these—the cosmos and governments—but the church does not.

The terms "kingdom" and "church" appear in the same context only a few times in the NT. The most prominent occurrence appears in ***Matthew 16:16-19***:

> 16*Simon Peter answered, "You are the Christ, the Son of the living God."*
>
> 17*Jesus replied, "Blessed are you, Simon son of Jonah, for this was not revealed to you by man, but by my Father in heaven.*
> 18*And I tell you that you are Peter, and on this rock I will build my church, and the gates of Hades will not overcome it.* 19*I will give you the keys of the kingdom of heaven; whatever you bind on earth will be bound in heaven, and whatever you loose on earth will be loosed in heaven."*

While some argue that the phrase *"I will give you the keys of the kingdom of heaven"* parallels Jesus' previous statement that *"on this rock I will build my church,"* a closer examination reveals not a parallel but a progression. On the foundation of Peter and the truth he confessed about Jesus' divinity (*"on this rock"*),[4] Jesus would build a community (*"my church"*) through whom He would unleash (*"I will give you the keys"*) His reign (*"the kingdom"*).

To equate the church with the kingdom risks reducing the kingdom—or at least our perception of it—to something that can fit within our walls, programs, and schedules. It risks reducing God's work in the world—or at least our involvement in it—to something we can manage in our committee meetings and on our laptops.

The kingdom operates in an adventurous, infinite realm, uncontrollable by humans. The kingdom compares to a raging river of whitewater rapids. The church compares to the raft that floats atop it. If those in the raft seek an existence they can control, they stay on shore, sit in the raft, play meaningless games, and argue with each other. If they seek the true adventure of the river, on the other hand, they push out into its rapids and discover thrill and excitement far beyond what they could have produced on their own.

The kingdom operates in an adventurous, infinite realm, uncontrollable by humans.

Biblical leaders discern the currents of the kingdom, and carefully guide their churches into these cur-

[4] For more discussion on this passage, including Jesus' wordplay with "Peter" and "rock," see the previous chapter.

rents. Instead of asking, "What can we do for God?" they ask, "What is God doing that we can join?" Perhaps God has stirred the hearts of college students in a particular town. How can a church in that town minister to those college students? Maybe the leaders of a church have sensed God's movement among those in China or Mexico. How can that church join these currents of the kingdom? Perhaps God has opened doors for ministry among the homeless or others with immediate physical needs. How can a church pursue these ministries?[5]

God's reign—the kingdom—provides opportunities for God's community—the church—to serve as tools in His hand to bring reconciliation and restoration to the world He so dearly loves.

THE KINGDOM ALREADY

A Balanced Perspective

The kingdom of God is both a present reality and a future hope. At present, God works in His world and among His people—His reign advances on the earth. In the future, all of creation will submit to His reign and His people will enjoy their full, eternal reward. In the present, the kingdom exists and advances; in the future, the kingdom will reach full consummation and glory.

If believers concern ourselves only with the present aspects of the kingdom, we will lose sight of eternal matters such as heaven and hell, and the conversion of people who do not know Christ. If believers concern ourselves only with the future aspects of the kingdom, we will lose sight of God's desire for peace, justice, and restoration in this world. The NT teaches the church to minister to people both in eternal matters (conversion) and in present matters (compassion).[6]

[5] Participants in such churches ("participants" seems a more appropriate designation than "members") serve and minister in unity—not because they focus only on relationships with one another, but because they partner in following the currents of the kingdom. This image further illustrates our discussion of the term *koinonia* in the last chapter. *Koinonia* does not refer to a friendly relationship between people, but to the partnership of those people in something larger than themselves.

[6] We do not minister in the present (compassion) only to further the eternal (conversion), as though we minister to people's immediate needs *only to* open the door for conversion. While this open door may come—and we pray it will—compassionately meeting people's needs exists as a ministry in its own right and as a significant way we obey the teachings of Christ to advance God's kingdom on earth.

The kingdom of God is "already" and "not yet." The church serves, ministers, and lives, therefore, to advance His kingdom in the present and with a hopeful eye on its future reward.

> **The kingdom of God is "already" and "not yet."**

Jesus and the "Already" Kingdom

Jesus spoke of the kingdom as something in the process of arriving. *"From the days of John the Baptist until now,"* He said, *"the kingdom of heaven has been forcefully advancing, and forceful men lay hold of it"* (***Mt 11:12***). When Jesus performed miracles through which He extended compassion to hurting people, He viewed such expressions as an advancement of the kingdom. *"If I drive out demons by the Spirit of God,"* He explained on one occasion, *"then the kingdom of God has come upon you"* (***Mt 12:28***). Through Christ, God began unleashing His reign—marked by peace, justice, and restoration—on the world. George Eldon Ladd affirmed,

> The future heavenly realm is already breaking into the world through Jesus in the form of wonderful, supernatural, coercive power operating from above. The Kingdom is not only the eschatological realm; it is also victorious, coercive power. The eschatological realm of salvation is already breaking into the world as divine *dynamis.* In the future age Jesus will become the heavenly Son of man; but he is already the agent of the present inbreaking power of the Kingdom. (***Presence*, 26**)

Jesus prayed, and taught His disciples to pray, *"Your kingdom come, your will be done on earth as it is in heaven"* (***Mt 6:10***). Jesus prayed that the perfect will of the Father—His reign, His kingdom—would so permeate the world that the condition of earth would mirror the condition of heaven. As peace reigns in heaven, may peace reign on earth. As those in heaven entirely submit to the Creator, may those on earth submit. As God's justice, righteousness, holiness, compassion, purity, and grace fill heaven, may they fill the earth.

Such advancement of the kingdom stands possible because of Jesus' death and resurrection, through which He conquered those forces that oppose the reign of God: *"Having disarmed the powers and authorities, he made a public spectacle of them, triumphing over them by the cross"* (***Col 2:15***). "When Jesus emerged from the tomb, justice, spirituality, relationship, and beauty rose with him," explains N.T. Wright.

"Something has happened in and through Jesus as a result of which the world is a different place, a place where heaven and earth have been joined forever. Gods' future has arrived in the present. Instead of mere echoes, we hear the voice itself: a voice which speaks of rescue from evil and death, and hence of new creation" (***Simply*, 116**).

TODAY'S CHURCH AND THE "ALREADY" KINGDOM

Just as Jesus recognized the presence of the kingdom in His earthly ministry, and just as He worked to advance it, so the contemporary church advances the kingdom through its ministry.

Each time the church injects God's righteousness, peace, and justice into the world, it claims one more bit of the created world for the kingdom. Every time a sinner confesses, a believer gives a cup of cold water, an addict seeks help, an executive chooses generosity over greed, a victim chooses forgiveness over revenge, a father chooses his child over a promotion, a friend extends a hug to one neglected, a missionary steps off of an airplane, and a teacher prays for her students . . . God's kingdom advances.

Sadly, many Christians focus only on the future, eternal aspects of the kingdom and miss these great joys of the journey. They compare to a busload of tourists traveling from the eastern United States to the Grand Canyon. They journey through the Kansas wheat fields and the glorious Colorado mountains. During this journey, however, the travelers keep the window shades down. Focused only on the future destination, they never bother to look out the windows (**Yancey, "Bus," 102**). Yes, the church's future destination holds great promise and hope; the journey to get there, however, also holds great purpose and beauty.

Focused only on the future destination, they never bother to look out the windows.

But why should the church worry about such temporal, earthly matters? Will not God simply destroy this earth, and all that goes with it? In short, no, He will not destroy everything. The Hebrews writer explains:

> [26]*At that time his voice shook the earth, but now he has promised, "Once more I will shake not only the earth but also the heavens."*

[27]The words "once more" indicate the removing of what can be shaken—that is, created things—so that what cannot be shaken may remain. [28]Therefore, since we are receiving a kingdom that cannot be shaken, let us be thankful, and so worship God acceptably with reverence and awe, [29]for our "God is a consuming fire." ***(Heb 12:26-29)***

God will destroy all that *is not* a part of His kingdom; but, *"we are receiving a kingdom that cannot be shaken."* All that *is* a part of His kingdom will remain. In fact, God may just use these elements of the kingdom that we have injected into the world as building blocks for the ultimate restoration, the new creation, He will one day bring. Consider this explanation and encouragement from N.T. Wright:

> What we can and must do in the present, if we are obedient to the gospel, if we are following Jesus, and if we are indwelt, energized, and directed by the Spirit, is to build *for* the kingdom. This brings us back to ***1 Corinthians 15:58*** once more: what you do in the Lord *is not in vain*. You are not oiling the wheels of a machine that's about to roll over a cliff. You are not restoring a great painting that's shortly going to be thrown on the fire. You are not planting roses in a garden that's about to be dug up for a building site. You are—strange though it may seem, almost as hard to believe as the resurrection itself—accomplishing something that will become in due course part of God's new world. Every act of love, gratitude, and kindness; every work of art or music inspired by the love of God and delight in the beauty of his creation; every minute spent teaching a severely handicapped child to read or to walk; every act of care and nurture, of comfort and support, for one's fellow human beings and for that matter one's fellow nonhuman creatures; and of course every prayer, all Spirit-led teaching, every deed that spreads the gospel, builds up the church, embraces and embodies holiness rather than corruption, and makes the name of Jesus honored in the world—all of this will find its way, through the resurrecting power of God, into the new creation that God will one day make. That is the logic of the mission of God. God's recreation of his wonderful world, which began with the resurrection of Jesus and continues mysteriously as God's people live in the risen Christ and in the power of his Spirit, means that what we do in Christ and by the Spirit in the present is not wasted. It will last all the way into God's new world. In fact, it will be enhanced there (***Surprised,*** **208**).

Implications of Kingdom Theology for Christian Ministry

L. Thomas Smith, Jr.[7]

CALLING:	A participation in the Christ-initiated, Spirit-empowered, "saving sovereignty" of God.
MISSION:	A proclamation of the Rule of God in word and deed.
OBJECT:	A reconciliation of all of humanity to God's design for creation.
TASK:	A manifestation of the ethics (values and behaviors) of the Reign of God.
METHOD:	A demonstration of the integrity of character (holiness), loving service, and perseverant suffering of a community of faith anticipating the consummation of the Kingdom of Heaven.
MOTIVATION:	An appreciation of what Christ has done and will do for us.
ATTITUDE:	An expression of Christian hope that is confident of God's work in both the future and the present.

Just as Jesus advanced the kingdom through his life, ministry, death, and resurrection, so the church advances the kingdom with every moment we give in full submission to the reign of God.

THE KINGDOM NOT YET

"Eternal Life" in John

The synoptic Gospels speak around one hundred times of the kingdom of Heaven (***Matthew***) and the kingdom of God (***Mark*** and ***Luke***), but the term "kingdom" appears in ***John***'s Gospel a scarce four times (***3:3,5; 18:36a,36b***). John replaces the emphasis on the kingdom with an emphasis on eternal life. While the synoptics speak often of entering and receiving the kingdom (such as ***Mt 5:20; 7:21; Mk 9:47; 10:15; Lk 12:32; 18:24***), John speaks often of having and receiving eternal life (such as ***Jn 3:16; 5:24; 6:47; 12:25; 17:2***).

[7] From "A Theology of the Kingdom," a workshop presented by Dr. Smith at the 2009 Johnson Bible College Homecoming. Used by permission.

In fact, in two of John's few uses of the term "kingdom," Jesus parallels it with "eternal life": *"No one can see the kingdom of God unless he is born again. . . . No one can enter the kingdom of God unless he is born of water and the Spirit. . . . Everyone who believes in him may have eternal life"* (***Jn 3:3,5,15***). Timothy Keller comments on this passage, "We see that 'entering the kingdom of God' and 'receiving eternal life' are virtually the same thing. . . . Conversion, the new birth, and receiving the kingdom of God 'as a child' are the same move" (**76**).[8]

While life in Christ begins at the moment of conversion, John's frequent use of the phrase "eternal life" points his readers, also, to the future, eschatological implications of that life in Christ.

Understanding the "Not Yet" Factor

As stated above, the kingdom is both a present reality and a future hope. Through Christ and His church, God has already unleashed His reign of peace, righteousness, and justice in the world. At present, however, we experience the kingdom only in a partial manner. The kingdom maintains an eschatological element because it will arrive in its full, glorious, ultimate expression when Jesus returns. *"Now we see but a poor reflection as in a mirror;"* wrote the Apostle Paul, *"then we shall see face to face. Now I know in part; then I shall know fully, even as I am fully known"* (***1Cor 13:12***). Paul often spoke of the kingdom in the future tense (***2Th 1:5; 2Tm 4:18***), particularly when he confronted vices such as immorality and idolatry: *"I warn you, as I did before, that those who live like this will not inherit the kingdom of God"* (***Gal 5:21***; see also ***1Cor 6:9-10*** and ***Eph 5:5***). Peter, writing from a more positive perspective, pointed his readers toward the day when they *"will receive a rich welcome into the eternal kingdom of our Lord and Savior Jesus Christ"* (***2Pet 1:11***). Though, at present, some submit themselves to

At present we experience the kingdom only in a partial manner.

[8] Why does John emphasize eternal life in his terminology while the Synoptics emphasize the kingdom? "As many scholars have pointed out, John emphasizes the individual and inward spiritual aspects of being in the kingdom of God. He is at pains to show that it is not basically an earthly social-political order (***John 18:36***). On the other hand, when the Synoptics talk of the kingdom, they lay out the real social and behavioral changes that the gospel brings" (**Keller, 76**).

the reign of God, we look forward to the day when *"at the name of Jesus every knee should bow, in heaven and on earth and under the earth, and every tongue confess that Jesus Christ is Lord, to the glory of God the Father"* (***Php 2:10-11***).

The kingdom is, and it will be more fully.

The Kingdom Eternal

When the kingdom arrives in its fullness, it will bring to a climax God's work of restoration that He has advanced since the Garden of Eden. He will bring to fruition the peace, righteousness, and justice that He desired for His creation in the beginning. God will replace the former creation—marred by sin and its consequences of death, disease, and disharmony—with a new creation. He hinted toward such a day in Isaiah,

> [17]*Behold, I will create*
> *new heavens and a new earth.*
> *The former things will not be remembered,*
> *nor will they come to mind.*
> [18]*But be glad and rejoice forever*
> *in what I will create,*
> *for I will create Jerusalem to be a delight*
> *and its people a joy.*
> [19]*I will rejoice over Jerusalem*
> *and take delight in my people;*
> *the sound of weeping and of crying*
> *will be heard in it no more.* (***65:17-19***)

God gave John a more detailed peek into this future restoration:

> [1]*Then I saw a new heaven and a new earth, for the first heaven*
> *and the first earth had passed away, and there was no longer any*
> *sea.* [2]*I saw the Holy City, the new Jerusalem, coming down out of*
> *heaven from God, prepared as a bride beautifully dressed for her*
> *husband.* [3]*And I heard a loud voice from the throne saying, "Now*
> *the dwelling of God is with men, and he will live with them. They*
> *will be his people, and God himself will be with them and be their*
> *God.* [4]*He will wipe every tear from their eyes. There will be no*
> *more death or mourning or crying or pain, for the old order of*
> *things has passed away."*
>
> [5]*He who was seated on the throne said, "I am making every-*
> *thing new!" Then he said, "Write this down, for these words are*
> *trustworthy and true."* (***Rev 21:1-5***)

The new creation, the culmination of the kingdom, will remain free of sin and all of its consequences. Most significantly, the King will be fully present in the kingdom. Those who belong to the kingdom, therefore, will experience life eternally in all the fullness, glory, and bliss God intends for His creation.

This future kingdom John describes differs from the image of heaven often portrayed in movies, books, and even churches. Stanley Grenz explained,

> The biblical picture of the renewed cosmos differs from the vision many Christians articulate. They conceive of our eternal home as an entirely spiritual, non-material locale. To distinguish it from earthly, physical existence, they commonly call it 'heaven.' Consequently, they picture eternity as a realm inhabited by purely spiritual beings.
>
> As the texts we cited indicate, however, the prophets of both Testaments anticipated a new earth blanketed by a new heaven (***Isa. 65:17; Rev. 21:1***). Rather than resurrected believers being snatched away to live forever with God in some heavenly world beyond the cosmos, the seer of ***Revelation*** envisioned exactly the opposite. God will take up residence in the new creation (***Rev. 21:3***). The dwelling of the citizens of God's eternal community, therefore, will be the renewed earth. (**841**)

The Hope of What's to Come

Throughout Scripture, biblical writers point their readers toward the future fulfillment of the kingdom as a means of eliciting hope, thereby enabling perseverance. Though believers can experience and advance the kingdom in the present, this experience always falls short of our ultimate longings for life. This world includes broken relationships, broken dreams, and broken hearts. We face pain, disease, and death. *"In this world you will have trouble,"* Jesus promised. *"But take heart! I have overcome the world"* (***Jn 16:33***). In Titus, Paul wrote of our *"faith and knowledge resting on the hope of eternal life"* (***1:2***). In ***Romans,*** he wrote of the patient endurance of both creation and individual believers within creation, an endurance enabled by hope:

> *[18]I consider that our present sufferings are not worth comparing with the glory that will be revealed in us. [19]The creation waits in eager expectation for the sons of God to be revealed. [20]For the creation was subjected to frustration, not by its own choice, but by the will of the one who subjected it, in hope [21]that the creation*

itself will be liberated from its bondage to decay and brought into the glorious freedom of the children of God.

[22]We know that the whole creation has been groaning as in the pains of childbirth right up to the present time. [23]Not only so, but we ourselves, who have the firstfruits of the Spirit, groan inwardly as we wait eagerly for our adoption as sons, the redemption of our bodies. [24]For in this hope we were saved. But hope that is seen is no hope at all. Who hopes for what he already has? [25]But if we hope for what we do not yet have, we wait for it patiently. (***Rom 8:18-25***)

To persevere in faith, believers need to live this life—though fully, purposefully, and fruitfully—with one eye on eternity. Runners sprint fastest when they keep an eye on the finish line; basketball teams practice most diligently when they keep an eye on the championship; Christians persevere most faithfully and minister most fruitfully when they keep an eye on the eternal kingdom. Such hope "is not a form of escapism or wishful thinking," C.S. Lewis famously wrote. "If you read history you will find that the Christians who did most for the present world were just those who thought most of the next. . . . It is since Christians have largely ceased to think of the other world that they have become so ineffective in this" (***Mere*, 118**).

Christians are at their best when they keep an eye on the eternal kingdom.

We live most effectively for the present kingdom when we maintain hope for the future kingdom.

THE KINGDOM PARABLES

A discussion of the kingdom remains incomplete until it includes the kingdom parables. Jesus sometimes began His parables with the words, *"The kingdom of heaven is like . . ."* The heaviest concentration of such parables appears in ***Matthew 13***.

The Sower and the Soils
Matthew 13:1-23

Matthew 13 begins with the parable of the sower and the soils. While this parable does not begin with the phrase *"The kingdom of heaven is like . . . ,"* as do the following series of parables, it contains intriguing teaching about the kingdom and sets the stage for the remainder of the chapter.

The parable itself offers fairly direct, understandable teaching. Like a sower who spreads seed, God and His followers spread the message of the kingdom. Like assorted types of soil who receive seed, various listeners receive the message in differing ways. Some do not understand and the evil one snatches it away (the path). Some receive it with joy, but do not allow it to take root; therefore, they fall away when trouble or persecution comes (rocky soil). Others hear the message but allow the worries of life to choke it out (thorny soil). And others hear the message, understand it, and the message produces great fruit (good soil). The seed stays constant throughout the parable—the power of the message of the kingdom remains unchanged. The variable lies in the soils which receive the seed.

The more intriguing portion of the text appears between the parable itself (***Mt 13:1-9***) and Jesus' explanation of it (***Mt 13:18-23***). In ***verses 10-17***, Matthew records:

> [10]*The disciples came to him and asked, "Why do you speak to the people in parables?"*
>
> [11]*He replied, "The knowledge of the secrets of the kingdom of heaven has been given to you, but not to them.* [12]*Whoever has will be given more, and he will have an abundance. Whoever does not have, even what he has will be taken from him.* [13]*This is why I speak to them in parables:*
>
> *"Though seeing, they do not see;*
> *though hearing, they do not hear or understand.*
> [14]*In them is fulfilled the prophecy of Isaiah:*
> *"'You will be ever hearing but never understanding;*
> *you will be ever seeing but never perceiving.*
> [15]*For this people's heart has become calloused;*
> *they hardly hear with their ears,*
> *and they have closed their eyes.*
> *Otherwise they might see with their eyes,*
> *hear with their ears,*
> *understand with their hearts*
> *and turn, and I would heal them.'*
>
> [16]*But blessed are your eyes because they see, and your ears because they hear.* [17]*For I tell you the truth, many prophets and righteous men longed to see what you see but did not see it, and to hear what you hear but did not hear it.*

Jesus' disciples possessed *"the knowledge of the secrets of the kingdom of heaven,"* something *"many prophets and righteous men longed to see."* Others listened with calloused hearts and were, therefore, *"ever hearing but never understanding . . . ever seeing but never perceiving."* Recognizing the presence of these various listeners in His audience, Jesus taught in parables. D.A. Carson explains why by connecting ***verses 10-17*** with the parable of the soils:

> The parable of the soils not only says that the kingdom advances slowly and with varied responses to the proclamation of that kingdom but implicitly challenges hearers to ask themselves what kinds of soil they are. Those whose hearts are hardened and who lose what little they have do not participate in the messianic kingdom they have been looking for, and for them the parable is a sentence of doom. Those who have ears to hear, to whom more is given, perceive and experience the dawning of the Messianic Age; and for them the parable conveys the mysteries of the kingdom. In the varied responses given to the challenge of the parables, God's act of judgment and his self-disclosure in Jesus are both seen to be taking place in exactly the same way that various 'soils' respond to the 'seed,' which is the message about the kingdom. (**310**)

Jesus' parables enlightened, enriched, and challenged those who possessed the knowledge of the kingdom. For those with calloused hearts, the same parables met with blank stares and closed ears. The parables themselves helped distinguish, therefore, between those committed to the kingdom and those not committed.

For those committed to the kingdom, Jesus continued with a series of additional parables, each of which begins with the phrase, *"The kingdom of God is like . . ."*

THE WHEAT AND THE WEEDS MATTHEW 13:24-30, 36-43

"The kingdom of heaven is like a man who sowed good seed in his field," Jesus begins. *"But while everyone was sleeping, his enemy came and sowed weeds among the wheat, and went away"* (***Mt 13:24-25***). When the landowner's servants wanted to pull the weeds, the landowner refused, saying, *"While you are pulling the weeds, you may root up the wheat with them. Let both grow together until the harvest. At that time I will tell the harvesters: First collect the weeds and tie them in bundles to be burned; then gather the wheat and bring it into my barn"* (***Mt 13:29-30***).

The surprising detail of the parable involves the landowner's refusal to pull the weeds. When my father was a boy, he worked on his grandfather's farm, often walking the fields to pull weeds. His grandfather kept binoculars in his truck, and regularly stopped along the road to scan his fields with binoculars to make certain no weeds remained—he even demanded that his workers pull all weeds from the wooded areas that adjoined his fields. Weeds restrict growth and diminish the harvest.

Yet, in Jesus' parable the landowner allowed the weeds and the wheat to grow together until the harvest. Jesus taught through this imagery that the *"sons of the kingdom"* and the *"sons of the evil one"* will coexist until the *"end of the age,"* when *"The Son of Man will send out his angels, and they will weed out of his kingdom everything that causes sin and all who do evil"* (***Mt 13:38,40-41***).[9]

In His first advent, Jesus brought salvation, not judgment (***Jn 3:17***). Judgment will come with the second advent (***Rev 20:11-15***). Groups such as Zealots and those in the Qumran community sought a Messiah who would immediately rid the earth of evil (e.g., Rome) to establish His earthly kingdom. Jesus taught a different perspective—for a time, good and evil would coexist, giving sinners an opportunity to repent.

Like Jesus exemplified, those who submit to His kingdom extend grace and advance the kingdom by loving their enemies and praying for those who persecute them (***Mt 5:44***). While we may, at times, feel tempted to judge and condemn those of the world, Jesus teaches through this parable that we should refrain from such judgment because we may inadvertently condemn someone who indeed belongs to the kingdom (***Mt 13:29***). Furthermore, we can trust God will make the proper judgment in the end (***Mt 13:30***).

We advance the kingdom by loving our enemies and praying for those who persecute us.

The Mustard Seed and the Yeast Matthew 13:31-33

The kingdom is like a small mustard seed that grows into a tree large enough for birds to perch on its branches. And, the kingdom is like yeast that works through a large amount of flour to make dough.

[9] We need to recognize that the field does not represent the church (as though it consisted of both believers and nonbelievers), but the world (*v. 38*).

Though it began small, the kingdom will experience enormous growth and influence.

We often witness microcosms of this lesson about the kingdom in various believers, tucked away in inconspicuous corners of the church. Ann Mills and Genny Rice, for example, have each taught children's Sunday School classes for the last fifty years. They serve with the Oak Grove Christian Church in Beckley, West Virginia. Ann teaches the babies, and Genny teaches the two- and three-year-olds. Neither has entertained offers from major publishers, nor have they appeared on network television newscasts or on the front pages of newspapers or magazines. Aside from an occasional hug, Christmas card, or plaque, Ann and Genny receive little acclaim. Instead of riches or fame, they choose instead to *"store up . . . treasures in heaven"* (***Mt 6:20***). Numerous children who passed through their classes have served as church leaders—ministers, teachers, deacons, missionaries—across the country and world.[10]

Ann Mills tells of one little girl who, almost weekly, disrupted the classroom with her unruly behavior—"I hate to admit it, but I often would hope she wouldn't come, and I'd actually shudder when she burst into the room." A couple of years ago Ann saw the girl—now grown into a fine woman—at a funeral. She hugged Ann, and said, "I've been wanting to write or call you to thank you for teaching me. You're the only happy memory I have of my childhood." Further, she said, "I homeschool my children, and I was hoping you could give me copies of the songs that you taught, so that I can teach them to my children."

The kingdom consists of countless individuals such as Genny Rice and Ann Mills, who together use the small and inconspicuous to advance the kingdom, and thus to change the world.

The Hidden Treasure and the Pearl of Great Value Matthew 13:44-46

The kingdom is like a man who found a treasure hidden in a field, then joyfully sold all he had to buy the field. And, the kingdom is like a merchant who found a pearl of great value, then sold everything he

[10] Ann Mills quipped, "You didn't ask this, but as far as I know I only had one that went to jail."

had to buy it. Those who truly discover the kingdom overflow with such joy that they sacrifice whatever necessary to obtain it. In these parables, explains Craig Blomberg, "Jesus defines most pointedly what separates real disciples from the 'wannabes' or hangers-on who don't really make the grade. Quite simply, *true disciples are those who recognize that God's kingdom is so valuable that it's worth sacrificing whatever it takes to be its citizens"* (133).

Those who truly discover the kingdom sacrifice whatever necessary to obtain it.

When a person truly grasps the glory and majesty of the kingdom, when he or she catches the exhilaration of pursuing the rushing currents of God's reign, everything—utterly everything—takes second priority to pursuing the kingdom.

I have the privilege of teaching at a Bible college where several hundred men and women gather every fall and spring to train for local church ministry, missionary work, and various other avenues of Christian service. Their high school teachers and counselors scratched their heads when these students mentioned Bible college. Most could have chosen other career paths that would have led to greater fortune and prominence. Some left such careers and lucrative paychecks to change direction midlife (see sidebar for testimonies from some career-change students). Some enrolled against the wishes of their families. Yet, they sensed God's call, and they came.

Testimonies of Kingdom Pursuers

I admire all who give their lives to vocational ministry. I have particular affinity and respect, however, for those who change course midlife, often sacrificing lucrative careers and the security that comes with regular paychecks to train for ministry. I asked a few nontraditional Johnson Bible College students why they made such sacrifices. They responded:

- *I retired from the Navy and built my retirement home. But God had different plans. As I meditated on His Word, I continually thought about those around the world who are spiritually lost. I felt God was calling me to preach and teach. I anguished for weeks before finally submitting to*

God's call. When I finally responded, "Here I am, send me," peace came over me. I willingly sacrificed because I am extremely thankful for Jesus' sacrifice, and I'm stepping out in confident faith, knowing that God will use me to advance His kingdom.

- *We owned our own business, but realized we were giving ourselves to something temporal. We responded to the call to ministry because that is where we could see eternal results. We want to see people come to know Christ and then help them grow to lead others to Christ. The fruit of one soul accepting Christ can lead to thousands down the road.*
- *When I gave my life to Christ, a flame for ministry was lit. After much prayer, anguish, tears, indecision, and fears were realized, I came to know that something bigger than myself is at work. Pieces fell into place in a sort of magical, coincidental way, but I knew that there is no such thing as magic or coincidences. I felt there was only one way to go, committed to it, and started down that path. I really do not see any other options. Nor do I want to.*
- *In my business—engineering/military—a retiree is worth quite a bit to companies doing military contracts. Despite the very high potential for income in a civilian life working for these companies, I can only think of serving others and helping them come to know how wonderful our Lord is. The call to serve the Lord in preaching is extremely powerful—my wife and I both find it unthinkable to turn the other direction. Storing treasures in heaven is more important to us than treasures here on earth.*
- *I lost nothing when I left my job other than a paycheck. I gave up trusting in my own abilities to manage my life. Why? Because there is such a thing as a good life and then there is a better life. I could not get ahold of the better until I let go of the good. I gave up all the things I thought were important to do the only thing I really ever wanted to do—love people! I want people to find what I found: that Jesus came to give us life—a life beyond our comprehension.*

The Net
Matthew 13:47-49

The kingdom is like fishermen who let a net down into the water, and retrieved the net full of all kinds of fish. When they pulled the net onto the shore, they placed the good fish in baskets, and threw the bad away.

George Beasley-Murray believed this parable carries an evangelistic emphasis, related to the picture of the fishermen letting down their nets to catch *"all kinds of fish"* (***Mt 13:47***). He explains:

> It represents God's gracious approach to the common people through Jesus. 'The kingdom of heaven is like . . .' is the theme. The modern counterpart would be . . . the church taking the good news of redemption to Skid Row, to the casinos of Las Vegas and Monte Carlo, to clubs where homosexuals and transvestites gather, to taverns and dance halls and discotheques where long-haired youths stamp to loud music, and to those thousand and one places where men and women gather for leisure and pleasure but where many Christians would not want to be caught dead, let alone alive. So far as many are concerned, the fishing boats have been transformed into arks, and the nets have been left on the shore to rot; it is understandable that such would come to believe that the parable was intended to address the church about the church. But in Jesus' day there were still *fishing* boats!" (***Kingdom*, 137**)

Furthermore, with the separation of the good and bad fish, Jesus provided the stark reminder that judgment will one day arrive. Jesus explained, *"This is how it will be at the end of the age. The angels will come and separate the wicked from the righteous and throw them into the fiery furnace, where there will be weeping and gnashing of teeth"* (***Mt 13:49-50***).

Through Jesus' series of parables in ***Matthew 13***, He painted pictures with robust textures and vivid hues—He painted pictures of the kingdom.

CONCLUSION

We began this chapter with the story of Dietrich Bonhoeffer. While Hitler's kingdom has faded from the newspapers into the history books, the kingdom to which Bonhoeffer devoted his life—the kingdom of Christ—continues undeterred. The late British journalist Malcolm Muggeridge wrote of Bonhoeffer, "Looking back now across the years . . . what lives on is the memory of a man who died, not on behalf of freedom or democracy or a steadily rising gross national product, nor for any of the twentieth century's counterfeit hopes or desires, but on behalf of a cross on which another man died 2,000 years before. As on that previous occasion on Golgotha . . . the only victor is the man who died" (205).

What had Bonhoeffer discovered about the kingdom of Christ that enabled his radical devotion? He explained, "Our action springs from the recognition of the grace of God, toward humankind and toward ourselves and our action hopes for the grace of God which delivers us from the distress of the time. . . . Only those who have once tasted the utter depth and distress of the kingdom of the world . . . long to be away, and they have one wish, 'Let this world pass away, thy kingdom come'" (*Testament*, 351).

What Do You Say?

1. What beliefs did Dietrich Bonhoeffer hold that led to his radical devotion to Christ? Why are examples such as Bonhoeffer so rare? Or, are such examples all that rare?
2. What is the relationship between Jesus and the kingdom?
3. What is the relationship between the church and the kingdom?
4. What does the chapter mean when it says the kingdom is "already"? How can the church advance the kingdom in the present?
5. What does the chapter mean when it says the kingdom is "not yet"? Why should the church keep an eye on this future aspect of the kingdom?
6. What did Jesus mean when He said, *"This is why I speak in parables: 'Though seeing, they do not see; though hearing, they do not hear or understand'"* (*Mt 13:13*)?
7. Summarize what lessons you believe Jesus intended to relate through the kingdom parables in *Matthew 13*, and consider the implications of these lessons for today's church.

CHAPTER EIGHT

MISSION FOCUSED

I recently traveled with some friends to central Mexico for a week-long mission trip. The missionaries we visited function like most I've encountered, focusing the bulk of their time and resources on ministering to their community. The leaders of this particular mission, and the churches they lead, conduct summer camps for native youth, provide a home for the elderly, lead medical teams into poverty-stricken communities, and conduct Vacation Bible Schools for children in area villages. They pour their efforts into ministering to people outside of the church walls.

One afternoon, while we bounced in the back of a pickup truck on our way to a village, I wondered aloud to my travel companions, "What would it look like if our church back home functioned more like this mission and less like an 'Americanized' church?" While the believers we met in Mexico funnel a majority of their time and resources into their communities, many American churches focus our time and resources internally—we conduct programs, hold classes, and plan activities for ourselves.

Christians like those I encountered in Mexico have much to teach the rest of us about mission-focused ministry. "I am convinced that the church is at its best on the mission field," observes Kennon Callahan. "The peace and tranquility, the pleasant programs and endless committee meetings

- I. Extending Jesus' Mission
  - A. Jesus' Mission
  - B. Jesus' Mission and the Cross
  - C. The Church Extending Jesus' Mission
  - D. Distractions to Our Mission
- II. Expressing Jesus' Love
  - A. Showing Compassion
  - B. Being Salt and Light
  - C. Loving Jesus by Loving Others
- III. Explaining Jesus' Gospel
  - A. The Mandate
  - B. Varying Starting Points
  - C. Unvarying Message
  - D. The Power of Witness
- IV. Conclusion

of a churched-culture church is not where the church is at its best. . . . On the mission field the church is lean and strong and has courage and vision. In a churched culture the church becomes lazy and weak, timid and cautious, bloated and bureaucratic" (27).

Imagine, for the sake of argument, that a church spends eighty percent of its time and resources on programs and activities geared toward church members, and twenty percent on efforts to extend Jesus' love to the hurting and unsaved outside its walls. What if that church dedicated itself to reversing these portions? How would it impact programming, budgeting, staffing, and planning?

I recognize the issue holds more complexity than this simple scenario expresses. And certainly God called His followers to minister to one another (as much of this book expresses). Jesus and the early church, however, managed to develop intimate relationships with one another, and to pursue their mission of drawing others into the fold. I fear many churches today—not all, but many—have allowed the pendulum to swing too far toward internal programming and activities and have lost sight of our external mission.

Many churches today swing the pendulum too far toward the internal and miss the external.

EXTENDING JESUS' MISSION

JESUS' MISSION

As the previous chapter explained, Jesus unleashed the kingdom of God into the world—the reign of God marked by peace, righteousness, and justice. Jesus brought the possibility of life as God intends it to the earth. Through Jesus, believers can begin to experience this kingdom life immediately. Such immediate experiences serve as a foretaste of the fully consummated kingdom life they will enjoy eternally.

In the pages of the Gospels, Jesus often summarized His kingdom mission:

> *"The scroll of the prophet Isaiah was handed to him. Unrolling it, he found the place where it is written: 'The Spirit of the Lord is on me, because he has anointed me to preach good news to the poor. He has sent me to proclaim freedom for the prisoners and recovery of sight for the blind, to release the oppressed, to proclaim the year of the Lord's favor'"* (**Lk 4:17-19**).

- *"The Son of Man came to seek and save what was lost"* (**Lk 19:10**).
- *"I have come that they may have life, and have it to the full"* (**Jn 10:10**).
- *"Father, the time has come. Glorify your Son, that your Son may glorify you. For you granted him authority over all people that he might give eternal life to all those you have given him"* (**Jn 17:2**).

By combining these passages and principles, we can summarize Jesus' mission as follows:

Jesus came to seek and save lost people
by proclaiming the good news of freedom, recovery, release,
and the Lord's favor, enabling them to immediately experience kingdom life
and to gain the hope of eternal life in the fully consummated kingdom
by means of His death and resurrection.

Jesus' earthly life and ministry proclaimed and prepared people for the kingdom of God. He loved, ministered, and showed great compassion to people He encountered in daily life, but always kept His eye on the larger, spiritual implications of these encounters. Those who enter His kingdom enjoy eternal life; those who do not enter it face eternal punishment. His compassionate call to repentance, therefore, stood at the heart of Jesus' message:

- *"'The time has come,' he said. 'The kingdom of God is near. Repent and believe the good news!'"* (**Mk 1:15**).
- *"I have not come to call the righteous, but sinners to repentance"* (**Lk 5:32**).
- *"Unless you repent, you too will all perish"* (**Lk 13:3**).

Because individuals' future destinies depended on their present decision concerning the kingdom, Jesus called them to make such decisions. He called the rich young ruler to *"sell everything you have . . . then come, follow me"* (**Lk 18:22**). He invited the Samaritan woman at the well to partake of the *"living water"* which becomes *"a spring of water welling up to eternal life"* (**Jn 4:10,14**). He confronted the crowds following Him, *"If anyone would come after me, he must deny himself and take up his cross and follow me. For whoever wants to save his life will lose it, but whoever loses his life for me and for the gospel will save it"* (**Mk 8:34-35**).

Jesus called on individuals to make the decisions that would direct their destinies.

When people refused His message, the eternal consequences of their refusal broke Jesus' heart:

> [37]*"O Jerusalem, Jerusalem, you who kill the prophets and stone those sent to you, how often I have longed to gather your children together, as a hen gathers her chicks under her wings, but you were not willing.* [38]*Look, your house is left to you desolate.* [39]*For I tell you, you will not see me again until you say, 'Blessed is he who comes in the name of the Lord.'"* (**Mt 23:37-39**)

Jesus' compassion toward sinful people drew harsh criticism from the religious leaders of His day. *"This man welcomes sinners and eats with them,"* muttered the Pharisees about Jesus (**Lk 15:2**; see the sidebar "Table Fellowship as Mission Strategy in the Life of the Kingdom"). Jesus responded by telling of a shepherd who lost one of his hundred sheep, searched until he found it, then called his friends to celebrate. *"I tell you that in the same way there will be more rejoicing in heaven over one sinner who repents than over ninety-nine righteous persons who do not need to repent,"* Jesus taught (**Lk 15:7**). Then He told of the woman who lost one of her ten coins, turned the house upside down until she found it, then called the neighbors to come celebrate. *"In the same way, I tell you,"* Jesus explained, *"there is rejoicing in the presence of the angels of God over one sinner who repents"* (**Lk 15:10**). Third, Jesus grew more pointed toward the Pharisees' criticism by telling of the rebellious son who took his father's inheritance, squandered it in the far country, then repentantly returned home to his father's grace-filled arms. *"Let's have a feast and celebrate,"* said the father. *"For this son of mine was dead and is alive again; he was lost and is found"* (**Lk 15:23-24**). The climactic third story, unlike the two previous stories, adds an additional character—the elder brother who grew jealous of the grace the father extended to the prodigal. As the parable closes, the father pleads with the elder brother to join the celebration. The parable ends, however, without telling what the elder brother decides. Will he repent of his jealousy, or will he remain on the outside? With this open-ended third story, Jesus called even the Pharisees to repent.

The climactic third story, unlike the two previous stories, adds an additional character.

Table Fellowship as Mission Strategy in the Life of the Kingdom

Jeff M. Brunsman

God's eternal purpose is for all people to experience the fullness of salvation in the eschatological kingdom that comes in Jesus Christ. Jesus commissions His disciples to proclaim this good news of God's redemption to all peoples of the world. It is no less true today than it was in Jesus' day that the success of that mission to call people into this community of God requires the breaking down of the various barriers that exist between the peoples of the world. Jesus and the early church utilized an expansive and open table fellowship as part of the evangelistic process of expanding the kingdom of God.

In first century Greco-Roman and Palestinian society, the boundaries of a social group or institution were sustained through their table fellowship practices. Eating a meal with others was not simply a matter of consuming physical nourishment; rather, commensality established, strengthened, and reinforced one's place as an accepted and integral part of a group. Likewise, segregation from table fellowship was indicative of one's exclusion from a group or institution. This was no less true within Judaism, and was particularly evident among groups such as the Essenes and Pharisees. One's table fellowship practices spoke volumes concerning the status of others in relation to oneself and in relation to God's kingdom. Jesus entered into this world and steadily worked to dissolve the ethnic and social barriers that promoted division rather than reconciliation.

Among the gospel writers, Luke especially highlights this social aspect of Jesus' ministry. Instead of being a "defensive person" who avoided all contact with impurity and uncleanness, Jesus practiced an open commensality with those considered holy as well as others regarded as impure and on the outer edge of Jewish society. Jesus found himself being criticized by the religious elite for eating and drinking with tax collectors and sinners (***Lk 5:29-30***). This criticism extended to his acceptance of women (***Lk 7:39***) and children (***Lk 18:15-17***), groups accorded lesser status among many in his day. Jesus appeared willing to transgress even the socio-cultural boundary between Jew and Gentile in ***Luke 7:1-10*** as He prepared to enter a centurion's home to heal his servant, thus accepting the hospitality traditionally offered with such welcoming, which would have included a meal.

By sharing meals with the outcasts of society Jesus challenged the socio-cultural boundaries that disenfranchised individuals from full acceptance as members of the community of God's people. He proffered a new classification system founded upon faith in Him as Israel's Messiah. Through His commensality, Jesus also prepared his followers for their role in proclaiming the good news of God's eschatological kingdom, open to all who place their faith in Him as the Christ.

As Luke continues his two-volume work, Luke–Acts, he includes narrative descriptions that reveal the church expressing, through their commensality, an evolving understanding of themselves as the people of God. In imitation of the table fellowship of Jesus, this growing fellowship of believers triumphed over the barriers of traditional religious and societal customs as they fulfilled the commission of their Master to proclaim the good news of God's kingdom to all nations and peoples. Inclusive table fellowship was an important ingredient in expanding the boundaries of the kingdom to include Hellenistic Jews (***Acts:6.1-7***), former enemies (***Acts 9:19***), God-fearing Gentiles (***Acts 10–11***), God-fearing women (***Acts 16:15***), and outright pagans (***Acts 16:34***) into the community of faith.

Shared meals are one of the constituting elements of God's Messianic community. In commensality a brotherhood of believers as God's people emerges around their common faith in Jesus as the Christ. The willingness and action of sharing together around the table demonstrates community and fulfills God's intention for an inclusive kingdom that encompasses people from all strata of society.

Jesus' Mission and the Cross

Less than halfway through ***Luke***'s Gospel, he uses narrative flair to inform his readers, *"As the time approached for him to be taken up to heaven, Jesus resolutely set out for Jerusalem"* (***Lk 9:51***). Though Jesus would continue to teach, minister, and travel, in just the ninth of Luke's twenty four chapters, Jesus, *"set his face towards"* (the literal Greek idiom used in ***Lk 9:51***) His death, resurrection, and ascension. Mark accomplished a similar narrative purpose by use of repetition. Beginning in the eighth of ***Mark***'s sixteen chapters, Jesus began a cycle of teachings about His impending death: *"He then began to teach them that the Son of Man must suffer many things and be rejected by the elders, chief priests and teachers of the law, and that he must be killed and after three days rise again"* (***Mk 8:31***). Jesus repeats the same teaching, adding a few details, in ***Mark 9:31*** and ***10:33-34***. In each of the three cycles, Jesus' teaching confuses the disciples—Peter rebuked Jesus (***Mk 8:32***); the disciples *"did not understand what he meant and were afraid to ask him about it"* (***Mk 9:32***); and James and John sought their own glorification by asking to sit at Jesus' right and left hand (***Mk 10:37***). Finally, at the foot of the cross, Mark describes one who did understand. A Roman centurion, surprisingly, *"heard his cry and saw how he died, he said, 'Surely this man was the Son of God!'"* (***Mk 15:39***).

The Gospel writers portray Jesus as a man on a mission that led Him straight to the cross. Some recent scholars have issued reminders not to neglect the life and teaching of Jesus—we need such reminders because His life, ministry, and teaching hold great significance. We must not go to an extreme, however, that neglects the cross, which Jesus Himself viewed as "the focal point and climax of his mission. He had come in order to die" (**Grenz, 438**). His kingdom mission included additional elements; however, His crucifixion, resurrection, and ascension held primary significance.

Jesus was a man on a mission that led Him straight to the cross.

If Jesus had simply ministered to hurting people, preached repentance, and announced the coming of the kingdom, His ministry would have been no different than a prophet's ministry. More than any other prophet, however, Jesus both proclaimed the kingdom and through His death brought the kingdom to fruition. Through the cross, "our Savior is Revealer, Effector, and Originator of God's eschatological community" (**Grenz, 457**). Jesus' death enacts the justification and reconciliation through which people enter the kingdom presently and eternally (***Rom 5:6-11***).

The Church Extending Jesus' Mission

Following His death and resurrection, Jesus passed the missional baton to His followers, commissioning them to *"go and make disci-*

ples of all nations" (***Mt 28:19***; see sidebar for additional discussion of ***Mt 28:19-20***). Jesus called the church to extend His mission. What He began when He walked the earth, He continues through us. The kingdom He revealed, effected, and originated, He continues to advance through His church.

Jesus' mission includes a global perspective, because of which we advance the kingdom to *"the ends of the earth"* (***Acts 1:8***). When God established His covenant with Abraham, He promised Abraham that *"all peoples on earth will be blessed through you"* (***Gen 12:3***). Through Jesus, who descended from Abraham, *"all mankind will see God's salvation"* (***Lk 3:6***), so that the final consummation of the kingdom will include *"a great multitude that no one could count, from every nation, tribe, people and language, standing before the throne and in front of the Lamb"* (***Rev 7:9***). Advances in technology and travel offer today's church historically unprecedented opportunities to minister globally. We might imagine the spark in the eye of the Apostle Paul had he enjoyed our accessibility to air travel, the internet, television and radio, and the numerous other opportunities for global ministry that churches enjoy today.

Additionally, Jesus' mission includes a great sense of urgency. When He walked the earth, Jesus ministered with the knowledge that, for every person He encountered, Heaven and Hell hung in balance. Today's church, to extend Jesus' mission, must minister with the same sense of urgency.

In 1879, Charlie Peace, a well-known criminal in London, faced execution by hanging. When he was marched to the gallows, an Anglican priest walked behind him. In keeping with custom, the priest read aloud a specified passage from the Anglican prayer book, "Those who die without Christ experience hell, which is the pain of forever dying without the release which death itself can bring."

When the priest read these chilling words, Charlie Peace stopped marching, turned to the priest, and shouted, "Do you believe that? Do you believe that?"

The startled priest stammered for a moment, then said, "Well . . . I suppose I do."

"Well I don't," said the criminal. "But if I did, I'd get down on my hands and knees and crawl all over Great Britain, even if it were paved with pieces of broken glass, if I could rescue just one person from what you just told me" (**Campolo, 53-54**).

If we really believe, as did Jesus, that eternal consequences hinge on the accomplishment of our mission, we will pursue that mission with utter passion and resilience. The lost need salvation. The hopeless need hope. Sinners need Christ. "The church cannot live when the heart of God is not beating within her," writes Erwin McManus. "God's heartbeat is to seek and save that which is lost" (**24**).

In ***2 Corinthians***, Paul offered the image of the ambassador to help his readers visualize their role in extending Jesus' mission. *"We are Christ's ambassadors,"* he explained, *"as though God were making his appeal through us"* (***5:20***). A dignitary, such as a king, sends an ambassador to represent him and the interests of the kingdom in an environment the king cannot physically visit. The ambassador attempts to do and say what the king would do or say if the king were physically present. The ambassador does not seek his own interests or advancement, but the advancement of the king and his interests.

Believers serve as Jesus' ambassadors. He commissioned us to do what He would do if He were (and as He did when He was) physically present on the earth. He placed every individual believer in our environments—neighborhoods, offices, schools—to do what He would do if He lived there. As His ambassadors, therefore, we constantly ask ourselves, "What would Jesus do if He were in my shoes?" If Jesus lived in my neighborhood, rode in my carpool, served in the parent's organization at my child's school, worked on my jobsite, received my paycheck, and encountered the people I encounter, what would He do? How can I best represent Him and His kingdom interests in my environment?

Furthermore, to carry this principle beyond its individual implications, the church corporately exists as Christ's ambassadors. As communities of believers, we must ask, how can we best represent Christ and His interests in our surroundings? How can our church most effectively extend Jesus' mission in our town? How would He plan our church program, utilize our resources, administer our budget, evangelize our neighborhood, extend our influence globally, express love to the hurting, and proclaim truth? Jesus placed every gathering of believers in our communities to represent Him and His interests, to extend His mission and His kingdom.

How can our church most effectively extend Jesus' mission in our town?

Distractions to Our Mission

Churches often allow temporal—sometimes even sinful—matters to distract us from our mission. Three distractions appear most frequently and prominently.

First, the details and busyness of life and ministry threaten to divert our attention from our primary mission. Some churches think of their mission as what they do with leftover resources and time. Once they pay the light bill, the mortgage, and ministers' salaries, they designate the remainder for "Missions"—one compartment in the budget. Once they fill their calendars with all the activities they enjoy—Sunday School class picnics, Christmas parties, and Vacation Bible Schools, they find the one remaining week out of the year to sponsor a trip to a third-world country or a Native American reservation.

Healthy, biblical churches, on the other hand, view their mission not as a compartment in the budget nor as a way to fill otherwise vacant spaces on the church calendar, but as the umbrella vision to which all of their resources and time submit. If such a church conducts a Vacation Bible School, for example, they do so as a deliberate furtherance of their mission. If they hire a staff member, they commission that leader with responsibilities that relate to the mission. When asked, "How much of your time and resources do you give to your mission?" they respond, "All of it." "Mission, however ambitious and expensive or modest and inexpensive," writes John Buchanan, "is not an optional activity for the church. It is not the work we do after we have taken care of our responsibility to ourselves and paid all our other bills. It is the reason we exist" (**35**).

Second, a primarily inward focus threatens to sidetrack our mission.[1] John Stott describes those who function as though "the local church somewhat resembles the local golf club, except that the common interest of its members happens to be God rather than golf. They see themselves as religious people who enjoy doing religious things together. They pay their subscription and reckon that they are entitled to certain privileges" (**51**). When we view the church as a

[1]To be clear, churches should maintain both an inward and outward focus—ministering to one another and reaching into the world. In fact, the two aspects of ministry intertwine and feed one another—evangelism includes continuing discipleship, and discipleship will lead growing believers to evangelize. This section of the chapter addresses the problem, however, of many churches who overemphasize internal matters while neglecting external matters.

club, or as an organization that exists primarily for our own enjoyment, we lose sight of our mission.

In *Reaching a New Generation,* Alan Roxburgh offers convicting commentary and passionate exhortation for churches who have allowed selfishness to sidetrack their mission:

> Despite all our protestations, the church in North America remains focused upon itself. Until this is changed, evangelization will continue to look like forays into the world in order to recruit members for our clubs. We must refocus the life of the church from the inside to the outside. . . .
>
> Ministerial leadership is not primarily called to look after the people of a congregation. Not at all. If a congregation exists for its neighborhood and not for itself, then the calling of leadership is to move out ahead, to refocus the congregation's life from itself to the context in which it is found. We need missionary leaders in our churches, not chaplains. . . .
>
> It is not a contradiction to say that the church must refocus life outside itself and, at the same time, recover the sense of being a pilgrim community. Indeed, the former demands the latter, and the latter only has vital life in the former. Community demands a pilgrim band who are on a journey, caught up in something fantastically bigger than themselves and their needs. **(128-129)**

Third, our fears of the outside world threaten to derail our mission. Because of a discomfort for dealing with nonbelievers, and perhaps a fear of falling into temptation, some Christians view the church as a safe harbor from the world more so than as a mission to the world. Rather than building bridges, they build walls. While the church does provide mutual encouragement and support among believers, we must use the church as a harbor from the world only temporarily, regaining the strength to continue the mission. A football team who remains in the huddle will never move the ball down the field. An acting troop that remains in rehearsal will never reach an audience with its message. A church in which believers focus only on one another will never reach a dying world for Christ.

"God did not give us a spirit of timidity," Paul wrote Timothy, *"but a spirit of power, of love and of self-discipline"* (***2Tm 1:7***). We can proceed on our mission assured that *"the one who is in you is greater than the one who is in the world"* (***1Jn 4:4***). Confident in their empowerment by

Build bridges, not walls!

God, churches caught up in their mission break the huddle and pursue the adventurous mission of Christ, the mission of advancing His kingdom.

Linguistic Insights on the Great Commission[2]

Then Jesus came to them and said, "All authority in heaven and on earth has been given to me. Therefore go and make disciples of all nations, baptizing them in the name of the Father and of the Son and of the Holy Spirit, and teaching them to obey everything I have commanded you. And surely I am with you always, to the very end of the age." (***Mt 28:18-20***)

Repetition of "All" (*pas*)

- *"All authority"* (***28:18***): Following the resurrection, the Father bestowed upon Jesus all authority in heaven and on earth. This universal authority provides the basis (note the connecting "therefore") for the commission that follows.
- *"All nations"* (***28:19***): God's covenant with Abraham included the promise to bless all nations (***Gen 12:3***). Christ made this blessing possible through His death and resurrection, then commissioned His disciples to extend that blessing globally.
- *"All things"* (***28:20***, NIV *"everything"*): When they make disciples of all nations, Jesus' followers relay to these new disciples everything Jesus taught.
- *"All the days"* (***28:20***, NIV *"always"*): Jesus completes the commission with the promise of His continual presence "all of the days" (*pasas tas hemeras*).

One Preceding Participle: "Go" (*poreuthentes*)

- The participle *poreuthentes* (***28:19***, NIV *"go"*) precedes the only imperative Jesus uses in the Great Commission ("make disciples"). Some assert that, as a participle, the term suggests we make disciples "as we are going" about our normal lives and routines, rather than calling believers to deliberately "go" out of our ordinary way to extend the gospel. This common misunderstanding falls short of linguistic integrity for two reasons:

[2] Sources consulted: *Matthew*, by D.A. Carson; "As You Go, Make Disciples?" by Roy Ciampa; "What Is the Church's Commission? Some Exegetical Issues in Matthew 28:16-20," by Robert D. Culver; and *A Manual Grammar of the Greek New Testament*, by H.E. Dana and Julius Mantey.

- ✧ When a Greek participle precedes an imperative, the participle usually gains an imperative force, and indicates an action that must take place before the imperative can be realized. Here "go" precedes the imperative "make disciples." Therefore "go" gains imperative force, and indicates that we must "go" if we are to "make disciples."
- ✧ If the participle in *28:19* appeared in the present tense, it would allow a stronger argument for a temporal interpretation ("*while* you are going," or "*as* you go"). The participle appears, however, in the aorist tense, which indicates a more deliberate, punctiliar action ("go").

✦ While the following imperative carries the strongest emphasis (*"make disciples"*), the text indicates we must deliberately "go" into the world to complete this task.

One Imperative: "Make Disciples" (*matheteusate*)

✦ As the text's only imperative, the command to *"make disciples of all nations"* serves as the axis around which the Great Commission revolves. Jesus ultimately intends that all peoples will accept His teaching, submit to His Lordship, and thereby enter into the reign of God.

✦ Jesus stated this imperative in the aorist tense, indicating a deliberate action that warrants immediate attention.

Two Subsequent Participles: "Baptizing" (*baptizontes*), "Teaching" (*didaskontes*)

✦ When Greek participles follow an imperative, rather than taking on full imperative force (as with the preceding participle, "go"), they usually characterize the imperative. "Baptizing" and "teaching," therefore, characterize "making disciples."

✦ The Greek text includes no "and" (*kai*) between "baptizing" and "teaching" (though the NIV adds an "and" at the beginning of *verse 20*). Rather than presenting the two concepts subsequently (we baptize and then we teach), the text linguistically weaves them together as a way to further understand what it means to "make disciples."

EXPRESSING JESUS' LOVE

Showing Compassion

When Jesus encountered people who claimed to follow God but lived hypocritically, He confronted them ruthlessly. At the Temple, moneychangers and animal sellers overcharged visitors who needed to purchase animals for sacrifice—Jesus toppled their tables and ran them off with a whip (*Mt 21:12-17*). He minced no words with the Pharisees, calling them blind guides and fools, and comparing them with whitewashed tombs and a brood of vipers (*Mt 23:13-36*).

When Jesus encountered sinful people who did not claim to follow God on the other hand, He treated them compassionately. The Pharisees and teachers brought a woman before Jesus who had committed adultery. Though the law called for her stoning, Jesus showed her tenderness and grace (*Jn 8:1-11*). When Jesus saw Zacchaeus—a tax collector apparently as conniving and crooked as most of his day—He shared a meal with Zacchaeus, a sign of acceptance and fellowship.

Jesus bluntly confronted those who claimed to follow God but lived hypocritically; He showed compassion to sinful people who did not yet claim to follow God. The church today often does the opposite. With fellow Christians we shy from accountability, and thereby condone much hypocrisy. With people outside of the church, however, we snub our noses and furrow our brows. With an air of self-righteousness we make certain these "sinners" see the wrath of God in our cold stares, cold shoulders, and hateful internet postings. At an extreme, some find justification in acts of violence, such as murdering abortion doctors, or acts of hate, such as spitting on homosexual activists and verbally condemning them to Hell. Less extreme but equally as damaging to kingdom advancement, we might refuse to associate with the family who lives across the street because we see them living sinfully.

Too often, we treat harshly those whom Jesus treated compassionately, and treat passively those whom Jesus confronted harshly.

Perhaps we have confused prisoners of the enemy with the enemy himself. People who do not know Christ are not the church's enemy—they are unknowing prisoners of the enemy. Brian McLaren offered a similar analogy: "We were like doctors who are furious at their patients for needing help: 'Why are you bleeding? You're not supposed to bleed! You should be ashamed of yourself for making this horrible mess'" (76). Rather than drawing battle lines against

People who do not know Christ are not the church's enemy but unknowing prisoners of the enemy.

the unsaved, churches who follow Jesus' example strategize concerning how they might compassionately reach and save them. They view people of the world through Jesus' eyes: *"When he saw the crowds, he had compassion on them, because they were harassed and helpless, like sheep without a shepherd"* (**Mt 9:36**).

Being Salt and Light

Jesus offered two helpful images to describe the interaction His followers should have with our surrounding world:

> [13]*You are the salt of the earth. But if the salt loses its saltiness, how can it be made salty again? It is no longer good for anything, except to be thrown out and trampled by men.* [14]*You are the light of the world. A city on a hill cannot be hidden.* [15]*Neither do people light a lamp and put it under a bowl. Instead they put it on its stand, and it gives light to everyone in the house.* [16]*In the same way, let your light shine before men, that they may see your good deeds and praise your Father in heaven.* (**Mt 5:13-16**)

Like salt flavors and preserves, the presence of Christians should make life on earth more palatable and pure. And, our service and ministry should function like light, showing people the way to the Father. The world—more specifically our neighborhoods, schools, communities, and everywhere else we set foot—should be more godly because of our presence and Christian influence.

Matt Friedman, who preaches in Jackson, Mississippi, accepted an invitation to serve on a panel for a local news program. A newscaster moderated the panel, which convened to discuss a rash of moral problems that plagued the Jackson community. The city council president and another councilman faced prison because of shady deals they made with a local exotic dance club. The panel moderator looked straight at Friedman and asked, "Matt, whose fault is all of this?"

"Suddenly, I became agitated," Matt reflects. "I prepared to tell her in dramatic on-air fashion that we are a nation of laws and that the council president trampled on those laws. If we were looking to place blame, there was only one place to put it—smack-dab in his lap as he sat in his well-deserved jail cell."

Before these words left his lips, however, another panelist spoke up—John Perkins. Perkins has gained national recognition as a Christian writer, teacher, and community developer. "It's my fault," Perkins blurted.

Everyone turned his direction.

"I have lived in this community for decades as a Bible teacher. I should have been able to create an environment where what our council president did would have been unthinkable because of my efforts. You want someone to blame? I'll take the blame. All of it" **(Friedeman, 40)**.

Our world does not yet reflect God's holiness. As Christians, we can respond to this reality by pointing angry fingers at the corruption and degradation. Or, we can accept our responsibility to function as salt and light, and actively, compassionately advance the kingdom of Christ. John Stott writes,

> So why don't we Christians have a more wholesome effect on society? We look at deteriorating trends around us. We see social injustice, racial conflict, violence in the streets, corruption in high places, sexual promiscuity, and the scourge of HIV/AIDS. Who is to blame? Our habit is to blame everybody except ourselves. But let me put it in a different way.
>
> If the house is dark at night, there is no sense in blaming the house for its darkness. That is what happens when the sun goes down. The question to ask is: where is the light?
>
> Again, if the meat goes bad and becomes inedible, there is no sense in blaming the meat for its decay. That is what happens when the bacteria are left free to breed. The question to ask is: where is the salt?
>
> Similarly, if society becomes corrupt (like a dark night or stinking fish), there is no sense in blaming society for its corruption. That is what happens when human evil is unchecked and unrestrained. The question to ask is: where is the church? Where is the salt and light of Jesus? **(133-134)**

Rather than viewing the unsaved as our enemies, Jesus calls us to view them in compassion, functioning as salt and light in our society.

Loving Jesus by Loving Others

How, specifically, might it look if we function as salt and light? What particular actions might we take? What ministries might we pursue? Again, Jesus offers pointed, convicting teaching to guide us.

Matthew 24 describes Jesus' taking a seat on the Mount of Olives. From this hillside He delivered a series of teachings that scholars label the Olivet Discourse, which spans from ***Matthew 24:3–25:46***. Jesus told His disciples of the day when, in AD 70, Jerusalem would face destruction. Jesus then taught about His future return to the earth. Because no one knows the day or hour of His return, we must always remain prepared. To prepare, we must make wise use of the resources He has put at our disposal, so that when He returns He will judge our stewardship and service as wise and faithful.

This teaching leads Jesus to a picture of the final judgment, and examples of ways He expects us to serve in preparation for His coming. When all nations gather before His throne, He will separate them like sheep and goats (***Mt 25:31-33***). To those on His right He will grant their inheritance—the kingdom—because *"I was hungry and you gave me something to eat, I was thirsty and you gave me something to drink, I was a stranger and you invited me in, I needed clothes and you clothed me, I was sick and you looked after me, I was in prison and you came to visit me"* (***25:34-36***). When did the righteous perform such ministries? *"Whatever you did for one of the least of these brothers of mine, you did for me,"* Jesus will respond (***25:37-40***).[3] Conversely, those on Jesus' left will face eternal punishment because they did not perform the very same ministries (***25:41-44***). *"Whatever you did not do for one of the least of these, you did not do for me"* (***25:45***).

When we minister to those in need, we minister to Jesus.

Eric Swanson, cowriter of *The Externally Focused Church*, tells of a time he and a friend, Donny, picked up ten men from a homeless shelter and took the men to their church building for the night. After they unloaded from the church van, Eric and Donny served the men snacks, and they all watched a funny movie. They then prayed with the men, set up some cots, and turned in for the night.

Donny rose at 4:30 the next morning, long before the men got up, to make his specialty—homemade cinnamon rolls. Soon the men awoke to the aroma of fresh coffee and oven-fresh cinnamon rolls,

[3] Scholars differ concerning the identity of the *"least of these brothers of mine."* Some believe Jesus spoke in a more limited manner, referring to His disciples only, or perhaps to them and others who served as missionaries for the gospel. With this interpretation, the passage commends those who offer hospitality and care for the traveling disciples and/or missionaries of the early church (this interpretation is based on Jesus' use of similar terminology elsewhere). Other scholars interpret *"the least of these brothers of mine"* in a less limited manner, believing it refers broadly to anyone who has need. This chapter proceeds assuming the second, less limited interpretation, understanding that even if Jesus spoke in a more limited sense here, He taught and exemplified elsewhere (such as with the parable of the Good Samaritan, and His own healing ministry) the importance of ministering compassionately to people's needs.

dripping with icing and butter. As they watched the men gobble down the cinnamon rolls, Eric asked Donny what he was thinking. Donny replied, "I was just thinking, Jesus sure likes cinnamon rolls" (**Rusaw and Swanson, 68**).

When we minister to those in need, we minister to Jesus.

Conversely, when we neglect those in need, we neglect Jesus.

Fred Craddock tells a story from his days of doctoral work at Vanderbilt University. One evening, while preparing for comprehensive exams, he took a study break around midnight. He visited a nearby diner. After he enjoyed a grilled cheese sandwich and a couple of refills of coffee, Craddock noticed someone at the end of the counter waiting to be served—an old, grey-haired African-American man.

Finally, the cook huffed to the man, "What do you want?" After he took the order, the cook scooped up a dark patty of ground beef from the back of the grill, placed it on a piece of old bread, and gave it to the African-American customer without any condiments or even a napkin. The old man paid for his sandwich, then shuffled out to sit on the curb next to the garbage can.

When we minister to those in need, we minister to Jesus.

"I didn't say anything," Dr. Craddock reflects. "I did not reprimand, protest, or witness to the cook. I did not go out and sit beside the man on the curb. I didn't do anything. I was thinking about my upcoming exam."

A few minutes later, Craddock paid for his meal and walked out of the diner. He glanced down and for a brief moment locked eyes with the man sitting on the curb. As if on cue, he heard a sound from the distant Tennessee hills—the piercing crow of a rooster. He remembered Jesus' words, *"Whatever you did for one of the least of these brothers of mine, you did for me"* (***Mt 25:40***) (**Craddock, 48-49**).[4]

How we treat "the least of these," we treat Jesus.

We extend the mission of Christ when we extend the love of Christ—serving as salt and light by compassionately ministering to the needs of those around us.

[4] Some details have been added based on Dr. Craddock's own verbal recitations of the story.

From Performance to Mission[5]

Walt Kallestad ministers with the Community Church of Joy in Phoenix. Their weekend services drew twelve thousand attendees each weekend, but Walt grew convicted that the church had merely gathered consumers who sought entertainment through the church's polished programs. They had failed to grow disciples. He explained:

> "Attracting consumers was consuming me—not the way vision consumes a leader. It was the opposite of that—I was losing sight of the vision. Our church was a great organization. But something was missing. We weren't accomplishing our mission; we weren't creating transformed, empowered disciples.
>
> "We'd put all our energies into dispensing religious goods and services. But our people weren't touching our community. If our church, with its sheer number of people, was populated with disciples, we would be feeding the hungry, building meaningful relationships with neighbors, and transforming our community. But we were neither salt nor light.
>
> "After pouring more than 25 years of my life into this church, I knew we weren't developing disciples who were taking up their crosses to follow Jesus. We'd produced consumers—like Pac-Man, gobbling up religious experiences, navigating a maze that was going nowhere in particular."

A mentor advised Walt, "You must die as a church and be born as a mission."

Through a radical, immediate, often painful change of direction and ministry model, Walt led the church to a change of focus. "In the old days, we protected people's anonymity; today we thrust them into community, doing life together. We used to invite them to attend church; now we invite them to be the church. I used to ask, 'What can we do to get more people to attend our church?' Now I ask, 'How can I best equip and empower the people to go be the church in the marketplace where God has called them to serve?'"

[5] Excerpt from "Showtime: Could Our Church Shift from Performance to Mission?" by Walt Kallestad (*Leadership* 29 [Fall 2008] 39-43). Copyright 2008 Walt Kallestad and Christianity Today International. Reprinted by permission of *Leadership* journal. www.leadershipjournal.net.

EXPLAINING JESUS' GOSPEL

THE MANDATE

We might begin pursuing Jesus' mission through compassionate ministries to our communities. Our mission remains incomplete, however, until it includes the proclamation of the Gospel. *"How, then, can they call on the one they have not believed in?"* Paul asked the Roman Christians. *"And how can they believe in the one of whom they have not heard? And how can they hear without someone preaching to them? And how can they preach unless they are sent? As it is written, 'How beautiful are the feet of those who bring good news!'"* (***Rom 10:14-15***).

This proclamation of the gospel can occur on a personal level, as in the case of Philip and the Ethiopian eunuch (***Acts 8:26-39***). It can happen through public proclamation to large crowds, as with Peter's sermon at Pentecost (***Acts 2:14-41***). Or, the local church can proclaim the gospel through its ministries, as Paul described concerning the church in Thessalonica: *"You became a model to all the believers in Macedonia and Achaia. The Lord's message rang out from you not only in Macedonia and Achaia—your faith in God has become known everywhere"* (***1Th 1:7-8***).

These and similar passages do not negate the need to express Jesus' love through ministries of compassion; they do, however, remind us that such ministries do not substitute for the verbal sharing of Jesus' truth. Jesus' mission—and, therefore, the church's mission—necessarily includes both elements.

An event that occurred early in the life of the church demonstrates this balance. One day when Peter and John approached the Temple, a crippled man begged them for money (***Acts 3:1-5***). *"Peter said, 'Silver or gold I do not have, but what I have I give you. In the name of Jesus Christ of Nazareth, walk'"* (***3:6***). At Peter's pronouncement, strength entered the man's feet, and he began walking, jumping, and praising God, leaving onlookers amazed (***3:7-10***).

The healing—an act of compassionate ministry—caused a stir. *"All the people were astonished and came running to them"* to see what had happened (***Acts 3:11***). Peter, never one to waste an opportunity to preach, told the gathered crowd of the power behind the healing—Jesus, the one these very people had crucified, but whom God resurrected (***3:12-18***). *"Repent, then, and turn to God so that your sins may be wiped out,"* Peter preached (***3:19***).

The Jewish officials, angered by the message, arrested Peter and John and threw them in jail (**Acts 4:1-3**). *"But many who heard the message believed, and the number of men grew to about five thousand"* (**4:4**). When called to testify before the Jewish officials the next day, Peter simply preached again:

> [10]*It is by the name of Jesus Christ of Nazareth, whom you crucified but whom God raised from the dead, that this man stands before you healed.* [11]*He is 'the stone you builders rejected, which has become the capstone.'* [12]*Salvation is found in no one else, for there is no other name under heaven given to men by which we must be saved.* (**4:10-12**)

The officials threatened Peter and John, and warned them against any further preaching (**4:13-18**). Peter and John responded, *"Judge for yourselves whether it is right in God's sight to obey you rather than God. For we cannot help speaking about what we have seen and heard"* (**4:19-20**).

Peter's missional efforts began with the healing, but did not end with the healing. He continued by proclaiming the truth of Jesus.[6] His ministry included both the compassionate meeting of people's needs, and the proclamation of the gospel—as will ours, if we hope to advance Jesus' kingdom.

Varying Starting Points

When NT believers shared the gospel story, they began the story in varying ways, depending on the knowledge base and perceptions of a particular audience. For example, in Peter's sermon discussed above, following the healing of the crippled beggar, Peter began,

> [12]*"Men of Israel, why does this surprise you? Why do you stare at us as if by our own power or godliness we had made this man walk?* [13]*The God of Abraham, Isaac and Jacob, the God of our fathers, has glorified his servant Jesus. . . .* [18]*This is how God fulfilled what he had foretold through all the prophets, saying that his Christ would suffer."* (**Acts 3:12-13,18**)

Peter recognized that his audience operated from a Jewish knowledge base; therefore, he connected Jesus' story to their story by reflecting

[6] **Acts 3 and 4** refer to the "name" of Jesus nine times. For example, Peter told the crowds, *"By faith in the name of Jesus, this man whom you see and know was made strong. It is Jesus' name and the faith that comes through him that has given this complete healing to him, as you can all see"* (**Acts 3:16**). Jesus' name represents Jesus Himself. The crippled beggar, the text seems to emphasize, did not just encounter Peter and John. Through Peter and John, the beggar encountered Jesus.

back to Abraham, Isaac, Jacob, and the prophets. In ***Acts 17***, however, Paul stood before the pagan Athenian philosophers. Rather than appealing to Jewish theology and history, which would have meant little to these philosophers, Paul appealed to their bent toward spirituality, to what might be observed about God through creation (which compares to Paul's argument in ***Romans 1–3***), and to observations made by their own poets:

> [22]*Paul then stood up in the meeting of the Areopagus and said: "Men of Athens! I see that in every way you are very religious.*
> [23]*For as I walked around and looked carefully at your objects of worship, I even found an altar with this inscription: TO AN UNKNOWN GOD. Now what you worship as something unknown I am going to proclaim to you.*
>
> [24]*"The God who made the world and everything in it is the Lord of heaven and earth and does not live in temples built by hands.* [25]*And he is not served by human hands, as if he needed anything, because he himself gives all men life and breath and everything else.* [26]*From one man he made every nation of men, that they should inhabit the whole earth; and he determined the times set for them and the exact places where they should live.*
> [27]*God did this so that men would seek him and perhaps reach out for him and find him, though he is not far from each one of us.*
> [28]*'For in him we live and move and have our being.' As some of your own poets have said, 'We are his offspring.'"* (**Acts 17:22-28**)

In both cases, the preachers arrived at the gospel of Christ. They began their presentations differently, however, based on their audiences.

Communicating the gospel effectively in today's culture requires similar sensitivity to our audience. Though we must arrive at the gospel of Christ, the starting point will vary depending on the experiences and perceptions of our audience. Christians cannot assume, for example, that those with whom we speak at the coffee shop or in the bleachers of a ballgame believe in the God of the Bible, or in the truthfulness and authority of the Bible itself. In such circumstances, to begin the conversation with, "God says . . .", or "The Bible teaches . . ." will have little impact. In some situations—primarily in years past—an evangelistic-minded believer might ask a stranger, "If you died tonight, do you know that you would go to Heaven?" Such questions might then open the door for valuable conversations. The question assumes, of course, that the listener believes in an afterlife, believes in a Heaven and Hell as the Bible teaches them, and believes that the person asking the question can be trusted to relate reliable information on how to avoid Hell and gain Heaven. An evangelist who makes these assumptions today will have little success. Similar problems exist with any canned gospel presentation given to strangers.

Our contemporary circumstances call—not for a change in the gospel story—but for a change in the ways we begin the conversations to lead to the gospel story. Contemporary circumstances call for apologetics within, and an apologetic of, relationship.

"Apologetics" refers to a reasoned defense of truth. Believers who effectively evangelize stand ready to explain why they believe what they believe. They can explain, for example, not just that God created the world, but why they believe this in the face of a scoffing scientific community. They can explain not only what the Bible teaches about Jesus, but also why they believe in the Bible's truthfulness and authority.[7]

Furthermore, they recognize that such conversations most effectively take place in the context of trusting, respectful relationships. The effectiveness of street corner preaching, passing out tracts, and knocking on strangers' doors has waned significantly over recent decades. Wise believers build authentic relationships with people who do not know Christ (not, we should note, manipulative relationships developed only for evangelistic purposes). In these relationships, wise Christians listen to their friends, seek to understand them, and then carefully address misconceptions and connect the friends' stories to Jesus' story, like Peter did with the Jews in ***Acts 3*** and Paul did with the Athenians in ***Acts 17***. "Our goal should be," proposes David Geisler, "to talk to people in such a way today that the next time they see us, they are eager to continue the spiritual conversation, not run the other direction!" (117).

Wise believers build authentic relationships with people who do not know Christ.

Peter's teaching bears repeating,

[7] Numerous resources exist to help believers in this area. I recommend books, articles, and websites from the following contemporary apologists: William Lane Craig, J.P. Moreland, Ravi Zacharias, Norman Geisler, Lee Strobel, and Sean McDowell.

[15]Always be prepared to give an answer to everyone who asks you to give the reason for the hope that you have. But do this with gentleness and respect, [16]keeping a clear conscience, so that those who speak maliciously against your good behavior in Christ may be ashamed of their slander. (***1Pet 3:15-16***)

Unvarying Message

How we begin the conversations in which we proclaim the gospel varies according to those with whom we speak; however, the gospel we eventually proclaim remains unchanged. We proclaim the same Christ that Peter and Paul proclaimed, the same narrative taught from ***Genesis*** to ***Revelation***.

The essence of the gospel story divides easily into four scenes:

1. Creation: God created a perfect world in which He enjoyed a perfect relationship with His creation—particularly with mankind, the pinnacle of creation whom He formed in His own image (***Gen 1:26-27***).
2. Fall: Mankind, beginning with Adam and Eve, rebelled against God and allowed sin and its consequences—including death, disease, and disharmony—to infiltrate God's creation (***Genesis 3***).
3. Redemption: God initiated a process through his covenant with Abraham (***Gen 12:3***) to redeem creation (***Rom 8:19-25***). This redemption centers on what Paul labeled as matters of *"first importance"*: *"For what I received I passed on to you as of first importance: that Christ died for our sins according to the Scriptures, that he was buried, that he was raised on the third day according to the Scriptures"* (***1Cor 15:3-4***). *"All have sinned and fall short of the glory of God,"* Paul further explains, *"and are justified freely by his grace through the redemption that came by Christ Jesus. God presented him as a sacrifice of atonement, through faith in his blood"* (***Rom 3:23-25***).
4. Response: Mankind can receive God's grace, given through Christ, in faith (***Eph 2:8***). Beyond simple cognitive assent, faith includes a commitment of one's entire self (***Jas 2:14-26; Mt 16:24***). Initially, this faith response includes matters such as repentance and baptism (***Acts 2:38***). Ongoing, faith includes growing relationships with God and His people (***Acts 2:42; 1Cor 15:58***).

The manner in which we relate this story will fluctuate with circumstances. As John Stott explains, however, "We simply do not share the gospel if we do not declare God's love in the gift of his Son to live our life, to die for our sins and to rise again, together with his offer through Jesus Christ, to all who repent and believe, of a new life of forgiveness and freedom, and of membership in his new society" (**63**).

The Power of Witness

The prospect of talking with an unbeliever about Christ frightens many Christians, even if that conversation grows from the context of a friendship. These believers might find comfort in considering themselves witnesses (*martus*)—a term used thirty-nine times in ***Acts***. In ***Acts 1:8***, for example, Jesus told His disciples, *"You will be my witnesses in Jerusalem, and in all Judea and Samaria, and to the ends of the earth."* A witness testifies about what he or she has experienced. Some people may have particular giftedness or charisma that enables them to publicly proclaim Christ, or to initiate evangelistic conversations with strangers. Any Christian, however, can attest to the work of Christ in his life. This witnessing does not require great charisma or assertiveness; rather, it requires the simple willingness to say, "Jesus has made a difference in my life, let me tell you how."

Jimmy Carter tells of a Southern Baptist Convention at which he spoke while he campaigned for President. The agenda that evening included three speakers—Carter, Billy Graham, and a truck driver. Each had a five minute time limit.

Carter and Graham spoke first, each speaking with great eloquence and polish. The truck driver sat on stage watching. When Carter returned to his seat, the truck driver whispered, "I don't think I can live through this. I just can't do it."

With shaking knees, but determination, he rose and walked to the podium. He stood silently for a moment, then began mumbling into the microphone. "I was always a drunk, and didn't have any friends. The only people I knew were men like me who hung around the bars in the town where I lived." He then described how someone loved him, helped him, and won him to Christ. Once he gave his life to Christ, the truck driver wanted to witness to others about what God had done for him. His heart ached for his old friends at the bar, so he went there. He testified of the difference Jesus made in his life. The bartender called him a nuisance and said he hurt business. At first his old friends laughed at him. Before long, however, they began asking questions. Eventually, the truck driver reported, "fourteen of my friends became Christians."

Carter wrote concerning the experience, "The truck driver's speech, of course, was the highlight of the convention. I don't believe anyone who was there will ever forget that five-minute fumbling statement—or remember what I or even Billy Graham had to say" (**Carter, 71-72**).

Witnessing to the work of Christ in our lives does not require the eloquence or charisma of Billy Graham or Jimmy Carter. It requires only the willingness to testify.

CONCLUSION

I wrote in the beginning of this chapter of my mission trip to Mexico. I also recently traveled to China, where I had the opportunity to speak at a couple of universities. China does not allow Christian missionaries, so I spoke rather generically about leadership principles, and included only occasional references to my faith, hoping to plant seeds and raise questions. After one such lecture, a group of six students remained in the auditorium, wanting to talk further. A young man asked me, "What kind of things did Jesus teach?" I tried to offer a brief summary of Jesus' teaching, and mentioned that Jesus often taught in stories. Someone else asked, "Will you tell us one of His stories?" I recounted the parable of the prodigal son. They wept. "We are very touched," one girl responded in broken English. "We have never heard this story before. Is this what your God is like?"

All over the world people walk the streets, sit in classrooms, and muddle through life, who have never heard of the prodigal son, and who have never met the loving Father. Jesus sent the church on a mission—His mission—to tell them.

What Do You Say?

1. What would it look like if your church functioned more like a mission?
2. How did the cross relate to Jesus' mission? How does it relate to ours?
3. Why do many churches operate without Jesus' sense of urgency—recognizing Heaven and Hell hang in the balance—in our evangelistic efforts? How can we regain this urgency?
4. What did Paul mean when he said we are Christ's ambassadors? How can you function better in this role in your own daily environments?
5. In what ways has your church functioned as salt and light, and ministered to *"the least of these"*? How might you grow in this kind of ministry?
6. What have been your personal experiences—good and bad—in talking with others about your faith? What did you learn from these experiences?
7. Why do we typically fear talking with others about Christ and the gospel story? How might viewing ourselves as "witnesses" help us overcome our fears?

CHAPTER NINE
SPIRIT EMPOWERED

In the late nineteenth century, John Muir explored the western coast of North America. He traipsed from the California Sierras to the Alaskan glaciers, experiencing the wonders of creation with childlike exuberance and worshipful wonder.

In 1874, Muir visited a friend who lived in a cabin in the Yuba River valley of the Sierra Mountains. In December of that year, a storm raged inland from the Pacific, bending massive pine and fir trees like blades of grass. The cabin provided a warm, comfortable refuge from the storm. Muir, however, seldom settled for warm and comfortable. He hiked out of the cabin, leaned directly into the storm, climbed a high ridge, then found a giant Douglas fir. He scrambled to the top of the tree and held on for dear life, lashed about by the raging winds. Why? He wanted to experience *weather* with all its energy, scents, colors, and power.

> I. The Holy Spirit in Both the Testaments
>   A. The Spirit in the OT
>   B. The Spirit in the NT
> II. The Spirit and the Birth of the Church
>   A. A Spirit-Filled Birth
>   B. A Spirit-Filled Story
> III. The Spirit and the Ministry of the Church
>   A. Continuing Jesus' Mission
>   B. Spiritual Gifts
> IV. The Spirit and the Edification of the Church
>   A. Teaching
>   B. Character Development
>   C. Unity
> V. Conclusion

Eugene Peterson writes, "The story of John Muir, storm-whipped at the top of the Douglas fir in the Yuba River valley, gradually took shape as a kind of icon of Christian spirituality for our family. The icon has been in place ever since as a standing rebuke against becoming a mere spectator to life, preferring creature comforts to Creator confrontations." Peterson continues by pointing out the source of such a life, "Spirituality has to do with life, *lived* life. For Christians, 'spirituality' is derived (always and exclusively) from Spirit, God's Holy Spirit" (7-8).

The biblical terms for spirit, in both OT Hebrew and NT Greek, also carry the image of "wind" or "breath." Jesus utilized this imagery when He said, *"The wind blows wherever it pleases. You hear its sound, but you cannot tell where it comes from or where it is going. So it is with everyone born of the Spirit"* (**Jn 3:8**).

The Holy Spirit—an unseen power who, like the winds whipped by a Pacific storm, makes an enormous impact—mystifies even the most accomplished scholars. Historically, the church has had difficulty defining and describing the Holy Spirit. The Apostles' Creed, for example, gives extended explanation of God the Father and Jesus the Son, then simply says, "I believe in the Holy Spirit," with no further explanation. In recent generations those of Pentecostal and Charismatic persuasions have developed more comprehensive doctrines of the Spirit. Those of other backgrounds find fault in the Pentecostal and Charismatic perspectives, but often fail to develop clear doctrines themselves.

This failure proves tragic, both for individuals and for the church community. Our confusion concerning the Spirit leads us to avoid discussing Him and to cower from relying on Him, thereby missing much of the power, mystery, and adventure of a Spirit-led, Spirit-empowered faith.

The confines of a single chapter will not allow a comprehensive theology of the Holy Spirit. Rather than tackling a comprehensive theology, therefore, in keeping with the purpose of the book, this chapter will explore a particular element of the overall theology—the role of the Spirit in the life of the community of God's people.

Word Study: *Pneuma* (Spirit)[1]

The Greek term *pneuma* refers to wind, breath, or spirit. The intention of the term—whether an author intends it to refer to wind, a person's breath, a person's spirit, an evil spirit, God's breath, or God's Spirit—depends on its context. Of the term's 379 occurrences in the NT, the NIV translates it as "spirit" or "spirits" 357 times. Of these occurrences, 92 pair *pneuma* with *hagion* ("holy"), a phrase translated as "Holy Spirit."

[1] Sources consulted: "Pneuma," by Stephen Renn; "Holy Spirit, Doctrine of," by Gary D. Babcock, and "Pneuma," by Spiros Zodhiates.

The NT sometimes uses other names to refer to the Holy Spirit, such as the "Spirit of God," the "Spirit of Christ," or sometimes simply the "Spirit." ***Romans 8:9***, for example, contains all three of these designations in a single verse, paralleling them with one another: *"You, however, are controlled not by the sinful nature but by the **Spirit**, if the **Spirit of God** lives in you. And if anyone does not have the **Spirit of Christ**, he does not belong to Christ"* (bold added).

The Bible directly connects the Holy Spirit with the triune God (***Mt 28:19; Rom 1:4***), demonstrating that the Spirit is one of the three persons of whom God consists—Father, Son, and Spirit. The Spirit dwells within believers (***1Cor 3:16***) to facilitate matters such as new life (***Jn 6:63***) and the development of Christian character (***Gal 5:16-26***).

THE HOLY SPIRIT IN BOTH THE TESTAMENTS

THE SPIRIT IN THE OT

The OT, unlike the NT, contains no direct teaching that explains the person or the role of the Holy Spirit. Instead, it offers occasional glimpses into His work through particular circumstances and people.

The Spirit first appears in the second verse of the Bible. **Genesis 1:1** explains what the remainder of the chapter unpacks: *"In the beginning God created the heavens and the earth."* "God" in this verse translates from *elohim,* and includes all three persons of the Trinity (Father, Son, and Spirit). Immediately after ***verse 1, verse 2*** describes the role of the Holy Spirit—one of the three persons of whom *elohim* consists—in the creation process: *"Now the earth was formless and empty, darkness was over the surface of the deep, and the Spirit of God was hovering over the waters."* The Spirit's role in creation is described by the term "hovering" (*rachaph*). This term appears only three times in the Bible (***Gen 1:2; Deu 32:11; Jer 23:9***). ***Deuteronomy 32:11*** uses the term to picture God like an eagle who "hovers" over the nest of her young, protecting and nurturing them. The term describes ongoing, nurturing attention. As God created, the Spirit's particular role in the process involved caring oversight.

Later, the OT depicts the Spirit as One who empowers and equips God's people—often temporarily—for particular ministries or events. For example, after God commanded Moses to construct the tabernacle,

The LORD said to Moses, [2]"See, I have chosen Bezalel son of Uri, the son of Hur, of the tribe of Judah, [3]and I have filled him with the Spirit of God, with skill, ability and knowledge in all kinds of crafts— [4]to make artistic designs for work in gold, silver, and bronze, [5]to cut and set stones, to work in wood, and to engage in all kinds of craftsmanship." (***Ex 31:1-5***)

The Spirit is the One who empowers and equips God's people for particular ministries.

Later, as Gideon began leading God's people against the Midianites and Amalekites, *"Then the Spirit of the LORD came upon Gideon, and he blew a trumpet, summoning the Abiezrites to follow him"* (***Jdg 6:34***). The Samson narrative includes the phrase *"The Spirit of the LORD came upon him in power"* three times, describing God's empowerment of Samson to tear a lion apart (***Jdg 14:6***), to strike down thirty men of Ashkelon (***Jdg 14:19***), and to strike down a thousand Philistines with the jawbone of a donkey (***Jdg 15:14***).

Furthermore, the Spirit empowered people to prophesy and to lead. Zechariah spoke of *"the words that the LORD Almighty had sent by his Spirit through the earlier prophets"* (***Zec 7:12***). On a particular occasion, when Moses felt overburdened by his leadership over the Israelites, the LORD told Moses to bring seventy elders who would share the responsibilities.

[16]Have them come to the Tent of Meeting, that they may stand there with you. [17]I will come down and speak with you there, and I will take of the Spirit that is on you and put the Spirit on them. They will help you carry the burden of the people so that you will not have to carry it alone. . . . [25]When the Spirit rested on them, they prophesied, but they did not do it again. (***Num 11:16-17,25***)

Old Testament believers viewed the Spirit of God as the effective power of God at work in the world and among His people. Scholars such as Gerhard Krodel, in fact, equate phrases such as *"the arm of the LORD"* and *"the hand of God"* (phrases preferred by Isaiah and Jeremiah, such as in ***Isa 8:11*** and ***Jer 32:17***) with *"the Spirit of God"* in OT terminology. Krodel goes on to discuss the Spirit's giving of both physical strength and ethical renewal to His people,

The spirit of God is understood in the Old Testament not only as the awe-inspiring power of God which intermittently takes possession of persons especially chosen and which is manifest in physical strength, courage, revelations, insights into God's counsel, wisdom, and will. It is also perceived as God's saving presence which renews individuals, or as an ethical force which establishes righteousness, justice, and a clean heart in Israel. (**16**)

Prophets of the OT looked forward to a new era that would include a more pervasive role of the Spirit in and among God's people. Joel prophesied, for example, concerning the coming Day of the Lord: *"I will pour out my Spirit on all people. Your sons and daughters will prophesy, your old men will dream dreams, your young men will see visions. Even on my servants, both men and women, I will pour out my Spirit in those days"* (***2:28-29***). In ***Acts***, Peter quotes Joel's words and applies them to the arrival of the Spirit at Pentecost.

The Spirit in the NT

In contrast to the OT, in which the Spirit typically came upon only certain believers in particular circumstances, the NT promises the indwelling of the Spirit for all who follow and obey Christ. Though the community of God's people in the NT holds great similarities to that community of the OT, "The primary spiritual distinctive of the new community is its possession of the Holy Spirit" (**Seccombe, 49**).

Jesus promised His disciples that He would send the Spirit after His death, resurrection, and ascension:

> [16]*I will ask the Father, and he will give you another Counselor to be with you forever—* [17]*the Spirit of truth. The world cannot accept him, because it neither sees him nor knows him. But you know him, for he lives with you and will be in you.* [18]*I will not leave you as orphans; I will come to you. . . .* [25]*All this I have spoken while still with you.* [26]*But the Counselor, the Holy Spirit, whom the Father will send in my name, will teach you all things and will remind you of everything I have said to you.* [27]*Peace I leave with you; my peace I give you. I do not give to you as the world gives. Do not let your hearts be troubled and do not be afraid. . . .* [16:7]*It is for your good that I am going away. Unless I go away, the Counselor will not come to you; but if I go, I will send him to you.* (***Jn 14:16-18,25-27; 16:7***)[2]

When Peter preached to the large crowd in Jerusalem at Pentecost—crowds who had observed the Spirit in the disciples and grown

[2]The term "Counselor" in verses ***14:16, 14:25, and 16:7*** translates from the Greek *parakleton*, "a somewhat technical word that refers to one who is called along side to assist" (**Grenz, 477**).

convicted of their sin—they asked Peter how they should respond. *"Peter replied, 'Repent and be baptized, every one of you, in the name of Jesus Christ for the forgiveness of your sins. And you will receive the gift of the Holy Spirit. The promise is for you and your children and for all who are far off—for all whom the Lord our God will call'"* (***Acts 2:38-39***). The Spirit works in believers to guide us into truth (***Jn 16:13***), produce godly character (***Rom 8:5-11; Gal 5:22-25***), assure us of our salvation (***Rom 8:16***), minister to others (***1Cor 12:4-11***), and to help us pray when we are weak (***Rom 8:26-27***).

In addition to teaching of the Spirit's work in individual lives, in passages such as those above the NT also describes the Spirit's indwelling in the church corporately. Paul taught the Ephesians that, in Christ, *"you too are being built together to become a dwelling in which God lives by his Spirit"* (***Eph 2:22***). They, "together," were built into a dwelling for the Spirit. In ***1 Corinthians 3:16-17***, Paul asks the believers in Corinth, *"Don't you know that you yourselves are God's temple and that God's Spirit lives in you? If anyone destroys God's temple, God will destroy him; for God's temple is sacred, and you are that temple."* Though English translations lose this nuance, these verses use the plural "you," not the singular. God's Spirit dwells in "you" collectively, corporately, communally. "You," together, house the presence of God and, therefore, are His sacred temple.[3] "The Spirit in Paul has a strongly communal character," explains Edgar Krentz. "He has been given primarily to the community. The individual Christian discovers that the Spirit does not lead to individual spiritualism, but rather to the life of loving service in the community of faith that edifies the neighbor" (52). Craig Van Gelder concurs,

> During the Reformation, Protestant churches tended to emphasize the work of the Spirit in the life of the individual believer. This emphasis was reinforced later through influences from Enlightenment thinkers. While the calling, saving, sealing, gifting, and empowering works of the Spirit can be developed biblically from the perspective of the individual, this is not the New Testament's primary focus in defining the relationship between the Spirit and the church. The Bible's

[3]A few chapters later, in ***1 Corinthians 6***, Paul uses the singular "you" to teach, during a discussion of sexual morality, *"Your body is a temple of the Holy Spirit"* (***1Cor 6:19***). This further illustrates that a correct doctrine of the Spirit includes both His presence in the community (as in ***1 Corinthians 3***) and His presence in the individual (***1 Corinthians 6***).

focus is not on individual Christians but on the formation of a new type of community, a new humanity that is indwelt by the Spirit. (*Essence*, 112)

The Spirit serves as the lifeblood in the body of Christ, invigorating each part of the body and, at the same time, the body on the whole. Just as a physical body without the flow of blood will cease to live, so a church apart from the empowerment of the Spirit will lose all power, significance, effectiveness, and life. Apart from the Spirit, the church does not exist—a gathering of people, perhaps, but not the church.

The Holy Spirit in Jesus' Ministry

- ✦ The Spirit prophesied of Jesus' coming (*Mt 22:41-46*).
- ✦ The Spirit conceived Jesus in Mary (*Mt 1:18-20*).
- ✦ The Spirit came on Jesus at his baptism like a dove (*Mt 3:16*).
- ✦ The Spirit guided Jesus (*Lk 2:27; 4:1*).
- ✦ The Spirit empowered Jesus' preaching and ministry (*Lk 4:14*).
- ✦ The Spirit empowered Jesus to cast out demons (*Mt 12:28*).
- ✦ The Spirit filled Jesus with joy (*Lk 10:21*).
- ✦ The Spirit was involved in Jesus' resurrection (*Rom 1:4*).
- ✦ The Spirit is given by Jesus to His followers (*Jn 15:26*).

THE SPIRIT AND THE BIRTH OF THE CHURCH

A Spirit-Filled Birth

Before the Day of Pentecost described in *Acts 2*, the community of God's people had existed for millennia. This particular Pentecost celebration gains the designation "the birth of the church," however, because it represents a critical transition in the empowerment (the Holy Spirit) and the purpose (proclaiming the death and resurrection of Christ) of God's community. The church—when understood as the body of Christ (*1Cor 12:27*), and the household of God with Christ as its chief cornerstone and with the indwelling of the Spirit (*Eph 2:20-22*)—springs into life in these opening paragraphs of *Acts*.

As *Acts* describes this birth of the church, it highlights the critical part played by the Holy Spirit, referring to the Spirit ten times in just the first two chapters:

① Jesus instructed the disciples *"through the Spirit"* (**Acts 1:2**).

② Jesus promised the disciples, *"In a few days you will be baptized with the Holy Spirit"* (**Acts 1:5**).

③ Jesus explained to the disciples, *"You will receive power when the Holy Spirit comes on you; and you will be my witnesses in Jerusalem, and in all Judea and Samaria, and to the ends of the earth"* (**Acts 1:8**).

④ Peter explained to the believers about Judas, *"The Scripture had to be fulfilled which the Holy Spirit spoke long ago through the mouth of David concerning Judas"* (**Acts 1:16**).

⑤ When the disciples gathered on the day of Pentecost, *"Suddenly a sound like the blowing of a violent wind came from heaven and filled the whole house where they were sitting. They saw what seemed to be tongues of fire that separated and came to rest on each of them. All of them were filled with the Holy Spirit"* (**Acts 2:2-4a**).

⑥ The disciples *"began to speak in other tongues as the Spirit enabled them"* (**Acts 2:4b**).

⑦ When Peter preached to the crowds, he reminded them of Joel's prophecy, *"'In the last days,' God says, 'I will pour out my Spirit on all the people'"* (**Acts 2:17**).

⑧ Joel's prophecy continued, *"Even on my servants, both men and women, I will pour out my Spirit in those days"* (**Acts 2:18**).

⑨ Peter explained that through His death and resurrection Jesus *"has received from the Father the promised Holy Spirit and has poured out what you now see and hear"* (**Acts 2:33**).

⑩ If the people would repent and be baptized, Peter explained they would *"receive the gift of the Holy Spirit"* (**Acts 2:38**).

Newsweek magazine asked storyteller Garrison Keillor to choose what he considered the five most important books in his life. He placed **Acts** at the top of his list. "The flames lit on their little heads and bravely and dangerously went they onward," he explained (17). Through the power of the Spirit, God gave life to this ragged band of believers, igniting the church movement—the advancement of Jesus' kingdom—that continues today and will continue until the kingdom's full consummation.

A SPIRIT-FILLED STORY

In addition to the ten references to the Holy Spirit in the ***first two chapters of Acts***, Luke peppers the remainder of ***Acts*** with an additional forty-seven references to the Spirit. Observant teachers often quip that the book should wear the label "The Acts of the Spirit" instead of "The Acts of the Apostles" because it goes to great lengths to emphasize the Spirit's critical role in empowering and guiding the church in its early stages. Luke Timothy Johnson writes, "Luke not only includes five separate accounts of the Spirit's dramatic 'outpouring' on believers (***2:1-4; 4:28-31; 8:15-17; 10:44; 19:6***)—demarcating, it will be noted, the geographical and demographical progress of the 'Word of God'—but also shows the Spirit actively intervening in the story, impelling and guiding it (see ***Acts 8:29,39; 10:19; 11:15; 13:2; 15:28; 16:6; 20:22; 21:4,11***)" (*Acts*, 14).

Preachers often attribute the following words to A.W. Tozer: "If the Holy Spirit was withdrawn from the church today, ninety-five percent of what we do would go on and no one would know the difference. If the Holy Spirit had been withdrawn from the New Testament church, ninety-five percent of what they did would stop, and everybody would know the difference." Sometimes we wonder why today's church fails to experience the excitement, adventure, and growth that the early church experienced. Perhaps, to answer this dilemma, we should look first at absence of the Spirit in our conversation, teaching, planning, and remembering. Consider this—if you were to write a history of your church, perhaps for your website or a church directory, would the term "Spirit" appear in your historical account as frequently as it occurs in ***Acts***?

Perhaps we lack the vibrancy of the early church because we lack their reliance on the Spirit.

Perhaps we lack the vibrancy of the early church because we lack their reliance on the Spirit. We rely on our own power, logic, and creativity—tackling only those ministries we know we can accomplish on our own—rather than depending on the Spirit to push us and empower us beyond our human abilities.

THE SPIRIT AND THE MINISTRY OF THE CHURCH

CONTINUING JESUS' MISSION

Jesus' own ministry began with His baptism, at which time the Spirit descended on Him like a dove. Luke points out that He returned from His baptism *"full of the Holy Spirit"* and from His temptations *"in the power of the Spirit"* (***Lk 4:1,14***). He then went to the synagogue in Nazareth and proclaimed (quoting Isaiah), *"The Spirit of the Lord is on me"* (***Lk 4:18a***). The Spirit, Jesus further explained, *"has anointed me to preach good news to the poor. He has sent me to proclaim freedom for the prisoners and recovery of sight for the blind, to release the oppressed, to proclaim the year of the Lord's favor"* (***Lk 4:18b-19***).

As the previous chapter explained, Jesus commissioned the church to continue His mission of advancing the kingdom. Jesus promised that the Spirit—the same Spirit that empowered and led His ministry—would empower and lead our ministry: *"You will receive power when the Holy Spirit comes on you; and you will be my witnesses in Jerusalem, and in all Judea and Samaria, and to the ends of the earth"* (***Acts 1:8***). N.T. Wright explains, "The Spirit is given so that we ordinary mortals can become, in a measure, what Jesus himself was: part of God's future arriving in the present; a place where heaven and earth meet; the means of God's kingdom going ahead. The Spirit is given, in fact, so that the church can share in the life and continuing work of Jesus himself" (***Simply*, 124**).

In addition to empowering believers to fulfill Jesus' mission, the Spirit also arranges circumstances and guides believers to missional opportunities. In ***Acts 8***, the Lord led Philip to the road from Jerusalem to Gaza. As a chariot approached that held the Ethiopian eunuch, *"The Spirit told Philip, 'Go to that chariot and stay near it'"* (***Acts 8:29***). Philip obeyed the Spirit's leading, told the eunuch about Jesus, then baptized him. Afterward, *"The Spirit of the Lord suddenly took Philip away"* (***Acts 8:39***).

Erwin McManus describes one instance when, he believes, the Spirit guided both people and circumstances toward the fulfillment of Jesus' mission. A few years ago his wife talked McManus into attending a taping of *The Price Is Right*. To his chagrin, they waited in the ticket line for five hours. Eventually they began speaking with the lady who sat in line next to them. She had immigrated to Los Angeles from Uzbekistan. In the course of the conversation, McManus asked about her spiritual background, and shared with her about Jesus Christ.

She asked, "How can I believe in a God who only comes to people in America and not to people around the world? What about the person in India or China who has never heard?" McManus writes concerning his response to her question:

> I summarized for her what was so obvious to me in that moment. God had brought me from El Salvador via Miami, to throughout the East Coast, to be sitting in Los Angeles in line at *The Price Is Right* to see a show that I didn't even want to go to. And here she was from the former Soviet Union, having lived in a small town in a nation-state whose name I could not pronounce. If God could bring her from one part of the world and me from another part of the world and move us to the exact same place at the exact same moment so that she could learn that Jesus Christ died for her, didn't she think that God was both creative and powerful enough to bring life to everyone who would cry out to Him? (**169**).

McManus, consistent with the imagery contained in the biblical terminology, then compares the Spirit to the wind: "The world looks different when you understand yourself to be a child of the wind. You realize that when your sail is up, God's wind blows you to places you never imagined, at just the right moment for someone else" (**ibid.**).

Jesus commissioned the church to continue advancing His Kingdom. And, He gave us the Spirit—the same Spirit that empowered Him—to empower and guide us toward the fulfillment of this mission.

Acts' Emphasis on the Church's Spirit-Empowered Growth[4]

- ***Acts 1:8***: *"You will receive power when the Holy Spirit comes on you; and you will be my witnesses in Jerusalem, and in all Judea and Samaria, and to the ends of the earth."*
- ***Acts 2:41***: *"Those who accepted [Peter's] message were baptized, and about three thousand were added to their number that day."*
- ***Acts 2:47***: *"And the Lord added to their number daily those who were being saved."*

[4] Modified from a similar list offered in **Van Gelder, *Ministry*, 155-156**.

- **Acts 4:4**: *"Many who heard the message believed, and the number of men grew to about five thousand."*
- **Acts 5:14**: *"More and more men and women believed in the Lord and were added to their number."*
- **Acts 6:7**: *"So the word of God spread. The number of disciples in Jerusalem increased rapidly, and a large number of priests became obedient to the faith."*
- **Acts 9:31**: *"Then the church throughout Judea, Galilee and Samaria enjoyed a time of peace. It was strengthened; and encouraged by the Holy Spirit, it grew in numbers, living in the fear of the Lord."*
- **Acts 11:21**: *"The Lord's hand was with them, and a great number of people believed and turned to the Lord."*
- **Acts 12:24**: *"The word of God continued to increase and spread."*
- **Acts 13:48-49**: *"When the Gentiles heard this, they were glad and honored the word of the Lord; and all who were appointed for eternal life believed. The word of the Lord spread through the whole region."*
- **Acts 14:1**: *"A great number of Jews and Gentiles believed."*
- **Acts 14:21**: *"They preached the good news in that city and won a large number of disciples."*
- **Acts 16:5**: *"The churches were strengthened in the faith and grew daily in numbers."*
- **Acts 17:12**: *"Many of the Jews believed, as did also a number of prominent Greek women and many Greek men."*
- **Acts 17:17,34**: *"So [Paul] reasoned in the synagogue with the Jews and the God-fearing Greeks, as well as in the marketplace day by day with those who happened to be there. . . . A few men became followers of Paul and believed. . . . Among them was Dionysius, a member of the Areopagus, also a woman named Damaris, and a number of others."*
- **Acts 18:8**: *"Many of the Corinthians who heard him believed and were baptized."*
- **Acts 19:9-10**: *"He took the disciples with him and had discussions daily in the lecture hall of Tyrannus. This went on for two years, so that all the Jews and Greeks who lived in the province of Asia heard the word of the Lord."*
- **Acts 19:20**: *"The word of the Lord spread widely and grew in power."*

> ✦ ***Acts 28:30***: *"For two whole years Paul stayed [in Rome] in his own rented house and welcomed all who came to see him. Boldly and without hindrance he preached the kingdom of God and taught about the Lord Jesus Christ."*

Spiritual Gifts

One way the Spirit empowers believers to continue Jesus' mission is through spiritual gifts—particular skills and abilities granted by the Spirit for use in ministry. The NT discusses gifts such as teaching, hospitality, mercy, and leadership—various ways the Spirit equips Christians to minister (see next sidebar for complete list). The NT nowhere presents a comprehensive list of spiritual gifts. The various passages that discuss them each give examples—examples that differ from passage to passage—of the kinds of ways the Spirit may equip believers to serve. Because the lists are more representative than comprehensive, this leaves open the possibility that the Spirit may equip a believer with gifts not mentioned in the NT, such as with musical or other artistic abilities.

The NT nowhere presents a comprehensive list of spiritual gifts.

Though the kinds of gifts vary, the purpose of the gifts remains consistent. God grants spiritual gifts to individuals "so that those individuals may use these gifts to meet the needs of God's covenant people as a whole" (**Cottrell, 395**). Paul taught the Ephesians that God grants spiritual gifts *"to prepare God's people for works of service, so that the body of Christ may be built up until we all reach unity in the faith and in the knowledge of the Son of God and become mature, attaining to the whole measure of the fullness of Christ"* (***Eph 4:12-13***).[5] The Spirit gifts us *"for the common good"* (***1Cor 12:7***); therefore *"each one should use whatever gift he has received to serve others"* (***1Pet 4:10***). A believer who serves according to his or her gifts will find more joy and ful-

[5]This passage—***Ephesians 4:12-13***—speaks specifically to those with leadership gifts such as apostles, prophets, evangelists, and pastors and teachers. Paul instructs these leaders to use their gifts to prepare others to serve. Such leadership results in corporate unity and maturity.

fillment in service; these, however, come as secondary benefits, not as the primary purpose. Primarily, the Spirit grants gifts not to benefit the individual but to enable the individual to benefit the community.

Furthermore, ***1 Corinthians*** teaches that *"God has arranged the parts in the body, every one of them, just as he wanted them to be"* (***12:18***).

The church should design its program and make its plans based on the gifts God has granted.

God equips believers to perform the ministries that He wants the community to pursue. This implies, then, that when churches plan their activities, programs, and ministries, they should begin by asking, "What has God equipped the individuals in our church to do?" Then, the church should design its program and make its plans based on the gifts God has granted. For example, the leaders of a church might recognize that God has given gifts of hospitality to various members of their community. The leaders should then ask themselves, "How might we design a program that enables these individuals to utilize their gifts?" Perhaps it will involve ministry to unwed mothers who need a place to stay, helping refugees grow acclimated to a new culture, or foster care.

Too often churches operate the other way around. They begin by planning programs, then seeking people—usually any warm bodies willing to volunteer—to fill the necessary holes. This results in weary, unfulfilled servants (because they serve in areas for which God has not gifted them) and fruitless ministries (because they have pursued ministries God did not intend them to pursue).

The Holy Spirit equips individual believers with gifts that enable them to serve the community, thereby enabling the community to advance the kingdom of Christ in the manner God intends.

Spiritual Gifts Listed in Scripture

- ✦ Prophesying (***Rom 12:6; 1Cor 12:10***)
- ✦ Serving (***Rom 12:7***)
- ✦ Teaching (***Rom 12:7; 1Cor 12:28; Eph 4:11***)
- ✦ Encouraging (***Rom 12:8***)
- ✦ Contributing to the needs of others (***Rom 12:8***)

- ✦ Leadership (***Rom 12:8***)
- ✦ Mercy (***Rom 12:8***)
- ✦ Message of Wisdom (***1Cor 12:8***)
- ✦ Faith (***1Cor 12:9***)
- ✦ Healing (***1Cor 12:9,28***)
- ✦ Miraculous Powers (***1Cor 12:10,28***)
- ✦ Distinguishing between Spirits (***1Cor 12:10***)
- ✦ Differing Kinds of Tongues (***1Cor 12:10,28***)
- ✦ Interpretation of Tongues (***1Cor 12:10***)
- ✦ Apostles (***1Cor 12:28; Eph 4:11***)
- ✦ Prophets (***1Cor 12:28; Eph 4:11***)
- ✦ Ability to Help Others (***1Cor 12:28***)
- ✦ Administration (***1Cor 12:28***)
- ✦ Evangelists (***Eph 4:11***)
- ✦ Pastors and Teachers (***Eph 4:11***)

THE SPIRIT AND THE EDIFICATION OF THE CHURCH

In addition to empowering the church for evangelism and service, the Holy Spirit also performs ministries that edify the church.

TEACHING

Before Jesus submitted to the cross, He knew His disciples faced fear and apprehension about His leaving. He comforted them, therefore, by telling them of the arrival of the Holy Spirit. In this portion of ***John 14***, quoted previously in this chapter, Jesus promised He would not leave the disciples as orphans (***Jn 14:18***), but would give them *"another counselor to be with you forever—the Spirit of truth"* (***Jn 14:16-17***). This designation, *"the Spirit of truth,"* emphasizes the Spirit's role in revealing the Word of God to man. The Spirit inspired human authors to compose Scripture (***1Pet 1:10-12; 2Tim 3:16***), and gifts some believers to teach Scripture (***Rom 12:7; 1Cor 12:28; Eph 4:11***). Furthermore, in His ***John 14*** conversation with the disciples, Jesus explained that the Spirit would enable believers to understand and remember His teaching: *"The Counselor, the Holy Spirit, whom the Father will send in my name, will teach you all things and will remind you* *of everything I have said to you"* (***Jn 14:26***). Though Jesus made the promise directly to His disciples, who needed particular empowerment by the Spirit as they began their ministries and as some of them wrote books of the NT, other passages reveal that the Spirit continues to serve in a teaching role for all believers (***1Jn 2:20; 1Cor 2:9-10***).

All three elements of the Spirit's work in revealing God's Word—inspiring writers, gifting teachers, and empowering learners—stand as critical in the learning process of Jesus' followers. Like the legs of a three-legged stool, each element is necessary, and without any one of the elements the process will crumble. If we discount the divine authority of the Word, our teaching will sway back and forth with fads and opinions and will have no foundation or power. If we neglect the giftedness of teachers, thereby neglecting the role of the community in interpreting and applying the Bible, our learning grows individualistic, subjective, and unreliable.[6] If we ignore the role of the Spirit in the mind and heart of the learner, we miss the Spirit's ability to enlighten listeners and to apply the Word to their hearts so that *"it penetrates even to dividing soul and spirit, joints and marrow; it judges the thoughts and attitudes of the heart"* (**Heb 4:12**). If, on the other hand, we submit to the divine authority of the Word, facilitate teaching in the community through Spirit-gifted teachers, and trust the Spirit's work of illumination in the hearts and minds of learners, such teaching will build up the body of Christ and lead it into maturity.

Character Development

Ludwig Nommensen traveled to begin mission work with a tribe in southeast Asia. The village chief welcomed Ludwig and said, "You have two years to learn our customs and convince us you have a message worth hearing."

After two years, the tribal leader asked the missionary how Christianity differs from the moral rules and traditions of the tribe. "We already know what is right," the chief explained. "We too have laws that say we must not steal, or take our neighbor's wives, or tell lies."

[6] We will discuss this matter further in chapter 13, "Word Driven." For now, however, let us recognize, "Understanding the Bible is not a matter of private judgment. Biblical truth is corporate truth. As believers study the Bible, it is important that they draw on historical understandings of the biblical story and engage in interpreting the Bible as a corporate faith community, with an interpretation consistent with the apostolic tradition" (**Van Gelder, *Essence*, 145**).

The missionary replied, "That's true. But my God supplies the power needed to keep those laws."

This startled the chief. "Can you really teach my people to live better?"

"No, I can't," responded Ludwig. "But if they receive Jesus Christ, God will give them the strength to do what is right." The chief invited him to stay another six months, during which Ludwig preached the gospel and taught villagers how the Holy Spirit works in the lives of believers.

"You can stay as long as you want," the chief finally announced. "Your religion is better than ours, for your God walks with men and gives them strength to do the things He requires" (**Zuck, 68**).

By means of His Spirit, God walks with believers and enables them to live new lives in Christ, lives of new character, ethics, and integrity. Paul explained to the believers in Rome,

> 9*You, however, are controlled not by the sinful nature but by*
> *the Spirit, if the Spirit of God lives in you. And if anyone does not*
> *have the Spirit of Christ, he does not belong to Christ.* 10*But if*
> *Christ is in you, your body is dead because of sin, yet your spirit*
> *is alive because of righteousness.* 11*And if the Spirit of him who*
> *raised Jesus from the dead is living in you, he who raised Christ*
> *from the dead will also give life to your mortal bodies through his*
> *Spirit, who lives in you.*
>
> 12*Therefore, brothers, we have an obligation—but it is not to*
> *the sinful nature, to live according to it.* 13*For if you live according*
> *to the sinful nature, you will die; but if by the Spirit you put to*
> *death the misdeeds of the body, you will live,* 14*because those who*
> *are led by the Spirit of God are sons of God.* (***Rom 8:9-14***)

In Galatians, Paul outlined more specifically how the change from indulging the sinful nature to living by the Spirit alters a believer's character:

> 19*The acts of the sinful nature are obvious: sexual immorality,*
> *impurity and debauchery;* 20*idolatry and witchcraft; hatred, dis-*
> *cord, jealousy, fits of rage, selfish ambition, dissensions, factions*
> 21*and envy; drunkenness, orgies, and the like. I warn you, as I did*
> *before, that those who live like this will not inherit the kingdom*
> *of God.*
>
> 22*But the fruit of the Spirit is love, joy, peace, patience, kind-*
> *ness, goodness, faithfulness,* 23*gentleness and self-control. Against*
> *such things there is no law.* 24*Those who belong to Christ Jesus*
> *have crucified the sinful nature with its passions and desires.*

[25]Since we live by the Spirit, let us keep in step with the Spirit. Let us not become conceited, provoking and envying each other. (***Gal 5:19-25***)[7]

As the believer submits to the Spirit, the Spirit works in that believer to remove the acts of the sinful nature, and to replace these acts with fruit in keeping with godly character. Dwight Moody once illustrated this principle in a sermon. Before a large audience, he held an empty drinking glass. He asked, "How can I get the air out of this glass?"

One man shouted, "Suck it out with a pump!"

"That would create a vacuum and shatter the glass," Moody replied.

After numerous other suggestions, Moody smiled, picked up a pitcher of water, and filled the glass. "There," he said, "all the air is now removed." Moody continued by explaining that we cannot remove the sinfulness of our lives by pumping out a sin here or there, but by being filled with the Holy Spirit.

The Holy Spirit edifies the community by facilitating character development within the individuals of the community.

Unity

In his first canonized letter to the church in Corinth—a group sharply and hatefully divided—Paul taught the limping congregation about the Spirit-based unity that God designed in the church: *"The body is a unit, though it is made up of many parts; and though all its parts are many, they form one body. So it is with Christ. For we were all baptized by one Spirit into one body—whether Jews or Greeks, slave or free—and we were all given the one Spirit to drink"* (***1Cor 12:12-13***).

Paul explains in the following paragraphs that the church consists of individuals who serve as various parts of the body (***1Cor 12:14-31***); however, the church remains one unified body in Christ because of the Spirit who unites us. Believers hail from varying backgrounds, serve

The church remains one unified body in Christ because of the Spirit who unites us.

[7] In keeping with the purposes of this book, we should note the communal implications of the fruit of the Spirit. The matters discussed—love, joy, peace, patience, kindness, goodness, faithfulness, gentleness, and self-control—are matters that an individual lives out *in community*.

with differing gifts, and even share opposing opinions. Even so, by the power of the Spirit that dwells within them—both as individuals and as a community—believers can unite in spirit and purpose.

CONCLUSION

The Holy Spirit dwells within the church, God's community. He empowers the church to minister on behalf of the Kingdom. Though this power holds incredible potential for congregations, too many neglect it and miss the adventure and the fruit that they could enjoy.

Bill Bright used to tell of a man named Ira Yates who lived during the Depression era. Mr. Yates owned a sheep ranch in West Texas. Like many ranchers of the era, he did not make enough profit to pay his mortgage and stood in danger of losing everything. His family lived on government subsidies. He continued raising his sheep, grazing them across the rolling West Texas hills, constantly worrying how he might pay his bills.

His worries subsided, however, when executives from an oil company knocked on his door and told Yates that they suspected oil reserves might rest beneath the surface of his fields. A crew arrived soon thereafter and drilled a well that produced 80,000 barrels a day. They drilled more wells, some that produced twice as much.

The oil had been available the entire time. Yates lived in poverty for decades, however, simply because he did not realize what lay at his disposal.

God empowers His church with His Spirit that we may advance His Kingdom. Rather than neglecting or ignoring this power, may the church seek steadfastly, drink deeply, and depend entirely on the Holy Spirit.

What Do You Say?

1. What might individual believers and church communities learn from the story of John Muir, which opened this chapter?
2. Why do you think many Christians and churches avoid speaking of the Holy Spirit? How might we overcome these hesitations?
3. How did the role of the Spirit change from the OT era to the NT era?
4. Imagine that you had been among the disciples in Jerusalem on the Day of Pentecost described in *Acts 2*. How would you have felt when the Spirit descended? How do you think this experience would have changed your Christianity?
5. The chapter included this quote, often attributed to A.W. Tozer: "If the Holy Spirit was withdrawn from the church today, ninety-five percent of what we do would go on and no one would know the difference. If the Holy Spirit had been withdrawn from the New Testament church, ninety-five percent of what they did would stop, and everybody would know the difference." Do you agree or disagree, and to what extent? Can you give examples from your own experience that support his contention? In contrast and/or comparison with the church in *Acts*, what would a Spirit-empowered church look like today?
6. What role should spiritual gifts play in the life of a church community?
7. How might a believer transition from indulging the acts of the sinful nature to living by the Spirit?

CHAPTER TEN

SACRAMENTALLY PARTICIPATING

THE CROSS AND THE COVENANT EXPRESSED

Beyond Symbolism

A megachurch in the Midwest decided to approach the Lord's Supper in an unusual manner. In keeping with their casual nature, they mixed a large batch of Kool-Aid and purchased various kinds of tasty crackers, then served them in the middle of the worship service. After the service, a first-time guest approached the preacher and shook his hand. "You know what I liked best about the service?" she asked. "I liked that you stopped what you were doing and we all had snacks in the middle. That was very nice." The comment took the minister by surprise, he reports, and a heartbreaking image flashed through his mind: "This is my snack, given for you" (**Witherington, *Meal*, x-xi**).

Christ ordained baptism and the Lord's Supper as momentous expressions of our entrance into and continual commitment to our covenant with God, made possible through the cross and empty tomb. These sacred practices deserve far more than a casual attitude.

The church mentioned in the first paragraph made the mistake that many contemporary churches teeter toward. In a desire for authenticity, we create what amounts to an unwarranted, unbiblical dualism between the physical and the spiritual realms. "What really matters is the heart," we explain, inadvertently (or perhaps intentionally) minimizing anything physical. As a result, matters such as baptism and the Lord's Supper hold only trivial significance, viewed as symbols of spiritual realities and not as significant realities in themselves. It seems heretical to contemporary ears to consider something physical—a dip in a pool of water or partaking of bread and juice—as sacred.

Jesus and the NT writers, however, held a different view. God gave the church baptism as the means through which we, in faith, enter into the new covenant of Christ. He gave the Lord's Supper as a means through which we find continual nourishment in our covenant relationship with Him. If we attempt to separate these physical expressions from inward matters of the heart, we risk either overemphasizing practices such as baptism and the Lord's Supper ("It doesn't matter what's in your heart, as long as you do these physical things.") or underemphasizing them ("It doesn't matter what you do physically, as long as your heart is right.").

In contrast to this dualism, biblical faith includes the heart and the hands, the inward and the outward. Baptism and the Lord's Supper serve as *aspects* of—not just *symbols* of—biblical faith.

Participation in Jesus' Story

Jesus incarnated into the physical world. He submitted to an actual Roman cross. His dead body was laid in an actual tomb, then He literally rose from the dead. Jesus did not symbolically die and resurrect, rather the cross and the empty tomb—matters of infinite spiritual implication—happened in the physical realm.

This same cross and empty tomb serve as common threads that bind together baptism and the Lord's Supper. Through these sacred practices, we participate in the death and resurrection of Christ (***Rom 6:3-4; 1Cor 10:16***).[1] "As symbols of his story which is now our story, baptism and the Lord's Supper form the practices of commitment within the community of faith," explained Stanley Grenz. "Through

[1] I recognize that this is a theologically "loaded" statement. We will unpack it as the chapter proceeds.

these two acts we enact our faith as we symbolically reenact the story of redemption. We memorialize the events of Jesus' passion and resurrection, we bear testimony to the experience of union with Christ which we all share in the community, and we lift our sights to the grand future awaiting us as participants in the covenant community of God" (**677**). Adds N.T. Wright, "The precise point of the sacraments are that these are the moments when the story comes to life" (**"Space"**).

Through these sacred practices, we participate in the death and resurrection of Christ.

SACRAMENTS OR ORDINANCES?

Chapter titles usually come with relative ease. My attempts to title this chapter, however, left me bumfuzzled. As the paragraphs above made obvious, this chapter will address the roles of baptism and the Lord's Supper in the life of the church community. Some traditions refer to these practices as "sacraments"; other traditions refer to them as "ordinances." Either designation can spark a heated debate.

When understood correctly, however, and apart from the layers of misunderstanding and bad theology that have piled onto the terms, both designations—in their pure forms—contribute to accurate theologies of baptism and the Lord's Supper.[2]

"SACRAMENT"

In the early centuries of the church, believers in the East used the Greek term *mysterion* ("mystery") to refer to baptism and the Lord's Supper. They cited texts such as ***Ephesians 3:2-3***, where Paul speaks of administering God's grace, *"that is, the* ***mystery*** *made known by revelation"* (bold added).

Believers in the West referred to the practices with the Latin *sacramentum*—a term borrowed from the secular world in which it referred to an oath or commitment. For example, the term described the oath of obedience taken by a soldier when enlisting in the military (**Grenz, 668**). At its most basic linguistic level, "sacrament" referred to an oath of allegiance.

[2] This section relies heavily on the research of Stanley Grenz (**667-677**).

Augustine and theologians who followed him combined the concepts of *mysterion* and *sacramentum*, and used "sacrament" to refer to the mystery of God's grace. This grace, they taught, comes internally but is symbolized by external practices such as baptism and the Lord's Supper. The sacraments, they taught, give visible signs of the invisible reality.

By the Middle Ages, many Christians grew to believe that practices such as baptism and the Lord's Supper infused God's grace into participants, regardless of the participants' spiritual condition. This grace came, they believed, "so long as the recipient did not resist the working of God in the sacraments. When duly administered these acts infused grace by their very operation" (**Grenz, 669**).[3]

"Ordinance"

Martin Luther and the reformers rejected the idea that the sacraments infused the grace of God, regardless of the heart of the participant. They emphasized that a person must have faith to receive God's grace. Luther himself continued to believe that, when accepted in faith, the sacraments infused God's grace. Some of his contemporaries, however, felt Luther did not go far enough in his theology and terminology. His critics—particularly the Anabaptists—argued for a severe break from sacramentalism, including a change in terminology. They began using the term "ordinance" (derived from "to ordain") to refer to the practices.[4] This terminology emphasized that Christ Himself ordained baptism and the Lord's Supper. Believers participate not to receive an infusing of God's grace, but simply out of obedience to Christ.

Sacramentalists emphasized God's work through the sacrament—the sacraments signify outwardly what God does inwardly. Others emphasized the human side—the ordinances signify man's obedience to Christ.

[3] In time, the church recognized these seven practices as sacraments: baptism, eucharist (Lord's Supper), confirmation, penance, marriage, holy orders (ordination), and anointing of the sick (last rites). The Roman Catholic church today continues to recognize these seven.

[4] Protestants typically reduce the list of seven to two—baptism and the Lord's Supper—as these are the only two of the seven that Christ commanded.

Fusing Two Perspectives

As often occurs, those who protested an incorrect theology took their own theology too far to the opposite extreme. At one extreme, some sacramentalists ignored the human side of the sacred practices and viewed them as means by which God injects grace into participants, regardless of their faith. At the other extreme, some ignored God's involvement in baptism and the Lord's Supper and viewed them as nothing more than human acts of obedience. Both extremes hold partial truth and partial misunderstanding.

Furthermore, both terms—sacrament and ordinance—hold partial truth and partial misunderstanding. The practices relate with God's grace (sacrament), and Christ ordained them (ordinance). Neither term, however, with the baggage they have accumulated over centuries of misunderstanding, depict an accurate and complete biblical theology. The practices in and of themselves do not infuse God's grace, and they are not entirely human-centered.

A correct perspective of baptism and the Lord's Supper recognizes that through these acts human participants, in faith, meet with and participate in the death and resurrection of Christ, through which God grants grace. The practices include both divine and human involvement.

These practices include both divine and human involvement.

For example, let us consider baptism. A sacramentalist might say that the simple act of baptism, regardless of the faith of the participant, infuses God's grace into the participant. God—not people—acts in baptism. Others would respond that through baptism the participant simply obeys Christ's command, outwardly demonstrating his inward faith. People—not God—act in baptism. A biblical theology, however, recognizes that the baptism event includes both human faith and divine grace. In ***1 Peter 3:21***, Peter taught that baptism is *"the pledge of a good conscience toward God"* (human faith element), which *"saves you by the resurrection of Jesus Christ"* (divine grace element). In ***Acts 2:37-38***, Peter taught those who *"were cut to the heart"* that they should *"repent and be baptized"* (human faith element), this would bring *"forgiveness of your sins"* and *"the gift of the Holy Spirit"* (divine grace element).

We should, therefore, hold to the original meaning of *sacramentum*, a pledge of obedience, and to the term's evolution when it gained the influence of *mysterion* and the mystery of God's grace. The later evolution of "sacrament," however, where it referred to an infusing of God's grace into a participant regardless of the participant's faith, holds no place in a biblical theology.

Moreover, we should hold to the idea of obedience to what Christ has ordained, emphasized in the use of "ordinance." We should not, on the other hand, view the practices only as acts of obedience, devoid of God's grace or involvement.

In the end, I decided to title this chapter "Sacramentally Participating" because such a title includes both the mystery of God's grace and the obedient participation of the believer.

CHRISTIAN BAPTISM

I chose to follow Christ and submit to baptism as a nine-year-old. On a Wednesday evening, I wore what I considered my very best clothes to church—a Dallas Cowboy T-shirt, blue jeans with a Dallas Cowboy patch on back, a belt with Cowboys belt-buckle, and tennis shoes with the Cowboy's emblem on the side. I sat with my mother in the adult service that night, and at the end of the service, during the second verse of "Just As I Am," I leapt into the aisle, and virtually ran to the front. My father waited with a tear in his eye. When the music stopped, my father asked me to repeat a confession of my faith. I stood tall—nervous, but tall—and spoke the words with full conviction and a cracking voice: "I believe that Jesus is the Christ the Son of the Living God." My father and I then changed clothes and descended the stairs into the baptistery, where he immersed me into Jesus Christ. My mother, with misty eyes, waited at the top of the stairs with a towel.

We should not view the practices only as acts of obedience, devoid of God's grace or involvement.

I will never forget the rush of the water over me, the scent of chlorine on the robes, and the embrace of my mother when I reached the top of the stairs. Even as a nine-year-old, I knew that something significant had changed in that moment.

Churches across the world include baptism as a significant part of their faith and practice. Why do we place such emphasis on baptism?

Jewish Backgrounds

To understand Christian baptism, we must begin by exploring its Jewish backgrounds.

The OT commanded certain ritual cleansings that may have served as predecessors to Christian baptism. For example, God commanded the high priest to bathe himself before donning, and after removing, the sacred garments on the Day of Atonement (***Lev 16:4,24***). Also on the Day of Atonement, *"The man who releases the goat as a scapegoat must wash his clothes and bathe himself with water; afterward he may come into the camp"* (***Lev 16:26***). Among other situations, the OT law commanded cleansings when a person had overcome a skin disease (***Lev 14:8***), after sexual intercourse (***Lev 15:18***), after eating anything found dead (***Lev 17:15***), and after touching anything unclean (***Lev 22:6***).

Beginning around the second century BC, some zealous Jews who held great passion for purity—including those who lived in the Qumran community—emphasized ritual washings as a part of their quest for holiness. Individuals submitted to baptism to indicate repentance of their sins and a commitment to live obediently. The Qumran community lived in the Jordan River valley, so many such baptisms took place in the Jordan River.

In a limited sense, the ministry of John the Baptist appears to have grown out of this context. Before too closely identifying John's baptism with these predecessors, however, we should note that the two held significant differences. Those of the Qumran community, for example, often "baptized" themselves three times a day (**Beasley-Murray, *Baptism*, 15**).[5] John's baptism appears to have been more decisive and not repeated multiple times. Furthermore, in Qumran and other Jewish baptisms, people dipped themselves under water. John's baptism differed in that the prophet did the dipping. "That key difference made clear the meaning of John's action: God was offering to cleanse his people from that which they could not wash away themselves: their sin" (**Weatherly, 5**).

Despite these differences, when NT preachers taught of baptism, their listeners had at least some familiarity with the concept.

[5] A person's *first* baptism in such communities involved more ceremony and significance, such as a strict examination by the community elders. Later baptisms, however—such as the three-a-day described here—involved far less ceremony.

John the Baptist and Jesus' Baptism

Baptism first appears in the NT through John's ministry. Mark explains, *"John came, baptizing in the desert region and preaching a baptism of repentance for the forgiveness of sins"* (***Mk 1:4***). Baptism held such prominence in John's ministry that he earned the nickname, "John the Baptist." John's baptism did not yet contain all the fullness of Christian baptism: baptism into the death, burial, and resurrection of Christ (***Rom 6:3-4***), and baptism that includes the granting of the Holy Spirit (***Acts 2:38; 19:1-6***). His baptism did, however, provide a significant step forward from those of Qumran. In his baptism ministry, John pointed to and prepared his followers for the immediate coming of the Messiah and His Kingdom. *"Repent,"* John preached, *"for the kingdom of heaven is near"* (***Mt 3:2***). Mark explains about John, *"This was his message: 'After me will come one more powerful than I, the thongs of whose sandals I am not worthy to stoop down and untie. I baptize you with water, but he will baptize you with the Holy Spirit'"* (***Mk 1:7-8***).

One day, while John ministered, Jesus approached him. John exclaimed, *"Look, the Lamb of God, who takes away the sin of the world!"* (***Jn 1:29***). Then John, though with feelings of reluctance and inadequacy, baptized Jesus in the Jordan River. Upon Jesus' baptism, *"heaven was opened, and he saw the Spirit of God descending like a dove and lighting on him. And a voice from heaven said, 'This is my Son, whom I love; with him I am well pleased'"* (***Mt 3:16-17***).

Why did Jesus submit to baptism? As a sinless man, He did not need to repent nor to seek forgiveness. Jesus provided this explanation to John, *"It is proper for us to do this to fulfill all righteousness"* (***Mt 3:15***). While others submitted to John's baptism in repentance and in preparation for the Messiah, Jesus submitted as the Messiah committing Himself to obediently following the path God laid out for Him (*"to fulfill all righteousness"*). Upon this submission, the Spirit came upon Jesus like a dove and the Father expressed His pleasure (***Mt 3:16-17***)—all three persons of the Trinity joined in the glorious inauguration of the Messiah's ministry.

Jesus as Messiah submitted to obediently following the path God laid out for Him.

The NT indicates that Jesus and His disciples continued to baptize in conjunction with their ministry (***Jn 3:22,26; 4:1***), but gives little indication concerning the nature of this baptism. Presumably, this baptism functioned similarly to John's—as a baptism of repentance and forgiveness in preparation for the coming kingdom (***Mk 1:4; Mt 3:2***).

The Role of Baptism in the New Covenant

Baptism gained an even deeper meaning after Jesus' earthly ministry, playing a significant role in the new covenant Jesus' established with His death and resurrection. Baptism continued to involve repentance and forgiveness, as it did previously, but it also gained the force of the cross and empty tomb, and the new covenant Jesus enacted through them.

In the Great Commission (***Mt 28:19***), Jesus instructed His disciples to baptize those who are becoming followers. Peter, similarly, refers to baptism as *"a pledge of a good conscience toward God"* (***1Pet 3:21***). Baptism, then, in the very least, expresses a person's intent to follow Jesus.

Additionally, the NT connects baptism with the grace of God made possible through the cross of Jesus. The NT expresses this connection in various ways. In baptism comes:

- Forgiveness of sin (***Acts 2:38***)
- Washing away of sin (***Acts 22:16***)
- Release from the power of sin (***Col 2:11-15***)
- Death to sin (***Rom 6:11a***)
- Life in Christ (***Rom 6:11b***)
- Union with Christ (***Gal 3:27***)
- Union with Christ's death and resurrection (***Rom 6:3-5***)
- Reception of the Holy Spirit (***Acts 2:38***)
- Entrance into the kingdom (***Jn 3:5***)
- Connection with the church (***1Cor 12:13***)
- Reception of salvation (***1Pet 3:21***)

In baptism, summarizes John Castelein, God acts "to bestow on the repentant believer the spiritual blessings achieved by Jesus Christ in his voluntary sacrifice for our sins on the cross." The person "submits to a physical action in baptism," and "appropriates for himself or herself the promises of God's Word" (130-131).

Though by itself baptism does not save, it holds a significant place in the process.

Baptism, by itself, does not save.

Jesus saves by the grace of the cross. In baptism, as a part of faith and accompanied by repentance, we respond to Jesus' gift. Though by itself baptism does not save, it does hold a significant place in the conversion process. Jon Weatherly asserts, "The scholarly community reflects a growing, significant convergence of opinion on baptism, one that crosses denominational lines. The thrust of the consensus is this: In its biblical setting, baptism belonged in the context of conversion. Early Christians understood that a person should be baptized *when becoming a Christian,* not before or after" (4).

Understanding the role of baptism in salvation requires grasping the relationship between baptism and faith; the NT links the two in a significant manner. In ***Galatians 3***, for example, Paul explains to his readers, *"You are all sons of God through faith in Christ Jesus, for all of you who were baptized into Christ have clothed yourselves with Christ"* (***3:26-27***). Paul connects *"faith in Christ Jesus"* with *"baptized into Christ"* and *"clothed yourselves with Christ."* Elsewhere Paul speaks of his readers *"having been buried with him in baptism and raised with him through your faith in the power of God"* (***Col 2:12***). Baptism and faith interweave. Baptism without faith serves no spiritual purpose; to think otherwise would constitute the misunderstanding of the sacrament discussed above, where the act infuses grace regardless of the faith of the recipient. Rightly understood, genuine faith includes baptism as a part of its initial expression. This understanding helps reconcile passages such as ***1 Peter 3:21***, which speaks of *"the baptism that now saves you"*; and ***Ephesians 2:8***, *"It is by grace you have been saved, through faith."* The salvation process includes baptism and faith intertwined. New Testament writers assumed one with the other. Faith is not merely a preparatory step that precedes baptism, nor does faith come as a result of baptism. Instead, genuine faith includes baptism.

Rightly understood, genuine faith includes baptism as a part of its initial expression.

Some draw an analogy between baptism and a contemporary wedding. Marriages begin with a ceremony. Much preparation precedes the wedding: the couple gets to know one another, commit their love, and make plans. Much will occur after the wedding: continued commitment, growth in love, and a deepening of the relationship. Even so, the wedding ceremony serves as the benchmark. At this point, on this day, at the moment when the couple exchanges vows, everything changes. The ceremony cements the relationship: two become one.

God gave baptism as a ceremony though which we unite with Him. A great deal precedes baptism, a lifetime of growth will occur afterward, but the baptism provides the benchmark of a cemented relationship. At this point everything changes.

Uniting with Christ's Death and Resurrection

The most extensive teaching about baptism in the NT occurs in ***Romans 6***. Like most NT teaching about baptism, these verses argue *from,* not *for,* baptism: Paul assumes his readers already understand the doctrine of baptism (in fact, he assumes they have already been baptized), and builds from that doctrine to teach them how to live righteously. Even so, these verses offer a peek into the doctrine that includes powerful and memorable images:

> [1]*What shall we say, then? Shall we go on sinning so that grace may increase?* [2]*By no means! We died to sin; how can we live in it any longer?* [3]*Or don't you know that all of us who were baptized into Christ Jesus were baptized into his death?* [4]*We were therefore buried with him through baptism into death in order that, just as Christ was raised from the dead through the glory of the Father, we too may live a new life.*
>
> [5]*If we have been united with him like this in his death, we will certainly also be united with him in his resurrection.* [6]*For we know that our old self was crucified with him so that the body of sin might be done away with, that we should no longer be slaves to sin—* [7]*because anyone who has died has been freed from sin.* (***Rom 6:1-7***)

In baptism we unite with Christ in His death and resurrection. Often when discussing this passage, teachers focus only on the symbolic parallel between Christ's death and our own spiritual deaths: "Like Christ died on the cross, so in baptism we die to our old selves and sins"—like Christ died, we similarly die spiritually. While we do, indeed, die to sin (***Rom 6:2***), by thinking only of our own spiritual deaths, and a symbolic parallel with the cross, we miss the significant reality that *"We were baptized **into his** death. . . . Our old self was crucified **with Him**"* (***Rom 6:3,6***, bold added). The death of our sins occurred on Golgotha, two thousand years ago. In baptism, we unite with that death and thereby receive what Christ's crucifixion effected—the death of our sins; and we receive what His resurrection effected—new life in Him. This happens actually in baptism, not just symbolically. Baptism unites us with Christ's death and resurrection; through baptism we identify ourselves—physically, actually, and resolutely—with the cross of Christ. Baptism, therefore, is not merely symbolic. "For Paul," explains David Smith, "what baptism symbolizes really occurs, and it occurs through the ordinance of baptism" (**274**).

Beyond just symbolism—beyond "an outward expression of an inward commitment"—baptism itself, when weaved together with faith, unites the believer with Christ.

Baptism as Related to Church Community

Baptism ushers new believers into covenant with Jesus Christ; and, by necessary implication, into Christ's body—the church. Believers do not submit to baptism into a particular congregation, as though someone might say, "I was baptized into Community Christian Church." We submit to baptism into Christ. Coming "into Christ," however, includes our incorporation into His universal church.

Baptism does not, therefore, involve only a believer and God. The NT makes clear that baptism carries significant communal implications. It plays a role in unifying believers (***Eph 4:5***), and making us *"all sons of God through faith in Christ Jesus,"* where *"there is neither Jew nor Greek, slave nor free, male nor female, for you are all one in Christ Jesus"* (***Gal 3:26,28***), *"for we were all baptized by one Spirit into one body"* (***1Cor 12:13***). Those baptized enter a new kind of community with members jointly committed to Christ and to one another. Matters which previously divided individuals, such as ethnic background, gender, or social rank, hold no standing among the community of the baptized.

Philip Yancey describes a particular baptism service in which he participated while a member of the LaSalle Street Church in Chicago. The congregation gathered on the shore of the always frigid Lake Michigan, alongside of roller skaters, bikers, and sunbathers. Yancey explains,

> In the midst of this beachfront scene, thirteen baptismal candidates lined up to speak. There were two young stockbrokers, husband and wife, who said they wanted to 'identify with Christ more publically.' A woman of Cuban descent spoke, dressed in all white. A tall, bronzed man said he had

been an agnostic until six months ago. An aspiring opera singer admitted she had just decided to seek baptism that morning and asked for prayer because she hates cold water. An eighty-five-year-old black woman had asked to be immersed against her doctor's advice ("Strangest request I ever heard," he said). A real estate investor, a pregnant woman, a medical student. . . .

> The bodies were dipped rather quickly. Each baptismal candidate emerged from the water trembling and goosepimply, eyes bright and large from the cold. Those of us on shore greeted them with hugs, and as a result wet spots soon appeared on our chests. 'Welcome to the Body of Christ,' we said. . . .

> That small scene at the beach, worked out before a curious crowd, became for me a symbol of the alternative society that Jesus inaugurated on earth so long ago. Chicago's beaches have their own pecking order: Hispanics to the north, yuppies near the lifeguard tower, gays by the rocks. Like gathers with like, families stick together. This small community, though, encompassed stockbrokers and Cubans, an opera singer, and an eighty-five-year-old granddaughter of slaves. (***Church*, 38-40**)

Baptism provides the benchmark when everything changes: a new believer's relationship with God and His covenant, and that new believer's relationship with the body of Christ, the church.

Word Study on *Baptizo* (baptize)[6]

The English term "baptize" transliterates—notably not translates—from the Greek verb *baptizo*, which carries the image of immersing, plunging, dipping, or sinking. The term originally described the dying of cloth, for example, when the worker dipped the cloth into a container of colored dye. A person walking in a river, with the water rising to his or her waist, was "baptized" up to the waist. A sinking boat was "baptized" when it had fully fallen beneath the surface of the water. Metaphorically, *baptizo* could refer to being overwhelmed or engulfed in something, such as debt or sorrow. Various denotations and connotations of the term fall

[6] Sources consulted: "Baptizo" in Bauer, *A Greek-English Lexicon of the New Testament and Other Early Christian Literature*, "Baptizo," by Spiros Zodhiates; "Believers' Baptism as the Biblical Occasion of Salvation," by John Castelein; *All God's People*, by David Smith (**380-383**).

within the same semantic domain—being completely surrounded by and engulfed in something.

Early Christians—and some of their Jewish predecessors—baptized new believers in water as a part of their repentance and faith. Ancient documents use *baptizo* to describe this action. Other Greek terms meant "pouring" or "sprinkling," but the NT never uses these terms to describe Christian baptism. Evidence suggests that in first-century baptisms, participants removed their clothes and jewelry, and women loosened their hair, all to ensure that the water drenched the participant's entire body.

Scholars of various faith traditions generally acknowledge that early Christians practiced full immersion. Catholic scholar Joseph Egan explained, "When the New Testament writers referred to baptism . . . their experience of baptism was in the context of . . . being baptized through immersion in water in the powerful name of Jesus." And, Karl Barth taught, "The Greek word *Baptizo* and the German word *taugen* (from *Tiefe*, depth), originally and properly describe the process by which a man or an object is completely immersed in water and then withdrawn from it again. . . . One can hardly deny that baptism was carried out as immersion" (**D. Smith, 381**).

In the second century, the *Didache* allowed for pouring when immersion was not possible, such as when no pools of water were available or when a person laid sick in bed. Such pouring bore the label "clinical baptism" ("clinical" derives from the Greek term for "bed"). For a time, the church did not recognize clinical baptisms as fully equivalent to immersion, and prevented recipients of clinical baptisms from partaking of the Lord's Supper until they also submitted to immersion.

Sprinkling and pouring gained official recognition as alternative, equivalent forms of baptism at the Council of Ravenna in 1311.

Churches today who practice immersion do so because of (1) the linguistic background of *baptizo*, (2) the testimony of church history concerning first-century baptisms, and (3) the imagery in passages such as ***Romans 6*** that parallel baptism with the death, burial, and resurrection of Christ.

Churches who practice sprinkling or pouring believe (1) *baptizo* has a wider linguistic range that would allow for pouring or sprinkling, and/or (2) the mode of baptism is not significant, and/or (3) sprinkling or pouring maintain the essence of the idea behind baptism—cleansing or washing.

THE LORD'S SUPPER

Baptism—a one-time event—marks the believer's entrance into the new covenant with Christ and His church. The Lord's Supper—an ongoing practice—enables the believer's continuing fellowship in covenant with Christ and His church.

The Lord enacted this ceremony of communion to provide an ongoing reminder of the covenant, and an ongoing means of spiritual nourishment and refreshment for His followers. While eating the Passover meal with His disciples on the evening before His crucifixion,

> [26]*Jesus took bread, gave thanks and broke it, and gave it to his disciples, saying, "Take and eat; this is my body."* [27]*Then he took the cup, gave thanks and offered it to them, saying, "Drink from it, all of you.* [28]*This is my blood of the covenant, which is poured out for many for the forgiveness of sins."* (***Mt 26:26-28***; see p. 262 for a sidebar on the Passover background of the Lord's Supper)

"Do this," Jesus commanded, *"in remembrance of me"* (***1Cor 11:24-25***).

The early church *"devoted themselves . . . to the breaking of bread"* (***Acts 2:42***). These believers observed the Lord's Supper in conjunction with a fellowship meal, the *agape* feast. Just as Jesus established the ceremony in the upper room in Jerusalem in conjunction with a celebratory feast, so the early believers gathered on the first day of the week, in celebration of Jesus' resurrection, and shared a meal. As a part of this meal—in fact, as the focal point of this meal—they shared a loaf of bread in remembrance of Jesus' body, and shared a cup in remembrance of His blood.

AN ACT OF REMEMBRANCE

The Lord's Supper leads participants to remember Jesus' crucifixion. "The bread and juice are distinct and yet complementary symbols of Christ's death," explains Johnny Pressley. "The broken bread brings to mind the tearing of Christ's body and the suffering that would accompany that ordeal. The poured juice brings to mind the flow of blood from his body, the ending of his life, and the presentation of his blood before God as an atonement" (NACC workshop).

Teachers have long known the value of providing students with tangible reminders of lessons taught. Likewise, throughout the Bible God uses tangible means such as the rainbow, animal sacrifices, and the lamb eaten at Passover, to remind His followers of His truths and

His work among His people. The Lord's Supper invites participants to hold and taste bread, broken from a loaf, and to look upon and drink from a cup of juice—Jesus' body broken, His blood shed.

The ceremony of remembrance holds such significance that Paul warned the believers in Corinth,

> [27]*Whoever eats the bread or drinks the cup of the Lord in an unworthy manner will be guilty of sinning against the body and blood of the Lord.* [28]*A man ought to examine himself before he eats of the bread and drinks of the cup.* [29]*For anyone who eats and drinks without recognizing the body of the Lord eats and drinks judgment on himself.* [30]*That is why many among you are weak and sick, and a number of you have fallen asleep.* (**1Cor 11:27-30**)

Paul's phrase *"an unworthy manner"* finds further definition in the subsequent phrase *"without recognizing the body of the Lord"* (**1Cor 11:29**). Scholars tend to interpret the latter phrase in one of two ways. First, *"the body of the Lord"* may refer to the physical body of Christ that soldiers nailed to the cross. The phrase's immediate context points toward this interpretation; in the previous paragraph, Paul recounted Christ's words in the upper room where He called followers to partake in remembrance of his broken body and spilled blood. ***First Corinthians 11:29*** warns, from this perspective, of "inadequate, inappropriate eating and drinking, in a manner that is unsuited to it and not in harmony with it. It is a question of respect for the true character of what is here called the bread and cup of the Lord, i.e., the sanctity of his table fellowship (cf. ***1 Cor. 10:21***)," explains Herman Ridderbos. The problem lies in "not recognizing the offering in its separateness and sanctity and not recognizing the sacrifice of Christ itself" (**426**).

A scene from the movie *Saving Private Ryan* illustrates an inadequate recognition of sacrifice. The movie depicts a small band of American soldiers in France searching for Private James Ryan in the days following D-day. In one particular scene, these soldiers sit in an open tent and sort through piles of dog tags from dead soldiers to see if Ryan had been killed. While they sort, they laugh and make jokes. Meanwhile, a company of airborne soldiers marches by and witnesses the disrespectful handling of the dog tags. The glares from the silent, marching airborne soldiers spoke volumes: these emblems represented the sacrifices of their fellow soldiers, and they deserved respect and admiration.

The reader can almost feel Paul's glare toward the church in Corinth for treating the Lord's Supper with a flippant attitude. The memory of the cross demands reverence.

The memory of the cross demands reverence.

An Act of Community

A second way that some scholars interpret that phrase *"the body of the Lord"* (***1Cor 11:29***) connects the phrase, not with the physical body of Christ on the cross, but with the church. These scholars explain that when Paul refers to the physical body of Christ on the cross, he typically speaks of both the body and the blood (as in ***1Cor 11:27***). When he uses only the term "body," however, Paul typically refers to the church (as in ***1Cor 10:17*** and ***12:12-27***). Furthermore, the wider context, including ***1 Corinthians 11:17-34***, demonstrates that the problem in Corinth related to their lack of unity while approaching the Lord's Supper—not a lack of focus on Christ, but on the unity of Christ's church. Finally, this interpretation better fits Paul's conclusion to the entire section: *"So then, my brothers, when you come together to eat, wait for each other. If anyone is hungry, he should eat at home, so that when you meet together it may not result in judgment"* (***1Cor 11:33-34***). This *"judgment"* in **verse 34** points back to ***verse 29***. "Judgment" (***vv. 29 and 34***) comes when one *"eats and drinks without recognizing the body of the Lord"* (***v. 29***), a recognition which includes waiting for one another *"when you come together to eat"* (***v. 34***).

To review, some scholars believe that when Paul spoke of participating in the Lord's Supper *"in an unworthy manner . . . without recognizing the body of the Lord"* (***1Cor 11:27,29***), he warned against approaching the ceremony in a flippant manner, not revering the sacrifice of Christ on the cross. Other scholars believe Paul warned against approaching the Lord's Supper while in disunity with other believers.

Could not Paul have utilized a play on the term "body" that incorporates both interpretations? Throughout this section of ***1 Corinthians***, Paul weaves in and out of discussion of church unity and of the crucifixion of Christ. He uses the term "body" in both contexts, forcing his readers to view their unity in light of Christ's sacrifice. A clear example of this interplay occurs in ***1 Corinthians 10***, just a chapter before the verse in question: *"Is not the cup of thanksgiving for which we give thanks a participation in the blood of Christ? And is not the bread that we break a participation in the* ***body*** *of Christ? Because there is one loaf, we, who are many, are one* ***body****, for we all partake of the one loaf"* (***1Cor 10:16-17***, bold added). In its first occurrence (***10:16***), "body" refers to the physical body of Christ on the cross. In its second occurrence, "body" refers to the unified community of believers. Paul deliberately incorporates both meanings—Christ's physical body, and the church—into the same teaching. This interplay provides a Christ-centered basis for the church's unity.

The particular problem in Corinth, which Paul confronted in the passage under discussion (***1Cor 11:17-34***), grew from a common practice in the NT era. The church celebrated the Lord's Supper as a part of a larger meal. Apparently the more affluent church members in Corinth arrived early on Sunday evenings—perhaps they did not have to work as long as the poorer members (Sunday was a work day). Perhaps these wealthier members brought most of the food to the meal, and began feasting before the poorer members arrived. When the poorer members arrived, therefore, carrying their meager contributions to the meal, little of the good food remained. Furthermore, the wealthy apparently became intoxicated. Paul summarized the situation, *"When you come together, it is not the Lord's Supper you eat, for as you eat, each of you goes ahead without waiting for anybody else. One remains hungry, another gets drunk"* (***1Cor 11:20-21***). Feasts in the Greco-Roman world commonly displayed this kind of social class distinction (**Witherington, *Meal*, 36**). For Christians, however, this distinction should dissolve in our unity in Christ, where *"there is neither Jew nor Greek, slave nor free, male nor female, for you are all one in Christ Jesus"* (***Gal 3:26-28***).

Paul rebuked the Corinthian believers (***1Cor 11:22***), reminded them of the centrality of Christ's death to the Lord's Supper (***1Cor 11:23-26***), then warned them to examine themselves before partaking of the Lord's Supper lest they participate *"in an unworthy manner"* (***1Cor 11:27-28***). *"For,"* Paul explained, *"anyone who eats and drinks without recognizing the body of the Lord eats and drinks judgment on himself"* (***1Cor 11:29***).

While partaking of the Lord's Supper, believers must recognize the physical body and blood that Christ sacrificed on the cross. And, they must recognize the church body made possible by that sacrifice.

A correct theology of the Lord's Supper, therefore, includes both a vertical element (recognizing Christ and His cross) and a horizontal element (recognizing the church). "For Paul," explains Leonard Vander Zee, "the Lord's Supper binds the participants together with Christ and with each other into a single body. This bond is not a mere symbol but actually points to the deepest reality of community" (**159**). The Lord's Supper does not involve only the individual believer and God—this sense grows from contemporary individualism, not from the NT. As the NT presents it, the Lord's Supper involves individuals in community, and their relationships with God and with one another.

Correct theology of the Lord's Supper includes a vertical element and a horizontal element.

Adds Herman Ridderbos,

> The Supper is no personal affair between the individual believer and Christ. It is the covenant meal. The congregational meal *par excellence*. And it points to the sacrifice made by Christ, the reconciliation that has taken place in his blood, as the only ground of this communion between God and his people and of the unity of the church. Only in the eating of the body thus understood and in the drinking of this cup representing the reconciling power of his blood is the church one. In that sense, therefore, the Supper is the foundation and criterion for the unity of the church as the new people of God. (**423**)

The congregation in which my family and I currently participate, Farragut Christian Church in Knoxville, Tennessee, attempts to emphasize this communal element of the Lord's Supper in the way we partake. Like some other churches, when individuals receive the communion elements, we hold them until everyone has been served. Then we partake together. The NT does not prescribe this particular approach, but I have grown to appreciate it. This approach joins—as did Paul in ***1 Corinthians 10 and 11***—the vertical and horizontal aspects of the Lord's Supper. We, the church—the body of Christ—partake in unity with one another, remembering the physical body of Christ sacrificed on the cross.

One of the most powerful ceremonies of the Lord's Supper in which I have participated occurred several years ago at the North American Christian Convention, held that year in the Hoosier Dome in Indianapolis. On the Sunday evening of the convention, more than forty thousand believers shared together in the Lord's Supper. In addition to believers gathered in Indianapolis, convention organizers had arranged for believers from all over the world, via satellite video, to partake together at the same time. Images of these believers from around the earth appeared on the giant video screen in Indianapolis. I recall feeling a connection with the global church—the community of Christ that stretches across oceans, languages, and ethnicities—beyond what I had ever sensed before. I sensed this connection while sharing in the Lord's Supper.

Four Views Concerning the Elements of the Lord's Supper[7]

1. Transubstantiation: The elements change in substance to the literal body and blood of Christ. By partaking, one ingests the grace of the cross. The Roman Catholic church holds this view.
2. Consubstantiation: While the substance of the elements do not change, the elements do contain the literal body and blood of Christ, coexisting with the bread and juice. This view is often connected to the teaching of Martin Luther (though he never used the term "consubstantiation").
3. Dynamic Presence: The elements do not literally change into nor contain the literal body and blood of Christ. The body and blood do, however, have a dynamic presence because the ceremony includes the transcendent and miraculous presence of Christ. He is fully present during the ceremony. Many in the Reformed tradition hold this view.
4. Symbolic: The elements simply symbolize Christ's body and blood. And, Christ is not present in the ceremony in any manner other than how He is present always. The ceremony leads those who partake to remember the cross and to recommit themselves to living faithfully until He returns. Many evangelicals hold this view.

[7] Modified from discussion in **D. Smith, 385-387**. It is granted that this is a simplification of complex issues.

An Act of Participation

One of the more mysterious and exciting aspects of the Lord's Supper appears in Paul's question to the Corinthian believers, "Is not the cup of thanksgiving for which we give thanks a participation in the blood of Christ? And is not the bread that we break a participation in the body of Christ?" (***1Cor 10:16***). Medford Jones commented on this thrilling concept:

> Without worrying about the doctrine of transubstantiation, note that Jesus took the cup and simply said, 'This is my blood of the new covenant.' Then, consider the impact of partaking of the cup when Paul says that it is a 'participation' in the blood of Christ. It is interesting that we have no record of Jesus or any apostle ever interpreting these statements. They did not say the cup and the loaf were 'symbols' or 'emblematic.' They simply quoted, 'This is my body,' and 'this is my blood.' The startling reality is that, by the grace of God, whenever Christians put the cup to lip they are closer to the blood of Christ than the spike driving soldier on Golgotha. When Christians hear the crunch of the loaf they should hear the hammer blows at Calvary. It is not possible for the sincere Christian to come to the table of the Lord and escape the crisis as they participate. (**148-149**)

When Jesus commanded His followers to partake *"in remembrance"* of Him (***1Cor 11:24-25***), this instruction called for more than a mental recollection of facts, as one might mindlessly quote the alphabet or the names of the American Presidents. Jesus calls us to deeply consider, contemplate, and meditate upon Him and His crucifixion. Such "remembrance," more than just a mental exercise, enables participation in Jesus' sacrifice.

The Passover meal—which Jesus celebrated with His disciples when He established the Lord's Supper—provides a picture of this kind of deep recollection. Traditionally, the Passover meal begins with a child asking, "Why is this night special above all other nights?" The family patriarch responds by telling of God's redemption of ancient Jews from Egypt. Notably, the patriarch tells the story in first person: "*We* were Pharaoh's slaves in Egypt . . . God brought *us* forth." Though the actual events took place centuries before, Jewish families relive them through the Passover. The annual Passover feast enables them to participate in the historical Passover event.

Similarly, through the Lord's Supper, Christians participate in the body and blood of Christ.

The Lord's Supper and the Passover Meal[8]

Jesus established the Lord's Supper during a Passover meal He shared with the disciples (***Mt 26:17-19; Lk 22:15***). This fact adds depth to our understanding of what occurred on that particular evening. At the Passover, participants commemorated and renewed the Mosaic covenant; Jesus used the occasion to establish, He explained, *"the new covenant in my blood"* (***Lk 22:20***). Furthermore, the Passover required the sacrifice and eating of a lamb to recall the lambs sacrificed during the last plague in Egypt, and the lambs' blood smeared across Jewish doorposts to save them from the plague; Jesus is the Lamb of God whose blood saves us. At the Passover, the family patriarch explained each part of the meal; Jesus took the elements of bread and wine and explained, *"This is my body. . . . This is my blood"* (***Lk 22:19-20***).

The Passover meal occurred in four phases:

1. A preliminary course: a spoken blessing, some food, the first cup of wine (cup of consecration), and the placing of the main course on the table.
2. The Passover liturgy: explanation of the elements included in the ceremony, recitation of the first part of the Hallel (***Pss 111–113***), and the second cup of wine (cup of proclamation).
3. The main meal: the lamb, blessing of the unleavened bread (the first bread eaten), and the blessing of the third cup of wine (the cup of thanksgiving).
4. The conclusion: additional food, the second part of the Hallel (***Pss 114–118***), and the fourth cup of wine (cup of consummation).

By assessing Jesus' words at the Last Supper, we can make an educated guess concerning where His words fell in the Passover ceremony. Mark reports, *"While they were eating, He took some bread, and after a blessing He broke it, and gave it to them, and said, 'Take it; this is My body'"* (***14:22***, NASB). The blessing and partaking of bread occurred during the third portion of the meal.

[8] Sources consulted: "The Daily and Weekly Worship of the Primitive Church: Part 2," by Roger Beckwith; *What the Bible Says about the Lord's Supper,* by Andrew Paris (**31-46**); *Christ, Baptism, and the Lord's Supper,* by Leonard J. Vander Zee (**144-150**); and *All God's People,* by David Smith (**384-385**).

Likewise, when Jesus connected a cup of wine with His blood, it also probably occurred during this third segment. Luke and Paul both report that Jesus took the cup ***"after supper"*** (***Lk 22:20; 1Cor 11:25***)—presumably after the main course—and Paul refers to it as *"the cup of thanksgiving"* (***1Cor 10:16***).

(For additional explanation of the Passover, see chapter four.)

An Act of Ongoing Proclamation

The multifaceted ceremony of the Lord's Supper also provides one means by which believers proclaim the gospel of Christ. *"Whenever you eat this bread and drink this cup,"* wrote Paul, *"you proclaim the Lord's death until he comes"* (***1Cor 11:26***). Paul's teaching does not imply that churches should always include preaching alongside of the Lord's Supper (not that this is a bad idea, by any means); rather, the Lord's Supper itself *is* proclamation. Through partaking of the emblems, Christians announce Jesus' Lordship, and that through His cross and resurrection He reigns victorious.

Though the Lord's Supper includes a somber element—recalling the death and agony of Christ—this somberness must not dominate the atmosphere. Early believers partook on the first day of the week to commemorate Jesus' resurrection. They shared in the Lord's Supper as a part of a celebratory, communal meal. Many believers refer to the ceremony as the Eucharist ("thanksgiving"). The death and resurrection of Christ changed history, in an abundantly good way. And, in addition to changing history, it changed our present and our future. N.T. Wright explains concerning ***1 Corinthians 11:26*** (quoted above), "The present moment ('whenever') somehow holds together the . . . past event ('the Lord's death') and the great future when God's world will be remade under Jesus' loving rule ('until he comes'). Past and future come rushing together into the present, pouring an ocean of meaning into the little bottle of 'now'" (***Meal*, 47**).

The death and resurrection of Christ changed history, in an abundantly good way.

The final phrase in ***1 Corinthians 11:26***, *"until he comes,"* assumes believers will continually, repeatedly proclaim Christ through the

Lord's Supper, until the day He returns. Though the NT does not command a particular cycle (such as weekly, quarterly, or annually), it does imply that the practice should hold an ongoing, valuable place in church life. The church in the NT era and in the following decades partook on the first day of each week, as noted above, in celebration of the resurrection. Though the NT does not command such a practice, it makes good sense: Why would the church want to gather to worship Christ without worshiping Him in the manner He asks?

The most common objection to weekly observance of the Lord's Supper involves a fear that the ceremony would grow too routine and mundane. In response: I recall talking with a couple on their fiftieth wedding anniversary. Both had retired, remained in fairly good health, and enjoyed spending this season of their lives together. Their relationship exhibited warmth and love. They often held hands, whispered in one another's ears, and laughed together. At the party to celebrate their golden anniversary, I asked the wife the question she had probably fielded several times that day, "What's your secret?" Despite my lack of originality, she smiled—well, she glowed—as she responded, "Every day of our marriage, for fifty years, he has given me a kiss and told me that he loves me." Every day. Had this practice grown routine and mundane for this wife? Had she tired of hearing those words, of tasting that kiss?

In a devoted relationship, expressions of love never grow tiresome. This holds true of a loving relationship with God, and the Lord's Supper.

An Act of Communing

We often refer to the Lord's Supper as a memorial—this designation holds partial truth. The ceremony does memorialize the cross of Christ. Memorials, however, point only to things in the past: past events or people who have died. The Lord's Supper holds a significant difference from just a memorial, however, because the one we remember still lives. "The Lord's Supper was no mere recalling of a memory from the past," explained C.F.D. Moule, "nor only a looking forward to the future, but a potent means of present contact with the risen Lord" (**36**).

The living Christ hosts the Supper. He invites us to join Him. When we partake—when we deliberately, consciously commune with

Him—our focus on His presence magnifies our intimacy with Him. Ben Witherington writes, "The Lord's Supper should be seen as a chance for a close encounter with Jesus, a chance for a moment of clarity and recognition in one's life that Christ comes to meet us, bless us, forgive us, over and over again, and that *we can and must actively participate in this joyful event.* It is not about magical rituals or medicinal elements; it's about the living presence of Christ" (***Meal*, 134**).

A well-known painting pictures a widow and her daughter standing at the Vietnam Veterans Memorial wall in Washington, D.C., reaching out to touch the name of their husband and father who died. The reflection from the polished granite, however, does not show the mother and daughter. The reflection shows the man they love who gave his life, reaching out and touching their hands.

The artist attempted to portray that, though the wall memorializes Vietnam veterans, it is more than a memorial. The wall provides a place where, because of love and relationship, past and present come together.

Similarly, the Lord's Supper is more than a memorial. In fact, the one we remember still lives, and He meets us there. The Lord's Table provides a place where heaven and earth come together.

The Lord's Supper is more than a memorial; the one we remember still lives, and He meets us there.

CONCLUSION

Baptism and the Lord's Supper allow believers to sacramentally participate in the death and resurrection of Jesus Christ. In baptism we enter a covenant with Jesus; in the Lord's Supper we renew the covenant and find nourishment in Him. In both, we meet Christ.

What Do You Say?

1. What are the dangers in separating the physical and spiritual aspects of our faith?
2. What is the difference in a "sacrament" and an "ordinance?" How can both terms inform our understanding of baptism and the Lord's supper?
3. What significance does baptism hold in a person's life and faith? If you have been baptized, what significance did it have for you when you were baptized? What ongoing significance does it have?
4. How does baptism relate with the church community? How would you respond if someone said, "It's just between me and God."
5. How does the Lord's Supper relate with the church community? How would you respond if someone said, "It's just between me and God?"
6. In what ways does the Lord's Supper allow a believer to participate in the body and blood of Christ?
7. What have you learned from this chapter that will help you better appreciate your participation in the Lord's Supper?

Part 3

The Church in the Epistles and Revelation

CHAPTER ELEVEN

PURPOSEFULLY DESIGNED

Members of the orchestra drift onto stage. Most arrive by themselves, others in twos or threes. Each artist reaches his or her position, then removes an instrument from a case—a violin, an oboe, a couple of clarinets, a bass. With an ear cocked to the side, the bassist tunes his instrument and plucks its strings. A trumpeter arrives, lifts the mouthpiece to his lips, and plays a scale. The violinist takes her bow in hand, then slides it across the strings of her violin. More artists arrive, and more tune their instruments, but none give attention to the rhythms or harmonies of any written piece or of other instruments.

The result? The dogs in the alley outside slap their paws across their ears. A husband glares at his wife; "I paid *how much*, for *this*?" Every corner of the symphony hall fills with painful discord and disharmony.

The dissonance escalates until a white-haired gentlemen in a tuxedo struts to the front of the orchestra. All falls silent. The artists on stage raise their instruments and fix their eyes on the conductor. When the conductor raises his baton, guests lean forward. As the baton lowers, the velvet melodies of the accomplished symphony drench the ears and souls of those who fill the auditorium.

- I. Christ the Head of the Body
- II. The Body of Believers
  - A. A Body with Functioning Parts
  - B. A Body with Valuable Parts
- III. Leaders within the Body
  - A. A Highly Structured Leadership?
  - B. An Unstructured Leadership?
  - C. A Recognized Leadership
  - D. Leaders of Integrity
  - E. Leaders Imitating Christ
  - F. Servant Leadership
- IV. The Elder as Shepherd
  - A. Overarching Image: Shepherd
  - B. Functional Role: Elder
    - 1. Elder Task: Guide
    - 2. Elder Task: Feed
  - C. Functional Role: Overseer
    - 1. Overseer Task: Give Care
    - 2. Overseer Task: Protect
- V. The Deacon as Servant

When various parts submit to a common leader, the resulting cooperation produces something spectacular.

The Bible applies the same principle to the church, using a different metaphor—the church functions like a human body, with Christ as its head. Various parts function in accordance with their gifts; yet, as they all submit to the head, they combine to form something spectacular—the community of God completing the purposes of God.

This picture of the church as the body of Christ stands as one of the more prominent and memorable biblical images, providing a basis for a discussion of God's purposeful design of the church.

CHRIST, THE HEAD OF THE BODY

Christ functions as, and provides the very essence of, headship to the church. If the church is a body, Christ is our head. Ephesians and Colossians, in particular, emphasize Christ's headship:

> *And he made known to us the mystery of his will according to his good pleasure, which he purposed in Christ, [10]to be put into effect when the times will have reached their fulfillment—to bring all things in heaven and on earth together under one head, even Christ.* (***Eph 1:9-10***)

> *And God placed all things under his feet and appointed him to be head over everything for the church, [23]which is his body, the fullness of him who fills everything in every way.* (***Eph 1:22-23***)

> *He is before all things, and in him all things hold together. [18]And he is the head of the body, the church; he is the beginning and the firstborn from among the dead, so that in everything he might have the supremacy.* (***Col 1:17-18***)

> *Do not let anyone who delights in false humility and the worship of angels disqualify you for the prize. Such a person goes into great detail about what he has seen, and his unspiritual mind puffs him up with idle notions. [19]He has lost connection with the Head, from whom the whole body, supported and held together by its ligaments and sinews, grows as God causes it to grow.* (***Col 2:18-19***)

The church is the body *of* Christ and one body *in* Christ.

The church is the body *of* Christ (***1Cor 12:27***) and one body *in* Christ (***Rom 12:5***). The first phrase emphasizes Christ's life-giving and authoritative roles over the church; the second phrase emphasizes His necessity to the unity of the church. A body without its head falls limp and lifeless.

If a church has fallen limp and lifeless, therefore, it should consider whether or not it remains connected to the Head. Does Christ stand as the center of our existence, our source of life, and our primary focus? Do we seek Him, worship Him, and serve Him above all? Do we speak of Him more often than we speak of anything else? Do we turn first to Him when a dilemma arises? Do others most know us for our exaltation of Christ, or for something else?

To ask more bluntly, is Jesus our mascot or our master? Do we simply use His name and logo (the cross) on our letterhead and church signs then proceed by our own power, advancing our own agendas, and relying on our own abilities? Or, do we submit everything—utterly everything—to His authority and direction? Unless Jesus holds the central position in church life—not just an ornamental position in our liturgy and on our tee-shirts, but a central position of focus, reliance, and proclamation—we have lost connection with the head. Dietrich Bonhoeffer lamented, "Christ has become a matter of the church, or, rather, of the churchiness of a group, not a matter of life" (***Testament***, **53**). Erwin McManus adds, "The diminishing influence of the American church on American society is not simply because fewer people are going to church, but fewer people are going to church because of the diminishing influence of Christ on the church itself" (**28**).

Is Jesus our mascot or our master?

A church built on the personality or charisma of its preacher, even a godly preacher, will eventually collapse. A church centered on a particular program, even a beneficial program, will one day crumble. A church primarily focused on a particular position, even a doctrinally correct position, will ultimately fold. A body remains alive only as it remains connected and submissive to the Head.

THE BODY OF BELIEVERS

As the body of Christ, the church serves as an extension of Christ. This imagery of the church as a body—exclusively Pauline in Scripture—appears most prominently in ***Romans 12:4-8*** and ***1 Corinthians 12:12-27***. *"Now you are the body of Christ,"* Paul summarizes, *"and each one of you is a part of it"* (***1Cor 12:27***).

Each individual congregation—in Rome, in Corinth, and by implication any particular community of believers—rightly wears the label "the body of Christ." Each congregation is the complete body. "The community at Corinth is not said to be part of a wider body of Christ or to be 'a body of Christ' alongside numerous others," explains Robert Banks. "It is '*the* body of Christ' in that place. This suggests that wherever Christians are in relationship, there is the body of Christ in its entirety, for Christ is truly and wholly there through his Spirit (***1Cor 12:13***). This is a momentous truth. We find here further confirmation of the high estimate Paul had of the local Christian community" (**59**).

Each congregation is the complete body.

Certainly a universal church exists, consisting of all believers from all places. The existence of this larger body, however, does not render local bodies incomplete. Each individual community of believers is the body of Christ. Each congregation—each local church—has a unique identity in Christ and manifests His body in its location.

A Body with Functioning Parts

The Spirit equips each believer—each part of the body—to fulfill a particular role. Paul wrote to the Romans,

> *4Just as each of us has one body with many members, and these members do not all have the same function, 5so in Christ we who are many form one body, and each member belongs to all the others. 6We have different gifts, according to the grace given us. If a man's gift is prophesying, let him use it in proportion to his faith. 7If it is serving, let him serve; if it is teaching, let him teach; 8if it is encouraging, let him encourage; if it is contributing to the needs of others, let him give generously; if it is leadership, let him govern diligently; if it is showing mercy, let him do it cheerfully.* (***Rom 12:4-8***)

God designs each member of the church body to function—to actively extend the ministry of Christ. The Holy Spirit gifts each Christian with particular abilities, such as serving, teaching, or showing mercy, and expects us to use these gifts to contribute to the ministry of the church.[1]

Several years ago Merv Griffin hosted a group of bodybuilders on his variety television show. Griffin stood to the side and watched as

[1] See chapter nine for additional discussion of spiritual gifts.

the guests flexed and posed their impressive physiques. Finally Griffin asked one of the bodybuilders, "What do you use all those muscles for?" The guest responded with another pose. "No, you don't understand, how do you *use* your muscles?" Again, the bodybuilder just flexed. A third time the guest responded to Griffin's question in the same way.

Too many Christians, similarly, fail to make productive use of their gifts. If God gifted you to teach, whom do you teach? If He gifted you to encourage others, whom do you encourage? If God gifted you with hospitality, whom have you invited to your house lately?

A fully functioning body involves hands, feet, noses, ears, and so on. Each part plays a vital role. If any part ceases to function, the body will continue, but it will continue impaired. If any believer does not function as God gifted him or her to function, the church will continue, but not to its fullest potential. God designed a body of functioning parts.

Furthermore, God designed each part of the body to function in harmony with one another. Imagine how the various parts of a human body coordinate to perform even menial tasks. A moment ago, I paused from typing to take a sip of coffee. My brain sent impulses to various muscles. My arm reached toward the cup, bending properly at shoulder, elbow, and wrist, with all related ligaments, cartilages, muscles, and bones functioning in harmony. My fingers grasped the cup—again with the synchronized mechanical functioning of all parts of my arm, wrists, hand, and fingers. Then I lifted the cup to my lips, and my wrist hinged to tilt the cup such that coffee poured into my mouth. The coffee spilled across my taste buds, which informed my brain of the coffee flavor (including a bit of vanilla chai spice creamer). The muscles in my esophagus sent the coffee toward my digestive system, where the remnants of former ulcers sent a message back to my brain reminding me that I shouldn't drink coffee.

Too many Christians fail to make productive use of their gifts.

Similarly, imagine how the various members of a church coordinate to perform a ministry. For example, the church in which my family participates operates a food pantry. Various church members donate food and money. Every Sunday morning, a group of young people move a bin into the church foyer to hold donations. Volunteers take any money given and shop for appropriate canned goods and other items. Additional volunteers then organize the food and stock the shelves. Greeters serve each week welcoming clients, discussing their needs, and giving them food to meet their needs—in the process, through both their words and the act of giving, they testify to the love and power of Christ. An additional volunteer takes phone calls, sends letters, and keeps records. Finally, a director organizes over forty volunteers, prepares reports, keeps communication lines open, and keeps the needs of the food pantry before the congregation. Numerous parts of the church body function harmoniously to place a can of green beans in the hands of a hungry family.

The body ministers as each part functions together.

A Body with Valuable Parts

While the Romans passage about the body of Christ, discussed above, emphasized the function of each part, Paul's use of the body image in ***1 Corinthians 12*** places greater emphasis on the value of each part:

> *[14]Now the body is not made up of one part but of many.[15]If the foot should say, "Because I am not a hand, I do not belong to the body," it would not for that reason cease to be part of the body. [16]And if the ear should say, "Because I am not an eye, I do not belong to the body," it would not for that reason cease to be part of the body. [17]If the whole body were an eye, where would the sense of hearing be? If the whole body were an ear, where would the sense of smell be? [18]But in fact God has arranged the parts in the body, every one of them, just as he wanted them to be. [19]If they were all one part, where would the body be? [20]As it is, there are many parts, but one body.*
>
> *[21]The eye cannot say to the hand, "I don't need you!" And the head cannot say to the feet, "I don't need you!" [22]On the contrary, those parts of the body that seem to be weaker are indispensable, [23]and the parts that we think are less honorable we treat with special honor. And the parts that are unpresentable are treated with special modesty, [24]while our presentable parts need no special treatment. But God has combined the members of the body and has given greater honor to the parts that lacked it, [25]so that there should be no division in the body, but that its parts should have equal concern for each other. [26]If one part suffers, every part suffers with it; if one part is honored, every part rejoices with it.* (***1Cor 12:14-26***)

Each part of the body, functioning in harmony with other parts to extend the ministry of Christ, holds great value. Often we consider more public gifts—such as teaching, preaching, or leading—more valuable than less public gifts. *"Those parts of the body that seem to be weaker,"* however, *"are indispensable"* (***1Cor 12:22***). Those who teach the toddlers, who stock the food pantry, who gather each Saturday morning to serve scrambled eggs to the homeless, and who stop by the widow's house to clean the gutters hold as much value to the church's ministry—even more value, arguably—than those who minister in more visible ways.

Each Christmas season in Morehead, Minnesota, the local community college holds a concert. And, each year, the community bands together to paint the backdrop for the choir—a painting one hundred feet wide and thirty feet high. The summer before, the town rents an empty building. Designers erect an enormous canvas, marked with tiny squares and numbers, and provide paint. Over the coming months, thousands of townspeople—from junior highers to senior citizens—stop by. Each person finds the number inside a square, chooses the correct paint color, then paints. Day after day, month after month, the "paint by the number" mosaic takes shape.

When the weekend arrives for the Christmas concert, those who helped paint arrive early to gloat over their painting. "See that little spot below the camel's foot?" someone whispers. "I painted that!"

At first glance, each tiny square appears insignificant. Six months later, after each individual contributes, the tiny squares combine to form a masterpiece (**Yaconelli, 118-119**).

Some ministries within the body may seem small and insignificant—helping with a preschool class, sending a card, or stopping by the hospital to encourage someone. When every part functions, however, including these apparently insignificant but infinitely valuable parts, the combined picture grows stunning.

When every part functions, the combined picture grows stunning.

KA8QEZ Is Standing By: The Ministry of a Man in a Wheelchair

Rachel Ronk

(My sister, Rachel Ronk, and her family served as missionaries in Haiti for eleven years. Often their only contact with family and friends in the United States came via ham radio. Skip Zutaut—a friend from our hometown in West Virginia—provided their most helpful radio contact in the States. Having been diagnosed with Multiple Sclerosis in 1976, Skip operated his radio from a wheelchair.

Skip passed from this life in 2004. When Rachel heard the news, she sat down with a pen and paper and reminisced. Rachel and Skip's widow, Mary Beth, graciously allowed me to share what Rachel wrote.)

Many of our outstanding memories of our eleven years in Haiti include Skip. We could barely begin to estimate the number of hours he devoted to our family and the mission work in Haiti.

Anything we asked him to do, he would. He might give a good chuckle first, but he was always willing to attempt whatever we needed; whether it was making phone calls to doctors or shipping companies, ordering something from J.C. Penney, researching what kind of truck would work well for us, or relaying all sorts of messages to family and friends. It might be a message as important as the details concerning supplies for a medical group coming in, or as "unimportant" as asking Grandma to send some M & M's. Whatever the message, we knew we could depend on Skip to pass it along. He was also willing to help other missionaries in our area who would come and use our radio. He and Mary Beth even allowed their daughter, Teresa, to spend six months with us in Haiti. Her ministry to our children was an encouragement as well.

During a three-year embargo which prohibited essential supplies from entering Haiti, Skip was literally our only connection with the outside world. He faithfully "met" us on the radio three times a week (and more if we requested) to put through phone patches to our family and friends. Our parents often said how thankful they were to actually get to hear our voices while we were so far away. They even commented that they sometimes talked to us more often than they talked to their children living in the States!

Skip's voice was a routine sound in our home. We would sit at the radio with our list of questions or requests, and start turning the radio dial until we heard the familiar deep voice, "HH7RLR . . . HH7RLR . . . HH7RLR . . . this is KA8QEZ standing by . . . KA8QEZ is standing by." We realized how often our children heard this when we listened to them playing in their room one day. Our daughter Sarah picked up a play telephone, and instead of saying "Hello," she said, "KA8QEZ, are you there?!" In her world, that was the way to communicate and get results!

Through our conversations Skip took a genuine and personal interest in what was happening, both with our family and the mission work. He remembered details and would keep up with what all was going on.

We'll never forget what happened one night just as we were "signing off" with Skip on the radio. One of our older girls screamed, "Rebecca just ate a bottle of medicine!" Our hearts started racing, and I quickly turned back to the radio. "KA8QEZ—are you there?!" He was! He put a phone patch through to the poison control center, and after we convinced them that we couldn't bring Rebecca into the Emergency Room, they instructed us on what to do. Our first response had been to force her to vomit the medicine, but it was the type of medicine that vomiting would have made more harmful. How thankful we were for that unusually-timed appointment with Skip; we believe it was a divine appointment.

Maybe some believe that a man confined to a wheelchair doesn't have much to contribute to ministry. We stand to testify differently. Skip's ministry blessed us and the Haitian community we served. God used him to lighten our load, probably even more than we will ever realize. When we remember our times in Haiti, Skip is a fond part of our reminiscing. The radio waves surely miss Skip.

How grateful we can all be for the hope Jesus Christ gives us, to know that this separation is not permanent. In fact, we can almost hear the words now, "KA8QEZ is standing by . . . KA8QEZ is standing by."

LEADERS WITHIN THE BODY

Within the body, some members function in leadership roles. *"It was he who gave some to be apostles, some to be prophets, some to be evangelists, and some to be pastors and teachers,"* wrote Paul, describing a few of the leadership functions pictured in the NT (***Eph 4:11***). Such leaders serve the body *"to prepare God's people for works of service, so that the body of Christ may be built up until we all reach unity in the faith and in the knowledge of the Son of God and become mature, attaining to the whole measure of the fullness of Christ"* (**Eph 4:12-13**).

A Highly Structured Leadership?

Bible scholars disagree significantly concerning the degree of organization that characterized the leadership structures of NT-era congregations.

At one extreme, some scholars believe congregations quickly developed complex, hierarchical leadership structures. Such scholars depend heavily on the writings of early church fathers who ministered soon after the NT era. J.B. Lightfoot, for example, cited ancient historical sources that describe bishops over churches or groups of churches within the first two centuries AD, beginning with James in Jerusalem and John in Asia Minor. Of John, for example, Lightfoot quoted Clement of Alexandria, who describes John traveling from city to city "in some places to establish bishops, in others to consolidate whole churches, in others, again, to appoint to the clerical office some one of those who had been signified by the Spirit." Lightfoot also quoted Tertullian, who said, "The sequence of bishops traced back to its origin will be found to rest on the authority of John" (**60**). Another example grows from the writings of Polycarp of Smyrna, who spoke of himself as a bishop over a group of presbyters. Polycarp's student Irenaeus wrote that Polycarp had "not only been instructed by Apostles and conversed with many who had seen Christ but had also been established by Apostles in Asia as bishop in the church at Smyrna" (**J.B. Lightfoot, 61**). Other examples include Theophilus of Caesarea, Cassius of Tyre, Clarus of Ptolemais, and Ignatius of Antioch. "The notices thus collected," Lightfoot concludes, "present a large body of evidence establishing the fact of the early and extensive adoption of episcopacy in the Christian Church. . . . Episcopacy is so inseparably interwoven with all the traditions and beliefs of men like Irenaeus and Tertullian that they betray no knowledge of a time when it was not" (**75**).

Those who advocate a more intricate leadership structure often teach of three hierarchical levels. The highest level includes a single *episkopos* (bishop, overseer), the second consists of a plurality of *presbyterous* (elders), and the third includes a group of *diakonois* (servers, deacons).[2] As noted above, this structure appears in the writings of some early church fathers; and, scholars who advocate this structure believe the NT epistles hint toward such hierarchy. For example, the Pastoral Epistles use the singular *episkopos* (bishop, overseer; ***1Tm 3:1-7; Tts 1:7-9***), and the plural *presbyterous* (elders; ***1Tm 4:14; 5:17; Tts 1:5***). This suggests, these scholars assert, that the bishop and the elders served distinct roles—probably, a single bishop rose from among the group of elders to serve as their overseer.

Those who advocate a more intricate leadership structure often teach of three hierarchical levels.

An Unstructured Leadership?

At the other extreme, some scholars believe that congregations during the NT era had little, if any, formal leadership structure. Robert Banks represents scholars who take this position. According to Banks, the only differentiation among believers visible in Paul's epistles—this in stark contrast to the hierarchical structure discussed above—lies in a distinction between the more and less mature, demonstrated in passages such as ***Galatians 6:1***, *"Brothers, if someone is caught in a sin, you who are spiritual should restore him gently"* (**Banks, 140**). To these mature believers, Paul describes particular functions they should perform within the body. The functional terms Paul uses include *poimenes* ("shepherds, pastors"), *episkopoi* ("overseers"), and *diakonoi* ("servants"), among others. These terms, Banks emphasizes, refer not to positions held but to functions performed: "Certainly no official positions in the church are in view" (**142**).

Paul calls other believers, Banks explains, to submit to these more mature believers—a submission that grows not from recognition of a formal position but from honor and gratitude for one's work and service. Paul called the Corinthians, for example, to submit to *"the household of Stephanas"* and to *"everyone who joins in the work."*

[2] These three levels are outlined from a local congregation's perspective. Each congregation within this leadership structure looks to a single bishop, a group of presbyters, and a group of deacons. Beyond the local level, however, a single bishop may oversee multiple congregations. And, every bishop stands on equal footing with other bishops in other locations.

Paul appointed mature believers to fulfill a task, not just to hold an office.

This submission came not because Stephanas and the others held formal offices, but because *"they have devoted themselves to the service of the saints,"* and because of the "labor" they perform (***1Cor 16:15-16***). When Paul and Barnabas appointed elders in various churches (***Acts 14:23***), they appointed these mature believers to fulfill a task, not just to hold an office.

Further, Banks responds to a potential objection to his position,

> Very frequently a basis for the idea of office is thought to be in Paul's greetings to "bishops" and "deacons" in Philippians and in the mention of pastors (*poimenes*) and Archippus' ministry (*diakonia*) in ***Ephesians*** and ***Colossians*** respectively. In Philippians, names are used to distinguish two groups of people from the rest of the community (***Phil 1:1***). Yet, the "saints" have precedence over "guardians" (*episkopoi*) and "servants" (*diakonoi*)—a strange order if the latter were the chief officeholders in the church. Also, and this applies to the words in ***Ephesians*** (*poimenes* and *didaskaloi*) as well, the Greek has no definite article with these terms. This means that they are not being treated as titles. Maybe only one group of people is in view. Further, with the sole exception of the reference to the "true yokefellow" whose task is to settle a personal dispute, in Ephesians, Philippians, and Colossians Paul always addresses the whole community. Nowhere does he entrust special responsibilities to any single group vis-à-vis the remainder.
>
> In any case the terms *episkopos* and *diakonos* themselves should be freed of the ecclesiastical connotations they have for us today, for they are not essentially different from the various other pastoral terms Paul uses. No real evidence exists to suggest these terms had any technical meaning at the time. (**Banks, 144**)

A Recognized Leadership

As with most scholarly debates, the truth probably lies somewhere between the two extremes. Where, precisely, does the truth lie? To what extent were the leadership structures of NT era churches formalized and organized? Quite simply, we cannot know for certain. Neither Jesus nor the apostles dictated a precise template for church polity, and demanded that all churches pattern themselves precisely to that template. Various congregations, then—in various parts of the Mediterranean world and at various stages of maturity and development—probably functioned in different ways, including their leadership structures. This explains why Paul addressed Philippians to the *"saints . . . overseers and deacons"* of Philippi and included extensive qualifications for elders and deacons in the Pastoral Epistles, while epistles such as ***Romans, 1*** and ***2 Corinthians, Galatians, Ephesians,*** and ***Colossians,*** make no mention of such leaders.[3]

The same variety marked churches in the generations that followed the NT era. Among the early church fathers, Clement wrote of plural "overseers and deacons," and apparently viewed overseers as synonymous with elders. Ignatius, on the other hand, presented a three-tiered structure including a single overseer, a group of elders, and a group of deacons. Polycarp wrote only of elders and deacons. Hermas spoke of apostles, overseers, teachers, and deacons (**Marshall, 177**).

While we cannot know the precise leadership structure of every congregation, and while individual congregations in the NT era probably differed from one another in regards to their organization, we can know that some kind of leadership structure did develop. The idea that NT churches functioned without the presence of leadership and structure—as though churches operated in an entirely free-flowing, communal manner—ignores numerous NT references to such leaders and such structures (***Acts 15; Rom 12:8; 1Cor 12:27-31; 1Th 5:12; 1Tm 3:1; Tts 1:5; Heb 13:17; 1Pet 5:1-4***). Luke Timothy Johnson explains, "Less important than the form of community structure is the conviction attested to both in Paul's letters, in ***Acts,*** and in other NT writings, that there is no essential incompatibility between a prophetic self-consciousness or a Charismatic awareness, and ecclesiastical structure. The narrative of ***Acts*** is surely historical in this broad sense, that Christian communities needed from the very beginning to establish local leadership" (***Acts,* 256-257**).

Individual congregations probably differed from one another in regards to their organization.

[3]The lack of mention of elders and deacons in these epistles does not necessarily mean they did not exist in these churches. Clement, in fact, himself a leader in the church of Rome, wrote in the late first century of elders in Corinth. The lack of mention does, however, illustrate that the apostles dictated no precise template for all congregations.

The organizational structures of local churches probably evolved naturally in a way that reflected the culture and experience of early believers, rather than by apostolic mandate of an entirely new system previously unknown to these believers. When Paul and Barnabas *"appointed elders for them in each church"* (**Acts 14:23**), and when Paul instructed Titus to *"appoint elders in every town"* (***Tts 1:5***), Paul used a term (*presbyterous,* "elders") familiar to both Greek and Jewish cultures. Greeks used the term simply to refer to older men (**Banks, 147**). Numerous OT references attest to the Jewish history of elders—the mature men of the tribes—offering wise council and leadership.

A community did not recognize a man as an elder via a single event, or on a particular occasion, as if one day a person was not an elder and the next day he was. Instead, a community's recognition of a man as an elder evolved over time as that man demonstrated his wisdom and maturity. "The best explanation," explains I.H. Marshall, "is that each recognizable Christian group has a group of senior persons out of which is crystallizing a leadership group" (**181**). By appointing elders in churches, therefore, Paul simply recognized a cultural reality and extended that reality into the church community, as if to say to those elders, "You have earned the respect of the community. Based on this respect, bring your wisdom and leadership to the church." And, Paul could then bid the churches, *"Now we ask you, brothers, to respect those who work hard among you, who are over you in the Lord and who admonish you. Hold them in the highest regard in love because of their work"* (***1Th 5:1-13***).

A community's recognition of an elder developed as he demonstrated wisdom and maturity.

A similar dynamic may stand behind the development of deacons. The NT uses the term *diakonos* in its various forms around one hundred times. In most cases, English translations depict the noun forms as "servant" or "ministry," and the verb form as "serve" or "wait on." In four of these one hundred occurrences, most English Bibles translate *diakonois* as "deacons" because, in these four cases, *diakonois* appears to refer to a particular group of people within the church (***Php 1:1; 1Tm 3:8,10,12***). While Christ calls all of His followers to serve and minister, apparently some in the NT church gained respect because of their extraordinarily faithful service, such that churches recognized their service by appointing them as servants/deacons.

These organizational structures probably began evolving fairly quickly: "Common sense and sociology alike confirm the validity of the observation that intentional groups move progressively from simpler to more elaborate, and eventually more legitimated, structures. But it by no means follows that such development requires decades. Analyses of communes have shown that they cannot survive much beyond a few years without strong boundaries, mechanisms for decision making, and social control. . . . The assumption of a great time-lapse between the founding of a Pauline church and the development of a stable structure is counterintuitive" (**Johnson, *Letters*, 15**).

The organizational structure visible in the NT, however, apparently does not reach the level of hierarchical intricacy demonstrated in the writings of some church fathers, and advocated by some contemporary scholars. For example, we discussed above a three-tiered system that includes a single overseer (*episkopos*) who exercises authority over a plurality of elders (*presbyterous*) and deacons (*diakonois*). The argument for this structure hinges, at least partially, on the use of the singular *episkopos* in the Pastoral Epistles (in contrast to the plural *presbyterous*): *"If anyone sets his heart on being an overseer, he desires a noble task"* (***1Tm 3:1***); *"Now the overseer must be above reproach"* (***1Tm 3:2***); and *"Since an overseer is entrusted with God's work, he must be blameless"* (***Tts 1:7***). Elsewhere in the Pastorals, however, Paul uses singular nouns to represent groups of people, particularly when outlining certain traits that should characterize the people discussed. For example, when speaking of ministry to widows (plural, ***1Tm 5:3***), Paul used the singular "widow" to describe them: *"If **a widow** has children or grandchildren . . ."* (***1Tm 5:4***, bold added). Furthermore, outside of the Pastoral Epistles, "overseers" appears in the plural (***Php 1:1; 1Pet 5:2***).

Rather than a three-tiered hierarchy during the time described in the NT (though this apparently developed in some places soon thereafter), the more plausible perspective understands the terms "overseers" and "elders" to refer to the same group of leaders. As we will discuss below, the different terms emphasize different aspects of their function, but the same group of leaders fulfilled these functions at that time. In fact, some passages use the terms "overseers" and "elders" interchangeably (***Acts 20:17 and 28; Tts 1:5 and 7; 1Pet 5:1-2***).

In sum, churches in the NT—though some particulars probably varied from church to church and from time to time—had an organized leadership that consisted of those recognized to function as elders/overseers, and those recognized to function as deacons.[4] While the structure later grew more complex and hierarchical, it does not appear as such in the NT itself.

Leaders of Integrity

The two most extensive discussions of elders and deacons in the NT—*1 Timothy 3:1-13* and *Titus 1:5-9*—focus not on their gifts or responsibilities, but on their character. Churches today would do well to follow suit. Too often, we place people into leadership positions solely because of their abilities ("Jim is a good businessman"), because of their tenure ("Jim has gone to this church a long time"), or because of their potential ("If we make Jim a deacon, maybe he'll get more involved"). Instead, we must look first to a person's character. Does "Jim" display Christlike integrity? Does he emanate the fruit of the Spirit? Do people look to him as a godly example?

The two most extensive discussions of elders and deacons focus on their character.

First Timothy 3 and *Titus 1* provide extensive lists of the moral characteristics that should mark those recognized as leaders in the church (see sidebar "Moral Characteristics of Elders and Deacons"). No one person, other than Christ Himself, could reach perfection in every characteristic. These traits, however, should typify the Christian leader.[5] Leaders, by definition, lead. Christian leaders guide people toward Christlikeness. If leaders have not, themselves, grown into Christlikeness, how could they lead others in that direction?

David Wheeler, a colleague of mine at Johnson Bible College, tells of a funeral procession that illustrates a leader's influence. Several years ago, David officiated a funeral in Indiana. In accordance with custom, after the funeral, the attenders filed out of the funeral home and into their waiting cars to form a processional to the cemetery. The

[4] For the sake of clarity, the remainder of the chapter will refer to the first group as "elders," understanding that in the NT this group also functioned as "overseers" and in other functions that will be discussed below. Because NT teaching about these leaders focuses more on function than position, however, their titles hold less importance than their ministries.

[5] In reality, these traits should characterize every Christian. The leader should set the pace.

hearse led the processional, followed immediately by David, then all of the deceased's family and friends. During the drive to the cemetery, however, David needed to stop at a restroom. He could not wait much longer, and, even if he did try to wait, few cemeteries have public restrooms available. So, as the processional came upon an old, abandoned roadside picnic area that included an outhouse, David veered into the picnic area to use the outhouse. He assumed the remainder of the processional would follow the hearse to the cemetery, then he would catch up. He assumed incorrectly. When he emerged from the outhouse, he discovered the long line of cars patiently waiting!

Churches with Christlike love have leaders with Christlike love.

People follow leaders. Where, churches must ask before placing people into leadership functions, will they lead? Do we want people following where this person's life will take them? Churches with Christlike integrity have leaders with Christlike integrity. Churches with Christlike compassion have leaders with Christlike compassion. Churches with Christlike love have leaders with Christlike love. Paul bid NT churches, therefore—and through them bids us—to choose leaders carefully, and based primarily on their character.

Moral Characteristics of Elders and Deacons

Elder:

- Above reproach (*1Tm 3:2*)
- Self-controlled (*1Tm 3:2; Tts 1:8*)
- Hospitable (*1Tm 3:2; Tts 1:8*)
- Able to teach (*1Tm 3:2; Tts 1:9*)
- Not violent but gentle (*1Tm 3:3; Tts 1:7*)
- Not quarrelsome (*1Tm 3:3*)
- Not a lover of money (*1Tm 3:3*)
- Not a recent convert (*1Tm 3:6*)
- Good reputation with outsiders (*1Tm 3:7*)
- Blameless (*Tts 1:6*)
- Not overbearing (*Tts 1:7*)
- Not quick-tempered (*Tts 1:7*)
- Loves what is good (*Tts 1:8*)
- Upright (*Tts 1:8*)

- ➤ Holy (*Tts 1:8*)
- ➤ Disciplined (*Tts 1:8*)

Elder and Deacon:

- ➤ Husband of one wife (*1Tm 3:2; Tts 1:6; 1Tm 3:12*)
- ➤ Temperate (*1Tm 3:2; Tts 1:7; 1Tm 3:8*)
- ➤ Respectable (*1Tm 3:2,8*)
- ➤ Not given to drunkenness (*1Tm 3:3; Tts 1:7; 1Tm 3:8*)
- ➤ Manages family well (*1Tm 3:4,12*)
- ➤ Sees that children obey (*1Tm 3:4-5; Tts 1:6; 1Tm 3:12*)
- ➤ Does not pursue dishonest gain (*Tts 1:7; 1Tm 3:8*)
- ➤ Holds to the truth (*Tts 1:9; 1Tm 3:9*)

Deacon:

- ➤ Clear conscience (*1Tm 3:9*)
- ➤ Sincere (*1Tm 3:8*)
- ➤ Tested (*1Tm 3:10*)

Leaders Imitating Christ

Ultimately, churches need leaders who can legitimately say, as Paul said to the believers in Corinth, *"Follow my example, as I follow the example of Christ"* (**1Cor 11:1**); and, as Paul bid the Philippians, *"Join with others in following my example, brothers, and take note of those who live according to the pattern we gave you"* (**Php 3:17**).

Paul's teaching rings consistent with the concept of leadership in the ancient world. Leadership—and teaching, for that matter—relied heavily on modeling. "Since virtue was learned by imitation," explains Luke Timothy Johnson,

> the teacher had no greater duty than to live in a fashion corresponding to the principle he enunciated. The contemporary collapse of such an understanding of moral instruction and the present-day flight from the responsibility inherent in being a teacher of others provide the grounds for reflection on the ways in which the ancient world may have been, in these respects, superior to our own. (***Letters*, 169**)

Churches need leaders who have progressed a few steps beyond most toward spiritual maturity—leaders who can, by example, demonstrate a godly lifestyle. Leaders should provide such an example that others, when faced with a moral decision, could ask concerning their leaders, "What would so-and-so do in this situation?"

One Sunday, a couple of years ago, I attended the church in West Virginia where I grew up, and where my father, Ken Overdorf, ministered. During Sunday School, the teacher told of a time he had traveled out of town on business. While on the trip, he faced a moral dilemma that he was unsure how to handle. "I asked myself," this teacher explained, "What would Ken Overdorf do in this situation?"

Churches need such leaders—godly people who provide godly examples that demonstrate for others how to live like Christ.

Servant Leadership

Christlike leaders lead in a sacrificial, loving, generous manner.

One additional aspect of Christlike leadership that deserves mention is the attitude of servanthood that Christ demonstrated and godly leaders emulate. Christlike leaders do not seek personal glory, nor do they lead through the exertion of domineering, coercive power. Instead, they lead in a sacrificial, loving, generous manner. Jesus taught the twelve to follow His sacrificial model:

> *[42]You know that those who are regarded as rulers of the Gentiles lord it over them, and their high officials exercise authority over them. [43]Not so with you. Instead, whoever wants to become great among you must be your servant, [44]and whoever wants to be first must be slave of all. [45]For even the Son of Man did not come to be served, but to serve, and to give his life as a ransom for many.* (***Mk 10:42-45***)

Paul, likewise, most often described himself and other leaders with the term *diakonoia*—the same term Jesus used of Himself in ***Mark 10:45***—which describes service, not prominence.

A few years ago, I received a graduate degree from Lincoln Christian University in central Illinois. In keeping with school tradition, during commencement I accepted a diploma and a towel. The diploma marked the completion of an educational milestone; the towel signified the lifetime of service to which graduates commit. The diploma—more accurately, the education it signifies—well equips students to lead. The towel, however, represents an even more important qualification for biblical leadership. For without Christlike humility no one can lead in a biblical manner.

THE ELDER AS SHEPHERD

Overarching Image: Shepherd

The overarching image that best depicts the function of the elder/overseer appears frequently in both testaments of Scripture—godly leaders function like shepherds. The OT compares God to a shepherd (***Ps 80:1; Eze 34:11-24***), and uses the shepherding image of kings (***2Sa 5:2; 1Chr 11:2***) and other leaders (***Jer 23:1-2; 1Chr 17:6***). In the NT, Jesus says of Himself, *"I am the good shepherd. The good shepherd lays down his life for the sheep"* (***Jn 10:11***). Paul later utilized the image in his instructions to the Ephesian elders: *"Keep watch over yourselves and all the flock of which the Holy Spirit has made you overseers. Be shepherds of the church of God, which he bought with his own blood"* (**Acts 20:28**). Peter, likewise, wrote, *"To the elders among you, I appeal as a fellow elder, a witness of Christ's sufferings and one who also will share in the glory to be revealed: Be shepherds of God's flock that is under your care, serving as overseers"* (***1Pet 5:1-2***). Lynn Anderson well describes the background of this shepherding image:

> While some may not feel comfortable thinking of certain people as sheep and others as shepherds, our discomfort will likely disappear when we realize that the shepherding model revolves around the relationship between the shepherd and the flock. It is not a figure of strong over weak or 'lords' over servants. Quite the contrary. The shepherd figure is one of love, service, and openness.
>
> Ancient, Middle-Eastern shepherds lived in the pasture with the flock and were as much a part of the land as the sheep were. Through a lifetime of shared experience, shepherds nurtured enduring trust relationships with their sheep. . . .
>
> The shepherd lived with the lambs for their entire lives—protecting them, caressing them, feeding and watering them, and leading them to the freshest pools and the most luxuriant pastures—day and night, year in and year out. So by the time the lamb grew to 'ewe-hood' or 'ram-hood', it naturally associated the touch of the shepherd's hands and the sound of the shepherd's voice with 'green pastures' and 'still waters,' with safety, security, love, and trust. Each sheep came to rely on the shepherd and to know his voice and his alone. They followed him and no one else.
>
> Of course, the lambs understood clearly who was in charge. Occasionally, the shepherd might tap an unruly lamb

on the ear with a shepherd's crook. But this was a love tap, embraced in an enfolding circle of relationship. The shepherd smelled like sheep! (**19-20**)

Elders serve a comparable function in the church body. The terms "elder" and "overseer" further define this overarching image of the shepherd. And, the functional roles of elder and overseer include specific shepherding tasks such as guiding, giving care, feeding, and protecting. The following diagram illustrates how these images, roles, and tasks relate:[6]

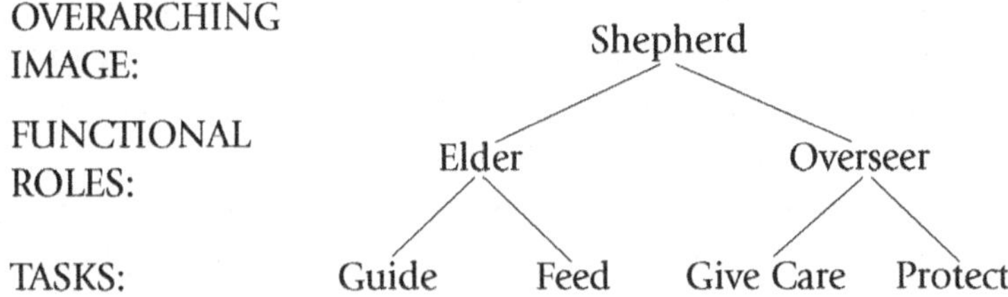

Functional Role: Elder

As explained above, the term "elders" (*presbyterous*) refers to those who have, through a life that demonstrates wisdom and maturity, gained the respect of the community. Such respect enables this person to lead through influence and example.

> **A church cannot elect someone into the functional role of an elder.**

This understanding of the biblical term implies that a church cannot elect someone into the functional role of an elder. Neither an election nor a title makes one this kind of leader. Certainly, a church can formally recognize (and this recognition could come through an election) that someone has gained respect and influence in the community. But such an acknowledgement only recognizes what has already existed in the life of the church. Churches cannot *make* a person an elder; rather they can *recognize* that a person *is* an elder—one who has gained godly influence in the community. Elders are those who have earned the respect of the church in such a way that people willingly and naturally follow their godly leadership.

[6] I grant that the conclusions represented in this diagram are debatable, and that the various terms and functions interrelate more than how they appear to on paper.

Moreover, when a community has recognized people as elders, those elders do not lead from an authority vested only in a title or a position; rather, they lead from an authority vested in gained respect and relationship. Ideally, people follow biblical elders not because they have to, but because they want to, because they have grown to love, trust, and respect them as leaders. "I'm not sure yet how I feel about this new ministry they talked about at church last Sunday," someone might say. "But John is the elder who's heading it up, and I trust John. I know he's a godly man, and that he cares about the church. So, I'm willing to follow along."

Elders lead because people have grown to trust them as leaders.

If people follow a leader only because that leader wears a title, they will follow only as far as they have to. If, however, people follow a leader because they have grown to love, trust, and respect him, they will follow as far as that leader can take them.

Two tasks naturally flow from the functional role of an elder.

Elder Task: Guide

An elder guides a congregation toward God's purposes. ***Acts 15*** demonstrates this elder task, as it describes the church facing a potentially divisive situation. Jewish believers differed in their opinions concerning how, precisely, to welcome Gentile believers into the church. Should the church require Gentiles to practice Jewish customs, such as circumcision? ***Acts 15:6*** explains, *"The apostles and elders met to consider this question."* A situation had arisen that required a significant decision concerning the direction of the church—a decision that carried enormous implications for later generations. The apostles who had sat at Jesus' feet and the elders who had gained the respect of the community met to resolve the issue. James spoke on behalf of the elders, *"We should not make it difficult for the Gentiles who are turning to God"* (***Acts 15:19***). They decided to instruct the Gentiles only to abstain from *"food polluted by idols, from sexual immorality, from the meat of strangled animals and from blood"* (***15:20***).

In the NT, only ***Acts 15*** describes elders making a decision. The role of the biblical elder finds its definition more in the hands-on care and teaching of the flock, and less in business meetings and decisions. Others should make most decisions that need made in a church. With most specific ministries within a church, those directly involved in a ministry, who have appropriate giftedness and insight, should have authority to make decisions. For example, a church's elders need not decide what brand of diapers to buy for the nursery (in most churches, you'd have the cheapest, ugliest, leakiest diapers available!). Those who serve in the nursery should make this decision. Elders need not decide what colors to paint the walls of a classroom. Those with decorating abilities should make such decisions.

In the NT, only Acts 15 describes elders making a decision.

However, when dealing with circumstances that relate to the overall direction and vision of a church, that community's elders—the seasoned, spiritually mature, and respected leaders—should provide primary guidance.

For example, I mentioned in a previous chapter that the church with which my family serves conducts an annual Prom of the Stars, a formal dinner and dance for mentally and physically disabled adults. Last fall, 100 volunteers from the church participated (plus numerous other volunteers from the community), hosting over 1,000 guests and their caretakers.

A few years ago, when the idea for the Prom of the Stars first surfaced, the elders of the church discussed the possibility of the new ministry. Would this further our mission as a church? Could we fruitfully serve the community through this activity? Has God equipped us with the necessary resources? Would it give us an opportunity to share Christ's love? Once they answered these questions, all in the affirmative, they involved others in carrying out the various details connected with the Prom. Each year, people other than the elders take leadership in fundraising, gathering donated dresses and tuxedos, arranging registration, marketing the event, coordinating with the civic center where the event takes place, making arrangements with caterers, and numerous other details. The elders made the big-picture decision, then empowered others to lead and serve in areas where they have gifts.

Elders, as a part of their shepherding, provide big-picture guidance and direction for the church.

Elder Task: Feed

An elder makes certain a church is properly fed and nourished with biblical truth. In both ***1 Timothy*** and ***Titus***, Paul included the ability to teach as a trait that should characterize elders (***1Tm 3:2; Tts 1:9***). Some elders apparently gave themselves primarily to preaching and teaching—such elders were *"worthy of double honor"* (***1Tm 5:17***). A church—both individual believers within a congregation and the community itself—simply cannot grow into maturity apart from the teaching of God's Word. God commissions leaders, therefore, to nourish the church *"so that the body of Christ may be built up until we all reach unity in the faith and in the knowledge of the Son of God and become mature, attaining to the whole measure of the fullness of Christ"* (***Eph 4:12-13***).

In the pasture, the shepherd devotes much attention and energy to the proper feeding and nourishment of the sheep. Such shepherds, particularly in biblical times, scoured the hillsides for lush grass and cool streams, then led the flock to them. Similarly, elders of the church community recognize the necessity of biblical teaching to maturing Christians and growing churches. They constantly ask themselves questions such as these: Are we providing biblical nourishment to our congregation? Have we recognized what members among us have teaching gifts, and placed these members in teaching roles? Do we equip our church members with tools for understanding and applying the Bible? Does the reading of Scripture hold a place of prominence in our public gatherings? Do our classes, groups, and worship services provide the meat of God's Word?[7]

Church bodies that have not received proper feeding grow frail and lifeless.

Like dehydrated, anemic, and malnourished human bodies, church bodies that have not received proper feeding grow frail and lifeless. Loving elders make certain this malnourishment never occurs in their churches.

Functional Role: Overseer

Beneath the overarching image of shepherding, two functional

[7] Chapter thirteen will discuss the role of the Word and teaching in greater detail.

roles emerge—elder (discussed above) and overseer. "Overseer" translates from *episkopos* (sometimes translated "bishop")—a fairly generic term, not necessarily religious, in the ancient world. Everett Ferguson explains about the term,

> "Bishop" was used in Hellenistic Greek for various kinds of managers, foremen, supervisors, and inspectors. It could refer to state officials with various civic functions, to supervisors at sanctuaries (but without cultic functions), to construction foremen, and in an educational context to tutors. It could also be used of a scout or watchman, and in that sense it was used for certain philosophers. (**322-323**)

Understood within its biblical, shepherding context, *episkopos* describes those who lovingly look after others' needs. It does involve overseeing, but not for the sake of exerting power or domineering (as might be the case when used in the secular sense). Robert Lowery, in fact, prefers to translate the term "caregiver," defining it as "a man who has responsibility for the care of someone" (**Lowery, "Elders"**). In ***Acts 20***, for example, Paul taught the Ephesian elders that the Holy Spirit had made them overseers of the church. This would involve being "shepherds," watching out for *"savage wolves,"* and being *"on your guard"* (***Acts 20:28-30***). *"An overseer,"* Paul explained to Titus, *"is entrusted with God's work"* (***Tts 1:7***).

Two tasks naturally flow from the functional role of overseer.

Overseer Task: Give Care

In the pasture, a careful shepherd watches over the flock. If a sheep has any briars or thorns in its wool, the shepherd removes them with loving care. If a sheep has any scrapes or cuts, the shepherd pours medicinal oil over these wounds.

Likewise, the overseer looks after and cares for the needs of those within the church. The image of the overseer compares more to a caretaker, less to an executive board room. Rather than passing down edicts, overseers best fulfill their roles when praying for the sick (***Jas 5:14***), and offering comfort.

Overseers best fulfill their roles when praying for the sick and offering comfort.

I recall one evening, during a period when I served in local church ministry, when the elders and I arrived at the church building for a meeting. When we all arrived, the chairman said, "Load up in the church van, gentlemen. Instead of meeting tonight, we're going to pray with a family who needs us." A particular family in the church faced multiple struggles—health problems, a rebellious child, and financial setbacks. The elders sat around the living room with the family and listened, provided guidance when appropriate, and cried with the family. Then, with the family sitting in chairs in the middle of the room, the elders circled around, placed their hands on the family members' heads and shoulders, and prayed for them.

These leaders were never more *episkopois* than on that evening. Biblical overseers spend more time in hospital waiting rooms than in meetings. They offer more prayers than policies, more words of comfort than of control, and have more concern for hugs than hierarchies. Certainly some circumstances call for meetings and policies, as described in *Acts 15* above, but matters of caretaking should eclipse such administrative duties in priority and energy.[8]

Biblical overseers spend more time in hospital waiting rooms than in meetings.

Overseer Task: Protect

The second task of oversight involves protecting the flock. A shepherd in the field kept a keen eye on the horizon, and watched behind every tree, shrub, and boulder for predators such as wolves and lions. He used his crook to fight off such predators. At night, a good shepherd would gather his flock into a pen or cave, then lay across the entrance to keep predators away from the precious sheep (***Jn 10:7-10***). Likewise, as Paul instructed the Ephesian elders,

> *[28]Keep watch over yourselves and all the flock of which the Holy Spirit has made you overseers. Be shepherds of the church of God, which he bought with his own blood. [29]I know that after I leave, savage wolves will come in among you and will not spare the flock. [30]Even from your own number men will arise and distort the truth in order to draw away disciples after them. [31]So be on your guard! Remember that for three years I never stopped warning each of you night and day with tears.* (***Acts 20:28-31***)

[8] Furthermore, when a group of elders have offered consistent care and concern, when circumstances call for administration people will more likely follow their leadership simply because the people know that their leaders love and care for them.

Paul warned the elders of the false teachers they would soon face. Like good shepherds, overseers must remain on guard against such threats. These threats might include false teaching that, like it infiltrated churches in Paul's day, stealthily infiltrates today's Sunday School classes, small group discussions, even pulpits. Other threats may include conflict (***Php 4:2-3***), bitterness (***Heb 12:15***), or immorality (***1 Corinthians 5***). Overseers watch for, and courageously confront, anything that threatens the health and growth of the flock.

THE DEACON AS SERVANT

In the strictest linguistic sense, any person who serves Christ and ministers to others is a "deacon." James Thompson explains concerning *diakonos*:

> Paul can use it as the umbrella term for describing all of the tasks within the body of Christ (***1 Cor. 12:4***). The term can be used for his special commission as an apostle (***2 Cor. 3:6***) and for the role of his coworkers in building churches (***1 Cor. 3:5; Eph. 6:21; Col. 1:7; 4:17***). It is also used in the gospel tradition for Jesus and his special mission (***Mark 10:45***) and for the work of his disciples (***Matt. 20:26***). The term is used in ***Hebrews*** and ***Acts*** for the church's service to human needs within the congregation (***Acts 6:2; Heb. 6:10***). According to ***Ephesians 4:12***, the various gifts are intended *"to equip the saints for the work of ministry."* (**144**)

As noted above, of the term's one hundred occurrences in the NT, ninety-six translate as general terms like "servant" or "ministry." In four uses on two occasions (***Php 1:1; 1Tm 3:8,10,12***), the term appears to refer to a particular group of people. These texts give little indication, however, concerning the precise responsibilities or role of the deacon.

A discussion of the deacon, therefore, should begin by granting that much of what we typically assume concerning deacons grows from culture and tradition rather than Scripture. Furthermore, this lack of scriptural instruction or mandate concerning the deacon allows freedom in the manner in which various congregations structure their ministries. For example, some churches designate certain

> **Much that we assume concerning deacons grows from culture and tradition rather than Scripture.**

members as "ministry leaders" or "servants," English terms that carry well the meaning of the Greek *diakonois*. Other churches use the term "deacons," a transliteration (rather than translation) of *diakonois*. Both congregations described remain within biblical bounds, and neither should think less of the other because of their different terminology. For another example, some churches include both elders and deacons in a church "board" that oversees the various ministries of a church (though usually these elders meet separately and lead in the overall vision and direction of the church). Other congregations do not include deacons in such a board and instead vest decision-making authority in elders and ministry teams. Scripture neither mandates nor prohibits either structure.[9] As long as elders function in the manner described above, and others so designated serve and minister, details of structure and functioning can be left to the discretion and wisdom of each congregation.

The NT teaching about the deacon, though sketchy, offers a glimpse into the value the early church placed on hands-on ministry and service to others. Some individuals served so faithfully in such ministries that congregations recognized their service by calling them deacons (servants, ministers).

My father wrote of a deacon in the church where he ministered:

> Among numerous others I could mention, one who comes to mind right now is J.R. Ellison. For decades, J.R. has served as a deacon in the church where I minister in West Virginia. For years a mentally challenged couple attended the church. They lived by themselves but needed help. Most people never knew, but J.R. stopped by their house frequently to make sure their bills were paid and their needs were met. Another couple had grown elderly, and was unable to drive. J.R. visited them at least once a week to do their grocery shopping or to take them to the doctor. J.R. has now retired from the medical profession. In his retirement he serves all the more—visiting shut-ins and nursing homes, caring for people in need. J.R. Ellison is a servant, a minister. He's a deacon. (**K. Overdorf, 80-81**)

During World War II, while Britain experienced its darkest days, the country struggled to keep coal miners in the mines. The men

[9] Though, I would point out that, in circumstances where a board of elders and deacons exist, such a board should not exercise authority over elders. In such circumstances, matters of overall church vision, mission, and direction—the "big picture"—should remain the responsibility of the elders.

wanted to walk from these jobs, which they viewed as thankless and insignificant, to join the military effort. Their work in the mines, however, stood critical to the war effort, both for the military itself and for the families left behind.

Winston Churchill, therefore, stood one day before thousands of coal miners and assured them of their vital role in the war effort. Churchill then described a scene he envisioned of the war's end. Following victory, Churchill imagined, a grand parade would honor those who had served so valiantly. First, the sailors of the Navy would march by, those who continued the long tradition of glorious battles on the sea. Next would follow the pilots of the Royal Air Force—Britain's best and brightest—who stood strong against the German Luftwaffe. On their heels would march the soldiers who battled at Dunkirk. Last would arrive men in miner's caps, covered in coal dust. Some might ask, "Where were they during the critical days of the struggle?" The voices of thousands would respond, "We were in the earth with our faces to the coal." As Churchill described this parade, even the most hardened men grew teary-eyed. They returned to their service with resolve, reminded by their leader of the critical role they played in Britain's success (**Maxwell, 19-20**).

The Bible says nothing of a similar parade in Heaven. If God chooses such a display, however, I can imagine the scene. Nursery workers and Sunday School teachers lead the way, followed by those who minister to the homeless, troubled teens, and prisoners. Next arrive missionaries who take the gospel to foreign soil, and those who care for the landscaping at the church building. Then a group of elders and deacons will march by, followed by those who prepare meals and send cards to the sick.

And somewhere in that parade is you.

God purposefully designed a body in which every part—each of infinite value—functions to further God's purposes in and through the community. Some serve as leaders; all minister as God has gifted them. And, all look forward to the ultimate commendation, *"Well done, good and faithful servant!"* (***Mt 25:21***).

What Do You Say?

1. Imagine someone asked you to design a list of questions, the answers to which would demonstrate whether or not your church had fully submitted to Christ, the head of the church body, and whether or not your church finds its life and power in Christ. What questions would you include on such a list? How would you answer each question for your church?
2. What did the Apostle Paul imply by using the image of a human body to describe the church? Why are these implications important for today's church?
3. Can you think of examples from your own experience of Christians whose gifts may seem insignificant from a worldly point of view, but who have made significant contributions to the kingdom?
4. What should churches take into account when choosing leaders?
5. What role should imitation ("follow my example as I follow the example of Christ") play in church leadership? Does this approach place too much emphasis on human leaders? Why or why not?
6. Contrast the image of elders serving as a board of directors with the image of elders serving as shepherds. Are some aspects of both images necessary for church leaders? To what extent should each image describe the function of an elder?
7. In four of its one hundred uses of *diakonos* ("servant, minister"), the NT apparently uses the term to identify particular people who were designated to serve. What should the contemporary church learn from this?

CHAPTER TWELVE

GRACIOUSLY UNITED

A few years ago I visited a couple in their home. Both husband and wife had lived most of their lives apart from Christ and His church. Their marriage—a second marriage for both—had grown rocky. The fifty-year-old husband faced a frightening battle with cancer, and neither partner handled the battle with the emotional health, vulnerability, or mutual support that such situations need.

- I. Barriers to Church Unity
  - A. Selfishness
  - B. The Unwarranted Exaltation of Human Leaders
  - C. A Focus on Nonessentials
  - D. Individualism
- II. A Church Unified
  - A. A Horizontal Implication of a Vertical Relationship
  - B. The Attitude of Christ
  - C. Unity and the Trinity
  - D. Unity and the Church's Mission
- III. Ethnic Harmony
  - A. Jews and Gentiles in the OT and Gospels
  - B. Jews and Gentiles in the Acts and the Epistles
  - C. An Ongoing Problem
  - D. Striving for Ethnic Diversity
    1. Proactive Not Passive
    2. Partnership Not Token Gestures
    3. Biblical Obedience Not Pragmatism

Their desperation led them to consider their spiritual needs. A friend invited them to church, and they came. The first Sunday they arrived late, sat in the back pew, then bolted for the door before the closing song ended. As weeks passed, however, they moved progressively toward the middle of the sanctuary and remained after the service long enough to mingle. After a few casual conversations about the weather, work, and local sports teams, I asked if I might visit them to talk further about their blossoming faith. They shuffled their feet and cleared their throats a time or two, then responded, "Yes, we would very much like to have that conversation."

I sat in their living room, sipped sweet tea, and attempted to make them comfortable with more talk of weather and baseball. After twenty minutes and a refill of tea, I awkwardly steered the conversation toward spiritual matters. "We've enjoyed having you at church. Is there anything about Christianity, Jesus, or the church that I could help you understand?"

The husband responded with carefully measured words that he had obviously practiced. "Jesus is attractive to me," he said, "but I struggle with the church. My grandmother sometimes dragged me to church when I was a kid. What I remember most are the arguments I'd hear in the parking lot and hallways. One person didn't like the preacher, another defended the preacher, another piped up with suspicions about the church treasurer. It was the same arguments, over and over, year after year."

The wife nodded her head and held his hand.

"Even today," he continued, now speaking more quickly, "I drive down the street near our house and come to ten different churches with ten different names on their signs. And the people in those churches barely talk to each other. People all around them are dying and going to Hell—or so they say they believe—but they just spend all their time arguing."

He then dropped the generic "they" and looked me in the eye. "Why should I believe what you all say when you can't agree on what to tell me?"

I stared at my tea, and shifted in my chair. I stammered through an answer that, frankly, did not satisfy me any more than it satisfied them.

Thankfully, this couple continued working through their questions, and we celebrated their baptism into Christ a few months later. How many, though, with similar questions, remain separate from Christ and His Church because the church is, itself, separate?

God designed a unified church. When we discuss unity, we often use faulty terminology. We preach, for example, about creating unity, or of building a unified church. God already created this unity, and built a unified church through the blood of Jesus Christ. Therefore, as Robert Banks explains, "Unity in the church is a reality to be acknowledged, not a potential to be worked towards" (**64**). We do

How many remain separate from Christ and His Church because the church is, itself, separate?

not create unity; rather, we acknowledge and seek to manifest the unity that already exists.

Paul bade the church in Ephesus, *"Make every effort to keep the unity of the Spirit through the bond of peace"* (***Eph 4:3***). "Keep" translates from the Greek *terein,* which implies "guard, hold, or preserve" (**BAGD, 814**). God calls the church to preserve the unity that He included in His original design. Paul continued in Ephesians, *"There is one body and one Spirit—just as you were called to one hope when you were called—one Lord, one faith, one baptism; one God and Father of all, who is over all and through all and in all"* (***Eph 4:4-6***). The church's oneness stands central to its identity.

The NT consistently warns believers against any behavior that threatens this unity. ***Galatians***, for instance, includes *"hatred, discord, jealousy, fits of rage, selfish ambition, dissensions, factions and envy"* in a list of vices that would prevent someone from inheriting the kingdom of God (***Gal 5:20-21***). When Paul heard of disunity in a church such as Corinth, therefore, he wrote them and began the letter (following his normal greetings) with a call for unity, *"I appeal to you, brothers, in the name of our Lord Jesus Christ, that all of you agree with one another so that there may be no divisions among you and that you may be perfectly united in mind and thought"* (***1Cor 1:10***). The apostles and early elders tenaciously guarded the unity of the church, such that "schism was regarded as a vile sin" (**D. Smith, 23**).

BARRIERS TO CHURCH UNITY

If God designed and desires a unified church, why have so many congregations—not to mention the church universal—grown fragmented? Scripture identifies at least four causes of disunity.

SELFISHNESS

James asked, *"What causes fights and quarrels among you?"* He then answered his own question, *"Don't they come from the desires that battle within you? You want something but don't get it. You kill and covet, but you cannot have what you want. You quarrel and fight"* (***Jas 4:1-2***). Similarly, Paul confronted the Philippians in the midst of a discussion on unity, *"Do nothing out of selfish ambition or vain conceit, but in humility consider others better than yourselves"* (***Php 2:3***). Perhaps the most common cause of bickering within communities is the selfishness of its members. Individual believers often elevate their own preferences and opinions above the needs of others, and above the needs of the community. Though we attempt to mask this selfishness with noble intentions—"I only want what's best for the church"—the façade of nobility dissipates in the heat of the argument, revealing (perhaps even to ourselves) our true motivations. Put simply, I want it the way I like it.

A few years ago my older son Peyton came home from Kindergarten and made an announcement. "Dad," he said, "I've figured out what 'good fighting' is." My ears perked. What—particularly for a six-year-old boy—could constitute "good fighting?" Thankfully, he explained, "Good fighting is when you fight for the other person to get their way."

Imagine a community in which individuals fought for the preferences of others, instead of their own preferences. Picture a church where someone stood up in a meeting and said to a brother or sister who had a different opinion about a program, a policy, or a style of music, "I want us to do what will put a smile on your face."

"Good fighting is when you fight for the other person to get their way."

Individuals in unified churches bury selfishness and thrive on selflessness.

The Unwarranted Exaltation of Human Leaders

Christ stands central to the teaching, worship, focus, and authority of healthy, unified churches. When churches place primary focus on anyone or anything else, they fragment.

The church at Corinth exalted human leaders to an inappropriate status. *"Some from Chloe's household have informed me that there are quarrels among you,"* Paul explained. *"What I mean is this: One of you says, 'I follow Paul'; another, 'I follow Apollos'; another, 'I follow Cephas'; another, 'I follow Christ.' Is Christ divided? Was Paul crucified for you? Were you baptized in the name of Paul?"* (***1Cor 1:11-13***).

This particular mistake litters church history—congregations exalting human leaders to a status, esteem, and level of authority that only Christ rightfully holds. Human leaders certainly hold some authority, and they deserve our devotion (as discussed in chapter eleven), but they hold this authority and deserve this devotion only as they point their followers to Jesus, and not when they take the place of Jesus. *"Follow my example,"* Paul taught later in ***1 Corinthians***, *"as I follow the example of Christ"* (***1Cor 11:1***). For the Corinthians and for contemporary churches, the latter phrase qualifies the former phrase. Christians follow leaders as—and only as—those leaders follow Christ.

Christians follow leaders as those leaders follow Christ.

Paul returns to the issue in the ***third chapter of 1 Corinthians***, and offers a metaphor to help his readers understand how human leaders cooperate with God in unified churches:

> *[3]For since there is jealousy and quarreling among you, are you not worldly? [4]Are you not acting like mere men? For when one says, "I follow Paul," and another, "I follow Apollos," are you not mere men? [5]What, after all, is Apollos? And what is Paul? Only servants, through whom you came to believe—as the Lord has assigned to each his task. [6]I planted the seed, Apollos watered it, but God made it grow. [7]So neither he who plants nor he who waters is anything, but only God, who makes things grow. [8]The man who plants and the man who waters have one purpose, and each will be rewarded according to his own labor. [9]For we are God's fellow workers; you are God's field, God's building.* (***1Cor 3:3-9***)

When leaders cooperate with one another and mutually submit to God, God brings growth. As a result, people unite as "fellow workers."

A Focus on Nonessentials

Some matters of faith serve as foundational to our identity as Christians and the church. Without a common agreement to these core beliefs, people remain different at the core and, therefore, divided. ***First Corinthians***—which, as we discussed above, Paul wrote to a divided community—provides additional insight. Paul referred to the essential doctrines of the faith, "the gospel," which consists of matters of "first importance":

> *[1]Now, brothers, I want to remind you of the gospel I preached to you, which you received and on which you have taken your stand. [2]By this gospel you are saved, if you hold firmly to the word I preached to you. Otherwise, you have believed in vain. [3]For what I received I passed on to you as of first importance: that*

Christ died for our sins according to the Scriptures, [4]that he was buried, that he was raised on the third day according to the Scriptures. (***1Cor 15:1-4***)

From Paul's divinely inspired perspective, some matters of faith hold greater importance than others: if matters of "first importance" exist, logic requires that matters of second importance also exist. What elements of faith, according to Paul, hold first importance? What is the gospel Paul preached? What essential beliefs will unify Christians? Paul's list of essential doctrines is, frankly, brief: *"Christ died for our sins according to the Scriptures . . . he was buried . . . he was raised on the third day according to the Scriptures."* This teaching reveals the essential matters of Christian faith: the authority of Scripture (*"according to the Scriptures"*), and Jesus' deity (He is the Christ), substitutionary death, and triumphant resurrection.

As believers place primary emphasis on this basic gospel, we will find unity with one another.

As believers place primary emphasis on this basic gospel, we will find unity with one another. As we place primary emphasis on secondary matters, we will remain divided.

I recognize that the previous paragraph presents an ideal that proves elusive. The ideal hinges on believers identifying secondary, nonessential matters of faith and practice, and allowing difference of opinion on these secondary matters while still viewing one another as brothers and sisters in Christ. Some issues fall with relative ease into this nonessential category, such as paint colors, music styles, and which translation of the Bible Christians should use.[1] Christians can hold varying opinions on these issues and still refer to one another as family in Christ. Other issues, however, prove more difficult to categorize as essential or nonessential, or as of primary or secondary importance. These issues might include the relationship between the sovereignty of God and the free will of man (Calvinism or Arminian-

[1] I use the phrase "relative ease" somewhat tongue-in-cheek concerning the nonessentiality of these matters. Churches have divided over these very issues. This only further emphasizes, however, the argument of this section of the chapter—a focus on nonessentials divides churches. One would—in my opinion—have to stretch Scripture significantly to include paint colors, music styles, and a particular Bible translation in a list of essential doctrines.

ism?), miraculous gifts of the Spirit (ceased when the apostles died or present today?), and the interpretation of end-times prophecies (premillennialism or amillennialism?). People disagree on these issues—people who call themselves Christian, who have submitted to the Lordship of Christ, and who agree with those doctrines Paul identified as holding first importance in ***1 Corinthians 15:3-4***.

Christians must wrestle with questions such as this: If I am an Arminian who believes miraculous gifts ceased when the apostles died, and who holds to an amillennial view of the end times, can I call someone a brother or sister who is Calvinist, believes miraculous gifts exist today, and who holds a premillennial view of the end times—assuming we both believe the basic tenets Paul set forth as "the gospel" in ***1 Corinthians 15:3-4***?[2] We will not achieve unity until we answer that question affirmatively.

Recognizing that some doctrinal matters hold primary importance, while others hold secondary importance, allows a definite standard for unity—I do not call everyone "brother" or "sister," but only those who believe the basic tenets of the gospel. It also keeps us, however, from holding a standard so strict that it prevents us from fellowshipping with Christians who have understood Scripture differently than we have regarding secondary matters.

Gaining this perspective will not necessarily result in the merging of congregations of different backgrounds. Unity on that level would require agreement on many secondary matters. This perspective will advance, however, our capacity to consider others as brothers and sisters in Christ. And, it will further our ability to say, "We are not the only Christians, but we are Christians only."

Individualism

The church in Corinth provides yet another example of a barrier to Christian unity. Apparently some in the congregation felt they did not need others. Paul confronted this individualistic attitude with the image of the body:

> *21 The eye cannot say to the hand, 'I don't need you!' And the head cannot say to the feet, 'I don't need you!' 22 On the contrary, those parts of the body that seem to be weaker are indispensable.*

[2] To be clear, these are not the only issues that make this discussion difficult; but, they are issues that arise often.

. . . [25]There should be no division in the body . . . its parts should have equal concern for each other. [26]If one part suffers, every part suffers with it; if one part is honored, every part rejoices with it. (***1Cor 12:21-22,25-26***)

Healthy bodies consist of healthy parts that rely on and support one another. A hand—though the hand maintains a distinct identity and serves a distinct purpose—functions not by itself but as part of a body. Separate from the body, the hand withers and rots. Each body part remains alive as it remains connected to and functions in accord with the others.

Like those in Corinth, many contemporary Christians struggle with this corporate aspect of Christianity. "We have been so soaked in the individualism of modern Western culture that we feel threatened by the idea of our primary identity being that of the family we belong to," explains N.T. Wright, referring to the church (***Simply*, 203**). Charles Colson agrees, explaining that some

> concentrate on personal obedience to Christ as if all that matters is "Jesus and me," but in doing so they miss the point altogether. For Christianity is not a solitary belief system. Any genuine resurgence of Christianity, as history demonstrates, depends on a reawakening and renewal of that which is the essence of the faith—that is, the people of God, the new society, the body of Christ. (**32**)

Individualism threatens the unity of the church. Healthy community requires significant effort. If a person felt no need for community, that person would not put forth the necessary effort. If people do not need one another, why love? Why forgive? Why serve? Why participate? Why support? Why encourage? Individualism results in a scattered, unconnected people who relate with one another only when convenient and only when relating would bring personal benefit. Such "relationships" offer little in the way of authenticity or support, and they do not last. Stated simply, such relationships are not church. Unchecked individualism develops into a cancer that kills the community.

Unchecked individualism develops into a cancer that kills the community.

A Church Reunited

A group of Christians in Lakeland, Florida, planted the Grove Park Christian Church in 1956. Six years later, in 1962, the church split. The disagreement had little to do with doctrine or theology; rather, about fifty members grew dissatisfied with the personality of the preacher and left to start another congregation, the Lakeland Christian Church.

From 1962–2007, each congregation thrived and grew to about two hundred members. Their church buildings sat about four miles from each other. The congregations maintained a friendly relationship over the years, even holding joint Christmas and Easter programs.

In 2006, the Grove Park church lost their preacher. Shane Hargrave—the preacher at the Lakeland church—instigated a meeting between the elders of the two congregations. "In a town this size," Hargrave said, "it makes no sense to have two congregations less than four miles from each other." After much consideration and discussion, the elders mutually decided to pursue a merger. Many additional meetings, including some difficult discussions, commenced over the coming months. The two congregations held no doctrinal differences, but each had evolved into differing styles, methods, and programs. Furthermore, each congregation had its own leadership, staff, and facilities.

Hargrave explained to a local news reporter, "There was a lot of trust-building that had to take place. We decided it had to be a mutual merger. There had to be a new name and a new logo" (**McMullen**).

Lakeland Christian Church had moved into a new facility in 2005. And, as merger discussions took place in 2006 and 2007, another congregation approached the Grove Park church about purchasing its property. The congregations' leaders decided, therefore, to sell the Grove Park property, and that the new, combined church—which would carry the name Legacy Christian Church—would meet in the building recently built by the Lakeland congregation.

On January 6, 2008, the Legacy Christian Church held its first service, reuniting the congregations that had divided forty-five years before. At the end of the service, Shane Hargrave—now the preacher of the reunited congregation—invited attenders to cross over a bridge erected at the front of the auditorium and place cards in a basket to demonstrate their commitment of membership to the church.

Hugs, handshakes, and tears abounded.

"Look around at those sitting on your left and right," Hargrave said to the congregation. "In fifty years, people still may be talking about this day" (**McMullen**).

A CHURCH UNIFIED

A Horizontal Implication of a Vertical Relationship

In his letter to the church in Philippi—a congregation apparently not as troubled as the one in Corinth, but facing at least one conflict (***Php 4:2-3***)—Paul presented church unity as an outgrowth of believers' unity with Christ: *"If you have any encouragement from being united with Christ, if any comfort from his love, if any fellowship with the Spirit, if any tenderness and compassion, then make my joy complete by being like-minded, having the same love, being one in spirit and purpose"* (***Php 2:1-2***).

In the original Greek text, the opening words of verse one include a *"therefore"* (*oun*; the NIV loses this nuance). A literal translation would depict this opening verse as, "If there is, therefore, encouragement in Christ. . . ." The "therefore" holds significance because it connects the opening paragraph of chapter 2 with the closing paragraph of chapter 1. In the closing paragraph of chapter 1, Paul encouraged the Philippian believers to remain faithful in the face of difficulty. *"Then,"* he explained, *"whether I come and see you or only hear about you in my absence, I will know that you stand firm in one spirit, contending as one man for the faith of the gospel"* (***Php 1:27***). Paul exhorted them to remain faithful, and to remain faithful together.

Chapter 2 then continues this flow of thought by reminding the believers of the basis of this unity—their relationship with Christ. Paul introduces four assumptions concerning their relationship with Christ, each beginning with "if." Paul uses the "if" rhetorically—he assumes that the believers indeed have unity with Christ, comfort from His love, fellowship with the Spirit, and tenderness and compassion (***Php 2:1***). Based on these four

Remain faithful, and remain faithful together.

foundations, Paul then bade them, *"make my joy complete"* (*2:2*). Paul already found joy in these believers (*1:3-4*), but the joy remained incomplete because, apparently, the church remained less than fully unified. The Philippians could complete Paul's joy by manifesting four implications that reflect the previous four assumptions. Because of their relationship with Christ (as spelled out in the four assumptions), believers should be like minded, have the same love, be one in spirit, and be one in purpose (*2:2*). As evidenced in the chart below, each of the four implications do not necessarily parallel each of the four assumptions (though the second and third seem to), but they at least reflect one another. And, the group of implications certainly grows from the group of assumptions.

If you have . . . (assumptions)	Make my joy complete by . . . (implications)
any encouragement from being united with Christ	being like-minded
any comfort from his love	having the same love
any fellowship with the Spirit	being one in spirit
any tenderness and compassion	being one in purpose

In short, believers' unity with Christ provides the basis for their unity with one another. A.W. Tozer illustrated this principle by describing a room full of pianos: "Has it ever occurred to you that one hundred pianos all tuned to the same fork are automatically tuned to each other? They are of one accord by being tuned, not to each other, but to another standard to which each one must individually bow." In the same way, one hundred believers who have all submitted to Christ will find themselves automatically unified with one another (**54**).

A hundred believers, all submitted to Christ, are automatically unified with one another.

The Attitude of Christ

Paul continued his encouragement to the Philippians by pointing to the attitude with which they treat one another: *"Do nothing out of selfish ambition or vain conceit, but in humility consider others better than yourselves. Each of you should look not only to your own interests, but also to the interests of others"* (***Php 2:3-4***).

Before Hudson Taylor spoke at a large Presbyterian church in Melbourne, Australia, a moderator introduced the famous missionary in eloquent and glowing terms, listing his accomplishments and presenting him as "our illustrious guest." Taylor, embarrassed, stood quietly for a moment, then opened his message with these words: "Dear friends, I am the little servant of an illustrious Master." When A.W. Tozer was presented to a congregation in a similar manner, he responded, "All I can say is, Dear God, forgive him for what he said—and forgive me for enjoying it so much!" (**Wiersbe, 29-30**).

Humility requires an accurate perspective of one's standing before God. And, as Paul more directly addresses in ***Philippians 2:3-4***, it requires a loving deference to other people—considering others better than ourselves, and looking first to their interests. Paul speaks here not of a false humility, or of an unrealistic view of our own gifts and abilities as they compare to others. He teaches, rather, that "our consideration for others must precede concern for ourselves" (**Kent, 122**).

Humility requires an accurate perspective of one's standing before God.

Our attitude, in fact, *"should be the same as that of Christ Jesus"* (***Php 2:5***). This thought launched Paul into what many scholars believe was an early Christian hymn, or perhaps a poem Paul himself penned. The christological masterpiece—one of the more memorable passages in all the Bible—paints a portrait of Christ's incarnation, humanity, death, resurrection, and exaltation. Furthermore, it demonstrates that Christ Himself provides the ultimate example of the humility necessary for unity among believers:

> [5]*Your attitude should be the same as that of Christ Jesus:*
> [6]*Who, being in very nature God,*
> *did not consider equality with God something to be grasped,*
> [7]*but made himself nothing,*
> *taking the very nature of a servant,*
> *being made in human likeness.*
> [8]*And being found in appearance as a man,*

he humbled himself
and became obedient to death—
even death on a cross!
9 *Therefore God exalted him to the highest place*
and gave him the name that is above every name,
10 *that at the name of Jesus every knee should bow,*
in heaven and on earth and under the earth,
11 *and every tongue confess that Jesus Christ is Lord,*
to the glory of God the Father. (**Php 2:5-11**)

Paul's appeal for unity among the believers in Philippi came not as superficial advice or casual suggestions. Paul roots his theology of Christian unity in believers' relationships with Christ, and with lofty theology of Christ himself. "No thoughtful reader can be unmoved by the complexity and seriousness of Paul's stirring appeal" (**Martin, 95**).

The "One Another" Passages

- *Love one another* (***Jn 13:34***).
- *Be devoted to one another* (**Rom 12:10**).
- *Honor one another* (**Rom 12:10**).
- *Live in harmony with one another* (**Rom 12:16**).
- *Stop passing judgment on one another* (**Rom 14:13**).
- *Accept one another* (**Rom 15:7**).
- *Greet one another* (**Rom 16:16**).
- *Agree with one another* (**1Cor 1:10**).
- *Have equal concern for each other* (**1Cor 12:25**).
- *Serve one another* (**Gal 5:13**).
- *Let us not provoke and envy each other* (**Gal 5:26**).
- *Bear with one another* (**Eph 4:2**).
- *Be kind and compassionate to one another* (**Eph 4:32**).
- *Forgive each other* (**Eph 4:32**).
- *Speak to one another with psalms, hymns, and spiritual songs* (**Eph 5:19**).
- *Submit to one another* (**Eph 5:21**).
- *Do not lie to each other* (**Col 3:9**).
- *Teach and admonish one another* (**Col 3:16**).
- *Encourage one another* (**1Th 5:11**).
- *Build each other up* (**1Th 5:11**).

- *Live in peace with each other* (**1Th 5:13**).
- *Spur one another on* (**Heb 10:24**).
- *Do not slander one another* (**Jas 4:11**).
- *Don't grumble against each other* (**Jas 5:9**).
- *Confess your sins to each other* (**Jas 5:16**).
- *Pray for each other* (**Jas 5:16**).
- *Offer hospitality to one another* (**1Pet 4:9**).
- *Clothe yourselves in humility toward one another* (**1Pet 5:5**).

Unity and the Trinity

Paul pointed to Jesus to encourage the Philippians toward unity. Our discussion would remain incomplete, however, without considering Jesus' own words on the matter. The ***seventeenth chapter of John's Gospel*** pulls back the curtains of heaven and invites readers to eavesdrop on a conversation between Jesus and the Father. This prayer, which Jesus lifted to the Father on the eve of His crucifixion, reveals what stirs God's heart when He looks upon His church. Early in the prayer, Jesus spoke to the Father concerning His own glorification on the cross. Next, He prayed for the protection of the disciples after He was gone. Then, beginning in ***verse 20***, Jesus looked ahead to the church across the ages:

> [20]*My prayer is not for them alone [the disciples]. I pray also for those who will believe in me through their message, [21]that all of them may be one, Father, just as you are in me and I am in you. May they also be in us so that the world may believe that you have sent me. [22]I have given them the glory that you gave me, that they may be one as we are one: [23]I in them and you in me. May they be brought to complete unity to let the world know that you sent me and have loved them even as you have loved me.* (**Jn 17:20-23**)

Jesus envisions His community unified in a manner that reflects the Trinity (*"just as you are in me and I am in you"*). God Himself—Father, Son, and Spirit—has experienced community throughout eternity. John Ortberg explains, "The life of the Trinity is an unceasing offering and receiving of self-giving love. The Father holds the Son in his heart, and the Son does the same with the Father . . . and the Spirit holds and is held as well." They are "offering themselves to one another in ceaseless, joy-filled, mutually submissive, generous, creative, self-giving love—this is what the Trinity has been doing from before the beginning of time" (37). The three persons of the Trinity dwell in unity; Jesus prayed that the church will experience the same.

The three persons of the Trinity dwell in unity; Jesus prayed that the church will experience the same.

Beyond just pointing to the Trinity as an example of church unity, however, Jesus also desires that His followers join in the Trinity fellowship: *"May they also be in us . . . that they may be one as we are one: I in them and you in me"* (***Jn 17:21-23***). By inviting us into fellowship with Him, God widens the circle of the Trinity's fellowship to include the church.[3] This circle of fellowship leads believers "to a fuller experience of the Father and the Son" (**Morris, 650**).

Our admittance into this fellowship cost God significantly. The perfect holiness of the fellowship cannot tolerate sin. Our admittance, then, required the cleansing of our sin. The Son accepted the cross, the Father watched the Son endure the anguish of death. As Jesus accepted the guilt of sin, the Father and Son—for the first time in eternity—faced alienation from one another. The resulting cleansing we receive from Jesus' blood enables us, then, to enjoy eternal fellowship with the Father, Son, and Spirit; and with one another.

Unity and the Church's Mission

Jesus' prayer in ***John 17*** offers an additional, critical insight concerning the unity of the church. Jesus prayed that we would remain unified *"so that the world may believe that you have sent me"* (***17:21***). He continued, *"May they be brought to complete unity to let the world know that you sent me and have loved them even as you have loved me"* (***17:23***). According to Jesus' prayer, the church's ability to complete our mission hinges on our unity. A unified church can reach the world with the message of Christ; a divided church cannot. Our unity will convince the world that our message is valid; our division convinces the world otherwise. John Stott explains, "We cannot proclaim the gospel of God's love with any degree of integrity if we do not exhibit it in our love for others. Perhaps nothing is so damaging to the cause of Christ as a church which is either torn apart by jealousy,

[3]This does not intend to imply, by any means, that Christians become deified. Though we enter fellowship with God, we remain His finite creation.

rivalry, slander and malice, or preoccupied with its own selfish concerns" (**69**).

Bob Russell wrote of a church who, years ago, bickered over the use of a piano. Some wanted to use a piano during Sunday worship, others did not. The disagreement grew sharp, and the church divided over the issue. One Sunday, when members arrived for church, they discovered a new piano on stage. To the horror of half the congregation, someone played the piano during the service. These furious members marched out of the building in protest. The following Sunday, everyone returned to church, but the piano no longer sat on the stage. Those who bought the instrument could not find it, and immediately pointed fingers toward those who did not want the piano. For months, the piano remained lost. Accusations flew and tempers flared.

Six months later, someone finally found the missing piano . . . in the baptistery, where it had sat undiscovered the entire time. When a church fights, baptisteries remain unused. "I doubt," Russell lamented, "that God ever blesses a bickering church" (**149**).

When a church fights, baptisteries remain unused.

In contrast, Luke described the early church's togetherness: *"All the believers were **together** and had everything in common. . . . Every day they continued to meet **together** in the temple courts. They broke bread in their homes and ate **together** with glad and sincere hearts"* (**Acts 2:44,46**, emphasis added). As a result, *"The Lord added to their number daily those who were being saved"* (**Acts 2:47**).

While God may never bless a bickering church, He will bless a united church with kingdom fruit. As long as people walk the earth outside of Christ, therefore, the church's unity matters.

ETHNIC HARMONY

I recently preached in a chapel service at Carver Bible College—a school in downtown Atlanta that targets African American students who seek training in Bible and ministry. I preached the same message I had preached at my own congregation the prior Sunday. Two thoughts struck me. First, I did not have to change a word of the sermon. God's Word to the students at Carver Bible College is the same as God's Word to the predominantly white congregation in which I participate. Second, I felt unusually refreshed afterward. Though I preached essentially the same message, at the college it received more "amens" and "praise Gods" than it did at my church (a little more gravy for the meat!). The students' passion for worship and the Word energized me.

Carver Bible College's most well known graduate, Dr. Tony Evans, preaches at the Oak Cliff Bible Fellowship in Dallas. Dr. Evans has written extensively, preached at numerous Promise Keepers and other events, and leads "The Urban Alternative," a radio, television, and internet ministry. While Evans attended Carver during the 1960s, one Sunday he visited a white congregation. The church board told Evans, "You're not welcome here. Don't come back." A few years ago the current preacher of that church scheduled a service of repentance. Among other gestures, he wrote a letter of apology to Tony Evans, which Evans graciously accepted.

Today this still predominantly white congregation has moved from downtown Atlanta into the suburbs. Ironically, they sold their building to an African-American congregation. These events are a microcosm of the American church. We have made some progress in ethnic relations—the white church confessed their guilt, demonstrated repentance, and asked forgiveness. We still have a ways to go, however: the white church and black church continue to worship separately.

Jews and Gentiles in the OT and Gospels

The Bible speaks clearly and repeatedly concerning the relationships between believers of different ethnic backgrounds.

Though God established the old covenant with a particular people—the descendants of Abraham—even that covenant demonstrated His heart for people of all ethnicities. *"All peoples on earth will be blessed through you,"* God promised Abraham. Later, through the prophets such as Isaiah, God proclaimed, *"Let no foreigner who has bound himself to the LORD say, 'The LORD will surely exclude me from his people'"* (**Isa 56:3**). God added a few verses later,

> [6]*And foreigners who bind themselves to the LORD*
> *to serve him*
> *to love the name of the LORD,*
> *and to worship him,*

all who keep the Sabbath without desecrating it
and who hold fast to my covenant—
[7]these I will bring to my holy mountain
and give them joy in my house of prayer.
Their burnt offerings and sacrifices
will be accepted on my altar;
for my house will be called
a house of prayer for all nations. (***Isa 56:6-7***)

Though God began to work out His plan through a particular people group, He never intended for His plan to include only that group.

When Jesus arrived on the earth, the Gospel writers make clear that His mission carried implications for people of all backgrounds. Matthew and Luke include Gentiles in Jesus' genealogy (Tamar, Rahab, Ruth, and possibly Bathsheba; ***Mt 1:1-17; Lk 3:23-38***).[4] Gentile Magi visited and worshiped Jesus in Bethlehem (***Mt 2:1-12***). When Jesus began His ministry in Nazareth, He attended the synagogue and read aloud from Isaiah's prophecy about the coming Messiah (***Lk 4:18-19; Isa 61:1-2***), then boldly proclaimed that these prophecies applied to Himself, *"Today this scripture is fulfilled in your hearing"* (***Lk 4:21***). In response, *"All spoke well of him and were amazed at the gracious words that came from his lips"* (***4:22***). Jesus' claim of being the Messiah met with warm agreement. Jesus continued, however, by describing God's heart for people other than just the Israelites, demonstrated through Elijah's ministry to a widow in Zarephath and Elisha's ministry to Naaman the Syrian (***4:24-27***). Though the listeners smiled and nodded when Jesus claimed Messiahship, they snarled and raised their fists when He pointed to God's heart for Gentiles: *"All the people in the synagogue were furious when they heard this. They got up, drove him out of the town, and took him to the brow of the hill on which the town was built, in order to throw him down the cliff"* (***4:28-29***). Despite the prejudice displayed by His fellow Jews, Jesus spent much time ministering to Canaanite women, Roman centurions, and numerous other Gentiles. Jesus shared the Father's heart for all nations.

Gentile Magi visited and worshiped Jesus in Bethlehem.

[4]The fact that each of these are women carries additional significance. Jesus' mission and concern includes both genders, as well as all nations.

Jews and Gentiles in Acts and the Epistles

Despite Jesus' example, some early Jewish Christians had difficulty extending grace to Gentiles. Jewish Christians viewed the acceptance of Jesus as Messiah as the top of the mountain their ancestors had climbed for centuries—to accept Christ brought one's Jewishness to full culmination. For a Gentile to accept Christ, therefore, logic required that Gentile to begin at the bottom of the mountain and experience Jewishness. Then, that person could accept Christ. For a Gentile to simply accept Christ through faith and baptism seemed preposterous—far, far too easy, and unfair to those who had devoted their lives to laws and rituals of the Jewish faith.

Acts confronts this misunderstanding in several places; two hold most prominence—***Acts 10*** and ***Acts 15***. ***Acts 10*** begins by introducing readers to Cornelius—a centurion of the Italian regiment, and a Gentile. *"He and all his family were devout and God-fearing; he gave generously to those in need and prayed to God regularly"* (***Acts 10:2***). Apparently, though, his faith remained incomplete because he did not yet know about Jesus. Through a vision, God instructed Cornelius to send for Peter (***10:3-8***).

Meanwhile, God prepared Peter for the encounter by sending Peter a vision of unclean foods, and instructing him, *"Get up, Peter. Kill and eat"* (***Acts 10:13***). Peter refused because, as a devout Jew, he had never eaten unclean food. The heavenly voice responded, *"Do not call anything impure that God has made clean"* (***10:15***). This exchange took place three times, then the sheet carrying the unclean animals returned to heaven (***10:16***). While this vision confronted the Jewish Christians' attitude toward old covenant dietary restrictions, as Peter would soon learn, it also confronted the Jewish perspective of Gentile converts.

While Peter contemplated the significance of the vision, Cornelius's messengers stopped at the gate outside of the house, and called for him. When they explained why they came, *"Peter invited them men into the house to be his guests"* (***Acts 10:23***). The next day, they traveled together to Cornelius's home, where Peter said to a large group who gathered,

> *[28]You are well aware that it is against our law for a Jew to associate with a Gentile or visit him. But God has shown me that I*

should not call any man impure or unclean. . . . [34]I now realize how true it is that God does not show favoritism [35]but accepts men from every nation who fear him and do what is right. (***10:28,34-35***)

Peter's words indicate that he understood the meaning of the vision—it not only had to do with animals, but also with people. Peter preached to those gathered in the house, including Cornelius, then the Holy Spirit descended on them, and Peter instructed that they be baptized (***10:36-48***). Peter remained for a few days (***10:48***), a significant detail that demonstrates Peter's transformation. He stayed with and enjoyed table fellowship (***11:3***) with Gentiles—an act of fellowship in which Peter would not have partaken prior to receiving the vision from God.

The vision not only had to do with animals, but also with people.

A second significant event regarding Jew and Gentile relationships in ***Acts*** occurs in ***chapter 15***. Some Jewish believers from Judea had taught Gentile believers in Antioch, *"Unless you are circumcised, according to the custom taught by Moses, you cannot be saved"* (***Acts 15:1***). Paul and Barnabas opposed this message, and traveled with a few other believers to present the matter to the apostles and elders in Jerusalem. In Jerusalem, some Christians who had background as Pharisees concurred with the Jews in Antioch: *"The Gentiles must be circumcised and required to obey the law of Moses"* (***15:5***). When the apostles and elders met to consider the issue, Peter stood and told of his own experiences:

[7]Brothers, you know that some time ago God made a choice among you that the Gentiles might hear from my lips the message of the gospel and believe. [8]God, who knows the heart, showed that he accepted them by giving the Holy Spirit to them, just as he did to us. [9]He made no distinction between us and them, for he purified their hearts by faith. [10]Now then, why do you try to test God by putting on the necks of the disciples a yoke that neither we nor our fathers have been able to bear? [11]No! We believe it is through the grace of our Lord Jesus that we are saved, just as they are. (***Acts 15:7-11***)

After some additional discussion, James spoke on behalf of the Jerusalem leaders, *"We should not make it difficult for the Gentiles who are turning to God. Instead we should write to them, telling them to abstain from food polluted by idols, from sexual immorality, from the meat of strangled animals and from blood"* (***Acts 15:19-20***). The Jerusalem leaders required the Gentile Christians to comply in four areas that related to personal holiness and/or issues that might cause them to be stumbling blocks to their new Jewish brothers and sisters. Otherwise, Gentiles would not have to submit to the law of Moses.

In sum, Gentiles did not have to undergo circumcision or submit to old covenant ceremony to receive Christ. They did, however, need to live in a holy manner, and act kindly and compassionately toward their new Jewish brothers and sisters.

As happens with most deeply ingrained, difficult issues, the Jerusalem council of ***Acts 15*** did not completely settle the matter. Misunderstandings and old prejudices sometimes reappeared. In his epistles, therefore, Paul had to occasionally remind both Jew and Gentile believers of their equal standing in Christ, and of their unity in Him. Perhaps Paul's clearest and most powerful teaching on this matter came in ***Ephesians 2***:

The Jerusalem council did not completely settle the matter.

> [11]*Therefore, remember that formerly you who are Gentiles by
> birth and called "uncircumcised" by those who call themselves
> "the circumcision" (that done in the body by the hands of
> men)— [12]remember that at that time you were separate from
> Christ, excluded from citizenship in Israel and foreigners to the
> covenants of the promise, without hope and without God in the
> world. [13]But now in Christ Jesus you who once were far away have
> been brought near through the blood of Christ.*
>
> [14]*For he himself is our peace, who has made the two one and
> has destroyed the barrier, the dividing wall of hostility, [15]by abol-
> ishing in his flesh the law with its commandments and regulations.
> His purpose was to create in himself one new man out of the two,
> thus making peace, [16]and in this one body to reconcile both of
> them to God through the cross, by which he put to death their
> hostility. [17]He came and preached peace to you who were far
> away and peace to those who were near. [18]For through him we
> both have access to the Father by one Spirit.*
>
> [19]*Consequently, you are no longer foreigners and aliens, but
> fellow citizens with God's people and members of God's house-
> hold, [20]built on the foundation of the apostles and prophets, with
> Christ Jesus himself as the chief cornerstone. [21]In him the whole
> building is joined together and rises to become a holy temple in
> the Lord. [22]And in him you too are being built together to become
> a dwelling in which God lives by his Spirit.* (***Eph 2:11-22***)

A church that began Jewish struggled to incorporate Gentiles. Through God's direction and church leaders' insistence, however, the church began the difficult process of ethnic integration.

An Ongoing Problem

Sadly, almost two thousand years later, the process of ethnic integration remains incomplete. Though the theological depth of the issue may not appear as blatantly today—few would deliberately attempt to deny God's grace to someone simply because of their ethnicity—we do continue to flock with others who share our skin color and socioeconomic background.

I spoke recently with a friend who serves as a youth minister in Atlanta. He often visits local high schools to enjoy lunch with students—supporting those in his youth group, and seeking opportunities to connect with other teens who may not yet know Jesus. "Everyone thought this generation would not be so segregated," my friend said. "But from what I see in the cafeterias, not much has changed." Students congregate and eat with others who have the same ethnic or socioeconomic background. They seldom cross the stark lines.

I also spoke recently with an African American friend who serves on the ministerial staff of a predominantly white church. The church hired him, at least in part, hoping to build bridges and create a more ethnically diverse congregation. Though several black families have joined the church, my friend explained, the blacks and whites remain functionally separate—each in their own Sunday School classes and social groups. Despite church leaders' deliberate efforts, the divide remains, even though blacks and whites worship under the same roof.

As Douglas Foster explains, "The continued separation of the races in the church, regardless of all the reasons offered to maintain it, is rooted in sin. . . . Admittedly this is a complex problem, and the solutions are not quick or easy. But as Christians, we cannot be complacent" (**21**).

Building a Healthy Multi-Ethnic Church
Summarized from the book of the same name by Mark DeYmaz (San Francisco: Jossey-Bass, 2007)

1. EMBRACE DEPENDENCE: Diverse churches deliberately shun the individualism of the culture and pursue communities in which individuals depend on one another.

2. TAKE INTENTIONAL STEPS: Instead of only passively welcoming those of other backgrounds, ethnically diverse churches actively seek cross-cultural fellowship.
3. EMPOWER DIVERSE LEADERSHIP: True ethnic harmony involves diversity in all aspects of the church, including its leadership.
4. DEVELOP CROSS-CULTURAL RELATIONSHIPS: Believers in multiethnic churches develop authentic relationships with those of cultures different from their own.
5. PURSUE CROSS-CULTURAL COMPETENCE: In diverse churches, believers seek to understand one another's culture, background, and perspectives.
6. PROMOTE A SPIRIT OF INCLUSION: A multiethnic church creates an atmosphere in which people of various backgrounds feel welcome.
7. MOBILIZE FOR IMPACT: The diverse church stands uniquely prepared for effective ministry in the 21st century.

Striving for Ethnic Diversity

Ethnic harmony is not the primary goal of the church; however, the church cannot achieve our primary goal without it. We cannot reach the world for Christ, and we cannot exist and minister as God calls us to, without rediscovering the unity that God built into the foundations of the church. For, *"Here there is no Greek or Jew, circumcised or uncircumcised, barbarian, Scythian, slave or free, but Christ is all, and is in all"* (**Col 3:11**).

To rediscover ethnic harmony, today's church must address three areas.

Proactive Not Passive

The easy (though unsuccessful) approach to seeking a multiethnic church reveals itself in comments such as these: "People of other backgrounds are always welcome at our church. We would be glad to have them." In other words, "If they come to us, we'll gladly greet them." Churches should not approach ethnic harmony with this passivity any more than we would approach evangelism passively. If God calls us to seek the lost, as in the case of evangelism, this requires an active pursuit. If God calls us to church unity, which necessitates ethnic harmony, this also requires active pursuit.

Partnership Not Token Gestures

Often churches make token gestures toward those among them who have different backgrounds—perhaps inviting someone to play in a praise band, help in the nursery, or serve with a cooking team.

Mark DeYmaz, pastor of the Mosaic Church of Central Arkansas in Little Rock (see sidebar "Building a Multi-Ethnic Church"), speaks about a conversation he shared with an African American preacher. The preacher told Mark not to think they had integration simply because they had diverse individuals on the staff of their church:

> Mark, if you hire or otherwise empower African Americans only to lead your church in worship, you may inadvertently suggest to people, "We accept them as entertainers." If you hire or otherwise empower African Americans only to work with your children, you may inadvertently suggest, "We accept them to nanny our kids." And if you hire or otherwise employ African Americans only as janitors, you are quite clearly stating, "We expect them to clean up after us." It is only when you allow us to share your pulpit, to serve with you on the elder board or alongside you in apportioning the money, that we will be truly one with you in church. (**"Ethnic," 50**)

True integration involves a partnership in all areas of ministry and leadership, from top to bottom.

Biblical Obedience Not Pragmatism

In 1970, church growth guru Donald McGavran published *Understanding Church Growth*. The book contains many insightful, helpful principles garnered by McGavran from decades of experience and research. One principle, however, continues to cause controversy and debate forty years later. McGavran observed, "People like to become Christians without crossing racial, linguistic, or class barriers" (**163**). Based on this observation, McGavran urged churches to plant new congregations within various ethnic groups, rather than developing multiethnic communities. For example, if a white, middle-class church in America sought to reach the growing community of Hispanics in their town, they would reach more for Christ by planting a new Hispanic congregation than by incorporating their Hispanic neighbors into the existing church community.

This particular principle from McGavran has two problems—one theological, one pragmatic.

Theologically, as established earlier in this chapter, Scripture calls believers into fellowship with one another despite their differing ethnic backgrounds. This fellowship involves more than a friendly "hello" at the grocery store or perhaps worshiping together in an Easter sunrise service once a year. Biblical fellowship requires believers to serve one another, minister alongside one another, and rejoice and mourn together. It involves intimate, daily involvement in one another's lives. In Christ's church,

> [19]*You are no longer foreigners and aliens, but fellow citizens with God's people and members of God's household,* [20]*built on the foundation of the apostles and prophets, with Christ Jesus himself as the chief cornerstone.* [21]*In him the whole building is joined together and rises to become a holy temple in the Lord.* [22]*And in him you too are being built together to become a dwelling in which God lives by his Spirit.* (***Eph 2:19-22***)

When Paul visited Ephesus he did not plant one church among the Jews and another among the Gentiles. He planted one church. And he told them to work through their differences and celebrate their oneness in Christ.

In Ephesus Paul planted one church.

Even if McGavran's principle has some pragmatic validity—if churches grow more by keeping themselves separate and ethnically homogenous—churches faithful to Christ obey Him and the principles of His Word beyond pragmatism. Such churches move beyond a market-driven approach ("What will attract the biggest numbers?") and instead seek to develop communities that further God's ideals as presented in Scripture. We obey, and trust Him with the increase.

In addition to theological reasons, even a pragmatist would have to reevaluate his or her perspectives on multiethnic ministry based on recent research and cultural changes. Today's world differs significantly from the world in which McGavran wrote in 1970. Advances in travel and technology, and further integration of various ethnicities in society in general, have changed the landscape in which the church ministers and have changed the dynamics that best aid church growth. A study performed by the Hartford Institute for Religion Research in 2005 concluded that "while most congregations in America are composed of a single racial/ethnic group, those that are multi-racial are most likely to have experienced strong growth in worship attendance" (**DeYmaz, 119**).

Both theology and practical considerations push the church into a pursuit of ethnic harmony.

On the blood of Christ, God built a unified church. We have divided His body over numerous, sinful mistakes. Let us lay aside our selfishness, superficial arguments, individualism, and our prejudice that we might rediscover the joy of God's unified family—a family in which we together *"stand firm in one spirit, contending as one man for the faith of the gospel"* (***Php 1:27***).

What Do You Say?

1. Have you had a conversation similar to the one described in the opening paragraphs of this chapter? How did the conversation make you feel? Were you able to bring it to a resolution? If so, how?
2. Of the four barriers to unity given in the chapter (selfishness, unwarranted exaltation of human leaders, focus on nonessentials, and individualism), which do you believe poses the greatest threat to the contemporary church? Why?
3. Imagine you serve as a church member in one of the congregations in Lakeland, Florida, described in the sidebar. How would you feel when your leaders announced that you would be reuniting with the church from which you had divided forty-five years before? What would excite you? What would frighten you?
4. In what ways should the church's unity reflect the Trinity (the relationship between the Father, Son, and Holy Spirit)?
5. How does the unity or disunity of the church influence its ability to evangelize? How does this manifest itself in local congregations? How does it manifest itself in the church universal?
6. What progress have you seen regarding ethnic harmony in today's church? What evidence have you seen that progress is still needed?
7. Speaking as practically as possibly, what steps can your congregation take to actively pursue greater ethnic diversity?

CHAPTER THIRTEEN

WORD DRIVEN

A minister, new to the church, substitute taught the fifth grade boys Sunday School class while their usual teacher vacationed. The preacher decided to test the boys' knowledge, so he asked, "Who knocked down the walls of Jericho?" All the boys firmly denied any participation in the wall debacle.

Their biblical ignorance appalled the preacher. At the next church board meeting, he described what had happened in the Sunday School class. "Not one of those boys knows who knocked down the walls of Jericho," he said. The group of leaders remained silent, until a seasoned, longtime leader spoke up. "Preacher, it sounds like this is really bothering you. But I've known those boys since they were born—they're good boys. If they say they didn't knock down those walls, I believe them. Let's just take some cash out of the building repair fund, fix the walls, and let it go at that." A unanimous vote affirmed the recommendation.

Though most churches haven't fallen to the extreme depicted in this old story, many preachers wish their congregations had a better grasp of Scripture. Biblical churches are, well, *biblical*. They seek, study, and submit to God's Word.

Bob Russell describes how the leaders of the Southeast Christian Church emphasized this truth as the congregation relocated to their new building in 1998. Before the building received carpet, the staff met at the new facility wearing hard hats and carrying Bibles and magic markers. Staff members then went to the areas of the new facility where they would minister and wrote Scripture verses on the concrete floors. Those in children's ministry wrote passages such as, *"Let the little children come to me . . . for the kingdom of heaven belongs to such as these"* (**Mt 19:14**). In the music practice rooms, staff members penned, *"Let everything that has breath praise the Lord"* (**Ps 150:6**). The preachers wrote on the floors of their offices, *"Preach the word; be prepared in season and out of season"* (**2Tm 4:2**). A single lady who worked with the children wrote in her office, *"It is not good for the man to be alone"*! (**Gen 2:18**).

Russell explained to the staff, "Someday soon the scriptures will be covered with carpet. But I hope you will always remember what you have written today. And what we do today will be a visible reminder that we are always to stand on God's Word" (13).

THE AUTHORITY OF THE WORD

The Authority of God

God reigns as the sovereign king of the universe. He holds ultimate authority. Nothing or no one else possesses any authority except when granted such by God, *"for there is no authority except that which God has established"* (**Rom 13:1**). This principle holds true of the Bible. The Bible finds its authority not in its human writers, not in its antiquity, and not even in its subject matter. Scripture has authority only because of its origin: *"All Scripture is God-breathed"* (**2Tm 3:16**). *"No prophecy of Scripture came about by the prophet's own interpretation,"* wrote Peter. *"For prophecy never had its origin in the will of man, but men spoke from God as they were carried along by the Holy Spirit"* (**2Pet 1:20-21**). Paul acknowledges in a letter to Thessalonica that the instructions he and his companions gave the church, they gave *"by the authority of the Lord Jesus"* (**1Th 4:2**). When scholars speak of "the authority of Scripture," this phrase serves only as an abbreviated acknowledgement that God, who holds all authority, invested authority into His Word.

Scripture has authority only because of its origin.

This acknowledgement should lead the church to a more lofty perspective of Scripture than we sometimes exhibit. Often we treat the Bible as simply an answer book, a devotional work meant to elicit warm feelings, a checklist of rules to define our righteousness, or a mine of proofs for our doctrinal stances. Parts of Scripture may provide these things from time to time; however, such perspectives miss the ultimate transformative power of God's Word. Scripture reveals God—the sovereign, majestic, king. The Bible carries His authority and reveals His redemptive, loving, wise purposes. Furthermore, it beckons His followers to abandon all else to participate in His purposes. A trite, "Here is one of God's promises to make you feel good today," fades into relative inconsequence when measured against Scripture's weightier truths and higher aims. "God's authority vested in scripture is designed, as all God's authority is designed, to liberate human beings, to judge and condemn evil and sin in the world, to set people free to be fully human," explains N.T. Wright. "That's what God is in the business of doing. That is what his authority is there *for*. And when we use a shorthand phrase like 'authority of scripture' that is what we ought to be meaning. It is an authority with this shape and character, this purpose and goal" (**"Bible," 8**).

Scripture reveals God—the sovereign, majestic, king.

The Authority of the Apostles

In the New Testament era, God revealed His authoritative truth through Jesus' apostles. In the early days of the church, therefore, the believers *"devoted themselves to the apostles' teaching"* (**Acts 2:42**). Early Christians dedicated themselves to learning from apostles such as Peter, James, and John—those who sat at the feet of Jesus.

Christians today do not have the same privilege. Those who sat at Jesus' feet died long ago. We do, however, have the apostles' teaching recorded in the NT. The books of the NT come from the inspired pens of apostles such as Matthew, John, Peter, and Paul; and from the equally-inspired pens of those who recorded what they heard directly from the apostles, such as Mark (who ministered with Paul and Peter) and Luke (who ministered with Paul).

The church today continues to bow to apostolic authority by submitting ourselves to the Scriptures the apostles recorded. John Stott explained,

> The church is not 'over' the Holy Scriptures, but 'under' them, in the sense that the process of canonization was not one whereby the church conferred authority on the books, but one whereby the church acknowledged them to possess authority. And why? The books were recognized as giving the witness of the apostles to the life, teaching, death and resurrection of the Lord and the interpretation by the apostles of these events. To that apostolic authority the church must ever bow. (**25**).[1]

God holds all authority. He invested His authority, through the apostles, into the NT.

Inspiration and Illumination

The process by which God delivered His Word through and to humans includes the intimate involvement of the Holy Spirit. The Spirit spoke the truth of God through human writers (***2Pet 1:20-21***, quoted above) and reveals it to human readers and listeners (***1Cor 2:12***). These two tasks wear the labels "inspiration" and "illumination."

The Spirit led biblical writers to compose the Scriptures through the process of *inspiration*—"that work of the Holy Spirit in influencing the authors and compilers of Scripture to produce writings which adequately reflect what God desired to communicate to us" (**Grenz, 498**). When God invested His authority into Scripture, He did not simply deliver completed manuscripts, penned by His own hand, to printers around the world for distribution. Instead, His Spirit transmitted His authoritative Word through the pens, personalities, and experiences of human agents.[2] On some occasions, God dictated word-for-word

God delivered His Word by the intimate involvement of the Holy Spirit with humans.

[1] Stott credits this teaching to the bishops of the Anglican Communion, as stated during their 1958 Lambeth Conference.

[2] This mode of delivery for His Word places His truths in the nitty-gritty, day-to-day lives and experiences of real human beings. He could have, for example, given a list of bullet points to describe what a healthy church looks like: "Healthy churches submit to Christ; healthy churches include brotherly love;" etc. Instead God taught these truths through the tangible stories of churches such as those in Corinth, Philippi, and Ephesus. Through His Word, God shows (not just tells) us His truth. Furthermore, if God had given His Word in His own handwriting, without transmitting it through human people and circumstances, people would enshrine those manuscripts and worship Scripture, rather than He to whom Scripture points.

what the human authors wrote (***Ex 19:3***, et al.). On other occasions, human writers apparently had more input, though the process still occurred *"by the Holy Spirit"* (***Mk 12:36***, et al.). As a result, the Spirit's involvement ensures that the Bible consists of God's true and authoritative Word, and the involvement of human writers results in various writing styles, emotions, and a reflection of their experiences.

The Spirit's role of inspiration ended when the final words of Scripture appeared on paper. The Spirit continues to reveal Scripture, however, through the process of *illumination*—the ministry by which He aids the church in understanding and applying the truths of Scripture. In illumination, the Spirit does not add to Scripture; rather, He empowers our understanding of the truths that already exist. Jesus promised His disciples, *"The Counselor, the Holy Spirit, whom the Father will send in my name, will teach you all things and will remind you of everything I have said to you"* (***Jn 14:26***). And, Paul taught the Corinthians, *"We have not received the spirit of the world but the Spirit who is from God, that we may understand what God has freely given us"* (***1Cor 2:12***).

Who Decided What Books to Include in the Bible?
The Formation of the Canon of Scripture

The term "canon" transliterates from a Greek word that describes a rod used by a builder—a standard for plotting and measuring a straight line. Bible scholars use the term to describe the 66 books recognized by Christians as inspired by God and, therefore, authoritative.

The recognition of the OT canon proves difficult to trace historically. By the time Jesus lived on the earth, believers generally recognized the 39 books of the OT as authoritative (though some debate did take place).

The books of the NT began as writings and letters that circulated among early churches in the latter half of the first century. Though many letters and documents arose during that era, early believers recognized that those penned by apostles, or by apostle's companions, carried the authority of God. Peter, for example, referred to Paul's writings as Scripture (***2Pet 3:16***).

As an increasing number of heretical documents began circulating in the third and fourth centuries, the church saw the need to officially identify those books which had already been recognized as

Scripture. This identification of the NT canon occurred at the Council of Carthage in AD 397. To officially define the 27 books of the NT, church leaders primarily considered whether or not a book originated from an apostle. Furthermore, they considered whether or not a book held consistent with other revealed Scripture, and if the church had, over the years, recognized its authority.

In addition to the 66 books in the canon, the Roman Catholic, Anglican, and Greek Orthodox churches recognize an additional 15 books as deuterocanonical (second to the canon), called The Apocrypha. Though most do not believe these books carry the same authority as the 66 books of the canon, they feel the apocryphal books offer additional insight that helps believers understand biblical history and culture.

THE POWER OF THE WORD

Power in Its Encounter with God

The Lord promises that His Word will accomplish what He intends it to accomplish:

> [10]*As the rain and the snow*
> *come down from heaven,*
> *and do not return to it*
> *without watering the earth*
> *and making it bud and flourish,*
> *so that it yields seed for the sower and bread for the eater,*
> [11]*so is my word that goes out from my mouth:*
> *It will not return to me empty,*
> *but will accomplish what I desire*
> *and achieve the purpose for which I sent it.* (**Isa 55:10-11**)

What does God intend to accomplish through His Word? He intends to transform lives. One cannot encounter God's Word with a willing, open heart and leave the experience unchanged. *"For the word of God is living and active. Sharper than any double-edged sword, it penetrates even to dividing soul and spirit, joints and marrow; it judges the thoughts and attitudes of the heart"* (**Heb 4:12**). The Bible offers inspiring literature, informative history, and insightful

One cannot encounter God's Word with a willing, open heart and leave the experience unchanged.

wisdom. It takes readers to the heights of glory, romance, and mystery; and takes them through the valleys of guilt, regret, and heartache. It informs, frightens, mystifies, and motivates.

The previous three sentences, of course, could describe many Hollywood blockbusters and best-selling novels. The Bible's real power lies not in its potential to inspire or inform; rather, Scripture contains inexhaustible power because it offers mankind an encounter with the living Lord. In the Bible, we see Him. We learn from Him. We allow Him to reach into our craniums and chests and mold our minds and hearts with His tender, holy hands. As we wrestle with and meditate on biblical truth, God "breathes into our nostrils his own breath—the breath of life. And we become living beings—a church recreated in his image, more fully human, thinking, alive beings" (**N.T. Wright, "Bible," 13**).

Power in Its Mystery

God performs a work through His Word too grand and mysterious to easily explain or quantify. This does not imply that Scripture stands beyond understanding; ultimately God reveals—not conceals—Himself and His story through Scripture. It does imply, however, that we cannot always wrestle the glory of Scripture down into bullet points or bumper stickers.

Those of us who tend to approach Scripture in a primarily logical manner face particular temptation to provide quick, easy, logical answers to every Scriptural dilemma or mystery. Though we study, research, and reason with good intentions—and sometimes with helpful results—we risk inadvertently removing the sense of "otherliness" from God's majestic Word, denying its power and glory.

There is a risk of removing the sense of "otherliness" from God's majestic Word.

Imagine a biologist who visits a creek and catches a frog. She brings the animal back to her lab to study it. She lays the frog on a dissecting table and opens its body with a scalpel. She removes various organs, identifies internal systems, and records her findings. By the end of the afternoon, this biologist can explain the inner workings of a frog in great detail. The problem? The frog no longer jumps! Somewhere in the midst of the dissection, the biologist removed life and breath from the frog.

Bible scholars sometimes make a similar mistake. Though research and reasoning play a vital role in biblical scholarship, such scholarship should lead believers into greater awe of God, not just lead them through academic exercises.

Philosopher Paul Ricoeur described a three-stage process that should occur in Bible study. Tom Long explains this process:

> Paul Ricoeur has a notion that we move from naivety, to objectification, then to a second naivety. In the first naivety we say, "The Bible is the Word of God, it speaks God." Then, we objectify it when we say, "The Bible is an ancient document that speaks in a foreign language," and we dissect it. If the process freezes there, we've objectified biblical knowledge.
>
> Ideally, though, the exegesis leads us to *recover* what is now a second naivety: The Bible is the Word of God; I understand it through the cultural, historical, and sociological contexts; then it seizes me again with the same force it did originally (**Long in D. Overdorf, 106**).[3]

Too often, Bible scholars proceed from the first naivety to objectification, but stop before recovering the sense of awe that one should find when encountering God in His Word.

Power in Its Narrative

God delivered His Word to mankind as narrative. Scripture contains additional literary forms, such as prophecy, proverbs, psalms, and epistles. Even these nonnarrative genres, however, fit within the Bible's overall narrative framework. Scripture begins as story: *"In the beginning God created,"* (***Gen 1:1***). It ends with the ultimate happily-ever-after, as John describes the glory of the New Jerusalem and Jesus' promise to return. Between these bookends lies the story of God's redemption of a deeply flawed, but deeply loved, creation.

Scripture begins as story and ends with "happily ever after."

Story invigorates, and calls people into new worlds and new perspectives. It invites them to dream, imagine, and experience. Had

[3] Ricoeur discusses these ideas in ***The Symbolism of Evil*** (Boston: Beacon Press, 1967). It is granted that the process, in reality, is more dynamic and fluid than Ricoeur outlines. His categories, however, do help us guard against approaching Scripture only as academic exercise.

God given only a list of rules or a series of logical principles (as we often give in our explanations of Scripture), people may have simply ignored it or explained it away. Instead the story—His story painted with deep textures and majestic hues—energizes and transforms.

Furthermore, story invites readers to find themselves in, and to continue, the narrative. Richard Hays points to the Apostle Paul as an example for the church, "Paul reads Scripture in light of a narrative hermeneutic as a grand story of election and promise, the story of . . . God's covenant faithfulness reaching out to reclaim a fallen and broken humanity. . . . The church is called to find its identity and mission within this epic story stretching from Adam to Abraham to Moses to Isaiah to Christ to the saints in Paul's own historical moment" (147).

As God's people, we find our identity and purpose in God's story—the vigorous, effervescent, story of Scripture.

THE ORAL/COMMUNAL NATURE OF THE WORD

After I began planning toward this particular chapter, I drove by a church building in the town where I live. The sign in front of the church, in addition to the church name and service times, read, "The Bible is God's personal letter to you." Though I have read this elsewhere (and have probably taught it), on this particular day the words gave me pause.

The message on the sign contained some truth. Scripture can affect us in an intensely personal manner. And, personal Bible reading enhances a believer's daily walk with God. I have grown to understand, however, that if our study of Scripture remains entirely—or even primarily—a personal, individualistic practice, we stand in danger of using the Word of God in a manner other than how He intended. And, to consider Bible reading an exclusively individual matter misses the communal element that its Spirit-inspired writers intended.

Though we tend to read the Bible individualistically, an examination of the evidence reveals that it was written primarily to communities.

Our practice of Bible reading often misses the communal element intended by the writers.

The Historical Situation

Most people in biblical cultures could not read. The literacy rate ranged from around 5 percent to 20 percent, depending on the particular culture and era (**Witherington, *Word*, 7**). In most cases, therefore, one who composed a document intended for someone on the receiving end to read the document aloud to a group of people. Authors intended their words to be heard more so than read. "So far as we can tell," explains Ben Witherington,

Authors intended their words to be heard more so than read.

> no documents in antiquity were intended for 'silent' reading, and only a few were intended for private individuals to read. Ancient documents were always meant to be read out loud, and usually read out loud to a group of people. For the most part, documents were simply the necessary surrogates for oral communication. This was particularly true of ancient letters. (**ibid., 8**)

Believers understood this oral nature of Scripture even in the centuries beyond the NT era. For example, in his *Confessions* (AD 398), Augustine described an instance when he discovered his mentor, Ambrose, reading Scripture without moving his lips or making a sound. Augustine found the scene quite peculiar—people did not typically read silently to themselves.

Furthermore, even for those who could read, few could afford manuscripts of their own. Papyrus, ink, and able scribes proved more expensive than most could afford. Almost no one owned personal copies of Scripture. People received exposure to the Bible by hearing it read at public gatherings.

Therefore, we would more accurately view most biblical passages like sermons (written to be spoken) than books (written to be read). Hebrews provides a clear example. The author identifies Hebrews as *"my word of exhortation"* (***Heb 13:22***); refers to what he has said, not what he has written (***2:5; 5:11; 6:9; 8:1; 9:5; 11:32***); speaks of a lack of time for the message, not a lack of space (***11:32***); and uses rhetorical devices commonly found in spoken messages, such as alliteration (***1:1***, for example, contains five words that begin with the Greek letter *p*) and repetition (such as ***chapter 11***, which uses "by faith" 18 times).

Additional evidence for the oral nature of biblical documents rises from Paul's epistles, in which he repeatedly includes instructions to read Scripture—his letters and other Scriptures—aloud: *"Until I come, devote yourself to the public reading of Scripture"* (**1Tm 4:13**); *"I charge you before the Lord to have this letter read to all the brothers"* (**1Th 5:27**); and, *"After this letter has been read to you, see that it is also read in the church of the Laodiceans"* (**Col 4:16**).

In the ancient world, Scripture reading was a communal, oral experience, more so than a personal, silent experience.

The Contemporary Application

Contemporary culture—particularly in recent decades—has transitioned from primarily oral to primarily visual means of learning. In the field of education, for example, learning used to involve little more than students listening to a teacher. Now, education relies heavily on PowerPoints, videos, and websites. Online education gains more prominence every year, through which students learn by themselves in front of a computer, interacting with other students only occasionally, and through the virtual world. People used to gather information by listening, today they gather information by reading and watching, often by themselves.

Online education gains more prominence every year.

This transition is not necessarily morally wrong. Tools such as PowerPoint and video segments can enhance learning and, in the case of online education, offer opportunities to people who could not have furthered their education otherwise.[4]

The church should recognize, however, the implications of this transition on Bible reading among Christians. As a culture, we have grown more visual and private in our learning. The Bible, in contrast, is a primarily oral document, intended to be heard in community. To help people encounter the Word in its robust texture and depth, the church must recognize and deal with this reality. The following suggestions should help.

First, let us follow Paul's instructions to Timothy: *"Devote yourself to the public reading of Scripture"* (**1Tm 4:13**). Many church traditions include extended readings from various parts of Scripture in their

[4] I, myself, use such tools in the classroom, and sometimes from the pulpit. And, I teach online classes. These visual elements can be quite helpful.

weekly liturgy. Others, however, seldom read more than a verse or two in our gatherings. If Scripture bears the authority of our God and Father, and if Scripture drives living churches who passionately pursue the Lord and His purposes, why would we not devote significant portions of our services to Scripture reading?

Second, when we read Scripture publicly, let us read well. Too often, when people stand to read Bible passages aloud, they read poorly—without emotion, without passion, and obviously without having practiced. As a result, no one listens. In contrast, several years ago a member of the church I attended memorized the Sermon on the Mount, and recited it before our congregation. This man spoke the words as though he believed them. The pitch of his voice rose and fell to demonstrate the emphases of the text, his pace varied to reflect the rhythms of the text, and his gestures, movements, and facial expressions exposed the emotion of the text. The congregation leaned forward, perked their ears, and engaged their imaginations. They *listened*.[5]

When we read Scripture publicly, let us read well.

Third, when we read privately, let us read orally. Despite the emphasis in the previous paragraphs, private reading can benefit believers. It enhances our learning, growth, and devotion to God. It should not replace the public reading of Scripture, but it can serve as a helpful addition. Because of the oral nature of the Scriptures, however, we will find our private reading most impactful when we read orally. If the situation allows, we may actually read the words of Scripture aloud, allowing the rhythms, images, and other rhetorical devices to reveal the depth and textures the biblical writers intended. If the situation does not permit reading aloud, we can still read slowly enough that our minds can verbalize each word, so that we gain a sense of the texts' oral rhythms.

Finally, let us continually remind ourselves of the benefits of communal reading and study. When believers read and study the Word in community, we can challenge, comfort, and correct one another in a manner that is not possible when we read privately. Furthermore,

[5]Zondervan Publishers recently released *The Bible Experience*—an audio presentation of the entire Bible using the skilled voices of actors and musicians. Though many audio Bibles have surfaced over the years, in my opinion this surpasses the others in quality and power. Some congregations play portions during worship services, helping their members learn to listen to the Word.

such reading joins us with the community of God's people across the ages. We journey with Abraham out of Ur, we praise with David from the Psalms, we stand with the crowds in awe of Jesus' miracles, and we learn alongside of the Philippian believers as we hear Paul's epistle read.

David Block offered these convicting words to remind the church of the priority of the public reading of Scripture:

> Evangelicals must rediscover that in the reading of the Scriptures worshipers hear the voice of God. Despite our lofty creedal statements and our affirmations of the inerrancy, infallibility, and authority of the Scriptures, the relative absence of the Scriptures is one of the marks of contemporary evangelical worship. At best the Scriptures are read piecemeal and impatiently so that we might get on with the sermon, which suggests to the congregation that our interpretation of Scripture is much more important for them than the sacred word of God itself. At worst we do not open the Scriptures at all. In our efforts to be contemporary and relevant, we dismiss the reading of the Scriptures as a fossil whose vitality and usefulness has died long ago. . . . In the process we displace the voice of God with the foolish babbling of mortals, and the possibility of true worship is foreclosed. And then we wonder why there is such a famine for the word of God in the land (*Amos 8:11-14*). (435)

God delivered His Word to mankind as an oral document—words written to be read aloud in community. The church will experience the Bible's full power, then, when we hear it together. Together, we hear the Word. Together, we hear God. Together, we grow.

Suggestions for Using Scripture in Corporate Worship

- **Weekly Planning**: Every service should include Scripture reading. As leaders make weekly plans, they should include Bible reading along with other elements of a worship service. A lectionary can provide helpful guidance in choosing weekly readings.
- **Require Practice**: Those planning to read during a worship service should receive their assigned texts several days in advance,

and should practice the reading in front of others who can offer helpful critique.

- **Train Readers**: Churches would benefit from providing training sessions for those who read Scripture publicly. A speech teacher from a local school could provide this training.
- **Verbal and Nonverbal Communication Techniques**: Those who read Scripture aloud should take care to communicate effectively. Verbally, this includes deliberate use of pause, and variance in pitch, pace, and punctuation. Nonverbally, it includes facial expression, eye contact, gesture, and movement.
- **Introduce Passages**: Usually, readers should briefly introduce passages—even if just stating the book, chapter, and verses. A sentence or two of background may also prove helpful: "*Acts 2:42-47*, as Luke describes the fellowship of the church in its earliest days. . . ."
- **Dramatic Presentation**: Someone with acting skills may memorize an extended passage of Scripture and present it in a dramatic way.
- **Responsive Readings**: Scripture passages may be divided such that a leader reads certain portions, then the congregation responds with other portions. Many hymnals provide responsive readings, and others can be found online.
- **Congregational Reading**: Particularly with shorter passages, a leader might invite the congregation to read the entire passage aloud together. Words might be projected on a screen, or congregants might read from their own Bibles or those provided in a pew.
- **Begin and End with Scripture**: A worship service might begin with a passage that invites people into worship; it might end with a passage that appropriately draws the service to a close and/or leaves attenders with a final challenge.
- **Sprinkle Throughout**: Every part of a worship service can include Scripture. Churches might consider how to include, in various weeks, appropriate readings throughout the service.
- **Multiple Readers**: Two, three, or more readers might divide a passage into brief sections.
- **Multiple Characters**: When reading a narrative passage, multiple readers might each become a character in the text, reading the dialogue from that character. Another reader might serve as the narrator, reading the descriptive, nondialogue portions.

- **Introduce Songs with Scripture**: During portions of a service that include musical worship, leaders might read passages that relate to upcoming songs.
- **Use Songs with Lyrics from Scripture**: Many songs include direct quotations from Scripture, and can provide a meaningful way to worship and learn Scripture at the same time. When using such songs, leaders might point out which Scripture texts they quote.
- **Provide Musical Background to the Reading**: A talented musician could perform appropriate music during Scripture reading.
- **Have Congregation Stand**: To remind attenders to revere the Word of God, leaders might invite congregants to stand while it is read.

THE CENTRALITY OF THE WORD

John Beukema, a preacher in Illinois, tells of an evening he attended a showing of *The Passion of the Christ*. Like most believers who watched the movie, Beukema left the theater stunned by the images that depicted the suffering our Savior experienced on our behalf.

When he arrived home later that evening, Beukema opened his mail. The flier at the top of the pile came from a local church, inviting recipients to visit their "special community." The flier listed what made their community unique:

- No religious dogma—We encourage the freedom of individual thought and belief. A humanist view of life—Our faith is based on celebrating the inherent worth and dignity of every person.
- Warm, accessible services—Our Sunday services . . . typically include a mix of readings, music, moments of meditation or contemplation, and a sermon. . . .
- Our children's religious education program—We teach our kids to be accepting of differing beliefs and the importance of each person seeking his or her own truth. They study the world's major religions and draw on the core values of each faith tradition. . . .
- So if you're looking for a congregation that cherishes freedom of belief and opinion, with a warm sense of community and fellowship, please visit us!

"I had watched the horrific suffering of Jesus and heard him say, *'I am the way and the truth and the life. No one comes to the Father except through me,'*" explains Beukema. "Hours later I opened an invitation to visit a group where truth doesn't matter" (**"Church"**).

In an effort to appear relevant, some churches attempt to water down biblical truth. While they may have noble intentions, they miss the authoritative, transformative power of Scripture.

Proclaiming Biblical Truth

Paul taught Timothy concerning the usefulness of the Word, which grows from its divine authority, and encouraged Timothy to proclaim this Word despite those who turn away from truth:

> [14]*But as for you, continue in what you have learned and have become convinced of, because you know those from whom you learned it,* [15]*and how from infancy you have known the holy Scriptures, which are able to make you wise for salvation through faith in Christ Jesus.* [16]*All Scripture is God-breathed and is useful for teaching, rebuking, correcting and training in righteousness,* [17]*so that the man of God may be thoroughly equipped for every good work.*
>
> [4:1]*In the presence of God and of Christ Jesus, who will judge the living and the dead, and in view of his appearing and his kingdom, I give you this charge:* [2]*Preach the Word; be prepared in season and out of season; correct, rebuke and encourage—with great patience and careful instruction.* [3]*For the time will come when men will not put up with sound doctrine. Instead, to suit their own desires, they will gather around them a great number of teachers to say what their itching ears want to hear.* [4]*They will turn their ears away from the truth and turn aside to myths.* [5]*But you, keep your head in all situations, endure hardship, do the work of an evangelist, discharge all the duties of your ministry.* (***2Tm 3:14–4:5***)

Living, vibrant, fruitful churches hold to the truth passed down from God's prophets and apostles to generations of believers. They recognize that the Word *"is useful for teaching, rebuking, correcting, and training in righteousness"*; therefore, they *"Preach the Word . . . in season and out of season; correct, rebuke, and encourage."* Faithful churches unashamedly proclaim the Word from their pulpits, they diligently teach it in small groups and classes, they steadfastly rely on it in counseling offices, and they carefully seek its wisdom when making decisions. The Word drives faithful churches.

The Word drives faithful churches.

During his final sermons to the Israelites, Moses instructed God's people to pass along the teachings of God:

> [6]*These commandments that I give you today are to be upon your hearts.* [7]*Impress them on your children. Talk about them when you sit at home and when you walk along the road, when you lie down and when you get up.* [8]*Tie them as symbols on your hands and bind them on your foreheads.* [9]*Write them on the doorframes of your houses and on your gates.* (**Deu 6:6-9**)

The New Testament reveals the same emphasis on the teaching of the Word. Few people in the ancient world benefited from formal education, and (as noted above) most could not read. Teachers in the church, therefore, played significant roles. The early apostles placed such value on their teaching ministry that when other areas of service—valid as they were—interfered, the apostles designated other believers to fulfill those ministries so that they could *"give . . . attention to prayer and the ministry of the word"* (**Acts 6:4**). Teachers carried so much sway that James warned, *"Not many of you should presume to be teachers, my brothers, because you know that we who teach will be judged more strictly"* (***Jas 3:1***). Paul listed teachers as third, behind only apostles and prophets, in importance (***1Cor 12:28***), and included teaching among critical leadership functions (***Eph 4:11***).

Teaching holds such priority because God's community grows, finds nourishment, and bears kingdom fruit as it relies on and proclaims His Word.

A friend told me of a time in his life before he knew Jesus, but when he began to sense a gnawing spiritual hunger. He lived in California. One Sunday he opened the Yellow Pages to find a church. He randomly chose one, and arrived in time to hear the sermon. The preacher stood before the congregation and delivered a message about how to prepare for earthquakes—not spiritual earthquakes (he didn't use the term as a metaphor), but the earthquakes that sometimes shake California. He never opened a Bible. The message provided helpful information, but my friend walked away still spiritually hungry.

May no one ever walk away from our churches without having encountered the Word of God. May God's Word always stand central.

Let no one ever walk away from our churches without encountering the Word of God.

Combating False Teaching

During the NT era, just a few years after Jesus' ascension, false teachings about Christ began infiltrating the church. Jesus warned this would happen: *"Watch out for false prophets. They come to you in sheep's clothing, but inwardly they are ferocious wolves"* (**Mt 7:15**).

Circumstances in and around Ephesus in the latter half of the first century provide an example of NT congregations' battles against false teaching. In the late 50s,[6] Paul warned the Ephesian elders, *"Savage wolves will come in among you and will not spare the flock. Even from your own number men will arise and distort the truth in order to draw away disciples after them. So be on your guard!"* (**Acts 20:29-31**).

By the early 60s, what Paul warned of began to happen. Paul wrote to Timothy, *"Stay there in Ephesus so that you may command certain men not to teach false doctrines any longer"* (**1Tm 1:3**); *"The Spirit clearly says that in later times some will abandon the faith and follow deceiving spirits and things taught by demons. Such teachings come through hypocritical liars, whose consciences have been seared as with a hot iron"* (**1Tm 4:1-2**); and, *"If anyone teaches false doctrines and does not agree to the sound instruction of our Lord Jesus Christ and to godly teaching, he is conceited and understands nothing"* (**1Tm 6:3-4**).

By the mid 80s, John—probably the only apostle still living—served as a leader and patriarch for the church in Ephesus and other churches in the region. He wrote three letters to these churches (dated between the mid 80s and mid 90s), mincing no words about the false teachers, calling them "antichrists" and "liars": *"Who is the liar? It is the man who denies that Jesus is the Christ. Such a man is the antichrist—he denies the Father and the Son. . . . I am writing these things to you about those who are trying to lead you astray"* (**1Jn 2:22,26**). Later in the same letter, John warned his readers again, and identified the essence of the false teaching:

> *[1]Dear friends, do not believe every spirit, but test the spirits to see whether they are from God, because many false prophets have gone out into the world. [2]This is how you can recognize the Spirit of God: Every spirit that acknowledges that Jesus Christ has come in the flesh is from God, [3]but every spirit that does not acknowledge Jesus is not from God. This is the spirit of the antichrist,*

[6]The next few paragraphs contain several dates about which scholars debate. Even though the dates are debatable, the texts quoted demonstrate the progression of the false teaching in Ephesus.

which you have heard is coming and even now is already in the world. (***1Jn 4:1-3***)

John gives a basic litmus test to identify false teaching. If a teacher acknowledges that Jesus Christ came in the flesh, that teacher comes from God. If a teacher does not acknowledge Jesus' true identity, however, *"This is the spirit of the antichrist."* While false teaching may include other factors, this basic issue confronted John's readers.

Denying that Christ came in the flesh is a basic element of much false teaching.

The same basic falsehood marks false teaching today. Whether the teachings rise from popular movies or novels, or whether they rise from those who identify themselves as Christian teachers or churches, if any teaching attempts to diminish the deity of Jesus—that fact that Jesus is the Christ, fully God and fully man, our unique Lord who deserves our full submission—that teaching holds no place in a biblical, faithful church.

Additionally, false teachers are *"conceited,"* have *"an unhealthy interest in controversies and quarrels,"* and *"think that godliness is a means to financial gain"* (***1Tm 6:4-5***). They may teach that sin is inconsequential (***1Jn 3:7-10***), or deny the freedom believers enjoy in Christ (***Gal 2:4***).

Willem Van Gemeren contrasted the characteristics of true prophets and false prophets. Though his discussion grew from OT study, the basic elements of true and false teaching remain the same throughout both testaments (***Interpreting,* 63**):

True Prophets	False Prophets
Foundation: Revelation	Foundation: Revelation and Religion
Holistic proclamation	Selective proclamation
Independence from social structures	Depends on social structures
Focus on intermediating between God and man	Focus on the human ideal
Vision of the reality of the kingdom of God	Guardians of the status quo
God-centered ethics	Man-centered ethics
Suffering for the sake of God	Popularity and Power

Thoughts of false teaching might frighten us. They should, because false teaching continues circulating today. Our fear, however, should only raise our awareness of its existence, and propel us toward Christ and His Word. We need not let the fear paralyze us because, as John taught his readers, *"You, dear children, are from God and have overcome [the false teachers], because the one who is in you is greater than the one who is in the world"* (***1Jn 4:4***).

My high school basketball coach sometimes employed unusual techniques and ideas. The state championships he won, however, demonstrated the wisdom he brought to the game. One unique aspect of his approach involved his reluctance to "scout" other teams before we played them. Most coaches spend hours watching—either live or via film—the teams they will soon play, learning their offensive and defensive techniques and tendencies. My coach, however, chose to devote his attention to preparing his own team with proper basketball fundamentals. "If we play like we're supposed to play," he often said, "it doesn't matter who our opponent is or what they try. If we do the right things in the right way, we'll win."

Similarly, churches who remain true to Christ and faithfully teach and submit to His Word will never be derailed by false teaching. Instead, the Word of God, planted firmly in their communities, will bear kingdom fruit in and through them.

After the staff of Southeast Christian Church wrote Scripture passages on the not-yet-carpeted, concrete floors of their new building (as described in the opening of this chapter), the idea caught on. Hundreds of church members came to the new facility to write Scriptures on the floors. Teachers wrote on the floors where their classes would meet. Parents brought their children and wrote Scriptures together. Bob Russell concluded about this experience, "I believe the greatest reason God has chosen to bless Southeast Christian Church and thousands of other evangelical churches around the world is that we have been serious about upholding the absolute truth of God's Word" (13-15).

Churches who remain true to Christ and His Word will not be derailed by false teaching.

Faithful churches seek and submit to the authoritative Word of God.

What Do You Say?

1. If you were to write a Scripture passage on the floor of your church building, what would you write? What would you write beneath the pew where you sit, or the place where you serve? What would you write on the floor at your workplace? At your home?
2. In what ways might a person or a church treat Scripture as trivial? How could we make certain to treat it with the respect it deserves?
3. What does this chapter teach about the Spirit's roles of inspiration and illumination? How should recognizing these tasks of the Spirit influence the way we perceive, read, and apply Scripture?
4. Paul Ricoeur taught that Bible study should proceed from naivety (this is God's eternal Word), to objectification (this is an ancient document, originally written in a different language, influenced by history and culture), to a second naivety (this is God's eternal Word). Do you agree or disagree? What would happen if the process stopped with the initial naivety? What if it stopped after objectification? Why should the process end by readers recovering what Ricoeur called a sense of naivety?
5. If most of the Bible was written to be read aloud in a community setting (rather than read silently and individually), how should this influence the way we read the Bible today? Does this make it wrong to read individually? How can you incorporate more public reading of Scripture in your church?
6. Do you believe the ministry of teaching holds as much importance in today's church as it held in the NT church? Why or why not? Do you feel it should hold as much importance? If so, how might we give this ministry the emphasis it warrants?
7. What false teachings circulate today? How might we differentiate between a false teaching and a simple difference of opinion? What is the best means to combat false teaching?

CHAPTER FOURTEEN

RADICALLY PERSEVERANT

THE CHURCH AND SUFFERING

The Existence of Persecution

Along with several other friends and supporters, I recently received an email from a Christian in India. His words painted images of persecution, suffering, and martyrdom. He described how several members of one particular family were killed. One brother "was burned alive and his house was set on fire." Another brother was buried alive. "When they were putting soil over him, he pleaded for help, but they kept on putting the soil over him saying, 'You tell people that your Jesus has brought dead people to life. He can do that to you as well.'" Extremists beat Christians with clubs, torch their houses and church buildings, and order them to cease preaching Christ.

Though some believers in India turn away from the faith, many stand strong. As a result, God's church thrives. Blossoming from the soil of persecution, Christ's church continues to bear Kingdom fruit.

Though American Christians have, for the most part, enjoyed religious freedom and protection from persecution like that described above, the church universal has suffered since its inception. Never has a time existed when the church did not face persecution. In its earliest days, the church met opposition from unbelieving Jews (such as Saul). Soon thereafter, the Romans grew leery of the growing band of believers and, in time, persecuted the church severely. Throughout the remainder of history, up until this morning's newspaper, believers in various places around the globe have been pushed to the edges of society and have faced beatings, burnings, and martyrdom. "You've heard it said that the safest place to be is in the center of God's will," writes Erwin McManus. "I am sure this promise was well intended, but it is neither true nor innocuous. When we believe that God's purpose, intention, or promise is that we will be safe from harm, we are utterly disconnected from the movement and power of God" (32).

The church universal has suffered since its inception.

Biblical Warnings

Jesus warned His followers of this inevitable reality: *"All men will hate you because of me,"* He said (***Mt 10:22***). Later, Paul explained to a group of new believers, *"We must go through many hardships to enter the kingdom of God"* (***Acts 14:22***). Still later, the writer of Hebrews reminded his readers of the difficulties God's followers faced in prior generations:

> *[32]And what more shall I say? I do not have time to tell about Gideon, Barak, Samson, Jephthah, David, Samuel and the prophets, [33]who through faith conquered kingdoms, administered justice, and gained what was promised; who shut the mouths of lions, [34]quenched the fury of the flames, and escaped the edge of the sword; whose weakness was turned to strength; and who became powerful in battle and routed foreign armies. [35]Women received back their dead, raised to life again. Others were tortured and refused to be released, so that they might gain a better resurrection. [36]Some faced jeers and flogging, while still others were chained and put in prison. [37]They were stoned; they were sawed in two; they were put to death by the sword. They went about in sheepskins and goatskins, destitute, persecuted and mistreated— [38]the world was not worthy of them. They wandered in deserts and mountains, and in caves and holes in the ground.* (***Heb 11:32-38***)

Peter, likewise, instructed, *"To this you were called, because Christ suffered for you, leaving you an example, that you should follow in his steps"* (***1Pet 2:21***). And further,

> [12]*Dear friends, do not be surprised at the painful trial you are suffering, as though something strange were happening to you.* [13]*But rejoice that you participate in the sufferings of Christ, so that you may be overjoyed when his glory is revealed.* [14]*If you are insulted because of the name of Christ, you are blessed, for the Spirit of glory and of God rests on you. . . .* [16]*If you suffer as a Christian, do not be ashamed, but praise God that you bear that name.* (**1Pet 4:12-14,16**)

Despite the opposition they faced, early believers remained extraordinarily undeterred in their dedication to the cause of Christ. What enabled them to persevere? What has enabled the church to endure through the centuries that followed? What enables the church today, in the face of persecution in varying degrees around the globe, to persevere?

> **Early believers remained extraordinarily undeterred in their dedication to the cause of Christ.**

Answers to these questions will prove critical because current trends suggest the church's future on earth will not get any easier. To endure in a world increasingly hostile to the Christian faith, today's church must learn perseverance from the NT church.

OUR COMMISSION

The Apostles' Perseverance

In one of Luke's summary statements concerning the early church, he wrote, *"Day after day, in the temple courts and from house to house, they never stopped teaching and proclaiming the good news that Jesus is the Christ"* (**Acts 5:42**). Day after day, come what may, they never stopped preaching Christ.

The summary statement grows even more significant when understood in its context. The statement occurs at the end of a narrative in which these early Christians faced imprisonment, beatings, and further threats. The Jewish religious officials, jealous of the Christians' growing influence, *"arrested the apostles and put them in the public jail"* (**Acts 5:18**). *"But,"* the story continues,

> *during the night an angel of the Lord opened the doors of the jail and brought them out.* [20]*"Go, stand in the temple courts," he said, "and tell the people the full message of this new life."* [21]*At daybreak they entered the temple courts, as they had been told, and began to teach the people.* (**5:19-21**)

Jesus commissioned them to proclaim His name; therefore, they proclaimed.

This instruction from the angel gave specific expression to the commission Jesus gave His followers before He ascended into heaven, *"Go and make disciples of all nations"* (***Mt 28:19***). Jesus commissioned them to proclaim His name; therefore, they proclaimed.

Jesus' commission energized His disciples. When the Jewish officials discovered the disciples, whom they thought were in jail, preaching in the temple courts, they arrested the disciples again. *"We gave you strict orders not to teach in this name,"* they said (***Acts 5:28***). Peter and the others replied, *"We must obey God rather than men!"* (***5:29***). Though threatened with imprisonment and scourging, though ordered repeatedly to cease preaching in the name of Jesus, they charged forward because God, to whom they gave ultimate allegiance, had commissioned them.

At Peter's response (and his subsequent sermon about Jesus, ***Acts 5:30-32***), the infuriated officials wanted to execute the disciples. The Pharisee Gamaliel diffused the situation, and convinced the others to flog the disciples, order them again not to preach, and release them.[1] Then, *"The apostles left the Sanhedrin, rejoicing because they had been counted worthy of suffering disgrace for the Name"* (***Acts 5:41***). In this one brief narrative—not to mention events prior and subsequent to these—these apostles faced two arrests, beatings, humiliation, and were threatened twice to never again preach in the name of Jesus.

This narrative then leads Luke to the concluding summary statement noted above, *"Day after day, in the temple courts and from house to house, they never stopped teaching and proclaiming the good news that Jesus is the Christ"* (***5:42***)

The Lesson for Today's Church

The critical question: How did they persevere? What enabled them to continue *"day after day,"* and to *"never stop teaching and pro-*

[1] Gamaliel convinced the others with this logic: *"Leave the men alone! Let them go! For if their purpose or activity is of human origin, it will fail. But if it is from God, you will not be able to stop these men; you will only find yourselves fighting against God"* (***Acts 5:38-39***). Though his logic may have been flawed—sometimes efforts apart from God do meet with earthly success—it thankfully resulted in the disciples' release.

claiming the good news"? The answer rests in the narrative that precedes the summary statement. These apostles hung with tenacious allegiance to their commission from Jesus. Jesus Christ—the very anointed Son of God—called and commissioned them with a task of eternal consequence. This commission—their calling to proclaim the name of Christ—energized them and gave them reason to endure. A divine commission led to their divine allegiance to proclaim the divine message.

We have a divine commission for divine allegiance to the divine message.

Likewise, today's church finds strength to persevere in its divine commission. The salvation of the world rides the crest of the church's proclamation. The message must reach the ears of the nations. The church must proclaim it. Those who sense this calling operate with such determination, thrill, resolve, fortitude, and old-fashioned grit that they hang in there even when others would give up. Reggie McNeal wrote that those "secure in their call will charge Hell with a water pistol" (**96**).

Fred Craddock often says that he begins each day with a particular prayer. When he awakens, and throws his feet out onto the floor, he prays, "Lord thank you for giving me a way of life more important than how I feel about it on any given day." Every Christian can pray likewise. The church—God's faithful community—perseveres, impassioned by our commission.

OUR CONFIDENCE

Confidence Brings Boldness

Another clue concerning the early believers' ability to persevere amid persecution appears in **Acts 4**, in a chapter prior to the narrative described above. This chapter depicts another occasion—the first recorded in **Acts**—when Jewish officials imprisoned those who preached Christ. *"On their release,"* Luke explains,

> *Peter and John went back to their own people and reported all that the chief priests and elders had said to them. [24]When they heard this, they raised their voices together in prayer to God. "Sovereign Lord," they said, "you made the heaven and the earth and the sea and everything in them."* (**Acts 4:23-24**)

Their prayer continued by describing God's sovereignty as displayed in the crucifixion of Christ. Then, they asked, *"Now, Lord, consider their threats and enable your servants to speak your word with great boldness"* (***4:29***).

The disciples began their prayer by addressing God as *"Sovereign Lord"* (***Acts 4:24***). This English title translates from the Greek *despotes*, which occurs only 10 times in the NT, and depicts one who has absolute ownership of, authority over, and responsibility for another.[2] When the disciples address God as *despotes*, this particular word choice emphasizes their submission to and reliance on God's absolute ownership and authority over them. In unmitigated allegiance, they looked to God as king, ruler, master, and provider. They trusted this relationship—resting in the assurance of His dominion.[3]

God's sovereignty provides His church confidence to remain bold in proclamation and ministry. As ***Acts*** continues unfolding, it reveals the church's bold willingness to face further imprisonment, persecution, and martyrdom, empowered by their trust in the sovereign God.

Confidence Brings Obedience

The OT provides a vivid picture of trust in God's sovereignty through its depiction of Shadrach, Meshach, and Abednego in ***Daniel 3***. The three, with Daniel, suffered capture and captivity at the hands of Babylon. While in captivity, they worked themselves into positions of authority in the Babylonian government. Any sense of security these positions garnered, however, melted when they heard King Nebuchadnezzar's decree—when the instruments played, everyone in the kingdom must bow to an idol, else face a blazing furnace.

When the instruments played, Shadrach, Meshach, and Abednego stood tall—backs straight, chin up, shoulders back, and faith intact.

Furious, Nebuchadnezzar summoned the three men. He offered them another chance: *"Now when you hear the sound . . . if you are*

[2]Translators often depict *despotes* with the English "master" (the NT uses the term to describe a master/slave relationship), and less often as "Lord" or, in the NIV, "Sovereign Lord." The much more common term translated "Lord" is *kurios* (used 720 times in NT). Though *despotes* and *kurios* overlap in meaning a great deal, *kurios* has a wider semantic range that includes Lord and master at one extreme, but at the other extreme a simple expression of respect such as "sir" (**BADG, 458-460**; "sir" as in ***Mt 13:27; 25:11; 27:63;*** et al.). *Despotes*, on the other hand, remains more narrowly in the range of Lord, master, or owner (**BADG, 176**).

[3]Chapter 5 provides more insight into God's sovereignty over His community.

ready to fall down and worship the image I made, very good. But if you do not worship it, you will be thrown immediately into a blazing furnace. Then what god will be able to save you from my hand?" (**Dan 3:15-16**).

Undaunted, Shadrach, Meshach, and Abednego replied, *"If we are thrown into the blazing furnace, the God we serve is able to save us from it, and he will rescue us from your hand, O king. But even if he does not, we want you to know, O king, that we will not serve your gods or worship the image of gold you have set up"* (**Dan 3:17-18**).

What enabled such radical commitment?

First, Shadrach, Meshach, and Abednego trusted in God's ability: *"The God we serve is able to save us from it"* (**Dan 3:17**). They recognized that no earthly king or blazing furnace came near eclipsing the power of God Almighty. God's ability infinitely surpasses any person, circumstance, or authority of this world. No one and nothing can overpower Him.

No earthly king or blazing furnace came near eclipsing the power of God Almighty.

Additionally, they trusted God's sovereignty. Though they knew God could save them, they did not know for certain that God would save them. *"Even if he does not [save us], O king,"* they vowed, *"we will not serve your gods"* (**Dan 3:18**). The three men remained faithful to God, trusting His ability to save them from the furnace. But, they vowed to remain faithful even if God chose not to save them. They trusted that God, in His sovereignty, knew and would do whatever was best for His kingdom.

God's church perseveres when we trust God's ability and sovereignty.

Martin and Gracia Burnham served as missionaries in the Philippines. In May of 2001, terrorists captured the Burnhams and held them hostage. They remained captive for over a year. In June of 2002, the Philippine military raided the terrorist camp, sending the terrorists running, with the Burnhams in tow. Martin and Gracia endured seven days on the run with little food, trudging through torrential downpours. They finally reached a place where they could rest, and Martin strung a hammock for himself and Gracia at the top of a knoll. When they laid down, however, bullets began flying and ripped into both their bodies. They fell from the hammock and rolled to the bottom of the knoll, landing next to each other. Gracia survived, Martin did not.

A missionary colleague of the Burnhams described her own struggle with Martin's death. She had prayed faithfully for the couple for over a year, begging God to protect them. When news arrived of Martin's death, she prayed, "God, this isn't how I would've written the last chapter."

Through the conviction of her heart, God replied to her, "This isn't the last chapter." Someone else who heard her tell the story added, "And it's not your book!" (**Asimakoupoulos, "Hostage"**).

God unfolds His story—chapter by chapter—in accordance with His sovereign will. Though some pages along the way—even some entire chapters—may confound us, perseverant believers recognize that mankind has a limited perspective of life. They persist in faithful service trusting *"the author and perfecter of our faith"* (***Heb 12:2***).

Perseverant believers recognize that mankind has a limited perspective of life.

Confidence Brings Perseverance

The final book of the NT canon provides additional insight about how God's sovereignty enables our perseverance. In the latter third of the first century, the Apostle John led and ministered among churches in Asia Minor, such as the churches in Ephesus, Smyrna, and Philadelphia. Though the Roman persecution of the church would not reach its peak for a few more decades, the seeds of such persecution began sprouting in various places throughout the empire during John's lifetime. The Romans grew increasingly leery of the growing band of Christians—particularly their disbelief in the Roman gods, their refusal to bow to Caesar as ultimate lord, and their strange customs such as "eating flesh and drinking blood" and "loving" their brothers and sisters. A few believers had already faced martyrdom; many more faced threats and had been pushed to the edges of society. Churches feared for their safety.

Church leaders like John, however, feared something of greater consequence than the physical persecution. Robert Lowery writes of

> the greatest menace facing the Christians in John's day. It was not from direct persecution, but from temptation to compro-

> mise with their culture. . . . As the Jews in Daniel's day faced the threat of "Babylonization," so the Christians in John's day faced the threat of "Romanization." John saw Roman culture, like Babylon of old, as seductress, using all of its moral, social, economic, religious, political, and military might to lure Christians into complacency in serving God and loving one another. (***Revelation*, 59**)

When the Romans arrested John for his persistence in preaching the gospel, they exiled him to the island of Patmos, not far from the coast of Ephesus. John explains what happened during his exile:

> *9I, John, your brother and companion in the suffering and kingdom and patient endurance that are ours in Jesus, was on the island of Patmos because of the word of God and the testimony of Jesus. 10On the Lord's Day I was in the Spirit, and I heard behind me a loud voice like a trumpet, 11which said: "Write on a scroll what you see and send it to the seven churches: to Ephesus, Smyrna, Pergamum, Thyatira, Sardis, Philadelphia and Laodicea."* (***Rev 1:9-11***)

John then turned to see who spoke to him:

> *12bAnd when I turned I saw seven golden lampstands, 13and among the lampstands was someone "like a son of man," dressed in a robe reaching down to his feet and with a golden sash around his chest. 14His head and hair were white like wool, as white as snow, and his eyes were like blazing fire. 15His feet were like bronze glowing in a furnace, and his voice was like the sound of rushing waters. 16In his right hand he held seven stars, and out of his mouth came a sharp double-edged sword. His face was like the sun shining in all its brilliance.*
>
> *17When I saw him, I fell at his feet as though dead. Then he placed his right hand on me and said: "Do not be afraid. I am the First and the Last. 18I am the Living One; I was dead, and behold I am alive for ever and ever! And I hold the keys of death and Hades."* (***Rev 1:12-18***)

With this and other similar visions sprinkled throughout Revelation—images of our sovereign, majestic, brilliant Lord, who reigns above all evil in the present and in the future—John bolstered the seven churches' confidence in God, enabling them to persevere in their faith. John wrote specifically to the church in Smyrna, for example, *"Do not be afraid of what you are about to suffer. I tell you, the devil will put some of you in prison to test you, and you will suffer persecution for ten days. Be faithful, even to the point of death, and I will give you the crown of life"* (**2:10**). And, he encouraged the church in Ephesus, *"You have persevered and have endured hardships for my name, and have not grown weary"* (**2:2-3**). To all of the churches, John explained, *"If anyone is to go into captivity, into captivity he will go. If anyone is to be killed with the sword, with the sword he will be killed. This calls for patient endurance and faithfulness on the part of the saints"* (**13:10**).

Nothing and no one eclipses the power of our God.

Nothing and no one eclipses the power of our God. We can, therefore, proceed in confidence and faithfulness, despite the obstacles our culture—or even Satan himself—places in our path. He has and will conquer all forces that oppose His church.

The Seven Churches of Revelation

EPHESUS:	An urban center with a population around 350,000, Ephesus drew acclaim for its architecture and arts. Many consider its temple to Artemis (goddess of fertility) as one of the seven wonders of the ancient world. The church had done much good—working hard, persevering, and confronting false teachers. They had, however, forsaken their first love. In his epistles, John had encouraged his readers to combat false teaching, and to love one another. Apparently, those in Ephesus gave such attention to battling error that they neglected their love for one another and for God.
SMYRNA:	Smyrna rested on a mountainside above a harbor. The wealthy city boasted a street of gold stretching from one end of the city to another, connecting two pagan temples. The Christians in Smyrna apparently did not share in its wealth, for they faced affliction, poverty, and slander. Despite their poverty, they enjoyed spiritual wealth, and the promise that their continued faithfulness would bring eternal reward.
PERGAMUM:	Pergamum, a regional center for culture and justice, sat on a hill that dominated its area. A massive altar to Zeus was built just above the city (*"where Satan*

has his throne," Rev 2:13). Though the believers in the city did not renounce their faith, they compromised with some false teachings and gave in to immoral behavior. Jesus promised judgment if they did not repent. If they would repent, He promised to forgive and provide for them.

THYATIRA: Thyatira rested in the valley below Pergamum. More "blue collar" than Pergamum, the city included several trade guilds for workers such as potters, tailors, and coppersmiths. The church had grown in deeds, love, faith, and service. They had, however, tolerated false teaching and immorality. Jesus threatened severe punishment for a particular false teacher (*"that woman Jezebel, who calls herself a prophetess,"* **Rev 2:20**) and those who followed her, but promised authority and reward for those who remained obedient.

SARDIS: Sardis sat in a river basin with fertile soil. The city had previously grown wealthy from gold. More recently, it enjoyed flourishing commerce. Because the believers in Sardis had apparently become complacent—"a perfect model of inoffensive Christianity" (**Koester, 67**)—Jesus called them to *"wake up!"* (**Rev 3:2**). They had obeyed incompletely, now they must obey more fully, or else remain unprepared for Jesus' return. Those who kept themselves unsoiled, and therefore worthy, would walk with Jesus, wearing white robes.

PHILADELPHIA: Philadelphia rested in a fertile valley and enjoyed rich agriculture. Despite their hardships, Christians in Philadelphia stayed faithful to Christ and to His name. Because of their faithfulness, Jesus promised to punish those who persecuted them, and to protect them from an upcoming period of trial. Jesus promised concerning those who continued to persevere, *"Him who overcomes, I will make a pillar in the temple of my God"* (**Rev 3:12**). Two of the few remains still standing from ancient Philadelphia are giant pillars.

LAODICEA	Laodicea sat in a valley, alongside a river. The city grew wealthy from its production of black wool, textiles, and an eye salve. They took pride in their self-sufficiency—when an earthquake destroyed Laodicea in AD 60, they refused Rome's help to rebuild (Sardis and Philadelphia were also destroyed by an earthquake, but they sought Roman help). The city built water ducts to transport water from the hot springs of nearby Hieropolis, and cold water from Colosse. When the water arrived, however, it was all lukewarm. Jesus compared the church's faith to the lukewarm water—indecisive, noncommittal, and therefore useless. Christ hoped to reenter (*"I stand at the door and knock,"* ***Rev 3:20***), that he might fellowship with them again.

OUR CHILDHOOD

The Father's Love Lavished on Us

In addition to his exhortations to persevere found in ***Revelation***, John also encouraged the believers in Asia Minor in three epistles. In these epistles, John exhorted his *"dear children"* to persist in faith, despite the forces that battled against them. In the first epistle, he encouraged them to *"walk in the light"* (***1Jn 1:7***), stay free from sin (***2:1***), *"walk as Jesus did"* (***2:6***), love their brothers (***2:10; 4:11***), not love the world (***2:15***), stay faithful to truth (***2:22-24; 4:1***), minister to others in need (***3:17-18***), and to obey God's commands (***5:3***). His second and third epistles repeat similar themes.

In the midst of such encouragements, John reminded his readers of their relationship with God the Father: *"How great is the love the Father has lavished on us,"* he exclaimed, *"that we should be called children of God! And that is what we are!"* (***1Jn 3:1***). The church's spiritual childhood—our ability to call Him Father and rest in the assurance of His love and provision—provides additional empowerment to persevere. In the midst of struggle, temptation, even persecution, we can trust our sovereign

Our ability to call Him Father provides additional empowerment to persevere.

King, and we can rest in our Father's embrace. J.I. Packer feels this truth holds a central place in Christianity. "If you want to judge how well a person understands Christianity," he asserts, "find out how much he makes of the thought of being God's child, and having God as his Father. If this is not the thought that prompts and controls his worship and prayers and his whole outlook on life, it means that he does not understand Christianity very well at all" (**182**).

A Father's Love

May 4, 2000:

The Atlanta skyline sparkles above my right shoulder. I'm unable to sleep on one of those torturous recliners placed mercilessly in hospital rooms. Beside me, in the bed, lies my wife. Exhausted. Asleep. Her head rests on a pillow from home. She's more beautiful tonight than I've ever seen her.

On the other side of Carrie, in a clear plastic crib on wheels, wrapped tight in a cotton blanket—our son. Also exhausted. Also asleep. He's thirty-nine hours old, to the minute—just beginning to figure out this strange new world.

We're in room 646 of the Atlanta Medical Center. I write by the light of the city, on the back of some hospital forms that were left lying around. Within reach is a cup of cafeteria decaf and a bag of my favorite homemade cookies, hand-delivered by my mother. A blue balloon bounces in the window sill.

The labor and delivery were, in the doctor's words, "just perfect." Carrie was amazing. A real trooper. I was oh so proud of my wife of five years. I was confined to the role of cheerleader. I'd planned to be her coach—but the only two phrases I remembered from childbirth class were "breathe" and "you're doing great," so I think I was more of a cheerleader than a coach.

At 6:15 a.m. the doctor said, "I think we're going to have a baby."

I thought, "Might as well, we've driven all this way."

The next few moments were a blur, but I vividly remember when, fifteen minutes later, the sun rising just outside our seventh story window, Peyton Reid Overdorf entered our world.

Already I stare for hours. Every twitch of his face. Every glint in his swollen eyes. I've studied his toes, counting them over and over.

His little body is perfect. People say he's got my chin. I'm not sure how they can tell, but it sure makes me proud to hear it.

I thought I understood love. I love my wife, and my parents. Other family members. But this is different. It's hard to explain. It's love in a realm beyond what I could have imagined.

This is my son.

My hopes for Peyton soar. I hope he stays healthy (that used to seem like such a cliché, but now I understand). I hope, and have prayed, that someday God will lead him to a young lady who will love him, and whom he will love. His life will assuredly contain struggles; I hope they aren't overwhelming. I know he'll make mistakes; I hope they aren't devastating.

I know this already—nothing can separate him from my love.

I can hardly wait for the day he first calls me "Daddy." I can hardly wait until he begins to understand my love for him. Maybe one day he'll have a child of his own, and he'll understand.

A father's love for his son . . .

Could this be how God feels about me?

The Unlimited Capacity of a Father's Love

As we have discovered throughout this book, we risk overindividualizing biblical concepts such that we miss their communal implications. This holds true with the concept of God as our Father. God loves each of us individually, as a father loves each of his children individually. Additionally, however, God serves as the Father of His entire family. *"I will be a Father to you, and you will be my sons and daughters, says the Lord Almighty"* (**2Cor 6:18**; quoting **2Sa 7:14**). His individual love for each believer does not minimize His love for others; in fact, it enhances it.

I learned this lesson from my father's mother. My grandmother lost her life to cancer when I was seven years old. Though I never heard her tell this story, my father has often recounted it, each time with emotion and appreciation in his voice.

When pregnant with her second child, Grandma felt guilty. She loved her firstborn—Jeannie—with a nothing-held-back, no-holds-barred, give-absolutely-every-sinew-of-your-heart kind of love.

Grandma loved Jeannie with her fullest capacity to love. She feared, therefore, that she would not be able to love a second child as much as she loved her first. It did not seem fair, she reasoned, to bring another child into the world, knowing she had no more capacity to love—she had given it all to her firstborn.

But when she held her second child in her arms, Phil, she felt her heart expand. Her capacity to love doubled. She loved Phil just as much as she loved Jeannie; and, somehow, she did not love Jeannie any less.

She later gave birth to Ken (my father), then Connie and Tom. With each addition to her family, God granted additional capacity to love. Each son and daughter received the same boundless love she'd given her firstborn.

Grandma learned, and relished explaining, that God gives parents an unlimited capacity to love. Parents draw from a bottomless well. We give from an unbreakable account.

Grandma's wisdom proved true for me. When I held my firstborn, my heart exploded (see sidebar, "A Father's Love"). I loved Peyton—and still do—with all the love I can muster. Yet, when I held my second born, Tyler, my heart expanded. The same happened with the birth of my daughter, Claire. With every cry, cuddle, and conniption, each of my children captured my entire heart—all of it, all over again.

God gives parents an unlimited capacity to love. Parents draw from a bottomless well.

This unlimited potential to love should not surprise us. God created us in His image. He loves His children in the same way. He loves each of us, individually and fully. Yet, with each addition to His family, His love only expands—He loves every one of His children boundlessly. He loves His church—each individual part, and the body as a whole—fully.

I recall reading long ago that children have something similar to a tape recorder in their minds. Whatever their parents say to them most frequently replays in their thoughts for the rest of their lives. This brings devastating consequences if parents repeat things like, "You'll never be good at anything," or, "You're nothing but a problem."

I resolved to plant a different kind of thought in my children's minds. As I put them to bed at night, I will look into their eyes, or whisper in their ears, "Your daddy loves you, and I always will no matter what."

"Ah, Dad," they respond, "you always say that!" They protest, but with a smile.

I want them to remember, when they grow older and face temptations and valleys, that I love them.

God's church needs the same continual reminder. Our Father loves us. Regardless what we face, regardless how tenaciously the culture attempts to smother or seduce us, our Father's love continues gushing.

When the Fatherhood Image is Difficult

Because of unhealthy relationships with their earthly fathers, some Christians have found difficulty finding joy and assurance in the image of God as Father. Francis Chan discussed his poor relationship with his abusive father. "My goal in our relationship was not to annoy my father," he explains. "I would walk around the house trying not to upset him." He transferred this perspective to his relationship with God, "I had no aspiration of being wanted by God; I was just happy not to be hated or hurt by Him." Chan explains when his perspective changed:

> Thankfully, my relationship with God took a major turn when I became a father myself. After my oldest daughter was born, I began to see how wrong I was in my thinking about God. For the first time I got a taste of what I believe God feels toward us. I thought about my daughter often. I prayed for her while she slept at night. I showed her picture to anyone who would look. I wanted to give her the world.
>
> Sometimes when I come home from work, my little girl greets me by running out to the driveway and jumping into my arms before I can even get out of the car. As you can imagine, arriving home has become one of my favorite moments of the day.
>
> My own love and desire for my kids' love is so strong that it opened my eyes to how much God desires and loves us. My daughter's expression of love for me and her desire to be with me is the most amazing thing. Nothing compares to being truly, exuberantly wanted by your children.
>
> Through this experience, I came to understand that my desire for my children is only a faint echo of God's great love for me and for every person He made (**52-53**).

If someone does not have children of their own, however, that person may have more difficulty overcoming scars from an unloving earthly father. Finding healing and joy in God's Fatherhood hinges on the person transitioning from comparing to contrasting—from comparing God to their earthly fathers to contrasting them. As abusive, critical, or unhealthy as earthly fathers can be; the heavenly Father is tender, loving, and edifying. "Just as bad as my father was," such a person might grow to say, "the Father is good—in fact, He's infinitely greater."

God loves His church as the ideal father loves his children.

God loves His church as the ideal father loves his children. As the church continually reminds itself of this foundational, critical truth, we will find strength to persevere.

OUR CHOSENNESS

Aliens and Strangers

Peter wrote his epistles to an audience similar to John's—those in Asia Minor beginning to feel the pressure of Roman persecution. Peter reminded these believers that they were *"aliens and strangers"* in this world (***1Pet 2:11***; see also ***1:1,17***)—not because of their geographic location, but because their true identity rested in their citizenship in God's kingdom, rather than in their Roman citizenship. They lived as God's people in the midst of a grossly pagan culture that grew increasingly suspicious of their countercultural lifestyles. Their identity as aliens and strangers

> corresponds to the social alienation and hostility which the readers have suffered as a result of their conversion. In this society in which they were once fully at home (***4:4-5***) they are no longer at home, since their way of life no longer resembles their neighbours' (***1:14; 4:4***). They experience a variety of forms of discrimination and accusation from their pagan neighbours who now treat them with the hostility and suspicion which difference so often attracts (***2:12; 3:14,16; 4:12,14, 16***). (**Bauckham, 163**)

Peter explained that because the Christians no longer participated in the immoral aspects of their culture, those of the culture *"think it strange that you do not plunge with them into the same flood of dissipation, and they heap abuse on you"* (***1Pet 4:4***).

Christians who feel increasingly less at home in contemporary culture can find kinship with Peter's readers. The teenage girl who stands for purity, the salesman who stands for integrity, and the church who stands for biblical truth recognizes the feeling of alienness. Through its films, television programs, and books, contemporary culture often depicts Jesus' followers as a group to be ignored as irrelevant, pitied as naïve, shunned as suspicious, or attacked as dangerous. The question "Are you a Christian?" typically comes not with a twinge of hope and kinship, but with a sneer of denigration. Like Peter's readers, today's church lives like strangers and aliens in a foreign land.

Chosen By God

Peter's encouragements to his readers, therefore, hold great hope for believers today. Though we live as strangers here, we have received a

> [3]*new birth into a living hope through the resurrection of Christ from the dead,* [4]*and into an inheritance that can never perish, spoil, or fade—kept in heaven for you,* [5]*who through faith are shielded by God's power until the coming of the salvation that is ready to be revealed in the last time.* [6]*In this you greatly rejoice, though now for a little while you may have had to suffer grief in all kinds of trials.* (**1Pet 1:3-6**)

Though shunned by culture, *"You are a chosen people, a royal priesthood, a holy nation, a people belonging to God, that you may declare the praises of him who called you out of darkness into his wonderful light"* (**2:9-10**). Furthermore, God builds us into a *"spiritual house"* (**2:5**), a *"brotherhood of believers"* (**2:17**), the very *"family of God"* (**4:17**) called to *"love one another deeply from the heart"* (**1:22**). Though we live as strangers here, God chose us and gave us birth into His family—His church, which provides a present home and future hope.

Peter's words bring to mind what God told the Israelites through Moses more than a millennia prior: *"Now if you obey me fully and keep my covenant, then out of all nations you will be my treasured possession. Although the whole earth is mine, you will be for me a kingdom of priests and a holy nation"* (**Ex 19:5-6**). The church is shunned by the world, but chosen by God—ostracized by culture, but treasured by the Father.

The church is shunned and ostracized, but treasured by the Father.

Rubel Shelly tells of his friends Rick and Patty White, who traveled to a third-world country to adopt a little girl named Olona. After two years of effort and paperwork, the Whites stood before a judge who read cold words from an official document: "Inasmuch as Olona Morgan is orphaned and unwanted by any family in this country . . ." And, "Inasmuch as no citizen of this country wishes to have Olona Morgan . . ." When the awful recitation concluded, which gave the Whites custody of Olona, the loving couple dropped to their knees, hugged their new daughter, and promised, "You will never have to hear the word 'unwanted' spoken of you again." When they arrived back at home in Tennessee, they changed their daughter's name from Olona Morgan to Hope White (**Shelly, 161**).

"You and I are not unwanted orphans in a hostile universe," Shelly writes. "Dearly loved, sought after, and claimed, we are God's children. We have been given Christ's name as our own. We are secure because of him. On the authority of Jesus, we rest in confidence that we are more precious than we dared dream" (**ibid.**).

Peter comforted his readers—those shunned by culture because of their Christian lifestyles—by reminding them that God had chosen them as His treasured family.

Chosenness and Evangelism

Additionally, Peter challenged his readers to use their distinctiveness as means to evangelize the culture. He bid them, *"Live such good lives among the pagans that, though they accuse you of doing wrong, they may see your good deeds and glorify God on the day he visits us"* (***1Pet 2:12***).[4]

While the church may feel tempted to huddle with one another in the safety and comfort of togetherness—the NT consistently calls believers to assertively reach out to the culture for Christ. By exposing ourselves to the culture, we risk suffering. *"But even if you should suffer for what is right, you are blessed,"* Peter explained (***1Pet 3:14***).

[4] Peter mentions two particular circumstances in which people—in these cases people in socially subordinate positions—can influence even their pagan social superiors for Christ. These include the Christian wives of unbelieving husbands (***1Pet 3:1-6***) and the Christian slaves of unbelieving masters (***2:18-20***). Even in these difficult contexts, Peter encourages the believers not to disengage, but to engage the relationships in a godly, loving manner, thus using their behavior (more so than their words) to influence people toward Christ.

> [15]*But in your hearts set apart Christ as Lord. Always be prepared to give an answer to everyone who asks you to give the reason for the hope that you have. But do this with gentleness and respect,* [16]*keeping a clear conscience, so that those who speak maliciously against your good behavior in Christ may be ashamed of their slander.* (***1Pet 3:15-16***)

God scattered us throughout the world, even into difficult contexts, that we might influence these contexts on His behalf. Though we live here as strangers and aliens, God placed us purposefully. He does not intend us to remain detached, but to engage those around us that they might see Him through us. While our interaction with the culture will, at times, provoke hostility, Jesus called us to impact our environment the same way salt impacts meat—giving it flavor and preserving it; and to fill the world with goodness like light fills a dark house, that people might praise Him (***Mt 5:13-16***). The Christlike integrity, character, excellence, and joy that Christians display in their marriages, friendships, and careers can cause unbelievers to take notice, and to seek the fulfillment, hope, and peace that their own lives lack.

God scattered us even into difficult contexts, that we might influence them on His behalf.

Paul to Timothy: Hang In There!

An old preacher said to a group of young preachers, "When you're feeling discouraged, open Paul's letters to Timothy, and just read through the verbs." Some of the verbs that appear are listed below, demonstrating Paul's repeated encouragement to Timothy to persevere.

- Stay there.
- Fight the good fight.
- Hold on to faith.
- Train yourself to be godly.
- Don't let anyone look down on you.
- Set an example.
- Devote yourself.
- Do not neglect your gift.
- Be diligent.
- Give yourself wholly.

- Watch your life and doctrine closely.
- Persevere.
- Keep these instructions.
- Keep yourself pure.
- Pursue righteousness, godliness, faith, love, endurance, and gentleness.
- Fight the good fight.
- Take hold of eternal life.
- Keep this command.
- Guard what's been entrusted to your care.
- Fan into flame the gift of God.
- Do not be ashamed.
- Join with me in suffering.
- Guard the good deposit.
- Be strong.
- Endure hardship.
- Remember Jesus.
- Keep reminding them.
- Present yourself to God as one approved.
- Flee the evil desires of youth.
- Pursue righteousness.
- Continue in what you've learned.
- Preach the Word.
- Be prepared.
- Keep your head.
- Endure hardship.
- Do the work.

Peter wrote to a church facing circumstances that made perseverance difficult. He encouraged them to endure by reminding them that God had chosen and commissioned them.

OUR COMMUNITY

STANDING TOGETHER

While warning his readers against turning away from the faith, the Hebrews writer pointed to the significance of community to perseverance: *"See to it, brothers, that none of you has a sinful, unbelieving heart that turns away from the living God. But encourage one another daily, as long as it is called Today, so that none of you may be hardened by sin's deceitfulness"* (***Heb 3:12-13***). When we stand together, we stand tall. When we stand apart, however, like burning coals removed from the fire, we grow cold. Christianity "can only be lived in community," testifies Philip Yancey. "Perhaps for this reason, I have never entirely given up on church. At a deep level I sense that church contains something I desperately need. Whenever I abandon church for a time, I find that *I* am the one who suffers. My faith fades, and the crusty shell of lovelessness grows over me again. I grow colder rather than hotter. And so my journeys away from church have always circled back inside" (***Church*, 23**).

When we stand apart like burning coals removed from the fire, we grow cold.

The Great Cloud of Witnesses

In the ***eleventh chapter*** of the same letter, the Hebrews writer pointed his readers to faithful believers of the past—the community that stretches across generations—as examples of faithfulness. Abel, Enoch, Abraham, Moses, Rahab, and numerous others stood faithful in the face of temptation and suffering. *"Therefore,"* he continues, *"since we are surrounded by such a great cloud of witnesses, let us throw off everything that hinders and the sin that so easily entangles, and let us run with perseverance the race marked out for us"* (***Heb 12:1***). Like a victorious runner, a perseverant believer throws off anything that hinders her stride, soaks in the encouragement of the community of believers—past and present—and thereby gains the strength to finish the race.

I recall, when I played basketball as a youth, enduring preseason conditioning. Though we did occasional strength training in the weight room, most conditioning came on the outdoor track or inside the gymnasium, running. In the weeks prior to our formal conditioning, I would attempt to run on my own. Each year, my efforts to condition by myself proved futile. I could run faster and further, with greater passion and perseverance, when I ran with my team. We pushed each other, encouraged each other, and kept each other sharp. We persevered together.

When one believer puts his arm on another's shoulder and begins praying, when a Christian encourages his brother to make the righteous choice, when a disciple looks another in the eye and says the difficult but needed words of confrontation, when a Christ-follower sends a note to her sister exhorting her to "hang in there," community enables perseverance.

OUR CONCLUSION

Fixing Our Eyes on Jesus

After pointing his readers to the *"great cloud of witnesses,"* encouraging them to *"run with perseverance the race marked out for us"* (***Heb 12:1***), the Hebrews' writer then points his readers toward the finish line:

> [2]*Let us fix our eyes on Jesus, the author and perfecter of our faith, who for the joy set before him endured the cross, scorning its shame, and sat down at the right hand of the throne of God.* [3]*Consider him who endured such opposition from sinful men, so that you will not grow weary and lose heart.* (***Heb 12:2-3***)

Jesus authored and perfected the very faith in which His followers attempt to persevere. Now, He stands at the finish line urging us to follow His example, and to continue placing one foot in front of the other until the day we reach His embrace. Let us fix our eyes on Him.

Fanny Crosby wrote many of the hymns sung in churches around the globe, such as "To God be the Glory" and "Near the Cross." In "Blessed Assurance," she wrote, "Perfect submission, all is at rest, I in my Savior am happy and blest, watching and waiting, looking above, filled with his goodness, lost in his love." The image of her watching and looking above grows even more striking when we remember that she was blind.

When Fanny Crosby reached old age, a friend said, "If you'd been born today, with the medical technology available, they could have restored your sight." Instead of being bitter, she responded, "I don't know that I would change anything. Do you know the first thing I'm ever going to see is the face of Jesus?"

Home Awaits

Living with an eternal perspective empowers the church to persevere despite the hardships we face. *"Therefore we do not lose heart,"* wrote Paul.

> *Though outwardly we are wasting away, yet inwardly we are being renewed day by day.* [17]*For our light and momentary troubles*

are achieving for us an eternal glory that far outweighs them all. [18]*So we fix our eyes not on what is seen, but on what is unseen. For what is seen is temporary, but what is unseen is eternal.* (***2Cor 4:16-18***)

Elsewhere, Paul explained, *"We also rejoice in our sufferings because we know that suffering produces perseverance; perseverance, character; and character, hope"* (***Rom 5:3-4***). Suffering leads to hope. It reminds us that something has gone amiss—the world in which we live is not yet the world God desires for us. We can allow suffering to repel us from God. Or, we can allow suffering to remind us that this world is not our ultimate destination, and that Christ will return and welcome us into a new creation that contains *"no more death or mourning or crying or pain"* (***Rev 21:4***).

Life for aliens and strangers often involves pain and hardship, but home awaits. Keeping this reward in sight, we persevere.

Suffering leads to hope. It reminds us that something has gone amiss.

What Do You Say?

1. The opening paragraphs of this chapter include this quote from Erwin McManus:

   You've heard it said that the safest place to be is in the center of God's will. I am sure this promise was well intended, but it is neither true nor innocuous. When we believe that God's purpose, intention, or promise is that we will be safe from harm, we are utterly disconnected from the movement and power of God.

   Why would McManus make such a statement? Is there any sense in which the "safest place" is the center of God's will? In what sense is it a dangerous place?

2. What enabled early Christians, such as those described in ***Acts***, to persevere in their faith? What should the contemporary church learn from their example?

3. How does God's sovereignty relate with the church's ability to endure? What would change in the contemporary church if we displayed the trust in God's sovereignty that Shadrach, Meshach, and Abednego displayed?

4. Imagine you were a Christian living in Asia Minor during the latter half of the first century, when Roman persecution began appearing. Imagine that your church received John's ***Revelation***. How do you think you would have felt when you first heard passages such as ***Revelation 1:12-18***?

5. Why do you think God wants us to think of Him as "Father"? What assurances or truths rest in this image? How would you respond to someone who had difficulty with this image because they had an unhealthy relationship with their earthly father?

6. Can you offer an example from your own experience of when other Christians have helped you to persevere in your faith? How did they help you? What did their help mean to you?

7. Why do you think the Bible so often connects perseverance and hope? How can Christians make certain to follow Paul's example of focusing on unseen, eternal matters, rather than focusing on seen, temporary matters (***2Cor 4:18***)?

CHAPTER FIFTEEN

ETERNALLY WORSHIPING

One wet and dreary Friday afternoon, during the years when I ministered with a local church, I struggled to prepare for the weekend. The week's hectic pace, filled with activities and church business, left me scrambling on Friday to finish my sermon and a Sunday School lesson. While I hunched over my desk, unable to develop anything that resembled a sermon, the office phone rang. From the phone's earpiece came the shaky voice of an elderly lady who lived in the nursing home, Mrs. Robinson. She wanted me to visit.

I looked at my unfinished sermon, then at the clock, then back at the computer screen. I grimaced. "I'll be right over."

Mrs. Robinson served faithfully in our church for years. She had endured a difficult life. Her husband, who passed away several years before, abused her. They had one child—a daughter—who lost her life in a car accident. Mrs. Robinson had one grandson who lived out of state, but he had not contacted his grandmother in years. Though she resided in a nursing home full of people, she lived alone.

During the drive to the nursing home, I considered turning my pickup around and returning to the office. "She probably won't remember she called, anyway," I said aloud to myself. Primarily because

- I. A New Heaven and a New Earth
  - A. God's Ultimate Restoration Project
  - B. The Nature of the New Creation
  - C. A Reflection of Eden
- II. The Return of Christ
  - A. Christ Returning as Emperor
  - B. Christ Returning as Bridegroom
  - C. The Resurrection of Christ's Followers
- III. The Present Heaven
  - A. Immediately Present with God
  - B. Heaven's Worship
- IV. Worship on Earth as It Is in Heaven
  - A. God-focused
  - B. Humble
  - C. Awestruck
  - D. Joining with the Saints on Earth
  - E. Joining with the Saints in Heaven

of the guilt in my gut, however, I continued toward the nursing home—though with a frown. "I'll just make it a short visit, then I can get back to more important things."

I entered her room, sat in the recliner next to her bed, and asked Mrs. Robinson about her week. She raised her head briefly from her pillow and smiled. Wisdom stood behind the wrinkles on her face as she said, "Awful kind of you to visit an old lady." My shoulders and eyes dropped. "My week has been fine, thanks for asking," she continued. "The beautician came by and gave me a new hair style. Do you like it?"

"Very pretty," I responded, though I could tell no difference. I glanced at my watch.

We chatted briefly about the happenings at the nursing home, then Mrs. Robinson grew quiet. Her eyes focused somewhere beyond the room. "I'm tired, and I want to go home," she whispered. Her head turned toward me. "Is it okay to want to go home?"

My last conversation about heaven had involved a debate concerning various millennial theories. I doubt Mrs. Robinson could explain the differences in premillennialism and amillennialism. Her exegesis of Revelation will probably never appear in a major commentary. Mrs. Robinson's thoughts of eternity bypassed eschatological debate. To her, heaven meant home—a home for which her tired body and spirit ached.

"I'm tired, and I want to go home. Is it okay to want to go home?"

Is it okay to yearn for home? We sometimes long for our earthly homes. I grew up in West Virginia. Any time I hear John Denver's "Country Roads, Take Me Home," my heartbeat quickens, my nostrils begin sniffing for clean mountain air, and my taste buds cry for Mom's mashed potatoes and homemade noodles. Thoughts of home spur an odd blend of nostalgia and hope. Things once were better, and one day will be better—when we return home.

Is it okay to yearn for our heavenly home? The Apostle Paul did. He wrote that he *"would prefer to be away from the body and at home with the Lord"* (**2Cor 5:8**). Until that time, *"We groan, longing to be clothed with our heavenly dwelling"* (**2Cor 5:2**). At some point we all experience similar longings. As C.S. Lewis wrote, "There have been times when I think that we do not desire heaven; but more often I find myself wondering whether, in our heart of hearts, we have ever desired anything else" (*Pain*, 149-150).

The first fourteen chapters of this book have traced God's development of His community while this community thrives on earth. This final chapter will peer into the future, offering a glimpse of the church's destiny.

Before we dive into this study, three qualifications deserve mention. First, this chapter will not enter the debate of various end-times theories.[1] I intend only to provide hope concerning the church's eternal home. Second, any discussion of the future should acknowledge that the Bible provides no precise, indisputable, clear roadmap of the times that lie ahead. Biblical teaching about the future provides "simply a set of signposts pointing into a fog" (N.T. Wright, *Surprised*, xiii). This chapter will attempt to reveal the signposts with full acknowledgement of the fog. Third, the chapter will proceed chronologically backwards, discussing the church's ultimate eternal existence, Christ's return, the existence of believers who die before Christ's return, the present "heaven," and how this knowledge should affect the church at present, particularly regarding our worship.

Biblical teaching about the future provides "signposts pointing into a fog."

A NEW HEAVEN AND A NEW EARTH

God's Ultimate Restoration Project

God's prophets have long envisioned the day when God will restore, renew, even recreate the heavens and the earth. *"Behold, I will create new heavens and a new earth,"* God announced to His people through Isaiah. *"The former things will not be remembered, nor will they come to mind"* (*Isa 65:17*). Peter recalled such prophecies when he preached to those in Jerusalem that Jesus *"must remain in heaven until the time comes for God to restore everything, as he promised long ago through his holy prophets"* (*Acts 3:21*). Later, Peter wrote of this great *"day of the Lord"* when

[1]Those familiar with such debates may see my bias bleed through occasionally. I do not intend, however, to further a particular argument.

[10]the heavens will disappear with a roar; the elements will be destroyed by fire, and the earth and everything in it will be laid bare. . . . [12]That day will bring about the destruction of the heavens by fire, and the elements will melt in the heat. [13]But in keeping with his promise we are looking forward to a new heaven and a new earth, the home of righteousness. (***2Pet 3:10,12-13***)

In the Bible's final chapters, John describes the day when these prophecies will come to fruition, *"Then I saw a new heaven and a new earth, for the first heaven and the first earth had passed away"* (***Rev 21:1***).

We often picture our eternal existence as an entirely ethereal matter, as though we will exist as free-floating spirits among the clouds, drifting about in an eternal state of euphoric bliss. Such images grow from misunderstandings, fairy tales, and Saturday morning cartoons more so than from the Bible. Scripture pictures the church ultimately existing—following Christ's return—in a physical, renewed heavens and earth. The Apostle Paul described how creation itself longs for the liberation it will ultimately experience:

Scripture pictures the church ultimately existing in a physical, renewed heavens and earth.

[19]The creation waits in eager expectation for the sons of God to be revealed. [20]For the creation was subjected to frustration, not by its own choice, but by the will of the one who subjected it, in hope [21]that the creation itself will be liberated from its bondage to decay and brought into the glorious freedom of the children of God. (***Rom 8:19-21***)

John pictures *"the new heaven and the new earth"* (***Rev 21:1***), as *"the Holy City, the New Jerusalem, coming down out of heaven from God"* (***Rev 21:2***). This New Jerusalem will include a throne, from which the Lord will proclaim, *"Now the dwelling of God is with men"* (***Rev 21:3***), and *"I am making everything new!"* (***Rev 21:5***).

Stanley Grenz summarizes,

> The biblical picture of the renewed cosmos differs from the vision many Christians articulate. They conceive of our eternal home as an entirely spiritual, non-material locale. To distinguish it from earthly, physical existence, they commonly call it "heaven." Consequently, they picture eternity as a realm inhabited by purely spiritual beings.
>
> As the texts we cited indicated, however, the prophets of both Testaments anticipated a new earth blanketed by a new

heaven (***Isa. 65:17; Rev. 21:1***). Rather than resurrected believers being snatched away to live forever with God in some heavenly world beyond the cosmos, the seer of Revelation envisioned exactly the opposite. God will take up residence in the new creation (***Rev. 21:3***). The dwelling of the citizens of God's eternal community, therefore, will be the renewed earth (**841**).

The Nature of the New Creation

Some aspects of our present existence will remain in the new creation. ***Hebrews***, in its description of Christ's return, explains that God will destroy ("shake") the earth and the heavens; however, all that is a part of God's kingdom will stand:

> *[26]At that time his voice shook the earth, but now he has promised, "Once more I will shake not only the earth but also the heavens." [27]The words "once more" indicate the removing of what can be shaken—that is, created things—so that what cannot be shaken may remain. [28]Therefore, since we are receiving a kingdom that cannot be shaken, let us be thankful, and so worship God acceptably with reverence and awe, [29]for our "God is a consuming fire."* (***Heb 12:26-29***)

Similarly, while *"nothing impure will ever enter"* the new creation (***Rev 21:27***), *"the glory and honor of the nations will be brought into it"* (***Rev 21:26***). What presently exists as a part of God's kingdom—most prominently this includes the church, the community of *"those whose names are written in the Lamb's book of life"* (***Rev 21:27***)—will continue to exist in the new creation.

Much from the present creation, however, will have no place in the New Jerusalem. The chapters leading into ***Revelation 21***, quoted above, display the demise of all that opposes God and His people—Babylon the harlot (***Revelation 17–18***); the beast, false prophet, and their armies (***Revelation 19***); Satan (***Rev 20:1-10***); and even death itself (***Rev 20:11-15***). "The [new] creation is marked, in part, by an *absence* of powers that oppose God and diminish life" (**Koester, 192**). As a result, in the new creation, *"There will be no more death or mourning or crying or pain, for the old order of things has passed away"* (***Rev 21:4***).

Contrasting the absence of all that opposes God, ***Revelation*** emphasizes the presence of God Himself with His people in the New Jerusalem. John *"heard a loud voice from the throne saying, 'Now the dwelling of God is with men, and he will live with them. They will be his*

Revelation emphasizes the presence of God with His people in the New Jerusalem.

people, and God himself will be with them and be their God'" (**Rev 21:3**). The words used in this verse, particularly *"They will be His people, and God Himself will be . . . their God,"* reflects a promise that strings throughout the OT:

- *"I will establish my covenant . . . to be your God and the God of your descendants after you"* (**Gen 17:7**).
- *"I will take you as my own people, and I will be your God"* (**Ex 6:7**).
- *"I will walk among you and be your God, and you will be my people"* (**Lev 26:12**).
- *"So you will be my people, and I will be your God"* (**Jer 30:22**).
- *"My dwelling place will be with them; I will be their God, and they will be my people"* (**Eze 37:27**).
- *"I will bring them back to live in Jerusalem; they will be my people, and I will be faithful and righteous to them as their God"* (**Zec 8:8**).

The Bible's grand narrative—God's mission to dwell with His people as their God—reaches its climax in the new creation. God will live with His community. All of Scripture's other promises about heaven fade into relative insignificance when compared to the promise of God's presence with us. John Piper offers a convicting question concerning this truth:

> The critical question for our generation—and for every generation—is this: If you could have heaven, with no sickness, and with all the friends you ever had on earth, and all the food you ever liked, and all the leisure activities you ever enjoyed, and all the natural beauties you ever saw, all the physical pleasures you ever tasted, and no human conflict or any natural disasters, could you be satisfied with heaven, if Christ was not there? (**15**)

Ultimately, Piper teaches, *"The Gospel is the good news of our final and full enjoyment of the glory of God in the face of Christ"* (**14**).

Furthermore, the community of God's people will reach its own full, communal potential in the new creation. The absence of all that opposes God and His people will include the absence of pride, greed, envy, lust, and other such sins that drive wedges between believers, and in turn deteriorate the community itself. In contrast, "Peace, harmony, love, and righteousness will reign everywhere. Fellowship will characterize our experience as humans. Above all, we will enjoy eternal community with the God who makes his abode among us. Because we are reconciled with God, we will enjoy complete fellowship with each other as well, for the eternal community is a social reality" (**Grenz, 843**).

A Reflection of Eden

The renewed creation will reflect the Garden of Eden.[2] In Eden, prior to Adam and Eve's sin, God enjoyed perfect fellowship and presence with His people. The new creation brings restoration of this fellowship and presence. As such, John's description of the New Jerusalem includes several parallels with ***Genesis's*** description of the Garden of Eden. Consider John's description in ***Revelation 22***:

> [1]*Then the angel showed me the river of the water of life, as clear as crystal, flowing from the throne of God and of the Lamb* [2]*down the middle of the great street of the city. On each side of the river stood the tree of life, bearing twelve crops of fruit, yielding its fruit every month. And the leaves of the tree are for the healing of the nations.* [3]*No longer will there be any curse. The throne of God and of the Lamb will be in the city, and his servants will serve him.* [4]*They will see his face, and his name will be on their foreheads.* [5]*There will be no more night. They will not need the light of a lamp or the light of the sun, for the Lord God will give them light. And they will reign for ever and ever.* (***Rev 22:1-5***)

Several elements of this description also appear in the Garden of Eden: the river of life (***Gen 2:10; Rev 22:1***), the tree of life (***Gen 2:9; Rev 22:2***), the curse present then absent (***Gen 3:14,17; Rev 22:3***); and the visibility of God (***Gen 3:8; Rev 22:4***). The parallels between the Garden of Eden and the New Jerusalem indicate, in the very least, that the New Jerusalem will reflect the Garden of Eden. The perfection God created will find restoration.

An additional parallel between Eden and the New Jerusalem deserves comment. In ***Genesis 1:28***, God outlined the role that Adam and Eve would fulfill in creation—they would *"rule over"* it. In the new creation, God's people *"will reign for ever and ever"* (***Rev 22:5***; see

[2]The renewed creation will surpass Eden, of course, however it will reflect it in the ways described below.

Existence will involve active cultivation and stewardship of the new creation.

also *2Tm 2:11-12; Rev 5:10* and *20:4*). Though the particulars remain vague, this indicates that our existence will involve an active, tangible cultivation and stewardship of the new creation, similar to how Adam and Eve functioned in the Garden of Eden.

Our ultimate existence, the new creation, will bring God's original desire to fulfillment: perfect love and relationship shared between Him, His people, and His creation.

THE RETURN OF CHRIST

Christ's return to the earth will serve as the transition—a grand, glorious transition—between the present creation and the new creation.

Following His death and resurrection, Jesus commissioned His disciples to take His message to the ends of the earth. Then,

> [9]*He was taken up before their very eyes, and a cloud hid him from their sight.* [10]*They were looking intently up into the sky as he was going, when suddenly two men dressed in white stood beside them.* [11]*"Men of Galilee," they said, "why do you stand here looking into the sky? This same Jesus, who has been taken from you into heaven, will come back in the same way you have seen him go into heaven."* (**Acts 1:9-11**)

Jesus had already promised this return on multiple occasions (***Mt 16:27; 24:30-31; Jn 14:3***; et al.). Later, as John's vision in ***Revelation*** came to a close, Jesus promised three times in the Bible's last chapter that He would return soon (***Rev 22:7,12,20***). Jesus' final recorded words in the Bible, in fact, further this promise: *"Yes, I am coming soon"* (***Rev 22:20***).

Christ Returning as Emperor

Christ will return as a triumphant emperor. John's Revelation describes Jesus in this manner:

> [11]*I saw heaven standing open and there before me was a white horse, whose rider is called Faithful and True. With justice he judges and makes war.* [12]*His eyes are like blazing fire, and on his head are many crowns. He has a name written on him that no one knows but he himself.* [13]*He is dressed in a robe dipped in*

blood, and his name is the Word of God. [14]The armies of heaven were following him, riding on white horses and dressed in fine linen, white and clean. [15]Out of his mouth comes a sharp sword with which to strike down the nations. "He will rule them with an iron scepter." He treads the winepress of the fury of the wrath of God Almighty. [16]On his robe and on his thigh he has this name written: KING OF KINGS AND LORD OF LORDS. (***Rev 19:11-16***)

This image would have resonated with John's original readers, some of whom had watched Roman generals returning triumphant from war, riding white horses. On one particular occasion, Julius Caesar himself drove a chariot through Rome, pulled by white horses, to celebrate military victory. During such celebrations, citizens marched throughout the city wearing white robes (**Wilson, 356**). ***Revelation*** pictures Jesus similarly triumphant, and the armies of heaven dressed in white linens in celebration with their emperor.

Paul likewise pictures Jesus returning triumphantly. And, Paul describes how believers living at that time will meet him in the air:

[16]For the Lord himself will come down from heaven, with a loud command, with the voice of the archangel and with the trumpet call of God, and the dead in Christ will rise first. [17]After that, we who are still alive and are left will be caught up together with them in the clouds to meet the Lord in the air. And so we will be with the Lord forever. [18]Therefore encourage each other with these words. (***1Th 4:16-18***)

N.T. Wright describes how Paul's original readers would have understood these words, and clarifies a common misunderstanding about our meeting the Lord in the air:

When the emperor visited a colony or province, the citizens of the country would go to meet him at some distance from the city. It would be disrespectful to have him actually arrive at the gates as though his subjects couldn't be bothered to greet him properly. When they met him, they wouldn't then stay out in the open country; they would escort him royally into the city itself. When Paul speaks of "meeting" the Lord "in the air," the point is precisely not—as in the popular rapture theology—that the saved believers would then stay up in the air somewhere, away from earth. The point is that, having gone out to meet their returning Lord, they will escort him royally into his domain, that is, back to the place they have come from (***Surprised,*** **133**).

When Jesus returns, believers will escort the triumphant emperor back to creation.

When Jesus returns, those believers still living will meet Him in the air to escort Him—the triumphant emperor—back to creation, where He will dwell with us and *"make everything new"* (***Rev 21:3,5***).

Christ Returning as Bridegroom

The Bible pictures the church as the bride of Christ (***2Cor 11:2; Eph 5:22-33***) awaiting the return of Jesus, our bridegroom (***Rev 19:7; Mt 25:1-13***). In an ancient marriage ceremony, a bride and her attendants would prepare themselves then wait at the bride's home for the arrival of the bridegroom. The bridegroom's arrival brought great ceremony and celebration. Likewise, John envisions, *"The wedding of the Lamb has come, and his bride has made herself ready"* (***Rev 19:7***).

Though today's marriage and wedding customs differ from those of the ancient world, anyone who has experienced a blissful wedding understands the joy that emanates from such occasions. After officiating and attending a fair share of weddings, I have grown to cherish one particular moment. The organist begins the bridal march, and the congregation stands. All eyes dart to the back of the sanctuary toward the bride, who after months of dress shopping and experimentation with various hairstyles and applications of makeup, beams. When all eyes dart toward her, I look the opposite direction, toward the front of the sanctuary. I want to see the groom's eyes when he catches the first glimpse of his bride. He freezes, except for the corners of his lips, which turn slightly upward. His face turns flush. He tilts his head, and shifts his weight from one side of his body to the other. The rest of the world melts into blurry obscurity as his eyes drink the beauty of his bride, his love.

The bridegroom—the Lamb, the Messiah, the Son of God—longs for His bride with the same look in His eye.

Believers who grow disgruntled with the church and see only its faults need, if only for a brief moment, to turn toward the bridegroom and watch His eyes. In His eyes we discover nothing short of passion for His bride.

Joni Eareckson Tada, who since a diving accident as a teenager has lived and ministered from a wheelchair, wrote about the day of her wedding:

I felt awkward as my girlfriends strained to shift my paralyzed body into a cumbersome wedding gown. No amount of corseting and binding my body gave me a perfect shape. The dress just didn't fit well. Then, as I was wheeling into the church, I glanced down and noticed that I'd accidentally run over the hem of my dress, leaving a greasy tire mark. My paralyzed hands couldn't hold the bouquet of daisies that lay off-center on my lap. And my chair, though decorated for the wedding, was still a big, clunky gray machine with belts, gears, and ball bearings. I certainly didn't feel like the picture-perfect bride in a bridal magazine.

I inched my chair closer to the last pew to catch a glimpse of Ken in front. There he was, standing tall and stately in his formal attire. I saw him looking for me, craning his neck to look up the aisle. My face flushed, and I suddenly couldn't wait to be with him. I had seen my beloved. The love in Ken's face had washed away all my feelings of unworthiness. I was his pure and perfect bride.

How easy it is for us to think that we're utterly unlovely—especially to someone as lovely as Christ. But he loves us with the bright eyes of a Bridegroom's love and cannot wait for the day we are united with him forever (**Tada in Akers, 222**).

Jesus will return as triumphant emperor, and as loving bridegroom.

The Resurrection of Christ's Followers

When Christ returns, those who have died in Him will resurrect to dwell with Him in the new creation.

Except for those alive on the earth when Christ returns, everyone who has lived throughout history will have died.[3] Death is real. Our hearts will cease beating, our blood will grow cold, and our bodies will decompose. At the moment of death, we will join Christ in a spiritual realm (discussed further below), but only temporarily. When He returns, we will return with Him, and experience on that day a *physical* resurrection. The reality of death loses its sting in the reality of the resurrection. Paul pictures this glorious day in his first letter to the Thessalonians:

[3] Exceptions to this statement include Enoch, who *"walked with God; then was no more, because God took him away"* (***Gen 5:24***); and Elijah, who *"went up to heaven in a whirlwind"* (***2Kgs 2:11***).

> *[13]Brothers, we do not want you to be ignorant about those who fall asleep, or to grieve like the rest of men, who have no hope. [14]We believe that Jesus died and rose again and so we believe that God will bring with Jesus those who have fallen asleep in him. [15]According to the Lord's own word, we tell you that we who are still alive, who are left till the coming of the Lord, will certainly not precede those who have fallen asleep. [16]For the Lord himself will come down from heaven, with a loud command, with the voice of the archangel and with the trumpet call of God, and the dead in Christ will rise first. [17]After that, we who are still alive and are left will be caught up together with them in the clouds to meet the Lord in the air. And so we will be with the Lord forever. [18]Therefore encourage each other with these words.* (***1Th 4:13-18***)

For those who hesitate concerning the idea of a physical resurrection, in ***1 Corinthians*** Paul argues extensively that believers will physically rise. At Christ's return, God will clothe us with new, splendorous, imperishable bodies. Jesus' own physical resurrection exemplifies and enables our resurrection. The excerpts below trace Paul's argument:

> *[12]But if it is preached that Christ has been raised from the dead, how can some of you say that there is no resurrection of the dead? [13]If there is no resurrection of the dead, then not even Christ has been raised. [14]And if Christ has not been raised, our preaching is useless and so is your faith.* (***1Cor 15:12-14***)

> *[35]But someone may ask, "How are the dead raised? With what kind of body will they come?" [36]How foolish! What you sow does not come to life unless it dies. [37]When you sow, you do not plant the body that will be, but just a seed, perhaps of wheat or of something else. [38]But God gives it a body as he has determined, and to each kind of seed he gives its own body. [39]All flesh is not the same: Men have one kind of flesh, animals have another, birds another and fish another. [40]There are also heavenly bodies and there are earthly bodies; but the splendor of the heavenly bodies is one kind, and the splendor of the earthly bodies is another. [41]The sun has one kind of splendor, the moon another and the stars another; and star differs from star in splendor. [42]So will it be with the resurrection of the dead. The body that is sown is perishable, it is raised imperishable; [43]it is sown in dishonor, it is raised in glory; it is sown in weakness, it is raised in power; [44]it is sown a natural body, it is raised a spiritual body.* (***1Cor 15:35-44***).

> *[51]Listen, I tell you a mystery: We will not all sleep, but we will all be changed— [52]in a flash, in the twinkling of an eye, at the last*

trumpet. For the trumpet will sound, the dead will be raised imperishable, and we will be changed. [53]*For the perishable must clothe itself with the imperishable, and the mortal with immortality.* (***1Cor 15:51-53***)

N.T. Wright refers to this physical resurrection, and the ensuing existence in the new creation, as "life after life after death." He summarizes, "After you die, you go to be 'with Christ' ('life after death'), but your body remains dead. Describing where and what you are in that interim period is difficult, and for the most part the NT writers don't try. Call it 'heaven' if you like, but don't imagine that it's the end of all things. What is promised *after* that interim period is a new bodily life within God's world ('life *after* life after death')" (***Simply***, **218-219**).

"Call it 'heaven' if you like, but don't imagine that it's the end of all things."

Death Well Lived

My family and I recently visited my parents in West Virginia and worshiped with my home church. We sat next to Nellie Tolbert.

Life has dealt Nellie more than her share of struggles. Over the years she lost a daughter, granddaughter, and great-granddaughter to car accidents. Just a year prior to our visit, her daughter-in-law slumped over the dinner table, dead from a brain aneurism. Nellie's husband, Lewis, was unable to attend church the Sunday I sat with Nellie. Lewis had cancer, and had already outlived his doctor's prediction.

Yet, Nellie greeted me with a warm smile. She hugged me and grinned ear to ear, asking how life had been treating me.

I watched her out of the corner of my eye while the congregation sang. The smile never left her lips. Nellie closed her eyes when the choir sang, "Through it all, through it all, I've learned to trust in Jesus, I've learned to trust in God." She looked as though Jesus Himself had wrapped His arms around her shoulders. She rested in His embrace.

Nellie buried her husband, Lewis, a few days after our visit. I did not have a chance to talk with her after the funeral; but if I had, I could guess what she would have said: "Through it all, through it all I've learned to trust in Jesus, I've learned to trust in God."

The same day Nellie Tolbert buried her eighty-five-year-old husband in West Virginia, Sandra Hammock buried her twenty-four-year-old son, J.J. Landrum, in Georgia.

J.J. began having stomach problems a year before. Tests revealed cancer. His intense battle for life ended, and J.J. went home to be with Jesus.

In the couple of months leading into his death, J.J. and I talked a great deal about spiritual matters. J.J. was a quiet young man; even as his death approached, he said little. But he wanted to make certain of his relationship with God. Three weeks before his death, he asked me to lead him through a brief ceremony in which he would rededicate his life to Jesus. I asked J.J. to repeat a confession of his faith—the same confession he had repeated years earlier, on the day of his baptism. He confessed his belief that Jesus is the Christ, the Son of the living God. He confessed that Jesus was his Lord, his Savior.

I have led others through the same confession. As J.J. professed his belief, however, the words echoed with a depth I had never encountered. He and I both knew that in all likelihood he would soon speak the words not as a confession *about* Jesus, but as an expression of praise *to* Jesus. And he would make this confession, not in his mother's living room, but in his Father's throne room.

How can we remain faithful, even in the face of death? Nellie Tolbert and J.J. Landrum demonstrated it far more effectively than I could ever explain it. "Through it all, through it all, I've learned to trust in Jesus, I've learned to trust in God."

THE PRESENT HEAVEN

This chapter has proceeded chronologically backwards, discussing the church's ultimate existence in the new creation, the return of Christ which will initiate that new creation, then the resurrection of believers that will accompany the return of Christ. The question lingers, however, for those believers who die before Christ's return: How and where do believers exist between their deaths and Jesus' second coming?

How and where do believers exist between their deaths and Jesus' second coming?

Immediately Present with God

Upon our physical deaths, and prior to Christ's return, we will dwell with God in a spiritual realm. As discussed above, believers will receive resurrected, physical bodies upon Christ's second coming. Between our physical deaths and Christ's return, however, we will exist without physical bodies. The lack of a physical body during this period does not minimize the glory of our dwelling, because—and most importantly—we will dwell with God.

As evidenced in his letter to the ***Philippians***, Paul felt torn between living for Christ on this earth and dying to dwell with Christ. He wrote, *"I desire to depart and be with Christ, which is better by far; but it is more necessary for you that I remain in the body"* (***Php 1:23-24***). Paul recognized that upon his death he would dwell with Christ (***1:23***), but that this dwelling would no longer include a physical body (***1:24***). In a similar passage, written to Corinth, Paul stated that he and his companions *"would prefer to be away from the body and at home with the Lord. So we make it our goal to please him, whether we are at home in the body or away from it"* (***2Cor 5:8-9***).

Though the Bible uses the term somewhat fluidly, it often refers to this intermediate spiritual realm as "heaven." Scripture provides only sketchy details of heaven as it presently exists. Most of what we think of as heaven—such as streets of gold and gates of pearl—relate to the new creation, the New Jerusalem, that will arrive with the return of Christ. The Bible does reveal, however, that God (***Mt 5:16***), His angels (***Mt 18:10***), and those believers who have died (***2Cor 5:1***) presently reside in heaven.

God, His angels, and believers who have died presently reside in heaven.

One afternoon I visited a friend in the hospital—Radford Morris. He suffered from multiple health issues, primarily related to his lungs and breathing. His health had worsened such that the doctors gave little hope of Radford living much longer. His condition led him to increasingly consider the hope of heaven. During our visit on this particular afternoon, Radford described a dream he experienced the night before. He envisioned himself as a small boy. He reached up and grasped a hand. He could not see the face of the one whose hand he held, but as he walked around he told everyone who would listen, "This is my daddy! This is my daddy!" He spoke not of his earthly father, but of walking hand-in-hand with God.

As in our ultimate existence in the new creation—the new heaven and the new earth—the present heaven offers as its greatest hope, and its utmost reward, the opportunity to dwell with God. *"No eye has seen,"* wrote Paul, *"no ear has heard, no mind has conceived what God has prepared for those who love him"* (***1Cor 2:9***).

What the Bible Says about Heaven

- Jesus came from heaven (***Jn 3:13; 6:33***).
- Heaven opened at Jesus' baptism, and a voice spoke from there (***Mt 3:16-17***).
- The Father currently resides in heaven (***Mt 5:16,34,45***).
- Heaven is separate from earth (***Mt 6:10***).
- Heaven is where God's will is done (***Mt 6:10***).
- We can "store up . . . treasures in heaven" (***Mt 6:20***).
- Angels dwell in heaven (***Mt 18:10; Lk 2:15***).
- Jesus ascended to heaven (***Acts 1:11***).
- Jesus sits at the right hand of the Father in heaven (***Mk 16:19***).
- Believers will dwell in heaven when we die (***2Cor 5:1***).
- Our inheritance is kept in heaven (***1Pet 1:4***).
- Heaven involves reward for the faithful (***Mt 5:12***).
- Jesus will come from heaven when He returns (***Acts 3:21***).
- Heaven as it presently exists will pass away (***Lk 21:33***).
- A new heaven will emerge (***2Pet 3:13; Rev 21:1***).

Heaven's Worship

Though the Bible does not give abundant detail concerning the nature of the present heaven, God did allow the Apostle John to peek through the doorway and gain a glimpse of its brilliance and glory. John saw life as it exists in heaven; and, he discovered that it centers on the worship of God:

> [2]*At once I was in the Spirit, and there before me was a throne in heaven with someone sitting on it.* [3]*And the one who sat there had the appearance of jasper and carnelian. A rainbow, resembling an emerald, encircled the throne.* [4]*Surrounding the throne were twenty-four other thrones, and seated on them were twen-*

ty-four elders. They were dressed in white and had crowns of gold on their heads. [5]From the throne came flashes of lightning, rumblings and peals of thunder. Before the throne, seven lamps were blazing. These are the seven spirits of God. [6]Also before the throne there was what looked like a sea of glass, clear as crystal.

In the center, around the throne, were four living creatures, and they were covered with eyes, in front and in back. [7]The first living creature was like a lion, the second was like an ox, the third had a face like a man, the fourth was like a flying eagle. [8]Each of the four living creatures had six wings and was covered with eyes all around, even under his wings. Day and night they never stop saying:

"Holy, holy, holy
is the Lord God Almighty,
who was, and is, and is to come."

[9]Whenever the living creatures give glory, honor and thanks to him who sits on the throne and who lives for ever and ever, [10]the twenty-four elders fall down before him who sits on the throne, and worship him who lives for ever and ever. They lay their crowns before the throne and say:

[11]"You are worthy, our Lord and God,
to receive glory and honor and power,
for you created all things,
and by your will they were created
and have their being." (**Rev 4:2-11**)

"John the Seer is summoned to become for a while a spectator at the heavenly court," explains N.T. Wright about ***Revelation 4***, "watching as the whole creation pours out its ceaseless praise before its creator. This is not a vision of the ultimate future—that comes in ***chapters 21 and 22***—but of the heavenly dimension of *present* reality" (**"Freedom," 2**). This chapter of John's Revelation describes the worship that presently fills heaven—worship that continues day and night exalting the Lord God.

John's vision of heaven holds much similarity to visions given to Isaiah and Ezekiel. Isaiah

[1]saw the Lord seated on a throne, high and exalted, and the train of his robe filled the temple. [2]Above him were seraphs, each with six wings: With two wings they covered their faces, with two they covered their feet, and with two they were flying. [3]And they were calling to one another:

"Holy, holy, holy is the LORD Almighty;
the whole earth is full of his glory." (**Isa 6:1-3**)

Ezekiel, likewise, reports of a day when *"the heavens were opened and I saw visions of God"* (***Eze 1:1***). Like John in ***Revelation 4***, Ezekiel described four living creatures—winged, and of bizarre appearance that included faces like a lion, an ox, a man, and an eagle (***Eze 1:4-14***)—and an aura surrounding the throne that included images of a rainbow and brilliant light:

> *[25]Then there came a voice from above the expanse over their heads as they stood with lowered wings. [26]Above the expanse over their heads was what looked like a throne of sapphire, and high above on the throne was a figure like that of a man.[27]I saw that from what appeared to be his waist up he looked like glowing metal, as if full of fire, and that from there down he looked like fire; and brilliant light surrounded him. [28]Like the appearance of a rainbow in the clouds on a rainy day, so was the radiance around him* (***Eze 1:25-28***).

Isaiah's vision from 700 BC, Ezekiel's from 600 BC, and John's from AD 90 share striking similarities, offering further evidence that in ***Revelation 4*** John described heaven as it presently exists, not just as it will exist at some point in the future. Right now, as I write and as you read, the inhabitants of heaven surround the luminous throne of God, crying out in worship, *"Holy, holy, holy is the Lord God Almighty, who was, and is, and is to come"* (***Rev 4:8***).

As I write and as you read, the inhabitants of heaven surround the luminous throne of God.

WORSHIP ON EARTH AS IT IS IN HEAVEN

God gave John a vision of the heavenly realm so that John might relate this vision *"to the seven churches in the province of Asia"* (***Rev 1:4***). Readers often think of ***Revelation*** only as a mysterious—and often frightening—roadmap of our future. While ***Revelation*** includes some elements that will find fulfillment in our future (particularly in its final few chapters), God intended the book to provide immediate encouragement and instruction to believers who lived amid growing persecution in first-century Asia Minor.

God's means of providing this encouragement exceeded a menial "attaboy" or "hang in there." Instead, God offered these believers—and through them, offers us—a glimpse into His own majesty. A reader who gallops through ***Revelation*** alongside of the rider on the white horse and the slain lamb reaches the end of the vision with his jaw having dropped to the floor. With brilliant hues and striking images God astonishes, amazes, and dazzles readers with the magnificence of His glory. This glimpse of His glory enables readers to *"be faithful, even to the point of death,"* that they might receive from God *"the crown of life"* (**Rev 2:10**).

One particular element of John's ***Revelation***, that picture of worship presented in ***chapter 4***, bids earthly readers—both ancient and contemporary—to join with those who inhabit the heavenly realm in worship of His majesty. "This unutterably beautiful and impressive conception of the worship in heaven, connected in some way with the worship upon earth, was destined to bear fruit in the church's liturgy" (**Cabaniss, 52**).

The praise pictured in ***Revelation***, then, provides an informative basis upon which the contemporary church can develop a theology of worship. How does God intend us to worship on earth? He intends us to praise Him in a manner that reflects the worship in heaven.

God-focused

Revelation 4 leaves no doubt who stands central to Christian worship. All inhabitants of heaven surround the throne and *"give glory, honor, and thanks to him who sits on the throne and who lives forever and ever"* (**Rev 4:9**). They *"fall down before him who sits on the throne, and worship him"* (**Rev 4:10**). *"Day and night they never stop saying: 'Holy, holy, holy is the Lord God Almighty, who was, and is, and is to come"* (**Rev 4:8**). Bowed before the throne, they say, *"You are worthy, our Lord and God, to receive glory and honor and power, for you created all things, and by your will they were created and have their being"* (**Rev 4:11**).

Christian worship glorifies God—first, last, and only.

Perhaps the most damaging aspect of the worship controversies that have swirled throughout churches in recent decades lies in their misdirected focus. We have taught church attenders to evaluate worship services based on what they "get out of it," or how services make them feel: "Did I enjoy and benefit from today's service?" The elders and living creatures who surround God's throne in ***Revelation 4*** appear entirely unconcerned

Christian worship glorifies God—first, last, and only.

with what they might "get out of" the experience. They seek to exalt, glorify, and please the one who reigns from the throne. Whether or not the worshiper enjoys or benefits from the experience holds, at best, secondary importance. If we feel uplifted by the experience, we should view this feeling only as an enjoyable by-product. We have too often placed primary emphasis on the uplifting nature of an experience—in essence, placing primary emphasis on ourselves—and have neglected the Lord Almighty.

The elders and living creatures appear unconcerned with what they might "get out of" the experience.

Donald Whitney tells of his tenth birthday celebration. He invited eight friends. They played football and basketball, enjoyed hot dogs and hamburgers, then devoured ice cream and cake.

> The climax of this grand celebration was a gift from me to them. Nothing was too good for my friends. Cost was immaterial. I was going to pay their way to the most exciting event in town—the high school basketball game. I can still see us spilling out of my parents' station wagon with laughter on that cool evening and running up to the gymnasium. Standing at the window, paying for nine 25-cent tickets and surrounded by my friends—it was one of those golden moments in life. The picture in my mind was the perfect ending to a ten-year-old boy's perfect birthday. Four friends on one side and four friends on the other, I would sit in the middle while we munched popcorn, punched each other, and cheered our high school heroes. . . .
>
> Then the golden moment was shattered. Once in the gym, all my friends scattered and I never saw them again the rest of the night. There was no thanks for the fun, the food, or the tickets. Not even a "Happy Birthday, but I'm going to sit with someone else." Without a word of gratitude or goodbye, they all left without looking back. So I spent the rest of my tenth birthday in the bleachers by myself, growing old alone. As I recall, it was a miserable ballgame. (**79-80**)

"I tell that story," Whitney goes on to explain, "not to gain sympathy for a painful childhood memory, but because it reminds me of the way we often treat God in worship" (**80**).

In contrast to those who abandon the one who deserves centrality, consider again those in heaven who instead abandon themselves in adoration of the King. They demonstrate what true worshipers emulate—the sacrifice of self to exalt God.

Worship: Terms Defined

The English word "worship" consists of the term "worth" and suffix "-ship" (the condition or quality of something). It describes the identification of the worth of something. Christian worship, based on this understanding, involves attributing worth to God. The hosts of heaven sing, *"You are worthy, our Lord and God, to receive glory and honor and power, for you created all things, and by your will they were created and have their being"* (**Rev 4:11**). And, David proclaimed, *"Ascribe to the LORD, O mighty ones, ascribe to the Lord glory and strength. Ascribe to the LORD the glory due his name; worship the LORD in the splendor of his holiness"* (**Ps 29:1-2**).

The Biblical languages—OT Hebrew and NT Greek—use a multitude of terms to describe the act, attitude, and quality of godly worship. The most common Hebrew term used to describe worship in the OT (*shahah*) and the most common Greek term in the NT (*proskuneo*) offer pictures of one bowing before a superior. As a loyal subject might bow before a king, so a worshiper bows humbly and submissively before God. The OT uses several additional Hebrew terms to describe worship, such as *hodah* (give thanks), *yada* (know), *batah* (trust), *yare* (fear), *gur* (be in awe), and *avad* (serve). Likewise, the NT uses several additional Greek terms, such as *leitourgeo* (serve), *doxazontes* (glorify), *sebomai* (revere), and *ainountes* (praise) (**Webber, 4-16**).

HUMBLE

The twenty-four elders John describes in heaven *"fall down before him who sits on the throne"* (**Rev 4:10a**). In the ancient world—as in certain places in the contemporary world—bowing demonstrated humility. The Bible often connects this posture with worship. *"Come, let us bow down in worship,"* bids the Psalmist, *"let us kneel before the LORD our maker"* (**Ps 95:6**). In fact, in both OT Hebrew and NT Greek, the terms used most often in worship picture one bowing before a deity (see sidebar above).

After the elders in heaven fall before God, they *"lay their crowns before the throne"* (***Rev 4:10b***). History records numerous incidents of subjects presenting crowns to their rulers as acts of submission.[4] John's readers from the seven churches in Asia Minor would have understood clearly what the image from heaven implied—those who worship God approach Him in humble submission.

Ben Witherington explains,

> Worship is not about our cozying up to God, our buddy or pal. There is of course intimacy with Abba, but we are in no way being set up in a partnership of equals in worship. . . . Any experience which seeks to put us up on God's level is not worship. It is inappropriate and even shocking familiarity, indeed it can even be called idolatry. God condescends and remains God, we do not ascend and become as gods. . . . Worship inherently implies a distinction between the worshipper and the one worshipped. (**"Transfigured"**)

Though God invites us into an intimate relationship with Him, a relationship in which we can *"draw near to God with a sincere heart in full assurance of faith"* (***Heb 10:22***), this invitation to intimacy does not imply casual familiarity. We do not draw near to God in the same manner that we might plop down next to a buddy in front of a bowl of potato chips and a ballgame. His inviting us into a relationship does not lessen His majesty and glory. We must not mistake the opportunity for a relationship with God, therefore, as license to approach God nonchalantly. He deserves our utmost honor and respect. He deserves our humility.

His inviting us into a relationship does not lessen His majesty and glory.

AWESTRUCK

Furthermore, genuine worshipers' humility includes a sense of awe. In describing the scene around the throne, John includes fantastic images that inspire wonder:

> *[3]And the one who sat there had the appearance of jasper and carnelian. A rainbow, resembling an emerald, encircled the throne.*

[4]In 41 BC, for example, the Jews of Ephesus laid a crown before Mark Antony when he visited their city. Josephus records how various Jewish embassies presented crowns to the Romans. Tiridates, prince of Parthia, laid his crown before Nero in AD 63 (**Wilson, 282**).

. . . [5]*From the throne came flashes of lightning, rumblings and peals of thunder. Before the throne, seven lamps were blazing. These are the seven spirits of God.* [6]*Also before the throne there was what looked like a sea of glass, clear as crystal.* (**Rev 4:3,5-6**)

True worship grows from a sense of the transcendent—an awe of God's "otherliness." He is infinitely beyond our full comprehension—more beautiful, glorious, majestic, powerful, and holy than our minds can fathom. John Stott fears that today's church has lost this sense of awe:

> We seem to have little sense of the greatness and glory of Almighty God. We do not bow down before him in awe and wonder. Our tendency is to be cocky, flippant and proud. We take little trouble to prepare our worship services. In consequence, they are sometimes slovenly, mechanical, perfunctory and dull. At other times they are frivolous, to the point of irreverence. . . . We need such a sincere offering of praise and prayer, that God's people say with Jacob, *"Surely the LORD is in this place, and I was not aware of it"* (**Genesis 28:16**) and unbelievers present will fall down and worship God, exclaiming *"God is really among you!"* (***1 Corinthians 14:24-25***). (44)

At a church I once attended, an issue arose concerning a young man who played the guitar in the worship band. He often played on stage in bare feet. Some worried that his lack of shoes demonstrated a lack of reverence—perhaps he approached worship too casually. When a leader talked with the young man about the issue, however, he discovered just the opposite: "When I worship God," the young man gushed, "His holiness and majesty so overwhelm me that I feel like Moses before the burning bush. I feel compelled to remove my shoes, because standing before God is standing on holy ground."

We do not just worship, we worship God—the infinite, majestic, holy, powerful King of all kings. Anyone who fails to stand in awe fails to worship.

Anyone who fails to stand in awe fails to worship.

Joining with the Saints on Earth

Heaven, as John describes it in ***Revelation,*** involves the community of God's people worshiping God. Rather than individuals experiencing God separately, people from every ethnic background and every part of the globe join voices in adoration. In one scene, John describes *"a great multitude that no one could count, from every nation, tribe, people and language, standing before the throne and in front of the Lamb. They were wearing white robes and were holding palm branches in their hands"* (***Rev 7:9***).

Worship can occur individually. Scripture, however, more often presents worship in community. Paul, in fact, discusses some of the horizontal, "one another" implications of our worship: *"Speak to one another with psalms, hymns, and spiritual songs"* (***Eph 5:19***); and, *"Let the word of Christ dwell in you richly as you teach and admonish one another with all wisdom, and as you sing psalms, hymns, and spiritual songs with gratitude in your hearts to God"* (***Col 3:16***). Biblical worship centers on God, not on other people. When a community of people join hearts and voices to worship God, however, the experience inevitably results in mutual encouragement and edification among worshipers.

Michael Quicke, citing an image used by Peter, explains further, "Scripture claims worship is God's most significant way of building his community of living stones. Living stones are built into a spiritual house to be a holy priesthood offering spiritual sacrifices acceptable to God (***1 Pet. 2:5***)" (3). God uses corporate worship as one critical method of creating community among His followers. Despite varying backgrounds, ages, preferences, and abilities, those who join voices in praise of God find their own hearts joined together in community.

C.S. Lewis wrote that when he first became a Christian, he held little regard for corporate church gatherings. "I thought that I could do it on my own," he explained, "by retiring to my rooms and reading theology, and I wouldn't go to churches." He held disdain for church hymns, which he "considered to be fifth-rate poems set to sixth-rate music." As his faith matured, however, he grew to value gathering with other believers to worship. As his conceit diminished, he realized that these hymns were "being sung with devotion and benefit by an old saint in elastic-side boots in the opposite pew, and then you realize that you aren't fit to clean those boots. It gets you out of your solitary conceit" (***Miracle*, 36**).

God uses worship to destroy barriers and create community.

Joining with the Saints in Heaven

When we worship on earth, we join voices with the worshipers of heaven. ***Revelation 4*** makes clear that worship presently—at this very moment—fills heaven. When believers on earth lift their praise and adoration to God, therefore, He receives our worship as He simultaneously receives the worship of the heavenly hosts. We worship along with the elders and creatures who surround the throne, and the saints of past generations.

Worship at this very moment fills heaven. Worship here gives us a foretaste of home.

Ben Witherington describes an occasion when this truth impacted him. He had traveled with a group to tour Greece and Italy. The latter part of the trip included a visit to the catacombs in Rome, one hundred and fifty feet beneath the ground, where early Christian martyrs had been buried. Amid the vaulted arches and the niches cut into the walls where martyrs' remains once rested, the group began singing. The melodies and harmonies echoed throughout the halls. "The further we got into this worship, and the closer we came to the Eucharist, the more we sensed the presence of the saints being with us while we were worshiping God. It was a ***Revelation 4*** kind of moment." He went on to explain, "Worship on earth is a tune-up for worship in heaven. In fact, we don't have to wait—we're already there!" (**interview**).

Worship offers the opportunity to join those who already encircle God's throne; it gives us a foretaste of home.

Several years ago I traveled to Haiti for a ten-day mission trip. The visit occurred in early July, and happened to include July 4. Haitians have no need to celebrate American Independence Day, but the Americans who served in the particular town I visited—missionaries from various backgrounds, United Nations workers, and other relief workers—planned a gathering for that evening. The missionaries who hosted the celebration decorated their home with American flags and red, white, and blue streamers. They passed out noisemakers and Uncle Sam hats. After feasting on food commonly enjoyed in the United States (hamburgers and pizza, if I recall correctly), we sang a few patriotic songs.

I enjoyed the evening, but I sensed that those Americans who lived in Haiti found significance in the celebration deeper than my mild enjoyment. As they celebrated Independence Day, and as they ate hamburgers off of red, white, and blue paper plates, they knew that their loved ones at home celebrated in the same manner, and at the same time. Across miles of ocean waters, these Americans serving God in a foreign land celebrated with their family from home.

Worship offers earthly believers the same opportunity. When we who still serve on earth lift praise and adoration to God, we join in the worship of the heavenly hosts. We get a taste of home.

What Do You Say?

1. Why do Christians often refer to our eternal existence as "home?" What assumptions lie behind this terminology?
2. How does a biblical perspective of the church's ultimate existence—the New Jerusalem—differ from popular conceptions and ideas?
3. In what ways will the New Jerusalem reflect the Garden of Eden? How does recognizing these parallels inform our perspective of God's grand story?
4. How should recognizing that the church is the bride of Christ, and that He is our bridegroom, affect the manner in which we perceive the church? How should it affect how we relate to the church?
5. Why do you believe the Apostle Paul, in ***1 Corinthians 15***, went to such great lengths to teach that believers will physically resurrect? How does this knowledge affect your view of our eternal existence?
6. In ***Revelation 4***, John describes the worship that presently occurs in heaven. As you read this chapter, what images and emotions does it spur in you? In what ways should ***Revelation 4*** influence our theology of worship on earth?
7. What needs to change in your own worship to make it better reflect the worship of heaven?

WHAT OTHER AUTHORS SAY

ABC News. "Stephen King: I Want You to Care." November 15, 2007. Accessed May 22, 2008 at http://www.abcnews.go.com/Nightline/Story?id=3872181&page=2.

Aikman, David. "Trying to Catch Its Breath." *The American Spectator* 41 (Apr 2008) 40-43.

Aitken, Jonathan. "Beijing Bows to Belief." *The American Spectator* 38 (Oct 2005) 44-45.

Akers, John N., John H Armstrong, and John D. Woodbridge, Gen. ed. *This We Believe: The Good News of Jesus Christ for the World.* Grand Rapids: Zondervan, 2000.

Anderson, Francis I. *Job*. Tyndale Old Testament Commentaries. Downers Grove, IL: InterVarsity, 1981.

Anderson, Lynn. *They Smell like Sheep: Spiritual Leadership for the 21st Century*. West Monroe, LA: Howard, 1997.

Archer, Gleason, R. Laird Harris, and Bruce Waltke. *Theological Wordbook of the Old Testament.* Vol. 1. Chicago: Moody Press, 1980.

Asimakoupoulos, Greg. "Hostage Missionaries in God's Care." Accessed 1-18-10 at http://www.preachingtoday.com/illustrations/weekly/02-07-29/13783.html.

Associated Press. "Friend Turns Out to Be Mother." *The Buffalo News,* March 6, 1991.

__________. "Ventura: Organized Religion Attracts the Weak-Minded." *The Washington Post,* September 30, 1999.

Babcock, Gary D. "Holy Spirit, Doctrine of." In *Dictionary for Theological Interpretation of the Bible.* Ed. by Kevin Vanhoozer. Grand Rapids: Baker Academic, 2005.

Banks, Robert. *Paul's Idea of Community*. Peabody, MA: Hendrickson, 1994.

Barrett, C.K. *A Critical and Exegetical Commentary on The Acts of the Apostles*. Vol. 2. The International Critical Commentary on the Holy Scriptures of the Old and New Testaments. Edinburgh: T&T Clark, 1998.

Bauckham, Richard. "James, 1st Peter, Jude, and 2nd Peter." In *Vision for the Church: Studies in Early Christian Ecclesiology*. New York: Continuum International, 1998.

Bauer, Walter, W.F. Arndt, and F.W. Gingrich. *A Greek-English Lexicon of the New Testament and Other Early Christian Literature*. 2nd ed. Rev. by F.W. Gingrich and F.W. Danker. Chicago: University of Chicago Press, 1979.

Beasley-Murray, G.R. ***Baptism** in the New Testament*. Grand Rapids: Eerdmans, 1962.

__________. *Jesus and the **Kingdom** of God*. Grand Rapids: Eerdmans, 1986.

Beckwith, Roger. "The Daily and Weekly Worship of the Primitive Church: Part II." *The Evangelical Quarterly* 56 (July–September 1984) 139-158.

Beukema, John. "Church Advertises That Truth Doesn't Matter." Accessed 12-31-09 at http://www.preachingtoday.com/illustrations/article_print.html?id=25598.

Block, Daniel I. "Tell Me the Old, Old Story: Preaching the Message of Old Testament Narrative." In *Giving the Sense: Understanding and Using Old Testament Historical Texts*. Ed. by David M. Howard and Michael A. Grisanti. Grand Rapids: Kregel, 2004.

Blomberg, Craig. *Preaching the Parables: From Responsible Interpretation to Powerful Proclamation*. Grand Rapids: Baker, 2004.

Boling, Robert G. *The Early Biblical Community in Transjordan*. Sheffield: Sheffield Academic Press, 1988.

Bonhoeffer, Dietrich. ***Life** Together*. New York: Harper and Row, 1954.

__________. *A **Testament** to Freedom: The Essential Writings of Dietrich Bonhoeffer*. Ed. by Jeffrey B. Kelly and F. Burton Nelson. San Francisco: HarperSanFrancisco, 1990.

Briggs, Charles A. "The New Testament Doctrine of the Church." *The American Journal of Theology* 4 (January 1900) 1-22.

Brownlee, William H. *Ezekiel 1–19*. Word Biblical Commentary. Waco: Word Books, 1986.

Bruce, F.F. *The Book of the Acts*, rev. ed. The New International Commentary on the New Testament. Grand Rapids: Eerdmans, 1988.

Brueggemann, Walter. *Mandate to Difference: An Invitation to the Contemporary Church*. Louisville, KY: Westminster John Knox, 2007.

__________. "Rethinking Church Models through Scripture." *Theology Today* 48 (July 1991) 128-138.

__________. *Reverberations of Faith: A Theological Handbook of Old Testament Themes*. Louisville-London: Westminster John Knox, 2002.

__________. *A Social Reading of the Old Testament: Prophetic Approaches to Israel's Communal Life*. Minneapolis: Fortress Press, 1994.

Buchanan, John M. *Being Church, Becoming Community*. Louisville, KY: Westminster John Knox, 1996.

Cabaniss, Allen. "Liturgy-Making Factors in Primitive Christianity." *The Journal of Religion* 23 (Jan 1943) 43-58.

Caliguire, Mindy. *Spiritual Friendship*. Downers Grove, IL: IVP Connect, 2007.

Callahan, Kennon. *Effective Church Leadership: Building on the Twelve Keys*. San Francisco: Jossey-Bass, 1997.

Campolo, Tony. *Letters to a Young Evangelical*. New York: Basic Books, 2007.

Carpenter, Eugene. "Qhl." In *New International Dictionary of Old Testament Theology and Exegesis*. Ed. by Willem A. Van Gemeren. Grand Rapids: Zondervan, 1997.

Carson, D.A. *Matthew*. The Expositor's Bible Commentary. Grand Rapids: Zondervan, 1984.

Carter, Jimmy. *Sources of Strength: Meditations on Scripture for a Living Faith*. New York: Time Books, 1997.

Castelein, John D. "Believers' Baptism as the Biblical Occasion of Salvation." In *Understanding Four Views on Baptism*. Ed. by Paul E. Engle. Grand Rapids: Zondervan, 2007.

Chan, Frances. *Crazy Love: Overwhelmed by a Relentless God*. Colorado Springs: David C. Cook, 2008.

Ciampa, Roy. "As You Go, Make Disciples?" Aug. 18, 2008, accessed 6-13-09 at http://connect.gordonconwell.edu/members/blog_view.asp?id=190052&post=37543.

Clements, Ronald E. *Ezekiel*. Louisville, KY: Westminster John Knox Press, 1996.

Clines, David J.A. *Job 1–20*. Word Biblical Commentary. Dallas: Word Books, 1989.

Colson, Charles. *The Body*. Dallas: Word, 1992.

Cottrell, Jack. *Power from On High: What the Bible Says about the Holy Spirit*. Joplin, MO: College Press, 2007.

Craddock, Fred B. *Craddock Stories*. Ed. by Mike Graves and Richard Ward. St. Louis: Chalice Press, 2001.

Culver, Robert D. "What Is the Church's Commission? Some Exegetical Issues in Matthew 28:16-20." *Bibliotheca Sacra* (July–Sept 1968) 243-253.

Dana, H.E., and Julius Mantey. *A Manual Grammar of the Greek New Testament*. New York: MacMillan, 1955.

DeYamz, Mark. ***Building** a Healthy Multi-Ethnic Church: Mandate, Commitments, and Practices of a Diverse Congregation*. San Francisco: Jossey-Bass, 2007.

__________. "Ethnic Blends?" *Leadership* 29 (Spring 2008) 49-51.

Ferguson, Everett. *The Church of Christ: A Biblical Ecclesiology for Today*. Grand Rapids: Eerdmans, 1996.

Foster, Douglas. "The Point of Christianity 2: Racial Reconciliation." *Christian Standard* CXLIV (May 17, 2009) 20-21.

Friedeman, Matt. "Blame Me." In *More Perfect Illustrations for Every Topic and Occasion*. Carol Stream, IL: Tyndale, 2003.

Garrett, Leroy. "Dietrich Bonhoeffer at 100." Feb. 4, 2006, accessed 5-12-09 at http://www.leroygarrett.org/soldieron/number108.htm.

Geisler, David. "Conversational Apologetics: Evangelism for the New Millennium." In *Apologetics for a New Generation*. Ed. by Sean McDowell. Eugene, OR: Harvest House, 2009.

Gemser, Berend. "The Importance of the Motive Clause in Old Testament Law." *Vetus Testamentum*, Supplement Vol. 1 (1953) 50-66.

Grenz, Stanley. *Theology for the Community of God*. Nashville: Broadman and Holman, 1994.

Griesinger, Emily, and Mark Eaton, eds. *The Gift of Story: Narrating Hope in a Postmodern World*. Waco: Baylor University Press, 2006.

Hanson, Paul D. *The People Called: The Growth of Community in the Bible*. Louisville, KY: Westminster John Knox, 2001.

Harris, R. Laird. *Leviticus*. The Expositor's Bible Commentary. Grand Rapids: Zondervan, 1990.

Hartly, John E. *The Book of Job*. Grand Rapids: Eerdmans, 1988.

Hattaway, Paul. *China's Christian Martyrs*. Oxford, UK: Monarch Books, 2007.

Hays, Richard B. *The Conversion of the Imagination: Paul as Interpreter of Israel's Scripture*. Grand Rapids: Eerdmans, 2005.

Healy, Nicholas M. "Ecclesiology and Communion." *Perspectives in Religious Studies* 31 (Fall 2004) 273-290.

Hellerman, Joseph. *When the Church Was a Family: Recapturing Jesus' Vision for Authentic Christian Community*. Nashville: B & H Academic, 2009.

Henderson, Jim, and Matt Casper. *Jim and Casper Go to Church: Frank Conversations about Faith, Churches, and Well-Meaning Christians*. Carol Stream, IL: BarnaBooks, 2007.

Hitt, James. *Jungle Pilot: The Life and Witness of Nate Saint*. Grand Rapids: Zondervan, 1959.

Holladay, William L., ed. *A Concise Hebrew and Aramaic Lexicon of the Old Testament*. Grand Rapids: Eerdmans, 1988.

Hooks, Stephen M. *Job*. The College Press NIV Commentary. Joplin, MO: College Press, 2006.

Howard, Kevin, and Marvin Rosenthal. *The Feasts of the Lord*. Nashville: Thomas Nelson, 1997.

Humphreys, W. Lee. *The Character of God in the Book of Genesis: A Narrative Appraisal*. Louisville, KY: Westminster John Knox, 2001.

Hybels, Bill. *Courageous Leadership*. Grand Rapids: Zondervan, 2002.

Jobes, Karen H. *Esther*. The NIV Application Commentary. Grand Rapids: Zondervan, 1999.

Johnson, Luke Timothy. *The Acts of the Apostles*, Sacra Pagina Series 5. Collegeville, MN: Liturgical Press, 1992.

__________. *Letters to Paul's Delegates: 1 Timothy, 2 Timothy, Titus*, The New Testament in Context. Valley Forge, PA: Trinity Press International, 1996.

Jones, Medford. *Building Dynamic Churches*. Joplin, MO: College Press, 1991.

Kallestad, Walt. "Showtime: Could Our Church Shift from Performance to Mission?" *Leadership* 29 (Fall 2008) 39-43.

Kaminsky, Joel S. *Corporate Responsibility in the Hebrew Bible*. Sheffield: Sheffield Academic Press, 1995.

Keillor, Garrison. "My Five Most Important Books." *Newsweek* (December 24, 2007) 17.

Keller, Timothy. "The Gospel in All Its Forms." *Leadership* 29 (Spring 2008) 75-78.

Kent, Homer A., Jr. *Philippians*. The Expositor's Bible Commentary. Grand Rapids: Zondervan, 1978.

Kinnaman, David. *unChristian: What a New Generation Really Thinks about Christianity . . . and Why It Matters*. Grand Rapids: Baker, 2007.

Koester, Craig. *Revelation and the End of All Things*. Grand Rapids: Eerdmans, 2001.

Krentz, Edgar. "The Spirit in Pauline and Johannine Theology." In *The Holy Spirit in the Life of the Church*. Ed. by Paul D. Opsahl. Minneapolis: Augsburg, 1978.

Krodel, Gerhard. "The Functions of the Spirit in the Old Testament, the Synoptic Tradition, and the Book of Acts." In *The Holy Spirit in the Life of the Church*. Ed. by Paul D. Opsahl. Minneapolis: Augsburg, 1978.

Kutch, E.W. "Berit Obligation." In *Theological Lexicon of the Old Testament*. Ed. by Ernst Jenni and Claus Westermann. Trans. by Mark E. Biddle. Peabody, MA: Hendrickson, 1997.

Ladd, George Eldon. *The **Presence** of the Future: The Eschatology of Biblical Realism*. Grand Rapids: Eerdmans, 1974.

__________. *A **Theology** of the New Testament*, rev. ed. Grand Rapids: Eerdmans, 1993.

Lawrence, Carl, and David Wang. *The Coming Influence of China*. Artesia, CA: Shannon, 2000.

Lewis, C.S. *The Grand **Miracle**: And Other Selected Essays on Theology and Ethics from God in the Dock*. New York: Ballantine Books, 1986.

__________. ***Mere** Christianity*. New York: MacMillan, 1943.

__________. *The Problem of **Pain***. San Francisco: HarperOne, 2001.

Lewis, Jack P. "Qahal." In *Theological Wordbook of the Old Testament*. Ed. by R. Laird Harris, Gleason L. Archer, Jr., and Bruce K. Waltke. Chicago: Moody Press, 1980.

Lightfoot, J.B. *The Christian Ministry*. Wilton, CT: Morehouse-Barlow, 1983.

Lockyer, Herbert Sr., gen. ed. *Nelson's Illustrated Bible Dictionary*. Nashville: Thomas Nelson, 1986.

Lowery, Robert. "Biblical **Elders** Then and Now." Workshop presented at Second Church of Christ, May 1996.

__________. ***Revelation**'s Rhapsody: Listening to the Lyrics of the Lamb*. Joplin, MO: College Press, 2006.

Marshall, I.H. *A Critical and Exegetical Commentary on the Pastoral Epistles*. The International Critical Commentary on the Holy

Scriptures of the Old and New Testaments. London-New York: T&T Clark International, 1999.

Martin, Ralph P. *Philippians*, rev. ed. Tyndale New Testament Commentaries. Grand Rapids: Eerdmans, 1987.

Mavis, Brian. "Caring for America's Orphans." *Christian Standard* CXLIV (June 28, 2009) 10-12.

Maxwell, John. *The 17 Indisputable Laws of Teamwork: Embrace Them and Empower Your Team*. Nashville: Thomas Nelson, 2001.

McComiskey, Thomas E. "Qodesh." In *Theological Wordbook of the Old Testament*. Ed. by R. Laird Harris, Gleason L. Archer, Jr., and Bruce K. Waltke. Chicago: Moody Press, 1980.

McGavran, Donald A. *Understanding Church Growth*, 3rd ed. Rev. and ed. by C. Peter Wagner. Grand Rapids: Eerdmans, 1990.

McKnight, Scot. "Covenant." In *Dictionary for Theological Interpretation of the Bible*. Ed. by Kevin J. Vanhoozer, Craig G. Bartholomew, Daniel J. Treier, and N.T. Wright. Grand Rapids: Baker Academic, 2005.

McLaren, Brian. *The Church on the Other Side: Doing Ministry in the Postmodern Matrix*. Grand Rapids: Zondervan, 2003.

McManus, Erwin. *An Unstoppable Force*. Loveland, CO: Group, 2001.

McMullen, Cary. "A Congregation That Split in Two Decades Ago Prays Together Again." Published January 12, 2008, in The Ledger of Lakeland, FL. Accessed 12-21-09 at http://www.theledger.com/article/20080112/NEWS/801120371/1326.

McNeal, Reggie. *A Work of Heart: Understanding How God Shapes Spiritual Leaders*. San Francisco: Jossey-Bass, 2000.

Michener, James. *The Source*. New York: Random House, 1983.

Morgan, Timothy C., with David Neff. "China Arrests Dozens of Prominent Christians." Feb. 1, 2004, accessed Feb. 11, 2008 at http://www.christianitytoday.com/ct/2004/februaryweb-only/2-16-31.0.html?start=4.

Morris, Leon. *The Gospel according to John*, rev. ed. The New International Commentary on the New Testament. Grand Rapids: Eerdmans, 1995.

Moule, C.F.D. *Worship in the New Testament*. Richmond, VA: John Knox Press, 1961.

Muggeridge, Malcolm. *A Third Testament*. Toronto: Little, Brown, and Co., 1976.

Naude, Jackie A. "Qds." In *New International Dictionary of Old Testament Theology and Exegesis*. Ed. by Willem A. Van Gemeren. Grand Rapids: Zondervan, 1997.

Ortberg, John. *Everybody's Normal till You Get to Know Them*. Grand Rapids: Zondervan, 2003.

Overdorf, Daniel. *Applying the Sermon: How to Balance Biblical Integrity and Cultural Relevance*. Grand Rapids: Kregel, 2009.

Overdorf, Ken. *I Love the Church: I Really Do!* Kearney, NE: Morris, 2007.

Packer, J.I. *Knowing God*. Grand Rapids: InterVarsity, 1979.

Paris, Andrew. *What the Bible Says about the Lord's Supper*. Joplin, MO: College Press, 1986.

Peterson, Eugene. "Foreword." In *Church: Why Bother?* by Philip Yancey. Grand Rapids: Zondervan, 1998.

Piper, John. *God Is the Gospel: Meditations on God's Love as the Gift of Himself*. Wheaton, IL: Crossway Books, 2005.

Pressley, Johnny. "The Place of Grace: The Lord's Supper." Workshop presented at the North American Christian Convention, July 2, 2009, in Louisville, KY.

Quicke, Michael J. "Exploring the Architecture of Community Formation." Paper presented at 2009 Evangelical Homiletics Society Conference, October 16, 2009, at Southwestern Baptist Theological Seminary.

Raphael, Chaim. *Festival Days: A History of Jewish Celebration*. New York: Grove Weidenfeld, 1990.

Renn, Stephen. *Expository Dictionary of Bible Words*. Peabody, MA: Hendrickson, 2005.

Richards, Lawrence. "Covenant." In *Expository Dictionary of Bible Words*. Ed. by Lawrence Richards. Grand Rapids: Zondervan, 1985.

Ridderbos, Herman. *Paul: An Outline of His Theology*. Trans. by John Richard De Witt. Grand Rapids: Eerdmans, 1975.

Robinson, Anthony B., and Robert W. Wall. *Called to Be Church: The Book of Acts for a New Day*. Grand Rapids: Eerdmans, 2006.

Robinson, Haddon. *Biblical Preaching: The Development and Delivery of Expository Messages*, 2nd ed. Grand Rapids: Baker, 2001.

Robinson, Jackie. "Jackie Robinson Quotes." http://www.baseball-almanac.com/quotes/quojckr.shtml. Accessed 12-2-08.

Roxburgh, Alan. *Reaching a New Generation: Strategies for Tomorrow's Church*. Downers Grove, IL: InterVarsity, 1993.

Rusaw, Rick, and Eric Swanson. *The Externally Focused Church*. Loveland, CO: Group, 2004.

Russell, Bob. *When God Builds a Church: 10 Principles for Growing a Dynamic Church*. West Monroe, LA: Howard, 2000.

Schmidt, Karl Ludwig. "*Basileia.*" In *Theological Dictionary of the New Testament*. Ed. by Gerhard Kittell. Grand Rapids: Eerdmans, 1964.

Schwarz, Christian. *Natural Church Development: A Guide to Eight Essential Qualities of Healthy Churches.* Carol Stream, IL: ChurchSmart Resources, 1998.

Scott, Bruce. *The Feasts of Israel: Seasons of the Messiah*. Bellmawr, NJ: The Friends of Israel Gospel Ministry, Inc., 1997.

Scott, Mark. "Love the Church More Honestly." Sermon preached in the Ozark Christian College chapel, Joplin, MO, Spring 2008. Accessed online at http://occ.edu/Chapel/Archives/008/Scott_Mark_2008S.mp3, Nov. 25, 2008.

Seccombe, David. "Luke's Vision for the Church." In *A Vision for the Church: Studies in Early Christian Ecclesiology in Honour of J.P.M. Sweet*. Ed. by Markus Bockmuehl and Michael B. Thompson. Edinburgh: T&T Clark, 1997.

Shelly, Rubel. "God Responds to All Who Seek Him." In *Preaching the Sermon on the Mount: The World It Imagines*. Ed. by David Fleer and Dave Bland. St Louis: Chalice Press, 2007.

Smick, Elmer B. "*Berit.*" In *Theological Wordbook of the Old Testament*. Edited by R. Laird Harris, Gleason L. Archer, Jr., and Bruce K. Waltke. Chicago: Moody Press, 1980.

Smith, David. *All God's People: A Theology of the Church*. Wheaton, IL: Victor Books, 1996.

Smith, L. Thomas, Jr.. "A Theology of the Kingdom." Workshop presented at Johnson Bible College, 2009.

Stott, John. *The Living Church: Convictions of a Lifelong Pastor.* Downers Grove, IL: InterVarsity, 2007.

Stuart, Douglas, *Ezekiel*. The Communicator's Commentary. Dallas: Word Books, 1989.

Thompson, James. "Ministry in the New Testament." *Restoration Quarterly* 27 (1984) 143-156.

Tozer, A.W. *The Pursuit of God*. Camp Hill, PA: Christian Publications, 1982.

Trepp, Leo. *The Complete Book of Jewish Observance.* New York: Summit Books, 1980.

Vander Zee, Leonard J. *Christ, Baptism, and the Lord's Supper: Recovering the Sacraments for Evangelical Worship*. Downers Grove, IL: InterVarsity, 2004.

Van Gelder, Craig. *The Essence of the Church: A Community Created by the Spirit*. Grand Rapids: Baker, 2000.

_________. *The Ministry of the Missional Church: A Community Led by the Spirit*. Grand Rapids: Baker, 2007.

Van Gemeren, Willem A. *Interpreting the Prophetic Word.* Grand Rapids: Zondervan, 1996.

_________. *Psalms.* The Expositor's Bible Commentary. Grand Rapids: Zondervan, 1991.

Verbrugge, Verlyn. "*Basileus.*" In *The NIV Theological Dictionary of New Testament Words: An Abridgement of The New International Dictionary of New Testament Theology*. Ed. by Verlyn Verbrugge. Grand Rapids: Zondervan, 2000.

Weatherly, Jon. "What Baptism Requests." *Christian Standard* CXLIV (March 8, 2009) 4-7.

Webber, Robert E. *The Biblical Foundations of Christian Worship*. Nashville: Star Song, 1993.

White, William. *Stories for the Journey: A Sourcebook for Christian Storytellers*. Minneapolis: Augsburg, 1988.

Whitney, Donald. *Spiritual Disciplines for the Christian Life*. Colorado Springs: NavPress, 1991.

Wiersbe, Warren. *On Being a Servant of God*, rev. ed. Grand Rapids: Zondervan, 2007.

Wilson, Mark. "Revelation." In *Zondervan Illustrated Bible Backgrounds Commentary*, Vol. 4. Ed. by Clinton E. Arnold. Grand Rapids: Zondervan, 2002.

Witherington, Ben, III. *Making a Meal of It: Rethinking the Theology of the Lord's Supper*. Waco, TX: Baylor University Press, 2007.

_________. "Transfigured." Sermon published on website. Accessed 11-23-09 at http://www.benwitherington.com/personal.html#Transfigured.

_________. Unpublished interview conducted by Drew Keane and Daniel Overdorf in Lexington, KY, on August 12, 2008.

_________. *What's in the Word: Rethinking the Socio-Rhetorical Character of the New Testament*. Waco, TX: Baylor University Press, 2009.

Wright, Christopher J.H. *Old Testament Ethics for the People of God.* Downers Grove, IL: InterVarsity, 2004.

Wright, N.T. "Freedom and Framework, Spirit and Truth: Recovering Biblical Worship." Accessed 9-12-09 at http://www.ntwrightpage.com/Wright_Biblical_Worship.htm.

_________. "How Can the Bible Be Authoritative?" Presented at Griffith Thomas Memorial Lectureship at Dallas Theological

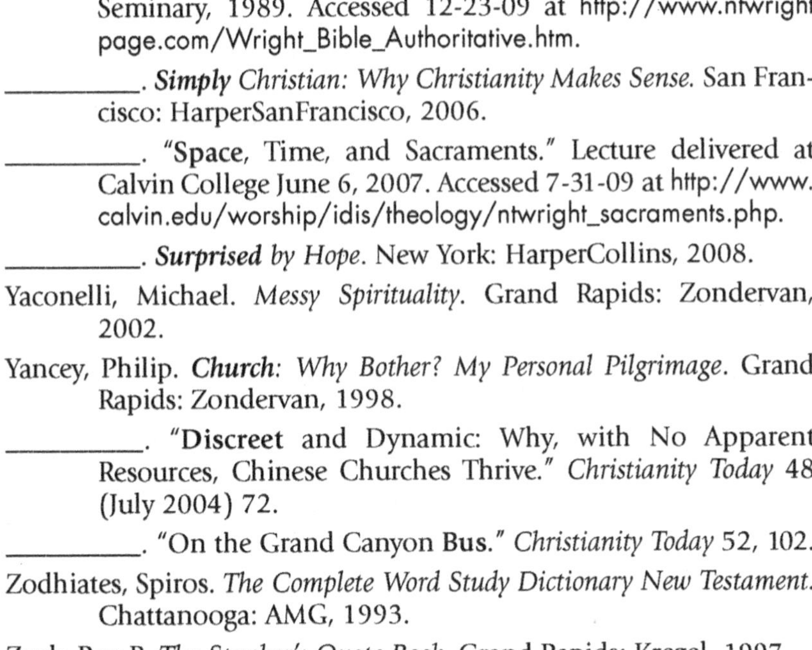

Seminary, 1989. Accessed 12-23-09 at http://www.ntwrightpage.com/Wright_Bible_Authoritative.htm.

__________. *Simply Christian: Why Christianity Makes Sense.* San Francisco: HarperSanFrancisco, 2006.

__________. "Space, Time, and Sacraments." Lecture delivered at Calvin College June 6, 2007. Accessed 7-31-09 at http://www.calvin.edu/worship/idis/theology/ntwright_sacraments.php.

__________. *Surprised by Hope*. New York: HarperCollins, 2008.

Yaconelli, Michael. *Messy Spirituality*. Grand Rapids: Zondervan, 2002.

Yancey, Philip. *Church: Why Bother? My Personal Pilgrimage*. Grand Rapids: Zondervan, 1998.

__________. "Discreet and Dynamic: Why, with No Apparent Resources, Chinese Churches Thrive." *Christianity Today* 48 (July 2004) 72.

__________. "On the Grand Canyon Bus." *Christianity Today* 52, 102.

Zodhiates, Spiros. *The Complete Word Study Dictionary New Testament.* Chattanooga: AMG, 1993.

Zuck, Roy B. *The Speaker's Quote Book*. Grand Rapids: Kregel, 1997.

Scripture Index

Mark

Luke

John

Acts

Romans

1 Corinthians

2 Corinthians

Galatians

Ephesians

Philippians

Colossians

Subject Index